RESEARCH HANDBOOK ON INTELLECTUAL CAPITAL AND BUSINESS

Research Handbook on Intellectual Capital and Business

Edited by

John Dumay

Professor of Accounting and Finance, Department of Accounting and Corporate Governance, Macquarie Business School, Australia; Nyenrode Business Universiteit, the Netherlands; Aalborg University Business School, Denmark

Christian Nielsen

Professor, Aalborg University Business School, Denmark

Morten Lund

Associate Professor, Aalborg University Business School, Denmark

Maurizio Massaro

Associate Professor, Department of Management, Ca' Foscari University of Venice, Italy

James Guthrie

Distinguished Professor, Department of Accounting and Corporate Governance, Macquarie Business School, Australia

EE Edward Elgar PUBLISHING

Cheltenham, UK • Northampton, MA, USA

Published by
Edward Elgar Publishing Limited
The Lypiatts
15 Lansdown Road
Cheltenham
Glos GL50 2JA
UK

Edward Elgar Publishing, Inc.
William Pratt House
9 Dewey Court
Northampton
Massachusetts 01060
USA

A catalogue record for this book
is available from the British Library

Library of Congress Control Number: 2021947684

This book is available electronically in the **Elgar**online
Business subject collection
http://dx.doi.org/10.4337/9781785365324

Printed on elemental chlorine free (ECF)
recycled paper containing 30% Post-Consumer Waste

ISBN 978 1 78536 531 7 (cased)
ISBN 978 1 78536 532 4 (eBook)

Typeset by Cheshire Typesetting Ltd, Cuddington, Cheshire

Printed and bound in the USA

Contents

PART II VISUAL METHODOLOGIES

PART III VALUE ADDED INTELLECTUAL COEFFICIENT (VAIC)

PART IV NOVEL APPROACHES

Contributors

Subhash Abhayawansa, Swinburne Business School, Swinburne University of Technology, Hawthorn, Australia.

Jackie Allen, School of Accounting, Finance and Economics, Division of Management, University of Waikato, Hamilton, New Zealand.

Laura Bini, Department of Economics and Management, Florence University, Florence, Italy.

Michela Cordazzo, Department of Management, Ca' Foscari University of Venice, Venice, Italy.

Paul Davis, School of Accounting, Finance and Economics, Division of Management, University of Waikato, Hamilton, New Zealand.

John Dumay, Macquarie Business School, Australia; Nyenrode Business Universiteit, the Netherlands; Aalborg University Business School, Denmark.

Susanne Durst, School of Business Administration, Tallinn University of Technology, Tallinn, Estonia.

Tatiana Garanina, School of Accounting and Finance, University of Vaasa, Vaasa, Finland.

Marco Giuliani, Department of Management, Università Politecnica delle Marche, Ancona, Italy.

Francesco Giunta, Department of Economics and Management, Florence University, Florence, Italy.

Viktoria Goebel, University of Edinburgh Business School, Edinburgh, UK.

James Guthrie, Macquarie Business School, Macquarie University, Sydney, Australia.

Henri Hussinki, LUT School of Business and Management, Lappeenranta-Lahti University of Technology LUT, Lappeenranta, Finland.

Gianpaolo Iazzolino, Department of Mechanical, Energy and Management Engineering, University of Calabria, Rende (Cosenza), Italy.

Alessandro Lai, Department of Business Administration, University of Verona, Verona, Italy.

Domenico Laise, Department of Computer, Control and Management Engineering, University of Rome 'La Sapienza', Rome, Italy.

Giulia Leoni, Department of Business Administration, University of Verona, Verona, Italy.

Zihan Liu, Swinburne Business School, Swinburne University of Technology, Hawthorn, Australia.

Rosa Lombardi, Department of Law and Economics of Productive Activities, University of Rome 'La Sapienza', Rome, Italy.

Mary Low, School of Accounting, Finance and Economics, Division of Management, University of Waikato, Hamilton, New Zealand.

Morten Lund, Aalborg University Business School, Aalborg, Denmark.

Maurizio Massaro, Associate Professor, Department of Management, Ca' Foscari University of Venice, Italy.

Jan Michalak, Department of Accounting, Management Faculty, Lodz University, Lodz, Poland.

Oren Mooneeapen, Department of Finance and Accounting, Faculty of Law and Management, University of Mauritius, Réduit, Mauritius.

Muhammad Nadeem, Otago Business School, University of Otago, Dunedin, New Zealand.

Christian Nielsen, Aalborg University Business School, Aalborg, Denmark.

Dinesh Ramdhony, Department of Finance and Accounting, Faculty of Law and Management, University of Mauritius, Réduit, Mauritius.

Gunnar Rimmel, Henley Business School, University of Reading, Reading, UK.

Göran Roos, Visiting Professor in Business Performance and Intangible Asset Management, Centre for Business Performance, Cranfield School of Management, Cranfield University, Cranfield, UK.

Federico Schimperna, Department of Economics and Law, University of Cassino and Southern Lazio, Cassino, Italy.

Umesh Sharma, School of Accounting, Finance and Economics, Division of Management, University of Waikato, Hamilton, New Zealand.

Lorenzo Simoni, Department of Economics and Business Studies, University of Genoa, Genoa, Italy.

Riccardo Stacchezzini, Department of Business Administration, University of Verona, Verona, Italy.

Stefania Veltri, Department of Business Administration and Law, University of Calabria, Rende (Cosenza), Italy.

Rashid Zaman, Lecturer at School of Business and Law, Edith Cowan University, Perth, Australia.

Foreword

Leif Edvinsson

It is a pleasure to write this Foreword to the latest *Handbook* on intellectual capital (IC) research. More than ever today, intangibles and IC are the drivers of economic, utility, social and environmental value. I am a foundational practitioner of IC. I was appointed as the World's First Director of Intellectual Capital in 1991 at Skandia Insurance Group, where I prototyped IC development for almost ten years. I was then appointed as the World's First Professor of Intellectual Capital at Lund University in 1990, followed by a Professorship at the Hong Kong Polytechnic University.

I have known the lead editor, John Dumay, for nearly a decade. I spent a sunny fall afternoon in Stockholm with John in 2012 as an interviewee for his latest research. At that time, John was already establishing himself as an IC scholar. We discussed how IC needed to go beyond the traditional metrics and how scholars needed to learn from cross-disciplinary initiatives, something I call IC foresearch, prototyped by platforms such as the Skandia Future Center. Since then, John and his colleagues, including Christian Nielsen and Morten Lund, have been paving a way forward to understand how IC research can continue to develop insights into how IC creates value; not just for companies but also for the wider community. This *Handbook* offers many such opportunities.

Thus, if you are looking for a book that will take you into the future of IC foresearch, this book is for you. Several familiar names are the authors of the chapters within. Other emerging scholars join them to offer innovative insights on how to keep IC foresearch relevant. We need to maintain relevance as we invest in a future where social and environmental sustainability goals transcend economic goals. Society 5.0 is demanding much more positive outcomes. This *Handbook* offers a way forward to start achieving those outcomes and impact through IC foresearch.

The World's First Professor of Intellectual Capital
Leif Edvinsson

Awarded Brain of the Year by Brain Trust,
UK, 1998, for pioneering IC

Introduction: welcome to the world of intellectual capital

John Dumay, Christian Nielsen and Morten Lund

Welcome to the world of intellectual capital (IC). It is a world where value is created from something we cannot touch but can identify and measure, manage and report. Ours is a world of ambiguity where value hides inside a company. Therefore, managers and academics need to carefully and intricately work on making IC visible. Through research on understanding IC and how it works, we make it less ambiguous and allow managers to incorporate it into practice. In a world where value creation mainly stems from intangible assets and where workflows and processes are ever more digital, understanding how IC creates value is critical.

IC research has a long and varied history based on the work of practitioners, journalists and academics such as Sveiby (1989), Kaplan and Norton (1992), Stewart (1997), Edvinsson (1997) and Guthrie and Petty (2000). These people have made significant contributions to the foundations of IC research, and most still do today. However, the challenge is how we continue to build on their contribution to understanding IC in a world where conservative accounting practices prevent the balance sheet from representing an enterprise's future value (Barker, 2015). In the following chapters, we take up the challenge by building on past IC research methodologies and introducing new opportunities to build understandings of IC that reach the future.

In academia, researchers are always under pressure to meet specific criteria from the journals and their editors. Sometimes these pressures tend to conform to methodological contributions and constrain them. Our objective with the *Research Handbook on Intellectual Capital and Business* is to provide a haven where methodological contributions to IC research can flourish. Our ambition is to publish a handbook that guides inexperienced IC researchers in their search for methodologies to help them make novel and timely contributions. For more established researchers, the *Handbook* offers an assembly of refreshing and straight forward contributions stripped of the traditional journal format constraints.

The chapters are written by leading IC academics and practitioners. The authors represented here all have an IC research specialisation or have developed novel approaches to IC research. By sharing their IC research knowledge with you, we hope to open up further developments in traditional IC research methodologies and inspire novel research to take its form in the future. Thus, we organise the book chapters within four parts, starting with traditional research methodologies and then expanding into novel IC research approaches.

PART I: CONTENT ANALYSIS

While being a traditional IC research methodology, content analysis has been the subject of critique and criticism (Dumay and Cai, 2014, 2015). The critique and criticism centres upon an abundance of research analysing annual reports for IC content in different industries and jurisdictions (Dumay, 2014). Alternatively, supporters identify content analysis as well established and not overly time-consuming; there is easy access to data; it is low-cost research; and still capable of developing insights not possible with other research methods (Guthrie, 2014). Thus, content analysis is not quite a dead end yet, and continues to transform and remain a legitimate IC research methodology (Goebel, 2015a, 2015b).

The chapters included in the content analysis part provide critique as well as examples of novel approaches. Continually reimagining content analysis as a methodology for IC research opens the door to new and exciting discoveries. Thus, we present chapters offering critique (Bini and Giunta, Chapter 1; Goebel, Chapter 2; Abhayawansa et al., Chapter 3) alongside chapters that offer novel approaches and new insights into conducting IC content analysis research (Hussinki et al., Chapter 4; Lai et al., Chapter 5; Rimmel and Cordazzo, Chapter 6; Simoni and Giunta, Chapter 7).

PART II: VISUAL METHODOLOGIES

A picture is worth a thousand words, says the old Chinese proverb and the ability to visualise intangibles might be worth thousands of dollars. IC research has more recently considered how visualising IC can help managers understand how their organisation creates and destroys value (Cuganesan and Dumay, 2009; Davison, 2014). However, visualising IC is challenging, and thus we need novel methodologies as there is no generic and widely known and accepted methodology for visualising IC. Thus, considering making the intangible visible is a challenge for IC researchers and practitioners, we include a chapter that offers an overview of research methodologies (Michalak, Chapter 8) and two chapters that help develop further research on this topic (Giuliani, Chapter 9; Low and Sharma, Chapter 10).

PART III: VALUE ADDED INTELLECTUAL COEFFICIENT (VAIC)

The VAIC methodology is another widely critiqued and modified IC research methodology (Ståhle et al., 2011). Pulic's (2000) original methodology's simplicity is both its greatest strength and greatest weakness as most critiques seek to change and add extra variables (Nadeem et al., 2019). VAIC also suffers critique similar to content analysis because many papers investigate different industries or jurisdictions, thus offering infinite research possibilities. Thus, we include chapters that continue the developing discourse expanding the original VAIC methodology (Iazzolino and Laise, Chapter 11; Mooneeapen et al., Chapter 12; Nadeem and Zaman, Chapter 13).

PART IV: NOVEL APPROACHES

Novel approaches, searching critiques and solutions that business, professional and scholarly communities demand are the things that create new discoveries (Guthrie, 2014). Thus, the last section includes chapters that offer these novel approaches because IC research needs to expand beyond its boundaries (Dumay et al., 2018). The chapters in this last part deal with such novel approaches by examining IC research relating to social networks (Lombardi and Schimperna, Chapter 14), different research methodologies (Durst, Chapter 15; Nielsen and Lund, Chapter 16; Veltri, Chapter 17) and building on theory (Roos, Chapter 18). Thus, these final chapters demonstrate novel approaches that expand beyond IC's boundaries. We hope these and the other chapters in this book inspire you to undertake IC research that makes a difference and ushers in a brand-new world of IC knowledge.

REFERENCES

Barker, R. (2015). Conservatism, prudence and the IASB's conceptual framework. *Accounting and Business Research*, *45*(4), 514–538. https://doi.org/10.1080/00014788.2015.1031983.

Cuganesan, S., and Dumay, J. (2009). Reflecting on the production of intellectual capital visualisations. *Accounting, Auditing and Accountability Journal*, *22*(8), 1161–1186. http://www.emeraldinsight.com/10.1108/09513570910999274.

Davison, J. (2014). Visual rhetoric and the case of intellectual capital. *Accounting, Organizations and Society*, *39*(1), 20–37. https://doi.org/http://dx.doi.org/10.1016/j.aos.2014.01.001.

Dumay, J. (2014). 15 years of the *Journal of Intellectual Capital* and counting: a manifesto for transformational IC research. *Journal of Intellectual Capital*, *15*(1), 2–37. https://doi.org/10.1108/JIC-09-2013-0098.

Dumay, J., and Cai, L. (2014). A review and critique of content analysis as a methodology for inquiring into IC disclosure. *Journal of Intellectual Capital, 15*(2), 264–290. https://doi.org/10.1108/JIC-01-2014-0010.

Dumay, J., and Cai, L. (2015). Using content analysis as a research methodology for investigating intellectual capital disclosure: a critique. *Journal of Intellectual Capital, 16*(1), 121–155. https://doi.org/10.1108/JIC-04-2014-0043.

Dumay, J., Guthrie, J., and Rooney, J. (2018). The critical path of intellectual capital. In J. Guthrie, J. Dumay, F. Ricceri and C. Nielsen (eds), *The Routledge Companion to Intellectual Capital: Frontiers of Research, Practice and Knowledge* (pp. 21–39). London: Routledge.

Edvinsson, L. (1997). Developing intellectual capital at Skandia. *Long Range Planning, 30*(3), 366–373. http://www.sciencedirect.com/science/article/B6V6K-4B38653-6/2/4063fb36f12daa98e33257f5049cc9ba.

Goebel, V. (2015a). Intellectual capital reporting in a mandatory management report: the case of Germany. *Journal of Intellectual Capital, 16*(4), 702–720. https://doi.org/doi:10.1108/JIC-02-2015-0011.

Goebel, V. (2015b). Is the literature on content analysis of intellectual capital reporting heading towards a dead end? *Journal of Intellectual Capital, 16*(3), 681–699. https://doi.org/doi:10.1108/JIC-04-2014-0048.

Guthrie, J. (2014). In defence of disclosure studies and the use of content analysis: a research note. *Journal of Intellectual Capital, 15*(2), 291–292.

Guthrie, J., and Petty, R. (2000). Intellectual capital: Australian annual reporting practices. *Journal of Intellectual Capital, 1*(3), 241–251.

Kaplan, R.S., and Norton, D.P. (1992). The Balanced Scorecard – Measures that drive performance. *Harvard Business Review, 70*(1), 71–79. http://search.epnet.com/login.aspx?direct=true&db=buh&an=9205181862.

Nadeem, M., Dumay, J., and Massaro, M. (2019). If you can measure it, you can manage it: a case of intellectual capital. *Australian Accounting Review, 29*(2), 395–407. https://doi.org/10.1111/auar.12227.

Pulic, A. (2000). VAIC™ – an accounting tool for IC management. *International Journal of Technology Management, 20*(5/6/7/8), 702–714.

Ståhle, P., Ståhle, S., and Aho, S. (2011). Value added intellectual coefficient (VAIC): a critical analysis. *Journal of Intellectual Capital, 12*(4), 531–551. https://doi.org/DOI: 10.1108/14691931111181715.

Stewart, T.A. (1997). *Intellectual Capital: The New Wealth of Organisations*. New York: Doubleday-Currency.

Sveiby, K.E. (1989). *The Invisible Balance Sheet: Key Indicators for Accounting, Control and Valuation of Know-How Companies (translation)*. The Konrad Group.

PART I

CONTENT ANALYSIS

1. Investigating intellectual capital disclosure through content analysis: reflections and suggestions for future research

Laura Bini and Francesco Giunta

BEYOND THE INTELLECTUAL CAPITAL STATEMENT: INTEGRATED REPORTS AND NON-FINANCIAL INFORMATION REGULATIONS

Over the years, the importance of intellectual capital has increased. Thus, when considering the value creation process, managers have shifted their focus from tangible to intangible capital (Abeysekera, 2006). This shift has also affected corporate reporting, which emphasizes intellectual capital disclosure.

Researchers have put considerable effort into developing an adequate framework for intellectual capital reporting. Starting from the early 2000s, many studies have focused on the measuring and reporting of intangibles. The Guidelines proposed by the Measuring Intangibles to Understand and Improve Innovation Measurement (MERITUM) (2002) project funded by the European Union (EU), and the final document of the Intellectual Capital Statement Project (Mouritsen et al., 2003), founded by the Danish Ministry of Science, Technology and Innovation, are considered as two seminal works. Academics in the field consider that these frameworks have failed to achieve their goals and they have not produced any significant change in financial accounting rules (Canibano, 2018; Schaper et al., 2017). Indeed, it is said that 'intellectual capital reporting appears to have died for listed companies', because companies have actually stopped preparing intellectual capital reports since 2011 (Dumay, 2016, p. 168).

While intellectual capital reports have gradually disappeared, a growing number of listed companies have started to voluntarily publish an integrated report. According to its proponents, the integrated report is 'a concise communication about how an organization's strategy, governance, performance and prospects, in the context of its external environment, lead to the creation of value over the short, medium and long term' (IIRC, 2013b, p. 7). In 2013, the International Integrated Reporting Council (IIRC) issued an IR Framework that has become the most used guideline for the preparation of an integrated report. The IR Framework identifies six different capitals a company needs to report on in order to provide stakeholders with a full picture of a company's value creation process.

The ongoing development of the integrated report offers interesting opportunities for intellectual capital disclosure research for a number of reasons. First of all, the IR Framework includes the publication of intellectual capital information. Three of the six capitals proposed in the IR Framework are closely related to intangible factors that are considered as major constituents of intellectual capital (Sveiby, 1997; Guthrie and Petty, 2000; Bontis, 2003): (1) intellectual capital, which includes both intellectual properties and tacit knowledge, systems, procedures and protocols; (2) human capital, which focuses on people's competencies, capabilities and experience, and their motivations to innovate; and (3) social and relationship capital, which deals with the relationships within and between communities, groups of stakeholders and other networks (IIRC, 2013b). Second, it seems that the integrated report is becoming one of the preferred channels for companies to disclose intellectual capital. The IR Framework has currently been tested in over 25 countries (IIRC, 2013a), and the number of companies regularly publishing an integrated report is increasing over time (Dilling and Harris, 2018). Lastly, integrated reporting is the subject of lively debate with conflicting positions. Proponents of integrated reporting believe that this document represents a radical innovation for corporate reporting, an opportunity to 'rethink the role of business and the interrelatedness of all its activities' (Painter-Morland, 2006, p. 363). They argue that integrated reporting is an essential requirement to achieve a more sustainable economy and greater accountability and transparency at a corporate level (Eccles and Krzus, 2010; IIRC, 2013b). The multiple capital model of the IR Framework is expected to shift the focus from meeting short-term financial goals to developing a long-term business strategy (Eccles and Krzus, 2010; Adams, 2015).

On the other hand, those who are sceptical about the opportunities related to integrated reporting advocate that beyond a well-established rhetorical infrastructure that emphasizes the benefits of integrated reporting, very little research has been conducted to assess the impact of integrated reporting and demonstrate the expected advantage of adopting such a framework (Flower, 2015; Dumay et al., 2016; Dumay, 2016; Maniora, 2017). It is also argued that the IR Framework only consists of general principles and provides little guidance on some crucial issues, such as the definition of value creation or the measurement of intangibles (Cheng et al., 2014). Certainly, these different positions call for research to clarify whether integrated reporting is a fashionable trend or whether it could play a major role in influencing corporate reporting practices.

Along with the development of voluntary intellectual capital disclosure practices, both national and international legislators have introduced new reporting regulations on non-financial information, which strongly relates to intellectual capital. For instance, companies are requested to disclose increasing amounts of information concerning employee-related matters, which are very close to the human capital pillar proposed in the intellectual capital reporting frameworks. Specific requirements on social and environmental matters, which are aligned with the relational capital pillar, have also been introduced. Lastly, the regulation about corporate governance systems, which are 'themselves systems of intellectual capital' (Keenan and Aggestam, 2001), has been widely strengthened.

In 2006, the United Kingdom (UK) standard setter issued a guideline for companies to prepare a management commentary (Operating and Financial Review). The guideline stated that companies should:

> set out the key strengths and resources, tangible and intangible, available to the business, which will assist it in the pursuit of its objective and, in particular, those items that are not reflected in the balance sheet. Depending on the nature of the business, these may include: corporate reputation and brand strength; natural resources; employees; research and development; intellectual capital; licences, patents, copyright and trademarks; and market position. (Accounting Standards Board, 2006, p. 51)

More recently, the European Union has issued Directive 2014/95, which obliges all large companies operating in an EU member country to disclose non-financial information in their annual reports. The set of non-financial items that the EU Directive requires includes environmental, social and employee matter; respect for human rights; and anti-corruption and bribery matters.

The introduction of these initiatives offers new research opportunities. These include the challenges posed by the regulation of intellectual capital information compared to financial information, as well as the identification of the qualitative characteristics associated to the reliability and the materiality of intellectual capital information, and the evaluation of the effects caused by a mandatory regime.

USING CONTENT ANALYSIS IN INTELLECTUAL CAPITAL DISCLOSURE RESEARCH

Content Analyses in Intellectual Capital Disclosure Research

Since intellectual capital disclosure is largely narrative in nature, content analysis is considered an appropriate method for investigation (Beattie and Thomson, 2007; Husin et al., 2012). Content analysis is a systematic method of identifying specific characteristics through the association of words with categories of the business environment, strategy, operations, human resources, and others, to build a classification scheme (Krippendorff, 2013).

Although content analysis is well established in the intellectual capital disclosure field of research, much criticism has been levelled against its use in previous studies. Beattie and Thomson (2007, p. 131) complain of 'a general lack of transparency in the content analysis methods used in the intellectual capital disclosure studies to date', while Dumay and Cai (2014, 2015) point out the conflicting results and call for more methodological precision to overcome inconsistencies. Lastly, Abeysekera (2006, p. 71) notes several issues that 'need to be resolved in order for intellectual capital disclosure research to be improved'.

The next section illustrates the principal phases that substantiate a content analysis, and considers some of the critical issues that have often been underestimated in previous studies, techniques that have not received substantial attention so far, and what might represent future research opportunities.

Investigating Intellectual Capital Disclosure in the Positive Paradigm

Contrary to other research methodologies, data in content analysis is not under researcher control (Dumay and Cai, 2015). Thus, the texts included in the analysis need to be identified simultaneously with the definition of the research question and the theoretical framework (Krippendorff, 2013) (see Figure 1.1).

The coherence between the research paradigm framework and the type of content analysis employed is a critical issue. Positivism is the dominant paradigm in accounting narrative research, including intellectual capital disclosure (Merkl-Davies et al., 2011). This is due, at least in part, to the fact that corporate intellectual capital disclosure is often explained by agency theory, a theoretical framework that mirrors a classical positivist approach. According to this framework, managers use intellectual capital disclosure as a mechanism to reduce investor uncertainty relating to the impact of intellectual capital on the firm's value (Welker, 1995). Therefore,

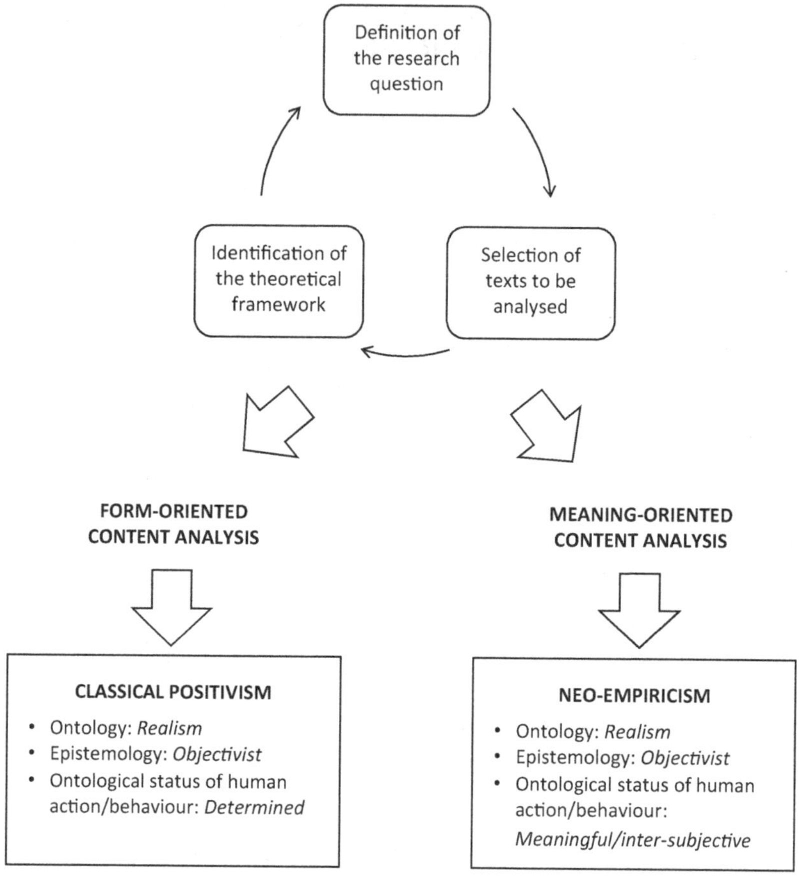

Source: Authors' elaboration based on Merkl-Davies et al. (2011).

Figure 1.1 Content analysis and research paradigms

high intellectual capital disclosure is expected to provide a more intensive monitoring package for a firm to reduce opportunistic behaviour and information asymmetry (Li et al., 2008). Studies adopting this framework usually use content analysis to assess the amount of intellectual capital disclosure and verify its association with information asymmetries or other company characteristics (Li et al., 2008; Whiting and Woodcock, 2011).

Positivism is characterized by a realist ontology, which states that social reality has an independent existence prior to human cognition, and an objectivist epistemology, assuming that the properties of the social reality can be measured through objective methods (Johnson and

Duberley, 2000). However, within the positivist paradigm, differences can be found in the beliefs regarding the ontological status of human action/behaviour (Jackson and Carter, 1993). In classical positivism, human action/behaviour is regarded as objective: that is, rational, purposeful and goal-oriented. In contrast, neo-empiricism considers the behaviour of organizational actors as subjective: that is, they act symbolically by attributing meaning to organizational outcomes and events (Boland and Pondy, 1983). As a result, under classical positivism, content analysis studies aim to produce objective evidence to be used for hypothesis testing. In contrast, in neo-empiricism content analysis objectively captures how organizational actors construct meanings, focusing on underlying themes in the texts (Merkl-Davies et al., 2011).

The choice between research paradigms noticeably influences the development of a content analysis study. Researchers who adopt a classical positivist framework perform the so-called 'form-oriented' analysis (Smith and Taffler, 2000). This analysis aims to convert narratives into numerical scores or indices 'to draw statistical inferences about the types and intent' of narrative disclosures (Craig et al., 2010). Thus, content analysis converts proxies for organizational disclosure behaviour into thematic or semantic indices (Pollach, 2012). Then, indices are used to investigate, by means of statistical tests, the characteristics of intellectual capital disclosure (Bozzolan et al., 2003; Vandemaele et al., 2005), its determinants (Brüggen et al., 2009; Kamath, 2017) and its relevance (Chen et al., 2005; Vafaei et al., 2011).

Melloni (2015), for instance, uses form-oriented content analysis to investigate intellectual capital disclosure within integrated reporting, positing two research questions, on how firms offer intellectual capital disclosure in integrated reports, and whether they resort to impression management strategies in doing this. The evidence of content analysis is used to calculate a disclosure index concerning the tone of disclosure, by means of which each company is graded with a score. This index is then used in a statistical test to verify the association of the tone of disclosure with several variables that are considered as incentives to manipulate disclosure.

Content analyses can be used in the classical positivist paradigm to test hypotheses that have been deductively stated before, but also in the neo-empiricist paradigm (Alvesson and Deetz, 2000). In this case, the goal is 'to develop inductively thick descriptions of the patterns in the intersubjective meanings that actors use to make sense of their everyday worlds and who investigate the implications of those interpretations for social interaction' (Johnson et al., 2006). In these contexts, content analysis is referred to as 'meaning-oriented' content analysis (Smith and Taffler, 2000), as outlined in Figure 1.1.

Abhayawansa and Guthrie (2014) use meaning-oriented content analysis to investigate the types of intellectual capital information that analysts consider important. Presenting their research design, the authors explain that 'meaning-oriented content analysis was performed whereby text units/information items were assigned to appropriate intellectual capital subcategories by gauging the meaning they convey with their context' (Abhayawansa and Guthrie, 2014, p. 71). The authors use the context within which the intellectual capital information is presented to infer why intellectual capital is important for analysts. For instance, they notice that analysts' references to the management team are generally 'forward-looking, and emphasize management's potential future contributions'. This fact leads the authors to induce that analysts consider management quality as a surrogate for the quality of human capital and corporate governance.

Another example of meaning-oriented analysis is represented by Campbell and Rahman (2010), who conducted a longitudinal case study of intellectual capital disclosure to examine where external events may have driven changes in reporting patterns. The authors use meaning-oriented content analysis, first, to classify intellectual capital disclosure according to a preordained classification framework that divides intellectual capital disclosure into three categories (structural capital, relational capital and human capital). Then, each piece of information is coded to record 'the nature of the information (narrative or quantitative/financial) and the level of factuality or judgement conveyed by the information' (Campbell and Rahman, 2010, p. 62). The authors report an overall upward trend in purely narrative content and an overall downward trend in intellectual capital themes expressed as factual information. They interpret this finding in relation to the increasing complexity of the messages being conveyed, 'whereas physical assets can often be described in simple terms (the age of an asset, for example), intangibles are, by their nature, more complex to describe' (Campbell and Rahman, 2010, p. 67).

It is claimed that the utility of content analysis lies mainly in its meaning-oriented applications, which are able to make valid inferences about hidden or underlying meaning and messages of interest (Weber, 1990; Johnson et al., 2006). In keeping with this, Guthrie (2014) states that the importance of content analysis in intellectual capital disclosure research is mainly grounded in the fact that it brings understanding to issues that other methods cannot, especially by finding something hidden within the text. Despite this, intellectual capital disclosure studies mostly consist of form-oriented content analyses (Husin et al., 2012). Thus, meaning-oriented content analysis represents one of the most interesting areas of development for future research on intellectual capital disclosure

(Merkl-Davies et al., 2011; Dumay and Cai, 2015). Marr and Chatzkel (2004, p. 227), for instance, call for 'rich, longitudinal case studies on intellectual capital disclosure that will allow us to understand the specific context which seems to be critical for the analysis of intellectual capital'.

Developing a Content Analysis Procedure

Content analysis used in the positivist paradigm is grounded in the assumptions of realist ontology and objectivist epistemology. This implies that the development of a content analysis framework (form-oriented or meaning-oriented) needs to follow a rigorous procedure in order to be accurate, precise, objective, reliable, replicable and valid (Berelson, 1952; Weber, 1990; Neuendorf, 2002; Krippendorff, 2013). Figure 1.2 illustrates the main steps of a content analysis design, according to Boyatzis (1998) and Weber (1990). Some critical issues concerning the phases in the content analysis procedure are presented and discussed below.

Selection of the unit of analysis

The first step in developing a content analysis procedure is to identify the unit of analysis. This requires selection of the section of a text used by

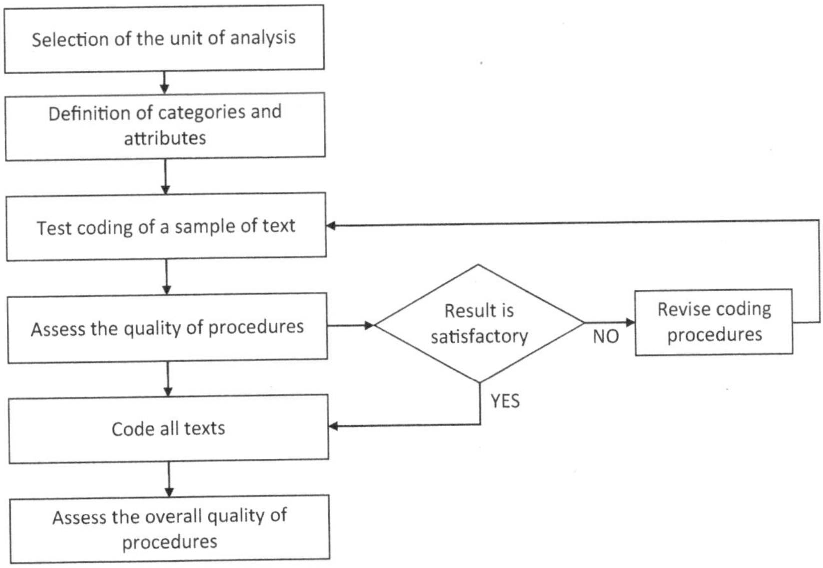

Source: Based on Boyatzis (1998) and Weber (1990).

Figure 1.2 Main steps in developing a content analysis

researchers to code a text (Husin et al., 2012). Several units of analysis have been used to examine intellectual capital disclosure (words, sentences, paragraphs, themes, and so on), but none has become dominant because each unit has its own strengths and weaknesses. Therefore, the unit of analysis should be selected to minimize the subjectivity involved and take into account the characteristics of the examined texts. Abeysekera (2006) demonstrates that different units of analysis lead to different evidence using the same source documents.

Steenkamp and Northcott (2007) argue that larger units, for instance paragraphs, enhance the researcher's ability to capture contextual meaning, but they show some problems in terms of the mutual exclusivity of categories in the coding of text. On the contrary, smaller units, such as words or sentences, reduce the concerns related to mutual exclusivity of coding but 'tend to abstract the analysis unit from its surrounding context' (Steenkamp and Northcott, 2007, p. 17). Guthrie et al. (2004, p. 288) support paragraphs as the most suitable unit because 'people establish meaning based on paragraphs instead of particular words or a sentence'. However, Beattie and Thomson (2007) raise doubts about the use of paragraphs and sentences, because they increase the level of subjectivity in the analysis. Since information pertaining to different intellectual capital sub-categories can be disclosed within the same sentence, the authors argue that a decision has to be made in relation to the dominant intellectual capital sub-category. This decision gives rise to the need for other coding rules to identify dominant themes that increase the level of subjectivity in the analysis (Beattie and Thomson, 2007, p. 142). Despite these limitations, sentences are largely used as units of analysis in intellectual capital disclosure studies (Bozzolan et al., 2003; Vandemaele et al., 2005; Abeysekera and Guthrie, 2005; Whiting and Miller, 2008).

To overcome the limitations related to using sentences as a unit of analysis, some authors propose the use of text units (also called themes) (Holsti, 1969; Beattie and Thomson, 2007; Steenkamp and Northcott, 2007; Campbell and Rahman, 2010; Husin et al., 2012). According to Beattie et al. (2004, p. 216), a text unit is defined as each group of words containing a 'single piece of information that was meaningful in its own right'. Campbell and Rahman (2010) maintain that text units offer considerable advantages because they allow the totality of the narrative to be categorized without the constraints of allocating meaning by words, sentences or paragraphs. If a sub-category is reported in a small number of words, this can be captured just as effectively as if it were an entire paragraph. As a result, the total number of sub-categories described in an intellectual capital narrative can be effectively captured.

However, since text units are not objectively identifiable like paragraphs and sentences, they need to be defined very clearly to minimize the subjectivity involved in the coding procedure (Steenkamp and Northcott, 2007). Carney (1972) recommends the use of illustrations to explain how text units are defined, rather than resorting to generalized, abstract terms.

The choice of the unit of analysis also depends on the use of an automated instead of a manual content analysis. Automated content analysis takes advantage of the development of specific software available since the 1980s. The use of automated content analysis may save time and effort, as the software makes it easier for researchers to conduct comprehensive analysis covering sizable samples (Abhayawansa, 2011). However, this is not a problem-free technique; for instance, automated coding processes are not able to recognize all possible synonyms and words with multiple meanings (Weber, 1990).

Definition of categories and attributes

The above-mentioned inconsistencies documented in intellectual capital disclosure studies (Dumay and Cai, 2015) are caused, at least in part, by the different coding procedures applied by researchers. The coding framework is the set of categories/taxonomies and the rules that support researchers in identifying and collecting target information within texts.

In the absence of an established definition of the intellectual capital concept, different intellectual capital frameworks have been developed over time (Abeysekera, 2006). Among these, the one elaborated by Guthrie et al. (2004) is the most well known. In keeping with Sveiby's (1997) classification of intellectual capital, Guthrie et al. (2004) renamed the categories (internal capital, external capital and human capital) and identified 18 separate intellectual capital attributes, six related to internal capital, seven to external capital and five to human capital (Table 1.1).

In reviewing the coding frameworks adopted in intellectual capital disclosure studies, Beattie and Thomson (2007) document a substantial agreement over the three categories of intellectual capital, but many discrepancies concerning specific intellectual capital attributes. They identified 128 different sub-categories that are used to describe the attributes that relate to the main three categories. Even if this long list includes synonyms, the authors argue that two main issues arise. The first issue concerns the broadness of the intellectual capital concept and the lack of an established definition; the second issue is a 'boundary' problem, as some attributes can be concurrently placed under different categories. Certainly, a more precise definition of the intellectual capital concept

Table 1.1 The intellectual capital coding framework

Internal capital	External capital	Human capital
Intellectual property	Brands	Employees
Management philosophy	Customers	Education
Corporate culture	Customer satisfaction	Training
Management processes	Company names	Work-related knowledge
Information/networking systems	Distribution channels	Entrepreneurial spirit
Financial relations	Business collaborations	
	Licensing agreements	

Source: Authors' elaboration based on Guthrie et al. (2004).

could facilitate comparisons between findings, reducing inconsistencies (Striukova et al., 2008). However, Goebel (2015) documents that results of prior studies are comparable regarding rankings and key findings as long as most of the widely used intellectual capital items are included in prior intellectual capital research frameworks. Thus, although the categories in a coding framework should be defined according to the analysed texts and the research objectives (Weber, 1990), widely used intellectual capital items included in previous studies can provide a valuable reference to developing a comparable coding framework.

Assess the quality of procedures

Once the coding framework is defined, it is tested on a pilot sample until sufficient validity and reliability are achieved (Weber, 1990). This step is crucial to conform to underlying positivist assumptions: 'content analysts need to demonstrate the reliability of their instruments and/or the reliability of the data collected using those instruments to permit replicable and valid inferences to be drawn from data derived from content analysis' (Milne and Adler, 1999, p. 238) (see Figure 1.3).

Validity, on the one hand, focuses on 'how well results of a study mirror reality' (Merkl-Davies et al., 2011, p. 23). Validity concerns the sample and the methodological tools used in the analysis. Thus, a large and stratified sample guarantees higher validity in terms of the representativeness of a certain population and, consequently, of the generalizability of results. A thorough selection of categories that are good proxies for abstract phenomena may validate the interpretation of results. Clear and detailed coding rules reduce mistakes and bias among coders, increasing the validity of data collected (Weber, 1990). Finally, computer-assisted content analyses are associated with a higher level of validity than manual content

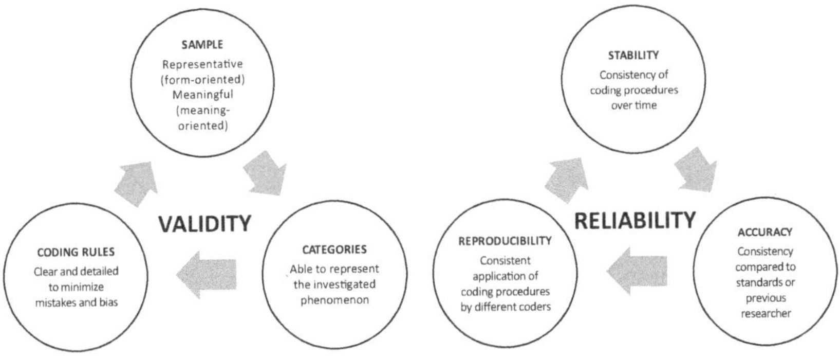

Source: Based on Weber (1990).

Figure 1.3 Evaluating a content analysis research design

analysis, as they reduce the presence of subjectivity and mistakes among collected data (Abrahamson and Park, 1994).

Reliability, on the other hand, 'is the extent to which data can be trusted to represent the phenomena of interest rather than spurious ones' (Krippendorff, 2013, p. 350). According to Krippendorff (2013), reliability deals with coding procedures adopted to content analyse texts. It consists of three different pillars: stability, reproducibility and accuracy. The first two pillars deal with the ability of a coding procedure to be consistently applied over time (stability) and by different coders (reproducibility). Accuracy 'involves assessing coding performance against a predetermined standard set' (Milne and Adler, 1999, p. 239), derived by previous literature or by a panel of experts.

Overall, these evaluation criteria are valid for both form-oriented and meaning-oriented content analyses, as both aim to permit replicable and valid inferences (Weber, 1990). However, some consideration should be given to specific points. Replicability and external validity (generalizability) issues in meaning-oriented content analysis and, more broadly, under neo-empiricist assumptions can be problematic due to the emphasis placed on the social setting where the research takes place. Any inferred interpretation is only valid within the specific setting and cannot be generalized to a wider context (Lewis and Ritchie, 2003).

This does not reduce the potential of research in the neo-empiricist paradigm, but influences the interpretation of results (Strauss, 1987). Form-oriented content analyses are based on statistical inference, where generalizability derives from sampling. On the contrary, meaning-oriented content analyses rely on logical inference, what Dumay and Cai (2015) refer to as abductive inference. This is based on rational and rigorous reasoning, which is used to propose an 'inductively generated and tested theoretical model' (Mitchell, 1983, p. 190). Abduction is a form of inference 'that goes from data describing something to a hypothesis that best explain or accounts for the data' (Josephson and Josephson, 1996). In this perspective, the conclusion of an abduction is 'logically justified' and contributes to generate knowledge by the force of its argument (Peng and Reggia, 2012).

Triangulation offers a possible way to improve intellectual capital research quality and overcome possible mistrust towards logical inference and meaning-oriented studies (Webb et al., 1966). Triangulation 'entails the contingent use of multiple researchers, multiple primary and secondary data sources and collection methods to cross-reference and substantiate the objectivity of findings by demonstrating their convergence and consistency of meaning' (Johnson et al., 2006, p. 139). The use of more than one method or multiple data sources strengthens the validation process as it ensures that the results obtained do not only depend on a specific dataset or method, thus they 'are valid and not a methodological artifact' (Bouchard, 1976, p. 268).

In their review of intellectual capital studies using content analysis, Dumay and Cai (2015) document little attention to validity by researchers. Gately and Cunningham (2014) use qualitative interviewing and qualitative content analysis to investigate relational capital. Buhr (1998) provides an example of triangulation in the field of environmental disclosure, where three research methods – historiography, interviews and content analysis – are used to develop a fuller and richer picture of environmental performance and related annual report disclosure in a case study.

ASSESSING INTELLECTUAL CAPITAL DISCLOSURE: OVERCOMING THE OVERLAP BETWEEN QUALITY AND QUANTITY

To assess companies' intellectual capital disclosure, extant research has mainly focused on disclosure frequency and volume, under the assumption that the frequency or volume of disclosure signals how important the writers of a report consider the issue to be (Unerman, 2000). Accordingly, the amount of space (whether in terms of words, sentences, paragraphs, and so on) devoted to intellectual capital disclosure has become the usual focus of content analyses (Beattie and Thomson, 2007).

Over time, many authors have highlighted the limitations related to the adoption of the volume/frequency of disclosure as a proxy for a complex, multifaceted concept such as disclosure quality (Beattie et al., 2004). For instance, several authors have highlighted that disclosure practices may differ not only in regard to the quantity of information released but also in terms of the modalities of presentation (Beretta and Bozzolan, 2008; Chatterjee et al., 2008). In the field of intellectual capital disclosure, this issue is particularly important, as 'the volume of disclosure is potentially misleading when it is the credibility and quality of disclosure that is important' (Beattie and Thomson, 2007, p. 141).

This awareness has resulted in the development of disclosure measures that take into account the nature of disclosure, distinguishing between quantitative and qualitative information. Guthrie et al. (2006), in their examination of voluntary reporting of intellectual capital by listed companies in Australia and Hong Kong, use an intellectual capital coding framework including 24 items. Each item was classified according to a four-element scheme: 0 if the item does not appear in the annual report; 1 if the item appears in a discursive form; 2 if the item is expressed in numerical terms; and 3 if it is quantified in dollar (currency) terms. Discussing their results, the authors noticed that nearly every instance of intellectual capital reporting involved expression in discursive rather than numerical terms, and explain this result in terms of 'the difficulty involved in trying to quantify what is, in many instances, essentially a qualitative item' (Guthrie et al., 2006, p. 268). They add that 'the low incidence of quantitative expressions of intellectual capital items seems to confirm the widely-held view that companies are not motivated to assign dollar values to intellectual capital' (Guthrie et al., 2006, p. 268).

Bozzolan et al. (2003) adopt a similar approach based on a three-element scheme that classifies items into three categories: 0 for the absence of the item; 1 for discursive information; and 2 for quantitative measures. Different to Guthrie et al. (2006), they use this framework as a weighting scheme, implicitly assuming that numerical information provides higher-quality disclosure than discursive disclosure.

However, linking quality with quantitative information might be inappropriate in the intellectual capital context (Beattie and Thomson, 2007), in part due to the difficulties in quantifying certain intellectual capital items, as the above quotation from Guthrie et al. (2006) emphasizes. Moreover, narrative theory, taken up in management and organizational studies (Tenkasi and Boland, 1993), stresses the role of discursive information in accounting disclosure. Narratives are considered as storytelling competences aimed at both convincing others to devote funds and other crucial resources to the company, and building the tangible and intangible worth of the company (O'Connor, 2002). In the context of intellectual capital disclosure, the value added of storytelling is the ability to explain the connections among key tangible and intangible factors (Mouritsen et al., 2001; Nielsen, 2010). Holland (2004, p. 47) maintains that 'intangibles that were invisible to outside monitors, were connected via the story to more visible intangibles and to tangibles as well as to output and performance measures'.

In light of this, the distinction between narrative and quantitative information is not sufficient to assess intellectual capital disclosure. A focus on narrative is needed to understand whether and to what extent it is able to convey intellectual capital information about a company. In keeping with linguistic studies, narrative can consist of both: effective narrative (Rhee and Lee, 2003), that is, information that focuses on relevant matters; and mere rhetoric, that is, 'words without commitment' (Eccles et al., 1992). Rhetoric should be weighted less when it is provided in large volume without commitment (Toms, 2002). Beattie and Thomson (2007) argue that intellectual capital research has never discussed this issue, paying no attention to the contents included in intellectual capital narrative.

Intellectual capital disclosure studies have also been criticized by Mouritsen et al. (2001) for the widespread use of the three-way model that splits intellectual capital into human capital, organizational (structural) capital and customer capital. The authors notice that this model assumes a strict separation between the three categories that is questionable, although it is valuable from a measurement perspective. The three elements of intellectual capital are complements, as they 'are part of a network of things and people that coproduce the effects of the whole network' (Mouritsen et al., 2001). Limiting the assessment to these three categories does not allow for the appraisal of the 'full' intellectual capital activated by companies, because a critical element, the interaction among factors (Roos et al., 1997), is left out. Therefore, the three-way model is unable to capture synergies that exist across the categories (Beattie and Smith, 2013) and that create what is known as the fourth intellectual capital element, the connectivity capital (Habersam and Piber, 2003; Bjurström and Roberts, 2007).

Moving from this criticism, Bini et al. (2016a) propose a new approach for assessing intellectual capital narratives grounded on two qualitative aspects: focus and connectivity. The former is aimed at identifying effective intellectual capital narrative based on the assumption that intellectual capital narratives should illustrate how intangible resources actively contribute to the company's value creation process (Björkdahl, 2009; Chesbrough and Rosenbloom, 2002). Thus, focused intellectual capital narratives exclude any generic description concerning intangible resources, as well as any intention, project or policy that is not referred to in terms of specific implemented activities and/or results.

The second dimension, connectivity, relies on the assumption that intellectual capital narrative should communicate the connections among key tangible and intangible factors, enabling market participants to gain an integrated view of that process over time (Holland, 2004). Therefore, this second aspect focuses on the presence of linkages within narratives, linkages that illustrate interactions, synergies, causal relations between intangibles or between intangible and tangible resources. Taken together these two aspects aim to assess the extent to which the story disclosed by companies is able to highlight the causal relationships among the elements involved in the value creation processes, presenting intellectual capital not 'on hold', but 'in action' (Chiucchi, 2013).

Bini et al. (2016a) use this framework to content analyse the disclosure included in the annual reports of 35 listed UK companies. To reduce subjective judgements, the authors develop a detailed scheme of coding to identify focused information. Analogously, they define specific rules to identify the linkages among the information (connectivity dimension). More precisely, they consider both explicit connections, expressed by connectives (that is, joining words used to connect phrases together into longer sentences) and implicit connections, provided by the text construction (Bini et al., 2016a, p. 91). Moreover, for both the aspects, they provide some practical examples of classifications, in keeping with Carney (1972) who recommends the use of illustrative examples to explain a coding framework. Results show that less than half of the information provided focuses on value creation, and companies rarely illustrate how resources, competences and activities are connected together to create value.

This first attempt to propose an alternative way to assess intellectual capital disclosure should stimulate researchers to break the conventional rules underpinning established methods. This seems particularly important as intellectual capital research has been criticized for producing controversial and inconclusive contributions (Abeysekera, 2006; Dumay and Cai, 2014).

MOVING INTELLECTUAL CAPITAL DISCLOSURE RESEARCH FORWARD

Intellectual capital disclosure has been and remains a main research topic in the field of accounting. Even though the project of an intellectual capital statement has been abandoned (Dumay, 2016, p. 168), companies keep communicating intellectual capital information. This offers future research opportunities, including both voluntary and mandatory disclosure. On the one hand, the growing popularity of integrated reporting among companies provides an opportunity to improve the knowledge about voluntary disclosure practices. On the other hand, the gradual rise of regulations for non-financial information poses new and interesting research challenges.

To date, most research on intellectual capital disclosure has been based on voluntary disclosure theory, as intellectual capital information has been provided by companies mainly on a voluntary basis. The issue of the Directive 2014/95 calls for research to shed light on intellectual capital regulation. Previous studies document that both voluntary and mandatory non-financial disclosure suffer from less credibility compared to quantitative financial information (Hirst et al., 1995; Hodge et al., 2006). This is related to the unavoidable discretion which characterizes non-financial information and gives managers incentives to report in an opportunistic way. According to Cormier et al. (2009, p. 73), 'firms may play on information attributes, such as precision level, to mitigate an external audience's tendency to discount the credibility of its discretionary disclosures and thus, enhance the persuasiveness and effectiveness of social and human capital disclosures'. In this vein, intellectual capital research may offer a relevant contribution to both companies which aim to enhance their disclosure, and regulators who need to guarantee high-level disclosure quality and identify opportunistic behaviours. Since intellectual capital disclosure is mainly narrative in nature, the content analysis technique is an appropriate tool of investigation.

On the other hand, the increasing number of companies issuing an integrated report (Gibassier et al., 2019) calls for research that looks at intellectual capital disclosure within integrated reporting to investigate, among other issues, its quality, its objective and its tone. High-quality content analyses, based on both form-oriented and meaning-oriented approaches, can contribute to better understand intellectual capital disclosure communicated by integrated reporting and its effectiveness in addressing stakeholders' information needs.

Lastly, communication devices represent another opportunity to enrich intellectual capital disclosure research. Content analysis studies largely focus on annual reports (Dumay, 2014). However, it is acknowledged that companies also use other channels to convey intellectual capital information, such as the company's website (Waters et al., 2009). To date, very few studies have focused on different communication tools. This includes information released via social media (Pisano et al., 2017; Lardo et al., 2017), initial public offering (IPO) prospectuses (Garanina and Dumay, 2017), earnings announcements and conference calls (Graaf, 2013), and analyst reports (García-Meca and Martínez, 2007; Abhayawansa and Guthrie, 2016).

Research opportunities can be identified in meaning-oriented content analysis, which has received little attention to date despite it being deemed the most useful in intellectual capital disclosure research (Guthrie, 2014). Beyond positivism and content analysis, other paradigms and methodologies should be explored to investigate intellectual capital disclosure (Roslender, 2004). For instance, Nielsen and Madsen (2009) use critical realism and discourse analysis to discuss the issue of transparency in intellectual capital reporting. Alternative instruments to investigate intellectual capital disclosure can be drawn from other disciplines, such as sociology and linguistics (Beattie, 2014).

Pollach (2012) argues that the process of opening up to new methodologies is still in its infancy in the accounting field. In this regard, corpus linguistics (Tognini-Bonelli, 2001) could represent an appealing tool for studying intellectual capital disclosure. Corpus linguistics is based on the perspective that a text is an integral part of its context, as communication cannot exist in isolation, detached from a specific environment (Sinclair, 1991). This technique combines both automated quantitative analysis, which usually focuses on the most frequent words in a text (keywords), and qualitative discourse analysis aimed at interpreting the keywords within the contextual words (Sinclair, 1991). These characteristics make corpus linguistics a flexible device that may be used in both positivist analyses of texts, and qualitative analyses anchored to other paradigms (Bini et al., 2016b).

Corpus linguistics has been used in the accounting field by Zappettini and Unerman (2016, p. 521) to explore sustainability disclosure in integrated reports with the aim to understand 'how discourses of sustainability have been recontextualized into financial and economic macro discourses and how different intertextual/interdiscursive relations have played out in linguistic constructions of "sustainability"'.

Recent reviews show that there is much work to be done to increase the quality of intellectual capital disclosure research (Dumay and Cai, 2014, 2015). Researchers seem to be reluctant to leave the comfort zone of descriptive and replicative analyses, which in many cases are methodologically questionable (Abeysekera, 2006).

Methodological rigour starts with an in-depth knowledge of the content analysis technique as well as of the assumptions on which it is based. Content analysis studies rarely discuss the research paradigm adopted, even though this strongly affects the development of the coding process, the evaluation criteria and the interpretation of findings. A more explicit explanation could be useful for researchers to guarantee the coherence of their research design within the paradigm adopted. Readers would benefit from a clear presentation of the framework in use as they can more easily interpret the results and identify the contribution of the work.

Additionally, the limitations of existing disclosure measures used to assess intellectual capital reveal that there is room for new approaches (Beattie et al., 2004). Bini et al. (2016a) propose alternative measures of intellectual capital narratives based on two key characteristics of intellectual capital disclosure: focus and connectivity. This approach could be used to assess intellectual capital disclosure with both form-oriented and meaning-oriented content analyses.

REFERENCES

Abeysekera, I. (2006), 'The project of intellectual capital disclosure: researching the research', *Journal of Intellectual Capital*, 7 (1), 61–77.

Abeysekera, I. and J. Guthrie (2005), 'An empirical investigation of annual reporting trends of intellectual capital in Sri Lanka', *Critical Perspectives on Accounting*, 16 (3), 151–163.

Abhayawansa, S. (2011), 'A methodology for investigating intellectual capital information in analyst reports', *Journal of Intellectual Capital*, 12 (3), 446–476.

Abhayawansa, S. and J. Guthrie (2014), 'Importance of intellectual capital information: a study of Australian analyst reports', *Australian Accounting Review*, 24 (1), 66–83.

Abhayawansa, S. and J. Guthrie (2016), 'Does intellectual capital disclosure in analysts' reports vary by firm characteristics?', *Advances in Accounting*, 35, 26–38.

Abrahamson, E. and C. Park (1994), 'Concealment of negative organizational outcomes: an agency theory perspective', *Academy of Management Journal*, 37 (5), 1302–1334.

Accounting Standards Board (2006), *Reporting Statement: Operating and Financial Review*, London.

Adams, C.A. (2015), 'The international integrated reporting council: a call to action', *Critical Perspectives on Accounting*, 27, 23–28.

Alvesson, M. and S. Deetz (2000), *Doing Critical Management Research*, London: SAGE.

Beattie, V. (2014), 'Accounting narratives and the narrative turn in accounting research: issues, theory, methodology, methods and a research framework', *British Accounting Review*, 46 (2), 111–134.

Beattie, V., McInnes, B. and S. Fearnley (2004), 'A methodology for analysing and evaluating narratives in annual reports: a comprehensive descriptive profile and metrics for disclosure quality attribute', *Accounting Forum*, 28, 205–326.

Beattie, V. and S.J. Smith (2013), 'Value creation and business models: refocusing the intellectual capital debate', *British Accounting Review*, 45 (4), 243–254.

Beattie, V., and S.J. Thomson (2007), 'Lifting the lid on the use of content analysis to investigate intellectual capital disclosures', *Accounting Forum*, 31 (2), 129–163.

Berelson, B. (1952), *Content Analysis in Communication Research*, Glencoe, IL: Free Press.

Beretta, S. and S. Bozzolan (2008), 'Quality versus quantity: the case of forward-looking disclosure', *Journal of Accounting, Auditing and Finance*, 23 (3), 333–376.

Bini, L., Dainelli, F. and F. Giunta (2016a), 'Business model disclosure in the Strategic Report', *Journal of Intellectual Capital*, 17 (1), 83–102.

Bini, L., Samson, C. and F. Giunta (2016b), 'Let the text talk: a corpus-driven analysis approach to investigate accounting narratives', *European Journal of Economics, Finance and Administrative Sciences*, 89, 81–96.

Björkdahl, J. (2009), 'Technology cross-fertilization and the business model: the case of integrating ICTs in mechanical engineering products', *Research Policy*, 38 (9), 1468–1477.

Bjurström, E. and H. Roberts (2007), 'The principle of connectivity: networked assets, strategic capabilities and bundled outcomes', in C. Chaminade and B. Catasús (eds), *Intellectual Capital Revisited: Paradoxes in the Knowledge Intensive Organization*, Cheltenham, UK and Northampton, MA, USA: Edward Elgar Publishing, pp. 45–60.

Boland, R.J. and L.R. Pondy (1983), 'Accounting in organizations: a union of natural and rational perspectives', *Accounting Organizations and Society*, 8 (2/3), 223–234.

Bontis, N. (2003), 'Intellectual capital disclosure in Canadian corporations', *Journal of Human Resource Costing and Accounting*, 7 (1), 9–20.

Bouchard, T.J. (1976), 'Unobtrusive measures: an inventory of uses', *Sociological Methods and Research*, 4, 267–300.

Boyatzis, R.E. (1998), *Transforming Qualitative Information: Thematic Analysis and Code Development*, Thousand Oaks, CA: SAGE Publications.

Bozzolan, S., Favotto, F. and F. Ricceri (2003), 'Italian annual intellectual capital disclosure: an empirical analysis', *Journal of Intellectual Capital*, 4 (4), 543–558.

Brüggen, A., Vergauwen, P. and M. Dao (2009), 'Determinants of intellectual capital disclosure: evidence from Australia', *Management Decision*, 47 (2), 233–245.

Buhr, N. (1998), 'Environmental performance, legislation and annual report disclosure: the case of acid rain and Falconbridge', *Accounting, Auditing and Accountability Journal*, 11 (2), 163–190.

Campbell, D. and M.R.A. Rahman (2010), 'A longitudinal examination of intellectual capital reporting in Marks & Spencer annual reports, 1978–2008', *British Accounting Review*, 42 (1), 56–70.

Canibano, L. (2018), 'Accounting and intangibles', *Revista de Contabilidad*, 21 (1), 1–6.

Carney, T.F. (1972), *Content Analysis: A Technique for Systematic Inference from Communications*, Winnipeg, MB: University of Manitoba Press.

Chatterjee, B., Tooley, S. and V. Fatseasa (2008), 'An analysis of the qualitative characteristics of management commentary reporting by New Zealand companies', *20th Asian-Pacific Conference on International Accounting Issues*, 9–12 November, Paris.

Chen, M.C., Cheng, S.J. and Y. Hwang (2005), 'An empirical investigation of the relationship between intellectual capital and firms' market value and financial performance', *Journal of Intellectual Capital*, 6 (2), 159–176.

Cheng, M., Green, W., Conradie, P., Konishi, N. and A. Romi (2014), 'The international integrated reporting framework: Key issues and future research opportunities', *Journal of International Financial Management and Accounting*, 25 (1), 90–119.

Chesbrough, H. and R.S. Rosenbloom (2002), 'The role of the business model in capturing value from innovation: evidence from Xerox Corporation's technology spin-off companies', *Industrial and Corporate Change*, 11 (3), 529–555.

Chiucchi, M.S. (2013), 'Intellectual capital accounting in action: enhancing learning through interventionist research', *Journal of Intellectual Capital*, 14 (1), 48–68.

Cormier, D., Aerts, W., Ledoux, M.J. and M. Magnan (2009), 'Attributes of social and human capital disclosure and information asymmetry between managers and investors', *Canadian Journal of Administrative Sciences*, 26 (1), 71–88.

Craig, R., Lehman, G., Milne, M. and H. Tregidga (2010), 'Analysing the quality, meaning and accountability of organisational reporting and communication', call for papers, *Accounting Forum*.

Dilling, P.F. and P. Harris (2018), 'Reporting on long-term value creation by Canadian companies: a longitudinal assessment', *Journal of Cleaner Production*, 191, 350–360.

Dumay, J. (2014), '15 years of the journal of intellectual capital and counting: a manifesto for transformational IC research', *Journal of Intellectual Capital*, 15 (1), 2–37.

Dumay, J. (2016), 'A critical reflection on the future of intellectual capital: from reporting to disclosure', *Journal of Intellectual Capital*, 17 (1), 168–184.

Dumay, J., Bernardi, C., Guthrie, J. and P. Demartini (2016), 'September. Integrated reporting: a structured literature review', *Accounting Forum*, 40 (3), 166–185.

Dumay, J. and L. Cai (2014), 'A review and critique of content analysis as a methodology for inquiring into IC disclosure', *Journal of Intellectual Capital*, 15 (2), 264–290.

Dumay, J. and L. Cai (2015), 'Using content analysis as a research methodology for investigating intellectual capital disclosure: a critique', *Journal of Intellectual Capital*, 16 (1), 121–155.

Eccles, R.G. and M.P. Krzus (2010), *One Report: Integrated Reporting for a Sustainable Strategy*, Hoboken, NJ: John Wiley & Sons.

Eccles, R.G., Nohria, N. and J.D. Berkley (1992), *Beyond the Hype: Rediscovering the Essence of Management*, Boston, MA: Harvard Business School Press.

Flower, J. (2015), 'The international integrated reporting council: a story of failure', *Critical Perspectives on Accounting*, 27 (1), 1–17.

Garanina, T. and J. Dumay (2017), 'Forward-looking intellectual capital disclosure in IPOs: implications for intellectual capital and integrated reporting', *Journal of Intellectual Capital*, 18 (1), 128–148.

García-Meca, E. and I. Martínez (2007), 'The use of intellectual capital information in investment decisions: an empirical study using analyst reports', *International Journal of Accounting*, 42 (1), 57–81.

Gately, C. and J. Cunningham (2014), 'Building intellectual capital in incubated technology firms', *Journal of Intellectual Capital*, 15 (4), 516–536.

Gibassier, D., Adams, C.A. and T. Jérôme (2019), *Integrated Reporting and the Capitals' Diffusion*, Report published by the French Accounting Standard Setter (Autorité des Normes Comptables).

Goebel, V. (2015), 'Is the literature on content analysis of intellectual capital reporting heading towards a dead end?', *Journal of Intellectual Capital*, 16 (3), 681–699.

Graaf, J. (2013), 'Colouring the numbers – on the role of intellectual capital in financial reporting', *Journal of Intellectual Capital*, 14 (3), 376–394.

Guthrie, J. (2014), 'In defence of disclosure studies and the use of content analysis: a research note', *Journal of Intellectual Capital*, 15 (2), 291–292.

Guthrie, J.E. and R. Petty (2000), 'Intellectual capital: Australian annual reporting practices', *Journal of Intellectual Capital*, 1 (3), 241–251.

Guthrie, J., Petty, R. and F. Ricceri (2006), 'The voluntary reporting of intellectual capital: comparing evidence from Hong Kong and Australia', *Journal of Intellectual Capital*, 7 (2), 254–271.

Guthrie, J., Petty, R., Yongvanich, K. and F. Ricceri (2004), 'Using content analysis as a research method to inquire into intellectual capital reporting', *Journal of Intellectual Capital*, 5 (2), 282–293.

Habersam, M. and M. Piber (2003), 'Exploring intellectual capital in hospitals: two qualitative case studies in Italy and Austria', *European Accounting Review*, 12 (4), 753–779.

Hirst, D., Koonce, L. and P. Simko (1995), 'Investor reactions to financial analysts' research reports', *Journal of Accounting Research*, 33 (2), 335–351.

Hodge, F., Hopkins, P.E. and J. Pratt (2006), 'Management reporting incentives and classification credibility: the effects of reporting discretion and reputation', *Accounting, Organizations and Society*, 31 (7), 623–634.

Holland, J. (2004), *Corporate Intangibles, Value Relevance and Disclosure Content*, Edinburgh: Institute of Chartered Accountants of Scotland.

Holsti, O.R. (1969), *Content Analysis for the Social Sciences and Humanities*, Reading, MA: Addison-Wesley.

Husin, N.M., Hooper, K. and K. Olesen (2012), 'Analysis of intellectual capital disclosure – an illustrative example', *Journal of Intellectual Capital*, 13 (2), 196–220.

International Integrated Reporting Council (IIRC) (2013a), *Integrated Reporting – The Pilot Programme 2013 Yearbook: Business and Investors Explore the Sustainability Perspective of Integrated Reporting*, London: International Integrated Reporting Council.

International Integrated Reporting Council (IIRC) (2013b), *The Integrated IR Framework*, London: International Integrated Reporting Council.

Jackson, N. and P. Carter (1993), '"Paradigm wars": a response to Hugh Willmott', *Organization Studies*, 14 (5), 721–725.

Johnson, P., Buehring, A., Cassell, C. and G. Symon (2006), 'Evaluating qualitative management research: towards a contingent criteriology', *International Journal of Management Reviews*, 8 (3), 131–156.

Johnson, P. and J. Duberley (2000), *Understanding Management Research: An Introduction to Epistemology*, London: SAGE.

Josephson, J.R. and S.G. Josephson (eds) (1996), *Abductive Inference: Computation, Philosophy, Technology*, Cambridge: Cambridge University Press.

Kamath, B. (2017), 'Determinants of intellectual capital disclosure: evidence from India', *Journal of Financial Reporting and Accounting*, 15 (3), 367–391.

Keenan, J. and M. Aggestam (2001), 'Corporate governance and intellectual capital: some conceptualisations', *Corporate Governance: An International Review*, 9 (4), 259–275.

Krippendorff, K. (2013), *Content Analysis: An Introduction to its Methodology*, Thousand Oaks, CA: SAGE.

Lardo, A., Dumay, J., Trequattrini, R. and G. Russo (2017), 'Social media networks as drivers for intellectual capital disclosure: evidence from professional football clubs', *Journal of Intellectual Capital*, 18 (1), 63–80.

Lewis, J. and J. Ritchie (2003), 'Generalizing from qualitative research', in J. Ritchie and J. Lewis (eds), *Qualitative Research Practice*, London: SAGE, pp. 263–287.

Li, J., Pike, R. and R. Haniffa (2008), 'Intellectual capital disclosure and corporate governance structure in UK firms', *Accounting and Business Research*, 38 (2), 137–159.

Maniora, J. (2017), 'Is integrated reporting really the superior mechanism for the integration of ethics into the core business model? An empirical analysis', *Journal of Business Ethics*, 140 (4), 755–786.

Marr, B. and J. Chatzkel (2004), 'Intellectual capital at the crossroads: managing, measuring, and reporting of IC', *Journal of Intellectual Capital*, 5 (2), 224–229.

Melloni, G. (2015), 'Intellectual capital disclosure in integrated reporting: an impression management analysis', *Journal of Intellectual Capital*, 16 (3), 661–680.

MERITUM (2002), *Guidelines for Managing and Reporting on Intangibles*, Tucson, AZ: TSER Programme, MERITUM.

Merkl-Davies, D.M., Brennan, N.M. and P. Vourvachis (2011), 'Text analysis methodologies in corporate narrative reporting research', working paper presented at 23rd CSEAR International Colloquium, St Andrews, UK.

Milne, M.J. and R.W. Adler (1999), 'Exploring the reliability of social and environmental disclosures content analysis', *Accounting, Auditing and Accountability Journal*, 12 (2), 237–256.

Mitchell, J.C. (1983), 'Case and situational analysis', *Sociological Review*, 31, 187–211.

Mouritsen, J., Bukh, P.N., Flagstad, K., Thorbjørnsen, S., Johansen, M.R., et al. (2003), *Intellectual Capital Statements in Practice – Inspiration and Good Advice*, Copenhagen: Danish Ministry of Science, Technology and Innovation.

Mouritsen, J., Larsen, H.T. and P.N. Bukh (2001), 'Intellectual capital and the "capable firm": narrating, visualising and numbering for managing knowledge', *Accounting, Organisations and Society*, 26 (7), 735–762.

Neuendorf, K.A. (2002), *The Content Analysis Guidebook*, Thousand Oaks, CA: SAGE Publications.

Nielsen, C. (2010), 'Conceptualizing, analyzing and communicating the business model', Working Paper No. 2, Department of Business Studies, Aalborg University, Denmark.

Nielsen, C. and M.T. Madsen (2009), 'Discourses of transparency in the intellectual capital reporting debate: moving from generic reporting models to management defined information', *Critical Perspectives on Accounting*, 20 (7), 847–854.

O'Connor, E. (2002), 'Storied business: typology, intertextuality, and traffic in entrepreneurial narrative', *Journal of Business Communication*, 39 (1), 36–54.

Painter-Morland, M. (2006), 'Triple bottom-line reporting as social grammar: integrating corporate social responsibility and corporate codes of conduct', *Business Ethics: A European Review*, 15 (4), 352–364.

Peng, Y. and J.A. Reggia (2012), *Abductive Inference Models for Diagnostic Problem-Solving*, New York: Springer Science & Business Media.

Pisano, S., Lepore, L. and R. Lamboglia (2017), 'Corporate disclosure of human capital via LinkedIn and ownership structure: An empirical analysis of European companies', *Journal of Intellectual Capital*, 18 (1), 102–127.

Pollach, I. (2012), 'Taming textual data: the contribution of corpus linguistics to computer-aided text analysis', *Organizational Research Methods*, 15 (2), 263–287.

Rhee, S.K. and S.Y. Lee (2003), 'Dynamic change of corporate environmental strategy: rhetoric and reality', *Business Strategy and the Environment*, 12 (3), 175–190.

Roos, G., Ross, G., Edvinsson, L. and N.C. Dragonetti (1997), *Intellectual Capital: Navigating in the New Business Landscape*, Houndmills: Macmillan Business.

Roslender, R. (2004), 'Accounting for intellectual capital: rethinking its theoretical underpinnings', *Measuring Business Excellence*, 8 (1), 38–45.

Schaper, S., Nielsen, C. and R. Roslender (2017), 'Moving from irrelevant intellectual capital (IC) reporting to value-relevant IC disclosures: key learning points from the Danish experience', *Journal of Intellectual Capital*, 18, 81–101.

Sinclair, J. (1991), *Corpus, Concordance, Collocation*, Oxford: Oxford University Press.

Smith, M. and R. Taffler (2000), 'The chairman's statement. A content analysis of discretionary narrative disclosures', *Accounting, Auditing and Accountability Journal*, 13 (5), 624–646.

Steenkamp, N. and D. Northcott (2007), 'Content analysis in accounting research: the practical challenges', *Australian Accounting Review*, 17 (43), 12–25.

Strauss, A. (1987), *Qualitative Analysis for Social Scientists*, Cambridge: Cambridge University Press.

Striukova, L., Unerman, J. and J. Guthrie (2008), 'Corporate reporting of intellectual capital: evidence from UK companies', *British Accounting Review*, 40 (4), 297–313.

Sveiby, K.E. (1997), *The New Organizational Wealth: Managing and Measuring Knowledge-Based Assets*, Oakland, CA: Berrett-Koehler Publishers.

Tenkasi, R. and R. Boland (1993), 'Locating meaning making in organizational learning: the narrative basis of cognition', in R. Woodman and W. Pasmore (eds), *Research on Organizational Change and Development* (Vol. 7), Greenwich, CT: JAI Press, pp. 77–103.

Tognini-Bonelli, E. (2001), *Corpus Linguistics at Work*, Amsterdam: John Benjamins.

Toms, J.S. (2002), 'Firm resources, quality signals and the determinants of corporate environmental reputation: some UK evidence', *British Accounting Review*, 34 (3), 257–282.

Unerman, J. (2000), 'Methodological issues: reflections on quantification in corporate social reporting content analysis', *Accounting, Auditing and Accountability Journal*, 13 (5), 667–681.

Vafaei, A., Taylor, D. and K. Ahmed (2011), 'The value relevance of intellectual capital disclosures', *Journal of Intellectual Capital*, 12 (3), 407–429.

Vandemaele, S.N., Vergauwen, P.G.M.C. and A.J. Smits (2005), 'Intellectual capital disclosure in The Netherlands, Sweden and the UK: a longitudinal and comparative study', *Journal of Intellectual Capital*, 6 (3), 417–426.

Waters, R.D., Burnett, E., Lamm, A. and J. Lucas (2009), 'Engaging stakeholders through social networking: how non-profit organizations are using Facebook', *Public Relations Review*, 35 (2), 102–106.

Webb, E.J., Campbell, D.T., Schwartz, R.D. and L. Sechrest (1966), *Unobtrusive Measures: Non-reactive Research in the Social Sciences*, Chicago, IL: Rand McNally.

Weber, R.P. (1990), *Basic Content Analysis* (2nd edn), Newbury Park, CA: SAGE Publications.

Welker, M. (1995), 'Disclosure policy, information asymmetry and liquidity in equity markets', *Contemporary Accounting Research*, 11, 801–828.

Whiting, R.H. and J.C. Miller (2008), 'Voluntary disclosure of intellectual capital in New Zealand annual reports and the hidden value', *Journal of Human Resources Costing and Accounting*, 12 (1), 26–50.

Whiting, R.H. and J. Woodcock (2011), 'Firm characteristics and intellectual capital disclosure by Australian companies', *Journal of Human Resource Costing and Accounting*, 15 (2), 102–126.

Zappettini, F. and J. Unerman (2016), '"Mixing" and "bending": the recontextualisation of discourses of sustainability in integrated reporting', *Discourse and Communication*, 10 (5), 521–542.

2. Has content analysis on intellectual capital reporting reached an impasse?

Viktoria Goebel

INTRODUCTION

The concept of intellectual capital (IC) has been discussed in the literature for more than 20 years, after the importance of intangible resources was first noted in early publications by Brooking (1996), Stewart (1997) and Sveiby (1997). IC reporting has become established as a separate research area, with content analysis being an important method to investigate narrative corporate reporting (for example, Guthrie et al., 2004). The development of content analysis studies on IC reporting has been criticised for stalling, rather than progressing, as the methodology of prior studies has mainly been applied to other research settings (for example, Dumay and Cai, 2014; Dumay, 2016). For nearly a decade, I have been following IC reporting research. A critical review of the literature on IC reporting research raises the question: is content analysis on IC reporting heading towards a dead end (Goebel, 2015a)? The following chapter critically evaluates IC reporting research and discusses how it can usefully be applied in the future. This chapter concludes with recommendations for how IC reporting research can be taken forward, and the role of content analysis.

WHAT IS IC REPORTING?

Initial studies concerning intangible resources established the idea of IC and highlighted its strategic importance (Brooking, 1996; Stewart, 1997; Sveiby, 1997). IC is a company's ability to react efficiently to the environmental situation by utilising its intangible resources (Brooking, 1996; Hall, 1992; Stewart, 1997). Due to the dynamic nature of IC, a comprehensive definition has not been provided, but different approaches exist. In a broad area of literature, IC is seen to equip the company with unique resources that cannot easily be imitated by competitors and represent a competitive advantage, which is reflected in strong corporate performance and high company value (Hall, 1992; Stewart, 1997; Sveiby, 1997).

Dumay's (2016, p. 169) definition even goes beyond company value, and sees IC as contributing to 'monetary, utility, social and sustainable value'.

IC is characterised as consisting of efficient internal structures, beneficial relations to primary stakeholders and human resources (Stewart, 1997; Brüggen et al., 2009). These features are widely categorised as structural, relational and human capital (Beattie and Thomson, 2007; Li et al., 2008). Structural capital supports the company to run by creating innovations (Guthrie et al., 2007). Relational capital constitutes favourable relations to important stakeholders, such as suppliers, customers, business partners and investors (Guthrie and Petty, 2000). Human capital represents people working for the company, their skills and development (Bukh et al., 2005).

IC reporting offers the opportunity for companies to tell the story of their IC-related resources and their importance within the business model. To approach IC reporting and to enable meaningful research, exploratory studies have been conducted, such as case studies (Mouritsen et al., 2001) and interviews with companies (van der Meer-Kooistra and Zijlstra, 2001). Early studies found that IC reporting should be embedded in a story describing its different aspects and roles inside an organisation (Mouritsen et al., 2001). A longitudinal study by Campbell and Rahman (2010), analysing over 31 years of annual reports in a retail company, sees a strong increase of IC information and a movement towards more narrative information. Their study also suggests that IC reporting has been rising along with the IC concept emerging in the literature.

People preparing corporate reports still consider IC reporting as an important tool to inform the market and stakeholders about a company's IC. To examine how IC reporting is perceived across corporate functions, Beattie and Thomson (2010) investigate IC reporting from the perspectives of the people preparing the reports. They find that most respondents regard IC as essential in the value creation process. Through questionnaires to finance directors, Beattie and Smith (2012) find that market considerations are seen to be relevant for IC reporting decisions. In a similar approach in a survey with banks, Wee and Chua (2016) identify the responsibility to enable stakeholders to make better decisions as important motivation for IC reporting. Therefore, IC reporting still offers research opportunities because it is a useful tool in practice.

CRITICAL REVIEWS OF CONTENT ANALYSIS ON IC REPORTING

The use of content analysis to study IC reporting has been critically reviewed in the literature. Given the narrative nature of IC reporting, content analysis has been a main research method in prior studies, as outlined by Guthrie et al. (2004). The studies by Dumay and Garanina (2013), Dumay (2014b) and Dumay and Cai (2014, 2015) have reviewed the developments and achievements in IC reporting research. These reviews highlight the wide range of approaches and perspectives across prior IC reporting studies. IC reporting research has introduced different perspectives without clear direction (Cuozzo et al., 2017; Dumay and Guthrie, 2017). Many studies have reused prior approaches to explore IC reporting in another country, or focused on another industry group, for example on universities, in recent years (Rossi et al., 2018).

Prior content analyses consider a diverse range of factors potentially associated to IC reporting and accordingly have gathered diverse data, without utilising all data collected. For their content analysis of IC reporting, Guthrie and Petty (2000) collect more criteria than analysed, for instance location of information. Due to unsystematic IC reporting practices, feasible comparisons and conclusions from this additional information might be hampered. Additionally, the acknowledged inherent drawbacks of content analysis, such as subjectivity (Krippendorff, 2018), add to non-comparable outcomes. For example, Striukova et al. (2008) record tone, type and location of disclosure; unfortunately they do not examine the implications of this for IC reporting. While Abeysekera and Guthrie (2005) introduce the idea of intellectual liabilities, they have not examined IC reporting for these intellectual liabilities. Thus, there appears to be a lack of clear focus in some studies.

The lack of clear focus causes some scholars to question whether this research area is still useful. Dumay (2016) even argues that IC reporting is dead among listed companies but is still popular among academics. Dumay and Cai (2014) and Cuozzo et al. (2017) critique IC content analyses as being illustrative rather than critical, particularly as prior studies have not utilised the content analysis results for critical investigations. Their critique is in line with prior calls by Mouritsen (2006, 2009) and Guthrie et al. (2012) that testing IC-related hypotheses and theories has been missing in IC reporting research.

INVESTIGATING IC REPORTING IN CONTENT ANALYSIS STUDIES

To approach IC reporting in content analyses, research frameworks have been introduced and represent the researchers' understandings of how to define IC for their studies. The elusive nature of IC poses a challenge for content analysis of IC reporting (Guthrie et al., 2004; Beattie and

Thomson, 2007; Lee and Guthrie, 2010; Guthrie et al., 2012). IC research frameworks include coding devices with predefined lists of IC items that are designed or chosen *ex ante* by the researchers as checklists. Numerous IC research frameworks have been developed for different IC reporting studies over time. Three influential studies are quoted frequently as a basis for developing IC research frameworks, namely Guthrie and Petty (2000), Bontis (2003) and Bukh et al. (2005). Decisions on reusing IC research frameworks of prior studies are also based on the same authors or author groups reusing their previous frameworks (Dumay and Cai, 2014).

It is difficult to conclude whether currently used frameworks show more uniformity with a decreasing number of newly proposed frameworks. Reusing previously developed frameworks has become common practice in IC research, as found by Guthrie et al. (2012). They interpret this development as a maturing process of IC research. Sometimes the frameworks of prior studies are used with modifications or combinations across different approaches (Goebel, 2015a). Adapting a certain IC research framework for a content analysis of IC reporting is driven by conceptual considerations, certain conditions given to the sample, certain author groups or trends in IC reporting research. Thus, IC research frameworks are often accepted uncritically and mentioned in the appendix of prior studies (García-Meca et al., 2005; Li et al., 2008).

Modifications to IC frameworks and unclear explanations about changes constitute a problem of transparency in IC reporting content analyses studies. Some studies do not provide details of the IC research frameworks applied, or they do not explain modifications to reused IC research frameworks (García-Meca and Martínez, 2007; Hidalgo et al., 2011). Modifications to IC research frameworks are rarely justified in discussions and subsequent researchers are not able to deduce the reasons for modifications. For example, García-Meca and Martínez (2007) altered Bukh et al.'s (2005) framework without providing reasons for their changes. Other studies introduce their IC research frameworks as being based on prior studies, but numerous amendments may result in different frameworks. While, for example, Hidalgo et al. (2011) claim to have adopted García-Meca et al.'s (2005) approach, the numbers of IC-related items differ and the classification of IC categories is changed, without presenting the final framework for comparison.

Another issue arising from comparing IC research frameworks of prior studies is that IC items are classified differently across prior frameworks (Goebel, 2015a). While some IC items are allocated to a certain category in one IC research framework, they may be classified differently in others, such as financial relations to structural or relational capital (Vandemaele et al., 2005; Lee and Guthrie, 2010). It is difficult to define appropriate boundaries because there are contentious points between IC categories, as Mouritsen (2009) highlights. Employee training on technology systems, for example, can be categorised as either human or structural capital. Furthermore, Mouritsen (2009) argues that interactions between IC items create difficulties to attribute individual items to certain categories. This may partly explain how diverse classifications have developed and how they continue to co-exist across IC research frameworks.

QUESTIONING TRANSPARENCY AND COMPARABILITY IN IC REPORTING STUDIES

Transparency is also an issue in IC reporting due to variations in content analysis procedures. Abeysekera (2006) questions the comparability of the results of prior IC reporting studies due to methodological aspects, such as sample compositions and decisions on content analysis procedures. The concern of non-comparability due to diverging procedures within IC content analyses is also raised by Beattie and Thomson (2007). Different decisions in the content analysis approach, such as counting occurrences of IC items with or without repetition in the narratives under review, various units of measurement and considerations of graphs, will result in different IC reporting scores. The coding procedures are normally mentioned briefly in prior studies; however, the chosen approaches may not be discussed in detail in subsequent papers as information on the coding device is often omitted (Hidalgo et al., 2011; Garanina and Dumay, 2017). Hence, IC reporting scores are not directly comparable across studies.

Non-comparability raises questions about the findings of prior studies. In a comparison of prior research frameworks, Goebel (2015a) suggests that widely used IC items across prior studies show a focus on a certain group of IC items in academia. However, if IC reporting in practice does not share this focus, the results from different IC research frameworks may deviate strongly. This consideration highlights the importance and variety of IC research frameworks in the IC content analysis (Guthrie et al., 2012). The question arises whether different IC research frameworks may even effectively analyse different areas of IC reporting.

Comparability of previous studies is also problematic because the development of IC reporting investigations shows a lack of agreement on how to assess corporate IC reporting. Dumay and Cai (2014) highlight that IC research frameworks are bound to be different due to different research settings. As a certain degree of subjectivity is inherent in content analyses (Krippendorff, 2018), the differences in IC research frameworks may increase this subjectivity. Hence, the comparability of prior content analysis studies of IC reporting may be considered questionable, or even inconsequential to developing knowledge about applying IC in practice. Table 2.1 shows a synoptic comparison of previous IC reporting studies in terms of their methodological considerations. This synopsis compares theories, country focus, communication channels, industry groups and sample size.

THEORIES RELATED TO IC REPORTING

Although reporting theories have been referred to or indirectly supported in the IC reporting literature, no strong theory seems to have been established for IC research. Theories related to IC reporting range from resource-based and actor-network approaches (Mouritsen et al., 2001) to cost of capital analysis (Bukh et al., 2005; Mangena et al., 2010). The most commonly mentioned theories are general reporting theories, such as agency, legitimacy or stakeholder theory (Beattie and Thomson, 2007; Garanina and Dumay, 2017; Guthrie et al., 2004; Rossi et al., 2018). However, describing IC reporting has been the focus of many studies that refer to but rarely test theories on IC reporting (Brüggen et al., 2009; Guthrie and Petty, 2000).

The theoretical background for an IC reporting study, based on general reporting theories, requires further explanation. Why would a company disclose information about its competitive advantage, as it may be commercially sensitive (Mangena et al., 2010; Singh and Van der Zahn, 2008), considering that IC is argued to support value creation (Dumay, 2016; Stewart, 1997; Hall, 1992)? Guthrie et al. (2004) tries to bridge theories of general disclosure to IC reporting, namely legitimacy theory and stakeholder theory. In their review, they conclude that theoretical developments are needed to enhance IC reporting research. Following their approach, theories of general disclosure can be further developed for the area of IC reporting research by logical argument to establish a framework for IC reporting. This theoretical framework can then be applied to investigate corporate motivations for IC reporting.

The prevalent lack of direct linkages between theories and IC reporting has been criticised, and calls for theory testing have been made (Marr et al., 2003; Mouritsen, 2006, 2009). Mouritsen (2006) argues that IC reporting theories change with the IC definition chosen. He does not claim that any theory is superior, but he promotes the position that a clear decision enhances IC reporting studies and encourages innovative research designs. Marr et al. (2003) also call for approaches to test theories on IC reporting to enhance IC reporting research. Goebel (2019) develops links between

Table 2.1 Synoptic table of previous content analysis studies of IC reporting

Studies	Theory	Country	Channels	Industry	Sample Size
Abeysekera and Guthrie (2005)	Explanatory	Sri Lanka	Annual report	not controlled	30 companies
Beattie and Thomson (2007)	Exploratory; refer to positive accounting, legitimacy, stakeholder theory	UK	Annual report		1 company
Bontis (2003)	Exploratory	Canada	Annual report	not controlled	10000 companies
Bozzolan et al. (2003)	Exploratory; refer to agency and signalling theory	Italy	Annual report	knowledge/ traditional	30 companies
Brennan (2001)	Exploratory	Ireland	Annual report	only knowledge based	11 companies
Brüggen et al. (2009)	Exploratory Implied agency theory	Australia	Annual report	9 industry groups	125 companies
Bukh et al. (2005)	Cost of disclosure theory	Denmark	IPO prospectus	knowledge/ traditional	68 IPOs
Cerbioni and Parbonetti (2007)	Agency theory, governance	Europe	Annual report	only biotechnology	54 companies
Duff (2018)	Institutional theory	UK	Annual review, CSR report, websites	professional accounting firms	20 companies

Garanina and Dumay (2017)	Agency theory	NASDAQ	IPO prospectus	technology companies	154 companies
García-Meca et al. (2005)	Agency and signalling theory	Spain	Analyst presentation	financial/ non-financial	257 reports
García-Meca and Martínez (2007)	Implied value-relevance	Spain	Analyst report	9 industry groups	260 reports
Goebel (2019)	Agency theory	Germany	Management reports	4 industry groups	428 companies
Guthrie and Petty (2000)	Exploratory	Australia	Annual report	6 industry groups	19 companies
Guthrie et al. (2007)	Exploratory; refer to stakeholder and legitimacy theory	Australia, Hong Kong	Annual report	not controlled	50 Australia 100 Hong Kong
Hidalgo et al. (2011)	Agency theory, governance, refer to signalling, capital market, cost–benefit theory	Mexico	Annual report	Industry dummies, number not specified	100 companies
Lee and Guthrie (2010)	Exploratory	Global	Annual report + Analyst reports	only IT sector	156 companies
Li et al. (2008)	Agency theory, governance	UK	Annual report	7 industry groups	100 companies

agency theory and IC reporting to test drivers for corporate IC reporting. The development of IC value is seen to cause information gaps between investors and managers aimed to be addressed by IC reporting. The issue of missing explanations on IC-related theories opens a potential research area to develop more focused theoretical approaches on IC reporting.

COUNTRY FOCUS IN IC REPORTING STUDIES

Single-country studies offer research settings to examine country-specific issues in IC reporting investigations. Guthrie and Petty (2000) mention amendments to the research framework due to country-specific considerations. In a study of IC reporting in Australia, they state that their framework is adjusted for 'items likely to be reported by Australian companies' (Guthrie and Petty, 2000, p. 245). Unfortunately, further studies cannot reproduce country-specific amendments with similar procedures, as they are not specified. Bukh et al. (2005) support that differences across countries affect reporting practices. They conduct a content analysis of Danish initial public offering (IPO) prospectuses over time, assuming that voluntary reporting practices have been well established in Denmark, and inferences may not be practical for analyses in a broader institutional context, partly due to national legislation and traditions.

The findings of cross-country studies are mainly descriptive because they cannot account for all possible factors that influence IC reporting in different countries. A study across different countries by Guthrie et al. (2007) shows that in Australia external and internal capital dominates corporate IC reporting, but Hong Kong companies report more on human capital. Although the findings are compared across the chosen countries, the results appear to be two separate studies describing general differences without identifying country-specific patterns. Other studies that compare IC reporting across countries show similar results, describing rather than explaining IC reporting divergences in different countries (Vandemaele et al., 2005; Vergauwen et al., 2007). Vergauwen and van Alem (2005) argue that IC reporting differences may be caused by different reporting regulations and auditor conservatism.

Strong arguments exist against international IC reporting studies. Different levels of technological progress and national IC value have been suggested as reasons why cross-country studies may be problematic (Lin and Edvinsson, 2010). Therefore, IC reporting may be more relevant in countries with higher technological levels. Additionally, reporting languages make cross-country comparisons difficult. The original language version of corporate documents may offer more detailed insights into IC reporting, compared to translated documents, as indicated by Goebel (2015b).

Particularly as IC reaches beyond the financial statements, regulation may vary strongly across countries between voluntary reporting, recommendations and detailed requirements. For example, Catalfo and Wulf (2016) compare German and Italian regulations and find that regulations on management reporting in both countries include aspects of IC, but the Italian approach was found to be more focused on recommendations. Goebel (2015b) also investigates IC reporting in the context of national requirements and recommendations in Germany. The findings indicate that requirements and recommendations seem to enrich IC reporting, as the cultural pressure and reputational risk may cause companies to report on recommendations. Therefore, regulations and even recommendations may influence IC reporting, reducing comparability across countries.

COMMUNICATION CHANNELS UNDER REVIEW

IC reporting studies on different communication channels add complexity to the question of comparability across prior studies. The scope of IC reporting instruments analysed ranges from IPO prospectuses (Bukh et al., 2005; Singh and Van der Zahn, 2008; Garanina and Dumay, 2017) to separately published IC statements (Mouritsen et al., 2001), integrated reports (Terblanche and Villiers, 2019), management reports (Goebel, 2019) and corporate websites (Rossi et al., 2018). Annual reports are the most commonly examined documents (Guthrie et al., 2012; Bozzolan et al., 2003; Guthrie et al., 2004). However, annual reports are criticised as being an inadequate source for corporate IC reporting, as companies often do not intentionally provide the overall picture of their IC in annual reports (Dumay and Guthrie, 2017).

To investigate reporting in extraordinary situations, such as public listings, communication means other than annual reports are more relevant for corporate purposes and different proxies are used for IC reporting studies. Investigations on IC reporting often focus on annual reports but have been broadened to include further communication channels. The review by Cuozzo et al. (2017) suggests that disclosure beyond regulated reporting may enhance IC reporting research. Bukh et al. (2005), Singh and Van der Zahn (2008) and Garanina and Dumay (2017) examine IPO prospectuses for forward-looking IC information provided to attract new potential investors. Analysts' reports are evaluated for the importance of IC value as perceived by analysts (García-Meca and Martínez, 2007).

Several channels of corporate communication are found to contain information on IC. Striukova et al. (2008) and Duff (2018) compare IC information provided in different communication channels available on corporate websites, including analyst presentations, annual and interim reports, corporate web pages and corporate social responsibility (CSR) reports. Dumay and Guthrie (2017) introduce the idea that 'involuntary disclosures' by interested stakeholders from outside the company may offer more information about corporate IC in comparison to corporate publications. They argue that new forms of media allow outsiders to easily publish information, opinions or rumours about companies. This situation affects corporate reputations and therefore IC. New communication channels, new media and new publishers of involuntary disclosures offer interesting research opportunities for IC reporting.

INDUSTRY GROUPINGS IN IC REPORTING STUDIES

The methodological issue of industry groupings may increase non-comparability of content analysis studies. Prior IC reporting studies arrange the samples into industry groups in a variety of ways. Since IC constitutes a competitive advantage (Stewart, 1997; Sveiby, 1997), competing companies within the same industry sector may aim to develop similar IC components. IC may be more important for some business models. Therefore, the industry grouping is essential for the set-up of comparing relevant IC items across companies. Additionally, diversified company segments hamper distinct classifications of industry groups as companies operate in more than one industry.

IC reporting may be less relevant for the financial sector. García-Meca et al. (2005) classify companies into financial and non-financial industry sectors. Their findings show no significant association to IC reporting in analyst presentations. This grouping may be too simplistic, as IC reporting may not play an important role for financial companies. Companies operating in the financial sector report least on IC, as found by Goebel (2015b). A potential reason is that corporate reporting is highly regulated for the financial sector, often with requirements on risk reporting. This may encourage financial companies to focus on regulated reporting rather than IC reporting.

Some studies may not be comparable because they focus on a single knowledge-intensive industry, such as information technology (IT) (Lee and Guthrie, 2010), biotechnology (Cerbioni and Parbonetti, 2007), universities (Rossi et al., 2018) or professional accounting firms (Duff, 2018).

Other studies distinguish between knowledge-intensive and traditional industries, such as high-tech and manufacturing (Bozzolan et al., 2003; Bukh et al., 2005; Vergauwen et al., 2007). A dichotomous distinction of knowledge-intensive and traditional industries may be chosen due to relatively small samples to indicate IC reporting patterns for general business models (Brennan, 2001; Williams, 2001; Bozzolan et al., 2003). These studies expect that knowledge-intensive companies report more on IC as their business models rely strongly on intangible resources, which is confirmed by Bukh et al. (2005) and Bozzolan et al. (2003). However, the definitions of high-tech companies are not always stated explicitly and may diverge between these studies.

Certain IC information in the content analysis research framework may be influenced by the nature of the businesses under investigation. Consequently, this may provide biased findings across the chosen sectors; for example, distribution channels may potentially be stronger in the retail sector. Many studies divide their samples into numerous industry groups according to different business models (Singh and Van der Zahn, 2008; Li et al., 2008; Goebel, 2019; Terblanche and Villiers, 2019). The findings by Striukova et al. (2008) deviate from their expectations, since IC reporting scores for companies from the retailing group surpass technology companies. Their study suggests that IC reporting might not entirely be related to knowledge sensitivity, but more towards maturity, as suggested by Secundo et al. (2015). Brüggen et al. (2009) find that only the IT and healthcare sectors are significantly positively associated with IC reporting. These results might be biased due to the high number of industry groups (nine in total) and due to the relatively small sample and the unstated sample distribution across industries.

SAMPLE SELECTION IN IC REPORTING STUDIES

The sample sizes and sample selection procedures vary widely across prior IC reporting studies. Sample sizes range from very small case samples of one company report (Beattie and Thomson, 2007) up to large samples of 10 000 reports (Bontis, 2003). Relatively small samples have initially been investigated in detail to explore IC reporting. Mouritsen et al. (2001) accompanied case companies in the process of creating IC statements and investigated IC reporting by means of observations and interviews. Some studies focus on a relatively small sample of large listed companies (Abeysekera and Guthrie, 2005; Bozzolan et al., 2003; Guthrie and Petty, 2000; Striukova et al., 2008). Small sample size is often given as a reason to avoid the question of generalisability, but Parker and Northcott (2016) advocate qualitative generalisability. They argue that social processes and concepts can be transferred to different settings and generalised in qualitative studies with logical reasoning and strong arguments.

As many studies conduct a manual content analysis, the sample size is certainly limited by the time-consuming procedures required (Brennan, 2001; Vergauwen et al., 2007; Duff, 2018; Rossi et al., 2018). To improve on inherent limitations of low statistical generalisability, extended content analyses have been undertaken. Larger samples may provide richer data sets for inferences and for testing IC-related hypotheses, as also advocated by Lee and Guthrie (2010). Software-aided coding may be a feasible tool for approaching this issue (Bontis, 2003; Lee and Guthrie, 2010). Dumay (2014a) even argues that refusing to use software-aided coding should not serve as an excuse for low statistical generalisability. However, computerised coding may be criticised for misinterpreting or omitting the IC context (Beattie and Thomson, 2007). Consequently, an explanation of the coding process is important to allow the readers to draw meaningful conclusions.

HOW TO INCREASE STATISTICAL GENERALISABILITY IN IC CONTENT ANALYSIS

The results of software-aided content analyses offer rich data sets for hypothesis testing. Computer-aided content analyses enable high volumes of narratives to be processed at a high level of consistency (Krippendorff, 2018). Software-aided coding has been criticised in the past by Weber (1985) and more recently by Beattie and Thomson (2007), as it may face problems with synonyms or pronouns. However, Krippendorff (2018) argues that the software-aided approach has advantages because it increases the degree of coding reliability and continuity. Furthermore, Dumay and Cai (2014) and Lee and Guthrie (2010) consider software-aided coding to have potential for enhancing IC content analyses, as they can be based on larger samples with extensive data. Content analysis results from software-aided coding can be used to statistically investigate the relationship between IC reporting and company criteria (Goebel, 2015c) or to test theory-based hypotheses on IC reporting (Goebel, 2019).

The issue of context sensitivity of IC for human coding aided by software on a computer can be reduced by undertaking certain steps. For example, Goebel (2015b) conducts a manual pilot content analysis for different industries and sizes. This pilot study approach provides the basis for the coding process to then investigate a high number of documents in a software-aided analysis. Krippendorff's (2018) alpha is a valid measure to ensure reliability, as it considers the relationship between observed disagreements and expected disagreements for different coding procedures; Krippendorff's alpha aims to be above 0.80 for reliability. The software results should be double-checked with manual coding from the pilot study and can then be gradually changed. Software codes for the search terms ought to be mutually exclusive for the IC components.

The coding process for IC reporting is exemplified by Beattie and Thomson (2007). After they found inconsistencies across prior IC content analyses, they highlight different aspects of coding procedures to be considered. Table 2.2 is based on these aspects, providing a checklist for IC content analyses. This checklist gives important information to the

Table 2.2 Content analysis procedures

Considerations	Procedures applied
Unit of analysis and measurement	Which unit level is the focus for coding and counting, e.g., words, sentences? How is non-narrative disclosure considered? Are headings and highlighted text considered to be equivalent to standard text?
Volume of disclosure	Are occurrences counted with repetitions? How is document length accounted for?
Type of disclosure	Are quantitative and qualitative information distinguished? Are intellectual assets and liabilities considered? How are graphs and tables taken into account?
Location of disclosure	Which reporting channels and which sections are of interest? Is the location of information used?
Language of disclosure	Which language is the original language for the sample? Is the reporting language appropriate for the applied coding?
Coding device	Software-aided coding or manual coding? How is the research framework designed?
Reliability checks	Is Krippendorff's alpha calculated and reported to measure reliability? Is the coding verified at different points in time to ensure stability? Is the coding process repeated by the independent coder for reproducibility? For software-aided coding: are electronic codes double-checked with manual coding?

Note: This table provides a checklist of the content analysis procedures for IC reporting, based on the considerations by Beattie and Thomson (2007).

reader to assess and evaluate the results of content analysis studies. These procedures are also elaborated on and recognised in other content analysis studies (Goebel, 2015a; Terblanche and Villiers, 2019), thereby increasing transparency. Furthermore, to account for differences in reporting length, the content analysis scores should be scaled by the number of pages or words of documents under review.

CONCLUSION

As IC reporting research and the comparability of IC reporting studies has been criticised, the question arises as to whether research on IC reporting can still be useful in the future. Furthermore, this question can be expanded to consider how content analysis may be used to take IC reporting research further. This chapter challenges content analysis studies on IC reporting on several levels. Investigations using different theories, samples, countries, industry groupings and communication channels contribute learnings and insights to different aspects of IC reporting. However, repeating prior studies and issues of non-comparability create the impression that IC reporting research has reached an impasse. Innovative approaches and new ideas are essential to utilise IC content analyses and to build upon prior knowledge. One recommendation for future IC reporting research is to utilise the remarkable amount of prior content analyses in meta-analysis studies to open new research discussions on IC-related hypotheses and theories. Furthermore, longitudinal studies have rarely been undertaken, and offer new insights into IC reporting developments and its perceived importance.

Content analysis can still be a useful method for IC reporting research, but safeguards for transparency and comparability need to be implemented. First, it is important to enable the reader to draw meaningful conclusions by clearly stating the content analysis procedures and providing the IC research framework applied. Second, comparability can be enhanced by making sure that the most widely used IC items, identified by Goebel (2015a), are included in the research framework. Third, the content analysis should be designed parsimoniously without gathering unnecessary data, a practice this chapter has criticised in prior studies. When these recommendations are applied, the reporting scores gathered in a content analysis provide the basis for further critical quantitative investigations. To approach and benefit from the extensive data available, software-aided coding is strongly recommended.

The literature on content analysis of IC reporting does not seem to have reached an impasse. Surveys and questionnaires by Beattie and

Smith (2012) and Wee and Chua (2016) show that companies still consider IC reporting to offer opportunities to inform the market about IC resources. But how can future IC reporting research agendas capture the nature of IC reporting? The broad IC definitions offer opportunities to interpret aspects of IC in the light of other research areas which might look at similar corporate features from different viewpoints. New insights are gained, for example, by applying a measure from mergers and acquisitions research to empirically investigate the role of IC value and mispricing (Goebel, 2015c, 2019).

Considering the idea of qualitative generalisability, IC reporting research still has many opportunities to generate further knowledge and insights. Qualitative studies have the potential to offer generalisations as they provide insights beyond the specific study settings and help to understand certain processes or concepts given certain circumstances. This is particularly interesting for developing IC-related theories for more insightful future research. Hence, qualitative generalisability supports qualitative studies, such as interviews or case studies, but it requires reasonable effort and strong arguments and explanations of how the findings are transferable and generalisable.

To conclude, future IC reporting research should find new ways to provide additional knowledge about IC rather than copying or adjusting prior studies. To take IC reporting research forward, this chapter advocates investigating communication channels in new media, longitudinal and meta-analysis studies, generalisable qualitative research and drawing inspiration from other research areas. This chapter strongly encourages new angles in IC reporting research inspired by different research areas, rather than repeating prior studies in new research settings. When IC reporting studies look beyond their field, the findings on IC reporting contribute to the body of knowledge on IC.

REFERENCES

Abeysekera, I. (2006), 'The project of intellectual capital disclosure: researching the research', *Journal of Intellectual Capital*, **7** (1), 61–77.

Abeysekera, I. and J. Guthrie (2005), 'An empirical investigation of annual reporting trends of intellectual capital in Sri Lanka', *Critical Perspectives on Accounting*, **16** (3), 151–163.

Beattie, V. and S.J. Smith (2012), 'Evaluating disclosure theory using the views of UK finance directors in the intellectual capital context', *Accounting and Business Research*, **42** (5), 471–494.

Beattie, V. and S.J. Thomson (2007), 'Lifting the lid on the use of content analysis to investigate intellectual capital disclosures', *Accounting Forum*, **31** (2), 129–163.

Beattie, V. and S.J. Thomson (2010), *Intellectual Capital Reporting: Academic Utopia or Corporate Reality in a Brave New World?*, Edinburgh: Institute of Chartered Accountants of Scotland.

Bontis, N. (2003), 'Intellectual capital disclosure in Canadian corporations', *Journal of Human Resource Costing and Accounting*, **7** (1–2), 9–20.

Bozzolan, S., Favotto, F. and F. Ricceri (2003), 'Italian annual intellectual capital disclosure: an empirical analysis', *Journal of Intellectual Capital*, **4** (4), 543–558.

Brennan, N. (2001), 'Reporting intellectual capital in annual reports: evidence from Ireland', *Accounting, Auditing and Accountability Journal*, **14** (4), 423–436.

Brooking, A. (1996), *Intellectual Capital: Core Asset for the Third Millennium Enterprise*, London: International Thomson Business Press.

Brüggen, A., Vergauwen, P. and M. Dao (2009), 'Determinants of intellectual capital disclosure: evidence from Australia', *Management Decision*, **47** (2), 233–245.

Bukh, P.N., Nielsen, C., Gormsen, P. and J. Mouritsen (2005), 'Disclosure of information on intellectual capital in Danish IPO prospectuses', *Accounting, Auditing and Accountability Journal*, **18** (6), 713–732.

Campbell, D. and M. Rahman (2010), 'A longitudinal examination of intellectual capital reporting in Marks & Spencer annual reports, 1978–2008', *British Accounting Review*, **42** (1), 56–70.

Catalfo, P. and I. Wulf (2016), 'Intangibles disclosure in management commentary regulation in Germany and Italy: a semantic approach', *Journal of Intellectual Capital*, **17** (1), 103–119.

Cerbioni, F. and A. Parbonetti (2007), 'Exploring the effects of corporate governance on intellectual capital disclosure: an analysis of European biotechnology companies', *European Accounting Review*, **16** (4), 791–826.

Cuozzo, B., Dumay, J., Palmaccio, M. and R. Lombardi (2017), 'Intellectual capital disclosure: a structured literature review', *Journal of Intellectual Capital*, **18** (1), 9–28.

Duff, A. (2018), 'Intellectual capital disclosure: evidence from UK accounting firms', *Journal of Intellectual Capital*, **19** (4), 768–786.

Dumay, J. (2014a), 'Reflections on interdisciplinary accounting research: the state of the art of intellectual capital', *Accounting, Auditing and Accountability Journal*, **27** (8), 1257–1264.

Dumay, J. (2014b), '15 years of the *Journal of Intellectual Capital* and counting: a manifesto for transformational IC research', *Journal of Intellectual Capital*, **15** (1), 2–37.

Dumay, J. (2016), 'A critical reflection on the future of intellectual capital: from reporting to disclosure', *Journal of Intellectual Capital*, **17** (1), 168–184.

Dumay, J. and L. Cai (2014), 'A review and critique of content analysis as a methodology for inquiring into IC disclosure', *Journal of Intellectual Capital*, **15** (2), 264–290.

Dumay, J. and L. Cai (2015), 'Using content analysis as a research methodology for investigating intellectual capital disclosure', *Journal of Intellectual Capital*, **16** (1), 121–155.

Dumay, J. and T. Garanina (2013), 'Intellectual capital research: a critical examination of the third stage', *Journal of Intellectual Capital*, **14** (1), 10–25.

Dumay, J. and J. Guthrie (2017), 'Involuntary disclosure of intellectual capital: is it relevant?', *Journal of Intellectual Capital*, **18** (1), 29–44.

Garanina, T. and J. Dumay (2017), 'Forward-looking intellectual capital disclosure in IPOs: implications for intellectual capital and integrated reporting', *Journal of Intellectual Capital*, **18** (1), 128–148.

García-Meca, E. and I. Martínez (2007), 'The use of intellectual capital information in investment decisions – an empirical study using analyst reports', *International Journal of Accounting*, **42**, 57–81.

García-Meca, E., Parra, I., Larrán, M. and I. Martínez (2005), 'The explanatory factors of intellectual capital disclosure to financial analysts', *European Accounting Review*, **14** (1), 63–94.

Goebel, V. (2015a), 'Is the literature on content analyses on intellectual capital reporting heading towards a dead end?', *Journal of Intellectual Capital*, **16** (3), 681–699.

Goebel, V. (2015b), 'Intellectual capital reporting in a mandatory management report: the case of Germany', *Journal of Intellectual Capital*, **16** (4), 702–720.

Goebel, V. (2015c), 'Estimating a measure of intellectual capital to test its determinants', *Journal of Intellectual Capital*, **16** (1), 101–120.

Goebel, V. (2019), 'Drivers for voluntary intellectual capital reporting based on agency theory', *Journal of Intellectual Capital*, **20** (2), 264–281.
Guthrie, J. and R. Petty (2000), 'Intellectual capital: Australian annual reporting practices', *Journal of Intellectual Capital*, **1** (3), 241–251.
Guthrie, J., Petty, R. and F. Ricceri (2007), *Intellectual Capital Reporting: Lessons from Hong Kong and Australia*, Edinburgh: Institute of Chartered Accountants of Scotland.
Guthrie, J., Petty, R., Yongvanich, K. and F. Ricceri (2004), 'Using content analysis as a research method to inquire into intellectual capital reporting', *Journal of Intellectual Capital*, **5** (2), 282–293.
Guthrie, J., Ricceri, F. and J. Dumay (2012), 'Reflections and projections: a decade of intellectual capital accounting research', *British Accounting Review*, **44** (2), 68–82.
Hall, R. (1992), 'The strategic analysis of intangible resources', *Strategic Management Journal*, **13** (2), 135–144.
Hidalgo, R., García-Meca, E. and I. Martínez (2011), 'Corporate governance and intellectual capital disclosure', *Journal of Business Ethics*, **100** (3), 483–495.
Krippendorff, K. (2018), *Content Analysis: An Introduction to Its Methodology*, 4th edn, Thousand Oaks, CA: SAGE Publications.
Lee, L.L. and J. Guthrie (2010), 'Visualising and measuring intellectual capital in capital markets: a research method', *Journal of Intellectual Capital*, **11** (1), 4–22.
Li, J., Pike, R. and R. Haniffa (2008), 'Intellectual capital disclosure and corporate governance structure in UK firms', *Accounting and Business Research*, **38** (2), 137–159.
Lin, C. and L. Edvinsson (2010), 'What national intellectual capital indices can tell about the global economic crisis of 2007–2009?', *Electronic Journal of Knowledge Management*, **8** (2), 253–266.
Mangena, M., Pike, R. and J. Li (2010), *Intellectual Capital Disclosure Practices and Effects on the Cost of Equity Capital: UK Evidence*, Edinburgh: Institute of Chartered Accountants of Scotland.
Marr, B., Gray, D. and A. Neely (2003), 'Why do firms measure their intellectual capital?', *Journal of Intellectual Capital*, **4** (4), 441–464.
Mouritsen, J. (2006), 'Problematising intellectual capital research: ostensive versus performative IC', *Accounting, Auditing and Accountability Journal*, **19** (6), 820–841.
Mouritsen, J. (2009), 'Classification, measurement and the ontology of intellectual capital entities', *Journal of Human Resource Costing and Accounting*, **13** (2), 154–162.
Mouritsen, J., Larsen, H.T. and P.N. Bukh (2001), 'Intellectual capital and the "capable firm": narrating, visualising and numbering for managing knowledge', *Accounting Organizations and Society*, **26** (7–8), 735–762.
Parker, L.D. and D. Northcott (2016), 'Qualitative generalising in accounting research: concepts and strategies', *Accounting, Auditing and Accountability Journal*, **29** (6), 1100–1131.
Rossi, F.M., Nicolò, G. and P.T. Polcini (2018), 'New trends in intellectual capital reporting', *Journal of Intellectual Capital*, **19** (4), 814–835.
Secundo, G., Perez, S.E., Martinaitis, Ž. and K.-H. Leitner (2015), 'An intellectual capital maturity model (ICMM) to improve strategic management in European universities', *Journal of Intellectual Capital*, **16** (2), 419–442.
Singh, I. and J.-L.W.M. Van der Zahn (2008), 'Determinants of intellectual capital disclosure in prospectuses of initial public offerings', *Accounting and Business Research*, **38** (5), 409–431.
Stewart, T.A. (1997), *Intellectual Capital: The New Wealth of Organizations*, New York, USA and London, UK: Currency and Doubleday.
Striukova, L., Unerman, J. and J. Guthrie (2008), 'Corporate reporting of intellectual capital: evidence from UK companies', *British Accounting Review*, **40** (4), 297–313.
Sveiby, K.E. (1997), *The New Organizational Wealth: Managing and Measuring Knowledge-Based Assets*, San Francisco, CA: Berrett-Koehler Publishers.
Terblanche, W. and C.D. Villiers (2019), 'The influence of integrated reporting and internationalisation on intellectual capital disclosures', *Journal of Intellectual Capital*, **20** (1), 40–59.

van der Meer-Kooistra, J. and S.M. Zijlstra (2001), 'Reporting on intellectual capital', *Accounting, Auditing and Accountability Journal*, **14** (4), 456–476.

Vandemaele, S.N., Vergauwen, P. and A.J. Smits (2005), 'Intellectual capital disclosure in the Netherlands, Sweden and the UK: a longitudinal and comparative study', *Journal of Intellectual Capital*, **6** (3), 417–426.

Vergauwen, P. and F. van Alem (2005), 'Annual report IC disclosures in the Netherlands, France and Germany', *Journal of Intellectual Capital*, **6** (1), 89–104.

Vergauwen, P., Bollen, L. and E. Oirbans (2007), 'Intellectual capital disclosure and intangible value drivers: an empirical study', *Management Decision*, **45** (7), 1163–1180.

Weber, R.P. (1985), *Basic Content Analysis*, Beverly Hills, CA, USA and London, UK: SAGE.

Wee, J.C.N. and A.Y.K. Chua (2016), 'The communication of intellectual capital: the "whys" and "whats"', *Journal of Intellectual Capital*, **17** (3), 414–438.

Williams, S.M. (2001), 'Is intellectual capital performance and disclosure practice related?', *Journal of Intellectual Capital*, **2** (3), 192–203.

3. Validity in content analysis-based intellectual capital disclosure research: a critical review

Subhash Abhayawansa, Zihan Liu and James Guthrie

INTRODUCTION

In 2000, Guthrie and Petty (2000) conducted the first investigation of intellectual capital disclosure practices using content analysis. Since then, more than 200 published studies have adopted content analysis (CA) to examine intellectual capital disclosure (ICD). CA is 'a research technique for making replicable and valid inferences from texts (or other meaningful matter) to the contexts of their use' (Krippendorff, 2004a, p. 18). While alternative methods of text analysis exist, such as discourse analysis, rhetorical analysis and narrative analysis, CA has been, and continues to be, a dominant approach in ICD research. Further, studies using this method receive more citations than those following other methods (Dumay, 2014).

CA has many benefits. For emerging scholars, CA is a well-established technique, with several significant articles demonstrating how it can be and has been applied (for example, Duriau et al., 2007; Lombard et al., 2002; Krippendorff, 2004b). For all researchers, CA is not an overly time-consuming method. Access to materials is relatively easy and most research activity is desk-based. As such, it is one of the cheapest forms of research and, when funding is limited, it may be one of only a few feasible options. Moreover, CA is flexible. It can be applied to any number of geographical contexts, organisational structures or document types (Lee and Guthrie, 2010) and there are many available theories through which to interpret the data and form insightful conclusions (Guthrie et al., 2012; Guthrie et al., 2017).

CA is founded on the understanding that language is central to human cognition (Sapir, 1944) and, hence, analysing the text a person writes reveals their cognitive schema (Huff, 1990). Of course, this requires judgement and interpretation on the part of the researcher (Weber, 1990). In ICD research, these judgements mainly fall into four categories: type, magnitude, frequency and quality. Type is the intellectual capital (IC) category to which a text unit belongs; magnitude is the prominence of the IC category within a text unit; frequency is how often an IC category occurs; and quality can be measured by many attributes, for example, tone, quantification and time-orientation.

In the CA method, data is 'made' by the researcher, not simply collected from a database. The implication is that the conclusions drawn from the data can be trusted only after demonstrating that they are not a result of 'irreproducible human idiosyncrasies' (Hayes and Krippendorff, 2007, p. 78). In other words, one must establish that the data is reliable. Moreover, the researcher must establish that the data fairly represent the underlying phenomenon. This is validity.

Commenting on the use of CA as a method for researching ICD, Guthrie et al. (2004, p. 288) highlight that: 'Those conducting CA need to demonstrate the reliability of their instruments and/or the reliability of the data collected using those instruments to permit replicable and valid inferences to be drawn from data derived from content analysis.' Likewise, it is equally important for researchers to explain, reflect on and justify the choices they made in 'making' the data so that readers can assess the merit of the conclusions drawn from that data.

A considerable body of work has been dedicated to guide and enhance reliability and validity in CA-based ICD research (for example, Dumay and Cai, 2015; Steenkamp and Northcott, 2007; Abeysekera, 2006; Beattie and Thomson, 2007; Guthrie et al., 2004). This is perhaps because CA is widespread in ICD research and its methodological weaknesses, such as a lack of procedural transparency, are well documented (Dumay and Cai, 2015). It is expected that methodological problems will dissipate as ICD studies continue to grow (Lee and Guthrie, 2010). However, anecdotal evidence and our experience in reviewing the papers discussed in this chapter highlight that, even after two decades of ICD research, reliability and validity with CA are still significant concerns. Supporting this view, Beattie and Thomson (2007), Dumay and Cai (2015) and others have argued that rigorous content analysis in ICD research is largely absent. On this basis, they concluded that most CA-based studies on ICD lack validity. Moreover, problems with reliability and validity might explain why there are only a few discernible patterns in ICD practices within and across jurisdictions, at least in some cases (Dumay and Cai, 2014). These problems might also be responsible for the mixed and contradictory evidence that exists over the determinants and economic consequences of ICD (Eddine et al., 2015; Dumay and Cai, 2014).

These issues aside, the purpose of this chapter is to understand the extent to which the ICD research conducted using CA is credible based on face validity and construct validity. Unlike prior reviews of ICD research, our focus is centred on whether the research meets the criteria to be considered valid. We use examples from the studies to demonstrate how method choices made or not made affect the validity of the inferences drawn. While we do not investigate the issue of 'reliability' in this chapter, validity is somewhat intertwined with reliability, which means that some evidence we provide may inform conclusions about the reliability of the research. Ultimately, our goal is to confirm or refute critiques of validity that have been made in prior reviews of ICD research and to extend the literature by quantifying the pervasiveness of the problem.

The remainder of this chapter is organised as follows. We first describe the concept of validity as applied in CA research. We then review papers providing methodological guidance for applying CA in ICD research. The research methods used are explained next, and the results are presented along with a discussion. Lastly, some concluding remarks and recommendations are provided.

VALIDITY IN CONTENT ANALYSIS

In CA, validity is the extent to which the inferences drawn from the text truthfully represent the phenomena to which they refer. McKinnon (1988, p. 36) states, 'Validity is impaired if the research design and/or conduct of the research are such that the researcher is unintentionally studying either more than or less than the claimed phenomena.' Thus, validity relates to both the research design and the data generation process. Validity in the research design is the extent to which an instrument is measuring what it is intended to measure. It is, therefore, dependent on appropriately formulating sampling units, recording units, content categories, operational definitions and coding rules.

Weber (1990) distinguishes between two types of validity: face validity and external validity. Face validity is the 'correspondence between investigators' definitions of concepts and their definitions of the categories that measure them' (Weber, 1990, p. 18). In ICD research, the face validity of CA relates to whether the IC content categories represent IC and its subcomponents as they are generally understood in the literature. Hence, if readers are to assess face validity, the researcher must define their coding categories and coding criteria.

External validity, Weber (1990) argues, is a much stronger form of validity than face validity as it more closely relates to the generalisability of inferences. He explains four types of external validity: hypothesis validity, predictive validity, semantic validity and construct validity, which

Krippendorff (2004a) calls correlative validity. Of these four categories, we have limited the scope of this study to construct validity and its two components: convergent validity and discriminant validity. Convergent validity is demonstrated by showing that two measures of constructs that theoretically should be related are, in fact, related. Discriminant validity is demonstrated by the opposite: that measures of different constructs are not correlated. We do not analyse the extent to which each study ensures hypothesis, predictive and semantic validities, as it is not possible to systematically investigate these forms of validity in a corpus of journal articles by only analysing the details reported in the articles.

REVIEW OF METHODOLOGICAL ARTICLES ON CA IN ICD RESEARCH

Several studies examine and critique how CA has been used in ICD research and, in doing so, suggest ways in which validity can be established and enhanced. Guthrie et al. (2004) was one of the first studies to shed light on the use of CA to inquire into ICD. The study is mainly an examination of various best-practice techniques in CA, drawing on CA textbooks, such as Krippendorff (2004a), and social and environmental accounting literature. This study highlights that improving validity involves having operational definitions for IC categories and decision rules for categorising content and ensuring coder reliability. Additionally, categorisation schemes should have greater situational specificity to control for the effects of size or the industry across samples of companies.

A few years later, Abeysekera (2006) reviewed the literature on ICD, highlighting, among other things, some of the methodological issues that affect the credibility and comparability of ICD research. He identified differences in how IC categories are defined, how ICD is measured and the composition of the samples as key issues that make comparisons between different ICD studies complicated. More recently, Cuozzo et al. (2017) reviewed the ICD research published between 2000 and 2017 to identify patterns in the use of CA, among other research methods. They criticised the overuse of corporate reports as the unit of analysis, and the Eurocentricity of the jurisdictions examined. By contrast, Guthrie et al. (2004) and Abeysekera (2006) advocate the use of corporate reports because they enable comparative analysis of management attitudes and policies across reporting periods.

Beattie and Thomson's (2007) critical review of how studies have applied CA in ICD research focuses on the reliability of the coding processes and transparency of categories of classification (hereafter: categorisation scheme) and coding criteria. They reveal problems with electronic keyword searches, measuring the volume of disclosures (as opposed to the variety), the units of analysis and units of measurement, along with the impact of all these considerations on inter-coder reliability. Using an illustrative example, the authors demonstrate that validity can be compromised by ignoring multiple disclosures (that is, only measuring single presence/absence of each IC category), conducting electronic searching of ICD and being vague or opaque about the IC categories and coding rules adopted. Beattie and Thomson (2007) advocate the use of 'text units' as the unit of analysis and unit of measurement to most comprehensively capture ICD, while highlighting how the choice of units of analysis and measurements can also impact upon reliability.

Steenkamp and Northcott (2007) illustrated and discussed three practical challenges encountered in applying CA: determining content categories and recording units; dealing with repetition; and interpreting and categorising ambiguous content. In particular, they advocate for pictures to be included in CA studies, and provide guidance on how to code pictures for IC content. They unpack the distinction between the presence and frequency of ICD and advocate for the use of 'themes' as the recording unit for coding ICDs. Their reasoning is that themes better reflect the nature of ICD, and using themes resolves some problems associated with repetitive content. They also suggest that using illustrative examples of how coding dilemmas are dealt with can benefit the reader. This call by Steenkamp and Northcott (2007) to include pictures and use themes as recording units is aimed at enhancing validity.

In Lee and Guthrie (2010), the focus was on setting practical boundaries for computer-based CA in ICD research. They describe four categories of CA tools for identifying relevant content, each varied in terms of its complexity and accuracy. For cases where documents with ICD need to be identified, as opposed to identifying the extent of ICDs within a document, they recommend concept-based or taxonomy-based tools. Although computer-based content analyses cannot identify ICD as comprehensively as human coders (Beattie and Thomson, 2007), according to Lee and Guthrie (2010, p. 11) it is a better method for making comparisons between firms, market sectors and countries. They argue that 'even if the CA method under-represents IC, it does so in a systematic way, which will not impact the validity of comparisons between different entities'.

Abhayawansa (2011) describes and illustrates a methodology for generating valid and reliable inferences from sell-side analyst reports, which he considers to be a communications device, not only a record of an analyst's decision-making processes. The methodology includes rationales for the most appropriate sampling, recording and measurement units; the process of developing a categorisation scheme and coding instrument; the data collection steps; and how to assess reliability and validity. Abhayawansa's (2011) methodology was designed to overcome the problems in applying CA in ICD research observed by Abeysekera (2006), Steenkamp and Northcott (2007) and Beattie and Thomson (2007), and to incorporate 'best practice' into CA research.

Husin et al. (2012) also tackled problems associated with validity in CA in ICD research. Echoing the recommendations of Steenkamp and Northcott (2007) and Beattie and Thomson (2007), these authors also proposed themes as the most appropriate recording and measurement unit for analysing ICDs in the form of narratives, numbers and especially images. They raise the point that using themes avoids the need for having different measurement and recording units and also makes it easier to code sentences/paragraphs that contain multiple types of ICDs. They illustrate that themes allow IC information presented in forms other than text to be coded, such as photographs, graphs, charts and diagrams (see Beattie and Thomson, 2007; Steenkamp and Northcott, 2007).

From a critique of studies using CA published between 1999 and 2013, Dumay and Cai (2014) conclude that, as a research method, CA has contributed little to advancing knowledge on ICD since the original seminal studies. They point out that ICD studies overwhelmingly focus on annual reports, cover shorter periods, adopt smaller samples and concentrate on a few Western jurisdictions, all of which have validity implications. Of relevance to this chapter are their findings on the main limitations of utilising CA in ICD research, as also identified in the papers reviewed in this section. The most commonly cited limitations are the validity of the ICD indices/categorisation schemes used, the subjectivity of the coding process, the reliability of the unit of analysis and problems associated with assessing the quality of the ICDs. Dumay and Cai (2014) further state that several articles in their sample call for researchers to supplement CA with other research methods, although only a few adopted methodological triangulation to enhance validity. What their observations highlight is that ICD researchers are aware of reliability and validity concerns when using CA.

In 2015, Dumay and Cai (2015) reanalysed the 110 CA-based ICD studies reviewed in their previous work (i.e., Dumay and Cai, 2014) to understand how different conceptual components of the CA methodology described by Krippendorff (2004a) have been used to investigate ICD. They conclude that 'there is much inconsistency and an absence of rigour in ICD studies applying CA as a methodology' (Dumay and Cai, 2015, p. 143), with little attention paid to validity. Dumay and Cai (2015) provide the perfect backdrop to undertake a detailed and critical examination of how validity is addressed in CA-based research on ICD.

In more recent research, Goebel (2015) focused on the differences in the various IC categorisation schemes used with ICD content analysis; a fact that has been discussed in several prior studies. She demonstrates that the results of prior studies are only comparable in terms of the relative importance of the main IC categories and even this depends on the extent to which certain widely used IC items are included in the IC categorisation scheme(s) used. Her analysis highlights the importance of ensuring construct validity by using more than one measure of ICD in CA studies.

Our study differs from the studies reviewed above in its focus on understanding the extent to which prior CA studies on ICD ensure face validity and construct validity. Our investigation, thus, reveals the validity of the instruments and processes used to generate the data.

RESEARCH METHOD

We conduct a CA of research articles on ICD in which CA is the primary research method. CA is suitable for this study because assessing validity requires the use of predetermined criteria to categorise aspects of the research designs of published studies. It also enables us to demonstrate how validity is maintained in our study, thus, 'walking the talk'.

Sample

Our data sample included articles published between January 2000 and September 2019 on IC and/or the main capitals of IC (human, relational and structural) that rely on CA as a primary research method. The first-ever study on IC to use CA was published in 2000 (Guthrie et al., 2012). Hence, our sample was intended to include the entire population of CA-based IC research. Relevant publications were identified in two steps: a database search followed by a filtering process.

First, we searched the academic journals in the ProQuest and EBSCOhost databases and the journal content platforms of five main publishers of academic journals: Emerald Publishing, Taylor & Francis Group, Springer Nature, Elsevier and SAGE Publications. When searching ProQuest and EBSCOhost databases, we used the keyword combinations 'intellectual/human/relational/structural capital report/disclosure' in the article title and 'content analysis' in the abstract or keywords. The journal content platforms did not provide the same level of search functionality as research databases. Hence, articles in these platforms were searched using the above-mentioned keyword combinations in the article title only, which necessitated manual screening of articles. We then reviewed the reference lists of all articles and included any relevant articles missed in the above searches.

With a set of 180 articles identified, we then began to examine the sample. First, we excluded 69 articles that were either ranked C or not ranked in the Australian Business Deans Council (ABDC) Journal Quality List 2016 to ensure that each paper met some commonly accepted criteria. The ABDC Journal Quality List 2016 includes 2777 peer-reviewed academic journals in various fields of business ranked as A*, A, B and C. We also excluded method papers that only included content analyses of ICD to illustrate methodological issues (five articles[1]) and papers using CA for purposes other than inquiring into ICD (two articles): for example, Gately and Cunningham (2014) who combine CA with interviews to examine how technology entrepreneurs build relational capital for a new venture. We excluded Abeysekera (2011), which explicitly claims to have adopted latent CA, as reliability and validity considerations for latent content analyses often differ from manifest content analyses. At the end of this process, 103 articles remained, which represent comprehensive coverage of two decades of CA-based ICD research.

The list of journals represented in the sample is shown in Table 3.1. Given the topic under study, most are accounting journals. Being the specialist journal in the field, the *Journal of Intellectual Capital* accounts for 60 per cent of the papers. Only 17 per cent of the papers were published in journals ranked A and A*. Most prior reviews of the ICD literature have either restricted their analyses to accounting journals or have covered significantly fewer journals than we have here (see Cuozzo et al., 2017; Guthrie et al., 2012). There are some exceptions, however, such as Dumay and Cai (2014) and Dumay and Cai (2015), who covered more journal articles than in this study, including those in C-ranked journals.

Variables of Interest

We investigated ten variables, each with nominal values. The variables were identified based on: a review of articles on CA in ICD research; articles focusing on validity in CA (Hayes and Krippendorff, 2007; Lombard et al., 2002; Krippendorff, 2004b); and our knowledge of the CA methodology having used this method in ICD research for many years. The variables are shown in Table 3.2.

Table 3.1 Journal titles relating to CA-based ICD articles

Journal title	ABDC ranking	No. of articles
European Accounting Review	A*	2 (2%)
Accounting and Business Research	A	3 (3%)
Accounting, Auditing and Accountability Journal	A	2 (2%)
British Accounting Review	A	5 (5%)
Critical Perspectives on Accounting	A	1 (1%)
International Journal of Accounting	A	1 (1%)
International Journal of Contemporary Hospitality Management	A	1 (1%)
Journal of Business Ethics	A	1 (1%)
Knowledge Management Research and Practice	A	1 (1%)
Sub-total		**17 (17%)**
Accounting Forum	B	2 (2%)
Advances in Accounting	B	3 (3%)
Australian Accounting Review	B	2 (2%)
Corporate Communications: An International Journal	B	2 (2%)
European Business Review	B	2 (2%)
International Journal of Productivity and Performance Management	B	1 (1%)
Journal of Accounting and Organizational Change	B	2 (2%)
Journal of Intellectual Capital	B	62 (60%)
Management Decision	B	6 (6%)
Managerial Auditing Journal	B	1 (1%)
Pacific Accounting Review	B	1 (1%)
The European Journal of Finance	B	1 (1%)
VINE: The Journal of Information & Knowledge Management Systems	B	1 (1%)
Sub-total		**86 (84%)**
Total		**103 (100%)**

Development of the Coding Instrument, Coder Training and Inter-Coder Reliability

We enhanced the reliability of coding by having pre-tested coding rules for all coding categories of the variables. We also ensured that the analyst was sufficiently trained and established inter-coder agreement on coding decisions. The lead co-author, who has extensive experience in applying

Table 3.2 Variables

Variable	No. of categories		No. of categories
Details about the categorisation scheme	3	Coding for extent and quality in the same dimension	2
Details about coding criteria	3	Type of CA	2
Categorisation scheme	4	Use of computer software	4
Measurement method	4	Recording unit	6
Measurement attributes	2	Supplementary research methods	2

CA to ICD research, developed and tested the initial draft of the coding instrument by coding ten articles from the sample. The coding instrument was refined and new coding categories were added. Then, the lead co-author and the second co-author each coded five articles using the revised coding instrument.[2] The two co-authors then discussed the coding problems and disagreements. Because of these discussions, the instrument was revised again and new coding categories and variables were added. The two co-authors repeated this process several times with different sample articles until there were no disagreements and the second co-author was sufficiently trained to code independently. By the time the two co-authors reached full agreement on the coding decisions for every variable, a total of 40 articles had been coded.

The remaining 63 articles were then coded by the second co-author. After about a third of these articles had been coded, ten were randomly selected by the lead co-author and coded, and a formal pilot test of inter-coder reliability was performed on these ten articles. The inter-coder agreement, measured using Krippendorf's alpha, was more than 0.9 for all variables, with most having a perfect alpha value. The ReCal OIR software program developed by Freelon (2011) was used to calculate the Krippendorf's alpha coefficients. Since the reliability levels from the pilot test were adequate, the second co-author proceeded with coding the remaining articles, after which the lead co-author randomly selected and coded another 11 articles to assess reliability. The Krippendorf's alphas for most of the variables were perfect scores and five were greater than 0.90. The one variable with a value lower than 0.9 was attributed to the second co-author incorrectly interpreting the meaning of a category in relation to computer-assisted CA. All 15 articles that used computer-assisted CA were coded again by the lead co-author for the 'technology' variable. The third co-author was involved in the data analysis.

RESULTS AND DISCUSSION

The results reported in Table 3.3 form the basis of this discussion.

Table 3.3 Categories of classification and results relating to validity

Variables and categories	No. of articles (%)
1. Details about the categorisation scheme	
1.1 Categories of classification disclosed	87 (84%)
1.2 Categories of classification partly disclosed	4 (4%)
1.3 Categories of classification not disclosed	12 (12%)
2. Details about coding criteria	
2.1 Coding criteria disclosed	35 (34%)
2.2 Coding criteria partly disclosed	11 (11%)
2.3 Coding criteria not disclosed	57 (55%)
3. Categorisation scheme	
3.1 Adopted from the literature without modification	26 (25%)
3.2 Adapted from existing coding schemes	29 (28%)
3.3 Self-generated	47 (46%)
3.4 Not disclosed	1 (1%)
4. Measurement method	
4.1 Single occurrence (Disclosure index method)	44 (42%)
4.2 No. of occurrences	50 (49%)
4.3 Other	2 (2%)
4.4 Multiple (single and no. of occurrences)	7 (7%)
5. Measurement attributes	
5.1 Only extent and/or type of ICD measured	64 (62%)
5.2 Also other qualitative attributes of ICD measured	39 (38%)
6. Coding for extent and quality in the same dimension	
6.1 Presence and quality of ICD coded together	25 (24%)
6.2 Presence of ICD coded separately or only presence of ICD is examined	78 (76%)
7. Type of CA	
7.1 Syntactical CA (word search)	15 (15%)

Table 3.3 (continued)

Variables and categories	No. of articles (%)
7.2 Semantical CA (meaning)	88 (85%)
8. Use of computer software	
8.1 Word search software	10 (10%)
8.2 Software with inbuilt dictionary and taxonomies	3 (3%)
8.3 Software assisting manual CA (Nvivo)	5 (5%)
8.4 No text analysis software used	85 (82%)
9. Recording unit	
9.1 One or a few words	15 (14%)
9.2 Sentence/line	15 (14%)
9.3 Information unit/theme/text unit	60 (59%)
9.4 Paragraph/Entire document	3 (3%)
9.5 Multiple	7 (7%)
9.6 Not stated	3 (3%)
10. Supplementary research methods	
10.1 Only content analysis applied	100 (97%)
10.2 Content analysis is supplemented with other research methods	3 (3%)

Face Validity

Categorisation schemes, coding rules and coding illustrations

With CA, the main research instrument is the categorisation scheme or disclosure index. Therefore, to ensure face validity, the researcher needs to make sure that what the IC categories/indicators purport to be measuring is what they are, in fact, measuring. For instance, Beattie and Thomson (2007) argue that due to the depth and breadth of the concept of IC and the lack of a common definitive language with which to describe it, the details provided about the categories must be precise. They claim that 'increased transparency in relation to the IC information found and how it is categorised would also clarify researchers' understanding of the IC concept and assist in the development of shared meanings' (Beattie and Thomson, 2007, p. 131).

Our analysis reveals that as many as 12 per cent of the studies do not list the IC categories and IC indicators included in the analyses, and 4 per cent only list the main IC categories but not the subcategories or IC indicators within them. While 84 per cent of studies disclosed the IC coding categories or indicators, 55 per cent of those only partly described these categories. Moreover, only a handful of studies provided examples to illustrate how complex coding dilemmas were handled. The absence of a sufficient description does not mean that a study has not taken adequate safeguards. However, detailed explanations can signal the quality and construct validity of the inferences made based on the data.

A quarter of the studies we analysed used a pre-existing IC categorisation scheme without any modifications. Twenty-eight per cent used a slightly modified version of a pre-existing scheme, and 46 per cent either used a self-constructed categorisation scheme or a substantially modified version of a pre-existing scheme. Some argue that if modifications are made to a previously used coding scheme, then the rationales for the additions, deletions and amendments should be outlined to demonstrate that only ICD is being measured and nothing else (Steenkamp and Northcott, 2007; Beattie and Thomson, 2007). However, only a very small percentage of studies explained how and why their modifications suited the context of sampling units, and even these often provided insufficient detail to be able to generalise or adapt the scheme to a different context (Goebel, 2015). For example, Hidalgo et al. (2011) claim that their IC categorisation scheme includes IC items found in García-Meca et al. (2005) and Nielsen et al. (2006), but they do not specify what items were included in the final categorisation scheme or explain the modifications made to suit the context of the study. Similarly, Guthrie and Petty (2000) did not explain how their IC categorisation scheme was adjusted to reflect items likely to be reported by Australian companies, despite claiming to have made modifications.

One way to increase face validity is to ensure that content categories are emic to the text being analysed. Husin et al. (2012, p. 198) claim that 'for most ICD studies, it is unclear whether the list developed in their IC index prior to conducting the research is definitive as there is no statement being made on a subsequent modification of the index on completion of their analysis'. They argue that the CA is only partial if the IC categorisation scheme (IC index, as they call it) is not revised to capture the context-specific ICD in the text, 'since the researcher only looks for certain type of information ignoring sections of the text that do not relate to the index' (Husin et al., 2012, p. 198).

Our analysis revealed only a few instances where the IC categorisation scheme was modified when new types of ICD were discovered during pilot testing, coder training or the coding stage itself. The subjectivity involved in defining an IC categorisation scheme makes it doubly important for the reader to know the nature of information included and/or excluded. Readers must be able to judge, from their own perspective, the extent to which ICD has been measured (Beattie and Thomson, 2007) and how appropriate that is to the context of the study. Our findings support Beattie and Thomson's (2007, p. 135) observation that 'there is a pervasive lack of explanation in previous studies of the detailed coding rules used to allocate information to IC categories'. Our findings lead us to concur with Beattie and Thomson (2007, p. 135) that 'it is impossible for the reader to judge which ICDs have been captured'. Hence, we conclude that most ICD research lacks face validity.

Measuring presence or frequency

The basis of CA in ICD research is to measure the presence or absence of a predetermined list of IC items and/or the frequency with which these references occur. These two measures of IC have important conceptual differences. While 'existence' captures the variety or range of IC types disclosed in a document, frequency is a measure of the extent to which some IC categories are emphasised over others. Given that some companies use repetition as a rhetorical device to communicate the significance of their IC (Davison, 2008), Husin et al. (2012) argue that frequency is a more appropriate, and probably more accurate, measure of the significance of ICD.

It has been argued that a simple presence/absence approach is a misleading measure of salience because: (1) it treats a company with one disclosure in a given category as equal to one that makes many; (2) it ignores different pieces of information relating to the same category; and (3) it ignores the repetition report preparers use to create emphasis (Hackston and Milne, 1996; Beattie and Thomson, 2007). Beattie and Thomson (2007) shed light on this issue by applying content analysis to an annual report of a United Kindom company, which showed that multiple disclosures exist for 45 out of 59 IC categories.

Our analysis shows that 42 per cent of the studies only measure the presence/absence of an IC item, ignoring frequency entirely, and 2 per cent of the studies merely check for the presence of IC items to categorise the sampling units as including or excluding IC. Measuring existence alone is justifiable if the intention is to examine variability, but a closer examination of the inferences made in these studies highlights that what the researcher intended to measure was salience. Additionally, when reporting their findings, many researchers who merely measured the presence of an item use the term frequency. When it is the presence that is measured, the researcher can only explain how many sampling units (for example, annual reports) in which types of IC is present. In contrast, when the frequency is measured, the findings relate to the extent of references to a given IC category.

Although Steenkamp and Northcott (2007) warn against misrepresenting measures of IC, our findings show that ICD studies consistently ignore this important methodological distinction. When a researcher purports to measure one thing but is measuring another, invalid inferences result. For instance, the inference we draw from the statement that 'Human capital is the IC category reported by the most number of companies' is different from the statement that 'Human capital is the most reported IC category by companies'. Given that the presence/absence approach to measuring ICD is at most partially meaningful, if not misleading, there is evidence that researchers may have misinterpreted their results. This raises serious concerns about the existing body of knowledge in this field. As measuring the presence/absence of IC items is considerably less time-consuming than measuring frequency, one can argue that IC researchers may be compromising the face validity of their research to save time and costs.

Measuring the quality or quantity of ICD

Beyond the quantity of IC disclosed, the quality of those disclosures is also a topic of inquiry. The most commonly studied attributes are tone (positive, negative and neutral), time-orientation (past-oriented, forward-looking and present) and quantification (qualitative, quantitative and monetary). In our sample, 62 per cent of the studies only investigated the type and extent of ICDs, while 38 per cent examined quality attributes in addition to type and extent. Of that 38 per cent, a quarter combined quantity with some qualitative attributes into one weighted 'ICD score' using ordinal scales. Quality represents the richness of information disclosed. Therefore, a composite measure that incorporates a qualitative assessment should not be interpreted in the same way as a pure ICD frequency measure. While it has been argued that a pure frequency measure of ICD and a measure that combined quality and frequency lead to the same conclusions about the salience of ICD, Husin et al. (2012) show that they generate differences at the IC subcategory or item level. However, most ICD researchers interpret the results of a weighted measure in the same way as they interpret pure quantity measures. For instance, Branswijck and Everaert (2012) compared ICDs in annual reports and IPO prospectuses using a weighted measure that adds 1 for presence, 2 for presence with additional detail, and 3 for presence with quantified information. Yet they make conclusions about the frequency of disclosure using this measure.

The problem of conflating quantity and quality and making sense of the resulting measure is intensified when the researcher only examines a single mention of the IC category within a text unit (that is, the existence approach). We find that 13 per cent of the studies that examine only existence also use an ordinal measure that incorporates some form of a qualitative attribute. Surely one cannot form a reliable conclusion about quality by randomly singling out disclosures in a given IC category, while ignoring other disclosures in the same category that may be of higher or lower quality. Thus, our results reveal that a significant proportion of ICD studies make invalid inferences.

Syntactic CA to measure ICD

All the articles we reviewed follow semantic CA, except for 15 (15 per cent), which use syntactic CA (that is, word searches). Two of these 15 involved a manual keyword search from a predetermined list of IC items, while 13 used software. ICD cannot be effectively investigated using syntactic CA because it limits the scope of the investigation to a list of words or word combinations. It is almost impossible to develop a list of words that reliably represents the multiplicity of possible references to IC. To identify most ICDs, text needs to be read for its meaning. The effectiveness of keyword searching is also impeded by organisation-specific jargon associated with ICD (Beattie and Thomson, 2007). Not to mention that even in semantic CA, it is common to find relevant information that does not fit into the original categorisation scheme. Searching for a set of predefined keywords will not find any information beyond what was originally envisaged. Moreover, Dumay and Cai (2015, p. 138) argue that, when applied to ICD, this kind of CA 'potentially misses what is hidden and only shows up that which is intentionally disclosed'.

Beattie and Thomson (2007) demonstrate the inferiority of syntactic content analyses in measuring ICD by comparing the results of an electronic keyword search and semantic CA of the same annual report. The authors report that 'an electronic search of 105 IC terms generated 264 hits compared to 906 pieces of information obtained from the manual search, and 107 of these (40 percent) were found to contain no IC content'. They also observed that one search 'hit' could relate to multiple pieces of information in multiple IC categories, which further undermines the validity of the data.

Lee and Guthrie (2010) argue that taxonomies or concept-based software tools for CA are superior to simple word searching methods, and that they can be effective when identifying the documents that contain ICDs as opposed to the extent of the ICDs within them. We examined the software tools used in the 13 computer-assisted syntactic studies and found that only three used a tool with an inbuilt dictionary or taxonomy. The other ten used software with a keyword in context (KWIC) search function, for example, Concordance, Wordstat, SPAD-T.8.2, atlas.ti, Leximancer and Nvivo. Moreover, all but one of these studies used keywords to examine the extent of the ICDs rather than for identifying documents that contained ICD, as recommended by Lee and Guthrie (2010).

Studies based on syntactic CA cannot be discarded completely as invalid without considering the research questions they address: as Lee and Guthrie (2010) show, if the intention is to make comparisons, then this method has merit. According to our analysis, only four of the 15 studies using syntactic CA were comparative. These observations lead us to conclude that syntactic CA's contribution to the ICD literature is minimal at best. At worst, it undermines face validity because, in many cases, the researchers are not adequately measuring the variable or construct they purport to be measuring.

Inappropriate use of recording and measurement units

Our analysis reveals that 59 per cent of the studies use information units, also referred to as text units or themes, as the recording and measurement unit, while 14 per cent use sentences. Another 14 per cent use a word or several words as the recording unit, and 7 per cent use multiple recording and measurement units.

As mentioned in the literature review, themes are the best units with which to identify and measure ICDs, because themes can capture visual disclosures, and they also capture narratives more comprehensively and reliably (Beattie and Thomson, 2007; Husin et al., 2012; Steenkamp and Northcott, 2007). Returning to Beattie and Thomson's (2007) example of Next PLC, the annual report contained 906 ICD text units as opposed to 260 sentence units. As such, Beattie and Thomson (2007, p. 146) describe the advantages of using themes (or text units) for coding narrative content: 'It enables the extent to which different categories of IC information are disclosed to be investigated; it avoids making decisions in relation to the dominant IC category disclosed in each sentence; and does not exclude the IC information which is less dominant.'

The problems associated with using words and sentences as the recording unit are somewhat averted with presence/absence type measurements. However, these types of studies only account for three out of the 30 studies using words and sentences as the recording unit (see Table 3.3). Hence, to the extent that words or sentences do not adequately capture the extent of ICD, at least 28 per cent of the studies are marred with face validity concerns.

Construct Validity

Our review of the literature indicates that researchers rarely report more than one measure of IC; thus, they fail to demonstrate construct validity. Abeysekera (2006) demonstrated that counting the number of lines relating to ICD resulted in different conclusions than counting the frequency with which IC categories are disclosed in annual reports, highlighting the need to adopt multiple measures of IC to ensure construct validity. Massaro et al. (2017) addressed construct validity by using computer-assisted CA to verify the data generated through a manual CA. This approach suited their study because they only classified posts on internet stock message boards as either containing or not containing any IC information; but it is worth reiterating that syntactic CA cannot generate a valid measure of the full extent of ICD even if the same verification strategy is applied.

Although not included in our sample as it is a method-related study, another exception is Goebel (2015) who used several different IC categorisation schemes and compared the results. The schemes included different combinations of IC items drawn from a consolidated item pool of 22 IC categorisation schemes found in the literature. Goebel (2015) chose this approach to understand whether the results of prior studies that had adopted different IC categorisation schemes could be reliably compared, but not to demonstrate construct validity. However, this would also be an acceptable way to ensure construct validity. Our analysis reveals that 74 per cent of the studies either adapted an existing categorisation scheme or generated their own, but none cross-checked their results with an alternative scheme. The failure to establish construct validity is intensified by the absence of a uniform definition and subcategories of IC (Beattie and Thomson, 2007).

Cuozzo et al. (2017) argue that ICD researchers should broaden their methodological repertoire and be innovative in their search for ICD. Supplementing CA with other research methods can ensure construct validity in ICD research. It can also be ensured by obtaining consistent results with different sampling units. This is especially important when the appropriateness of using annual reports, which are the most commonly used sampling unit in ICD research, has been questioned as they are likely to have been subjected to manipulation and contamination (Abeysekera, 2006; Dumay and Cai, 2015). In fact, analysing the content of disclosures made through other channels, conducting interviews or surveys or using experiments or field studies to corroborate one's findings from annual reports would also be good ways to enhance construct validity. Unfortunately, Dumay and Cai (2015) highlight that corroborating evidence from alternative sampling units or methods in addition to CA is scarce in ICD research. In their sample, only 8 per cent adopted such measures. In our sample, that number was only 3 per cent.

SUMMARY AND CONCLUSION

With this study of 103 articles using CA to inquire into ICD, we have examined the extent to which ICD studies generate valid inferences. Our results demonstrate that ICD research often fails to meet the level of validity required for an inference to be considered credible. Routinely, there are substantial problems in the way the content analysis has been designed and conducted. Moreover, there is a general lack of transparency about the methodological choices made.

First, a significant proportion of studies do not provide sufficient details to assess whether the CA technique adopted adequately captures the intended ICDs. In a field such as IC accounting, where a consensus on the meaning of the concepts is impossible to reach, it is the authors' responsibility to ensure that readers understand what they mean when they say 'ICD': what it comprises and how it is measured. Face validity cannot be established without this understanding. In CA studies, this must be done by fully explaining the categories of classification, their definitions, the criteria for deciding whether a given disclosure belongs in a particular category, how a modified categorisation scheme is situated within a new research context, and whether and how an ICD is indigenous to the analysed text.

Second, in a significant number of studies, what the researchers intended to measure and what they measured are not the same thing. One variant of this inconsistency is when a researcher intended to measure the extent of the ICDs but ends up measuring variability. In another variant, a composite measure of ICD that incorporates certain qualitative attributes of the communications is interpreted as a measure of the quantum of ICD. In 13 per cent of the studies we analysed, we found both of these errors, which further intensifies the threat to face validity. To overcome these problems, we propose that studies on the extent of ICD should code every disclosure in each document (that is, frequency), and that measures of quality and quantity should be kept separate.

Third, there are several instances where ICD researchers make methodological choices about CA that detract from their ability to measure what they purport to measure. Despite strong discouragement, ICD researchers still adopt syntactic CA or create measures of ICD that do not represent much of the ICD or the potential ICD that might be present in the analysed texts. Similarly, several studies use recording and measurement units that do not distinguish between multiple occurrences of ICD in a text, or cannot capture ICDs in all forms, such as images. We reinforce the recommendations made by other researchers to use semantic CA over syntactic CA and information units/themes as the recording and measurement unit.

Fourth, ICD researchers do not seem to appreciate the importance of construct validity as they rarely use an alternative measure of IC to highlight the robustness of their main ICD measure. Alternative measures of ICD include using different recording units, categorisation schemes and research methods.

As our analysis is based on what the researchers reported, rather than what they did, some of the studies we examined may have been based on exemplary method choices. However, because they did not provide sufficient details about their procedures and choices, we have concluded the research to be inadequate. This point illustrates that the CA method requires both an explicit description and reflexivity (Steenkamp and Northcott, 2007). When reporting the study, researchers should openly reflect on the challenges they experienced in applying CA. Incomplete and ambiguous reporting of the procedures and method choices, or a lack of reflection, prevents the reader from relying on or even evaluating the research findings.

Guthrie et al. (2004, p. 290) conclude their commentary on CA as a method for ICD research by stating that it 'is a method in need of further refinement and development if research advances are to be made in the field of ICR [intellectual capital reporting]'. We concur with Dumay and Cai (2015, p. 145) that 'the tools needed to ensure reliability and validity seem not to have been of concern to many ICD researchers, and this requires a return to the methodological drawing board as far as CA-based ICD studies are concerned'. After more than one and a half decades since Guthrie et al.'s (2004) article, our findings lead us to the conclusion that the application of CA in ICD research still needs further refinement and development. This time, however, it is not to advance the field; it is to ensure research in this field is valid enough to be taken seriously.

NOTES

1. These five papers were, however, included in the literature review above.
2. The coding instrument contains the operational definitions for each content category and coding rules for deciding when to code content into each category.

REFERENCES

Abeysekera, I. (2006), 'The project of intellectual capital disclosure: Researching the research', *Journal of Intellectual Capital*, 7 (1), 61–77.

Abeysekera, I. (2011), 'Civil war, stock return, and intellectual capital disclosure in Sri Lanka', *Advances in Accounting*, 27 (2), 331–337.

Abhayawansa, S. (2011), 'A methodology for investigating intellectual capital information in analyst reports', *Journal of Intellectual Capital*, 12 (3), 446–476.

Beattie, V. and S.J. Thomson (2007), 'Lifting the lid on the use of content analysis to investigate intellectual capital disclosures', *Accounting Forum*, 31 (2), 129–163.

Branswijck, D. and P. Everaert (2012), 'Intellectual capital disclosure commitment: Myth or reality?', *Journal of Intellectual Capital*, 13 (1), 39–56.

Cuozzo, B., Dumay, J., Palmaccio, M. and R. Lombardi (2017), 'Intellectual capital disclosure: A structured literature review', *Journal of Intellectual Capital*, 18 (1), 9–28.

Davison, J. (2008), 'Rhetoric, repetition, reporting and the "dot.com" era: Words, pictures, intangibles', *Accounting, Auditing and Accountability Journal*, 21 (6), 791–826.
Dumay, J. (2014), '15 years of the *Journal of Intellectual Capital* and counting: A manifesto for transformational IC research', *Journal of Intellectual Capital*, 15 (1), 2–37.
Dumay, J. and L. Cai (2014), 'A review and critique of content analysis as a methodology for inquiring into IC disclosure', *Journal of Intellectual Capital*, 15 (2), 264–290.
Dumay, J. and L. Cai (2015), 'Using content analysis as a research methodology for investigating intellectual capital disclosure: A critique', *Journal of Intellectual Capital*, 16 (1), 121–155.
Duriau, V.J., Reger, R.K. and M.D. Pfarrer (2007), 'A content analysis of the content analysis literature in organization studies: Research themes, data sources, and methodological refinements', *Organizational Research Methods*, 10 (1), 5–34.
Eddine, C.O.H., Abdullah, S.N., Hamid, F.A. and D.M. Hossain (2015), 'The determinants of intellectual capital disclosure: A meta-analysis review', *Journal of Asia Business Studies*, 9 (3), 232–250.
Freelon, D. (2011), *ReCal for Ordinal, Interval, and Ratio Data (OIR)*, Seattle, USA: DFreelon.org.
García-Meca, E., Parra, I., Larrán, M. and I. Martínez (2005), 'The explanatory factors of intellectual capital disclosure to financial analysts', *European Accounting Review*, 14 (1), 63–94.
Gately, C. and J. Cunningham (2014), 'Building intellectual capital in incubated technology firms', *Journal of Intellectual Capital*, 15 (4), 516–536.
Goebel, V. (2015), 'Is the literature on content analysis of intellectual capital reporting heading towards a dead end?', *Journal of Intellectual Capital*, 16 (3), 681–699.
Guthrie, J., Dumay, J., Ricceri, F. and C. Nielsen (2017), *The Routledge Companion to Intellectual Capital*, New York: Routledge.
Guthrie, J. and R. Petty (2000), 'Intellectual capital: Australian annual reporting practices', *Journal of Intellectual Capital*, 1 (3), 241–251.
Guthrie, J., Petty, R., Yongvanich, K. and F. Ricceri (2004), 'Using content analysis as a research method to inquire into intellectual capital reporting', *Journal of Intellectual Capital*, 5 (2), 282–293.
Guthrie, J., Ricceri, F. and J. Dumay (2012), 'Reflections and projections: A decade of Intellectual Capital Accounting Research', *British Accounting Review*, 44 (2), 68–82.
Hackston, D. and M.J. Milne (1996), 'Some determinants of social and environmental disclosures in New Zealand companies', *Accounting, Auditing and Accountability Journal*, 9 (1), 77–108.
Hayes, A.F. and K. Krippendorff (2007), 'Answering the call for a standard reliability measure for coding data', *Communication Methods and Measures*, 1 (1), 77–89.
Hidalgo, R.L., García-Meca, E. and I. Martínez (2011), 'Corporate governance and intellectual capital disclosure', *Journal of Business Ethics*, 100 (3), 483–495.
Huff, A.S. (1990), *Mapping Strategic Thought*, Chichester: John Wiley & Sons.
Husin, M.N., Hooper, K. and K. Olesen (2012), 'Analysis of intellectual capital disclosure – An illustrative example', *Journal of Intellectual Capital*, 13 (2), 196–220.
Krippendorff, K. (2004a), *Content Analysis – An Introduction to its Methodology*, Thousand Oaks, CA: SAGE Publications.
Krippendorff, K. (2004b), 'Reliability in content analysis – Some common misconceptions and recommendations', *Human Communication Research*, 30 (3), 411–433.
Lee, L.L. and J. Guthrie (2010), 'Visualising and measuring intellectual capital in capital markets: A research method', *Journal of Intellectual Capital*, 11 (1), 4–22.
Lombard, M., Snyder-Duch, J. and C.C. Bracken (2002), 'Content analysis in mass communication: Assessment and reporting of intercoder reliability', *Human Communication Research*, 28 (4), 587–604.
Massaro, M., Dumay, J. and C. Bagnoli (2017), 'When the investors speak: Intellectual capital disclosure and the Web 2.0', *Management Decision*, 55 (9), 1888–1904.

McKinnon, J. (1988), 'Reliability and validity in field research: Some strategies and tactics', *Accounting, Auditing and Accountability Journal*, 1 (1), 34–54.

Nielsen, A.C., Bukh, P.N., Mouritsen, J., Johansen, M.R. and P. Gormsen (2006), 'Intellectual capital statements on their way to the stock exchange: Analyzing new reporting systems', *Journal of Intellectual Capital*, 7 (2), 221–240.

Sapir, E. (1944), 'Grading, a study in semantics', *Philosophy of Science*, 11 (2), 93–116.

Steenkamp, N. and D. Northcott (2007), 'Content analysis in accounting research: The practical challenges', *Australian Accounting Review*, 17 (43), 12–25.

Weber, R.P. (1990), *Basic Content Analysis*, Newbury Park, CA: SAGE Publications.

4. Intellectual capital research: European versus North American approaches

Henri Hussinki, Tatiana Garanina and John Dumay

INTRODUCTION

Recent literature suggests that the international intellectual capital research community might not follow universally similar approaches to study intellectual capital and other intangible resources (Cuozzo et al., 2017). For example, Hussinki et al. (2017) highlight that the constituent elements of intellectual capital are perceived somewhat differently in countries with different cultural backgrounds, and Hussinki et al. (2020) demonstrate that scholars from different continents prefer quite diverse methodological and conceptual approaches to research intellectual capital. In addition, Cuozzo et al. (2017) point out terminological discrepancies between American, Australasian and European researchers, whereby American researchers are more likely to relate intellectual capital to 'intangible assets', whereas Australasian and European authors refer to intellectual capital in the traditional tripartite model of human, relational and structural capital. Thus, there are indications that there are fundamental differences in the way that intellectual capital scholars conduct research in different geographical regions (Garanina et al., 2021).

In this chapter, we compare the research output of two major intellectual capital jurisdictions – Europe and North America – by clarifying their scientific premises, methodological preferences and publication trends. Thus, the objective of our study is to analyse how different are the European and North American approaches to scholarly research on intellectual capital and intangibles. This is done by examining the different definitions of these ostensibly interchangeable terms. In our study we are also interested in how scholars treat intellectual capital and intangibles, as either an accounting or a management topic, particularly as limitations in the existing financial reporting system are prompting discussions of ways to measure, report and manage intellectual capital and intangibles (Petty and Guthrie, 2000). Further, we are acutely aware that North American scholars are more predisposed to conduct empirical and quantitative research, as opposed to Europeans who tend to do more theoretical and qualitative research than their North American counterparts (de Villiers et al., 2019; Garanina et al., 2021). This difference in research tradition also spills out into the specific journals that European and North American scholars publish in, so it will also be interesting to see how journals based in different geographical areas uphold these traditions when publishing intellectual capital and intangibles research. To meet these objectives, we conduct a systematic literature review on journal articles published from 2000 to 2017 in the top 20 international accounting and top 20 international management journals, using Google Scholar Metrics to select the journals as advocated by Massaro et al. (2016).

This chapter extends the emerging literature stream on the variance of global intellectual capital and intangibles research approaches by providing deeper coverage of European and North American literature than any prior review (for example, Cuozzo et al., 2017; de Villiers et al., 2019; Guthrie et al., forthcoming). Europe and North America have produced a clear majority of the post-2000 intellectual capital and intangibles research (Hussinki et al., 2020), which justifies the focus of this study. It is important to generate more discussion on the different approaches to view, research and interpret intellectual capital and other intangibles, as it could provide inspiration and options for the international intellectual capital research community to try something new in their quest to understand and explain the value and the role of intellectual capital and other intangibles in the contemporary economies.

METHODOLOGY

A systematic literature review methodology was applied for selecting and analysing the corpus of literature published in the leading accounting and management journals. By following the procedure developed by Massaro et al. (2016), we selected the relevant articles according to a structured seven-phase procedure.

Phase 1: Following the approach of Massaro et al. (2016), the 20 top academic journals in the fields of accounting and management were selected based on Google Scholar Metrics, which lists the top academic journals based on citations received in the last five years. According to Harzing and Alakangas (2016), Google Scholar Metrics provides a broad coverage of literature sources. Based on their quality, relevance and impact, the journals were considered for the literature selection process (see Table 4.1).

Phase 2: We searched the articles published from 2000 to 2017 from the selected journals' homepages. To attain a comprehensive body of

Table 4.1 Top 20 accounting and management journals according to Google Scholar Metrics

Top 20 accounting journals	Top 20 management journals
Accounting and Business Research	Academy of Management Journal
Accounting and Finance	Academy of Management Review
Accounting, Auditing and Accountability Journal	Entrepreneurship Theory and Practice
Accounting Horizons	Harvard Business Review
Accounting, Organizations and Society	Industrial Marketing Management
Auditing: A Journal of Practice and Theory	Journal of Business Research
Contemporary Accounting Research	Journal of Business Venturing
Critical Perspectives on Accounting	Journal of Corporate Finance
European Accounting Review	Journal of Management
International Journal of Accounting Information Systems	Journal of Management Studies
International Tax and Public Finance	Journal of Marketing
Journal of Accounting and Economics	Journal of Operations Management
Journal of Accounting and Public Policy	Journal of Product Innovation Management
Journal of Accounting Research	Journal of the Academy of Marketing Science
Journal of Business Finance and Accounting	Management Decision
Management Accounting Research	Management Science
National Tax Journal	Omega
Review of Accounting Studies	Organization Science
The Accounting Review	Strategic Management Journal
The British Accounting Review	Technological Forecasting and Social Change

Source: https://scholar.google.com/citations?view_op=top_venues&hl=en&vq=bus_accountingtaxation.

literature we used the following search keywords: 'intangible asset*', 'intellectual asset*', 'intangible capital', 'intellectual capital' and 'intangible*' as suggested by Eccles and Krzus (2010). After the initial search, removal of duplicates, and delimitation based on language (English), article type (only journal articles) and the year of publication, the number of potentially relevant articles was 2147 and 4172 for accounting and management journals, respectively. We then used the RefWorks reference management software to store and organise the title and abstract information of the articles.

Phase 3: Based on our assessment of the article's title, if it did not correspond with the accounting or managerial research objectives on intellectual capital or intangibles, the article was removed from the RefWorks database. After this, the number of potentially relevant articles was reduced significantly to 532 for accounting journals and 1561 for management journals.

Phase 4: Articles were excluded based on the abstracts. Here, we excluded book reviews, discussion articles and editorials/introductions because of their lack of rigorous methodological support, which may bias the results of further analysis. As a result, the list of articles was reduced to 349 for accounting journals and 427 for management journals.

Phase 5: Based on the full texts, we excluded remaining articles if they used intellectual capital or intangibles only as a side story, or did not reflect the role of intellectual capital or intangibles in the interpretation of the results. After this step, the number of articles became 325 for accounting journals and 265 for management journals.

Phase 6: The home country of the affiliated university of each first author was used to determine each article's country of origin.[1] After coding the home country information on each research article, we reorganised the articles into country categories, and we retained only European and North American articles for the analysis. Europe, including continental Europe and the United Kingdom, was represented by 190 research articles, whereas 'North America', that is, Canada and the United States of America, was represented by 258 articles.

Phase 7: We used NVivo software to code the abstracts and full texts of the chosen articles. The coding protocol for each reviewed article comprised the following information: name of author/authors, year of publication, country of origin of the first author and the applied research methods in each article.

RESULTS

As illustrated in Figure 4.1, the yearly research output has varied between European and Northern American research in the post-2000s literature. The American output peaked in 2002, whereas the European output decreased from 2001 to 2002. After that, the output of the European and North American researchers went up and down in an unsynchronised fashion until 2006, as they both saw their output increase from 2006 to 2007. In Europe, the years from 2010 to 2012 marked a recession of intellectual capital and intangibles research, as the yearly article volume decreased from its all-time high of 19 articles in 2010 to its lowest in the 2000s: four articles in 2012. One explanation as to why many European scholars may have lost interest in studying the topic by 2012 was that it was disinteresting to large companies. According to Dumay (2016, p. 173), intellectual capital reporting was dead by then as listed companies had lost interest in disclosing their intellectual capital publicly. By that time, a new form of reporting in the guise of integrated reporting, as per the International Integrated Reporting Council, was taking shape and providing plenty of fuel for academic research beyond intellectual capital, which appeared to become part of the wider integrated reporting framework (IIRC, 2013). According to Dumay et al. (2016), it was at this time that research into integrated reporting and its different variations started to take place.

Also, the North American output decreased significantly from 2011 to 2012 but started increasing again after 2012. Since 2012, the European research output has shown positive signs, with steady growth without major drops, but the North American output collapsed to its lowest level (six articles) in the post-2000s era in 2016. Unlike the dip in European research in 2012, we cannot offer any reason why the drop occurred in 2016. However, what is most notable is that the two lines do not share any symmetry, and while North American research dominates in most years, the lines cross in several places, signifying that intellectual capital and intangibles researchers in both geographical areas are motivated by different influences.

Figure 4.2 shows that North American researchers have published more articles in the leading accounting and management journals than their European counterparts, with the total number of publications being 258 and 190, respectively. Figure 4.3 shows that the differences in publication numbers for North America and Europe are most pronounced in the

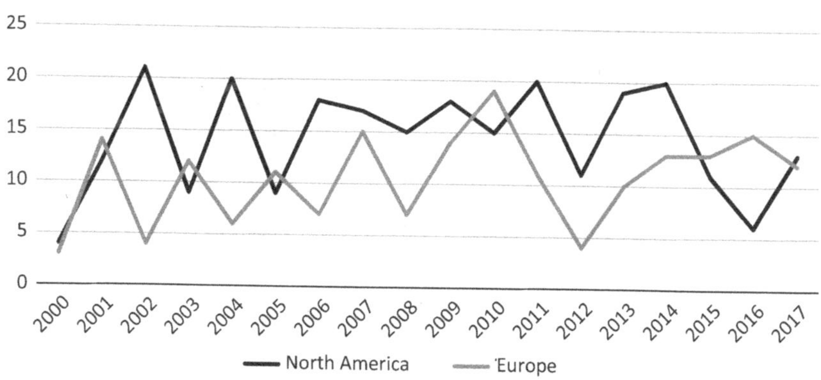

Figure 4.1 *Number of North American and European articles published from 2000 to 2017 in the leading accounting and management journals*

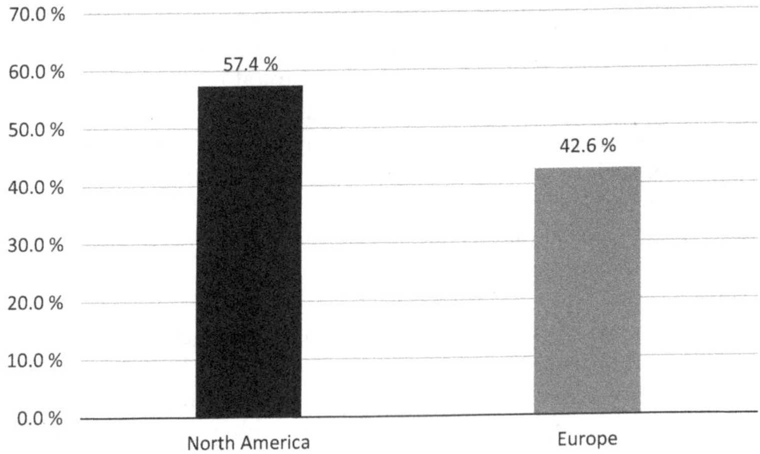

Figure 4.2 *Share of North American vs European research on intellectual capital and intangibles in the leading accounting and management journals*

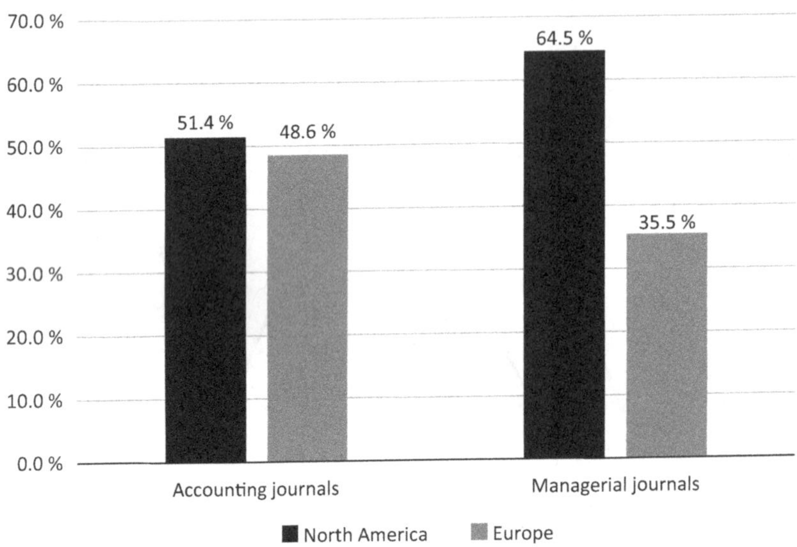

Figure 4.3 *Share of North American vs European research on intellectual capital and intangibles in the leading accounting and management journals*

leading management journals, whereas the number of articles published in the leading accounting journals is quite similar.

Figure 4.4 shows that studies published in the leading management journals focus on different managerial approaches to intellectual capital, whereas the articles published in the leading accounting journals are quite evenly split between managerial and accounting aspects of intellectual capital. Management is more prominent in the North American accounting journals, with the majority presenting research based on managing intellectual capital and intangibles than accounting for intellectual capital. This shows that, from an accounting perspective, North American researchers treat intellectual capital and intangibles as a management issue, compared to European researchers who treat it as a financial issue (for example, Barker, 2015). Unsurprisingly, research published in management journals is 97 per cent dominated by articles focusing on managing intellectual capital. Thus, when we consider all European and North American intellectual capital and intangibles research, it is evident that the managerial perspective is dominating intellectual capital and intangibles research in both Europe and North America (Figure 4.5).

This analysis shows that intellectual capital and intangibles researchers are more concerned about how to manage intellectual capital and intangibles than how to account for it. Thus, in intellectual capital and intangibles research it seems that the adage 'what you measure is what you manage' is not true (Dumay and Rooney, 2011), but rather, intellectual capital and intangibles emphasises management over measurement

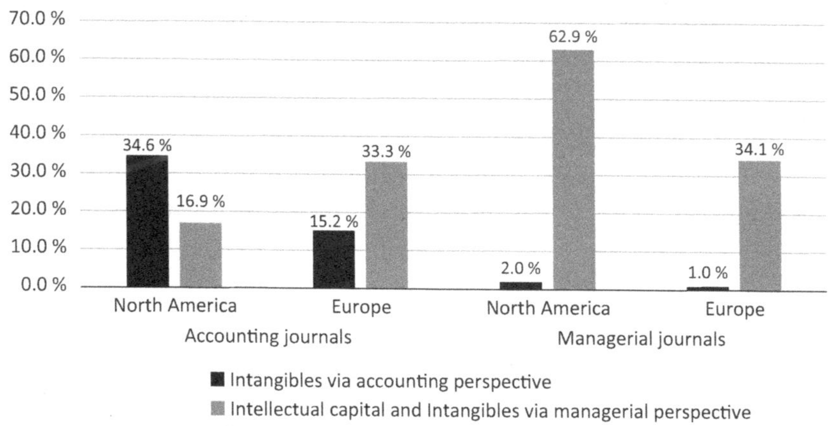

Figure 4.4 Accounting vs managerial perspective on intellectual capital and intangibles in the leading accounting and management journals

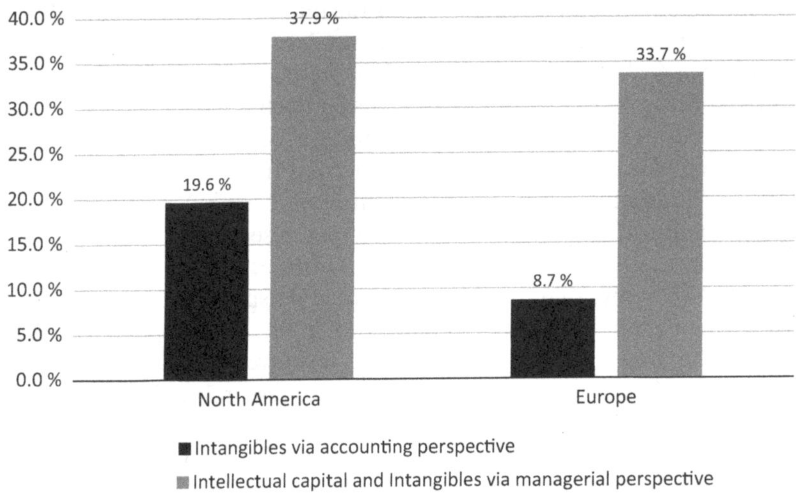

Figure 4.5 Accounting vs managerial perspective on intellectual capital and intangibles in the leading accounting and management journals – North America vs Europe

(Chaminade and Roberts, 2003). The management perspective is also consistent with early intellectual capital and intangibles research conducted by Mouritsen et al. (2001), who found that organisations participating in the Danish Intellectual Capital statement project were more interested in the internal benefits of managing intellectual capital than they were interested in measuring and reporting it. Thus, from the early days of intellectual capital and intangibles research there is strong evidence to argue that managing intellectual capital and intangibles is more important than measuring and reporting it (see also Schaper et al., 2017).

The managerial perspective towards intellectual capital and intangibles is what Guthrie and Dumay (2015) identify as a practice turn in intellectual capital research. The practice turn has its origins in European intellectual capital and intangibles research dating back to 2006, when Mouritsen (2006) began to theorise intellectual capital research based on Latour's (1986) differentiation between ostensive versus performative research. The new theoretical approach to intellectual capital and intangibles helped identify what Guthrie et al. (2012) term the third stage of intellectual capital research, which takes a performative and critical view of intellectual capital management practices based on their analysis of intellectual capital accounting research. Hence, the Guthrie et al. (2012) article identified that mainly European-based intellectual capital accounting researchers who had begun looking at intellectual capital and intangibles from an accounting perspective were increasingly realising that intellectual capital and intangibles research required a management approach much more than a measurement approach.

Table 4.2 shows the descriptive statistics highlighting the research methods applied by the European and North American intellectual capital and intangibles researchers. It demonstrates quite clearly that North American researchers prefer empirical quantitative research methods compared to their European colleagues. In more detail, out of all research on intellectual capital and intangibles published in the leading accounting and managerial journals from 2000 to 2017, 29.24 per cent is North American empirical research based on secondary data, and 8.71 per cent is North American empirical articles based on survey data. Conversely, the comparative figures for the European empirical research are 10.49 per cent and 6.03 per cent, which suggests a significant difference in the methodological approach between the two camps. Also, North American scholars are more active than their European colleagues in terms of essays and literature reviews, as the total share of publications is 11.16 per cent and 8.71 per cent, respectively. Moreover, European case studies (12.05 per cent) on intellectual capital and intangibles are more common than in North American (5.13 per cent), as is content analysis in Europe (5.14 per cent) compared to North American (3.36 per cent). Altogether, it seems that European researchers utilise more versatile approaches to study intellectual capital and intangibles than their North American colleagues, who have firmly focused on quantitative research methods.

Figure 4.6 visualises the statistics from Table 4.2. The horizontal bar for the North American empirical research is far ahead of any other bar. Additionally, European studies span a variety of research approaches, most notably case studies, essays, literature reviews, empirical research and different multi-method approaches.

DISCUSSION

This study compared the European and North American research on intellectual capital and intangibles to learn more about the scientific premises, methodological preferences and publication trends of the two major academic research geographical areas that research intellectual capital and intangibles. The data was collected from the leading international accounting and management journals, as they both include high-quality research on the subject matter. The systematic literature review methodology was applied to select an appropriate body of literature and to ensure

Table 4.2 Applied research methods in North American versus European articles (in number of articles, and percentage in brackets)

Journals Methods	Accounting journals		Managerial journals		Both types of journals	
	North America	Europe	North America	Europe	North America	Europe
Single-method approach						
Case study/interview/experiment	5 (2.06%)	16 (6.58%)	4 (1.95%)	2 (0.98%)	9 (2.01%)	18 (4.02%)
Content analysis	2 (0.82%)	8 (3.29%)	0 (0.00%)	1 (0.49%)	2 (0.45%)	9 (2.01%)
Empirical research	83 (34.16%)	36 (14.81%)	48 (23.41%)	11 (5.37%)	131 (29.24%)	47 (10.49%)
Essays and literature reviews	21 (8.64%)	29 (11.93%)	29 (14.15%)	10 (4.88%)	50 (11.16%)	39 (8.71%)
Multi-analysis approach						
Case study/interviews/other action methods	1 (0.41%)	14 (5.76%)	3 (1.46%)	3 (1.46%)	4 (0.89%)	17 (3.79%)
Case study or interviews and empirical study	1 (0.41%)	2 (0.82%)	9 (4.39%)	17 (8.29%)	10 (2.23%)	19 (4.24%)
Content analysis and literature review	0 (0.00%)	3 (1.23%)	2 (0.98%)	0 (0.00%)	2 (0.45%)	3 (0.67%)
Content analysis and empirical study	8 (3.29%)	8 (3.29%)	3 (1.46%)	3 (1.46%)	11 (2.46%)	11 (2.46%)
Survey and empirical study	4 (1.65%)	2 (0.82%)	35 (17.07%)	25 (12.20%)	39 (8.71%)	27 (6.03%)
Total	125 (51.44%)	118 (48.56%)	133 (64.88%)	72 (35.12%)	258 (57.59%)	190 (42.41%)

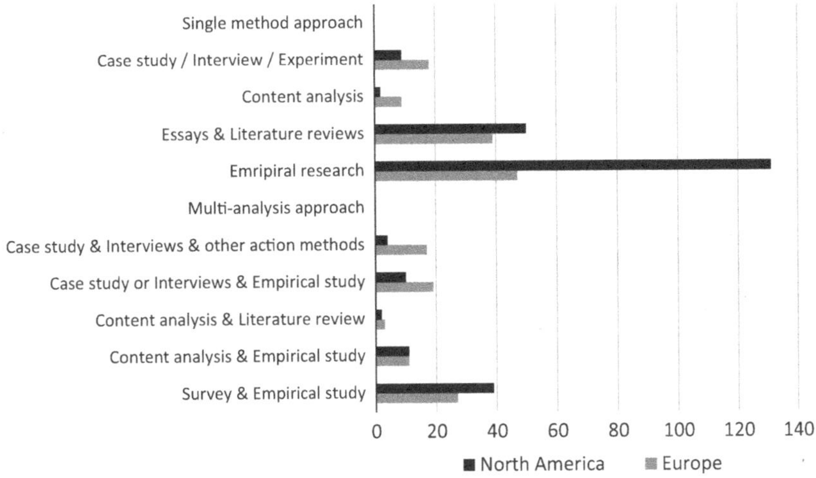

Figure 4.6 *Applied research methods in North American versus European articles in both types of journals*

the methodological rigour of the study. Altogether, we included 190 North American and 258 European research articles in the analysis.

The findings of our analysis show that European and North American researchers have published nearly equal quanitities of scholarly studies on intellectual capital and intangibles in the top 20 accounting journals, but the North American literature dominates the intellectual capital and intangibles discussion published in the top 20 management journals. Also, North American researchers give more attention to the accounting-related issues than their European counterparts, who tend to contribute to the managerial intellectual capital discussion. Regarding research methods, North American researchers tend to utilise publicly available databases to write empirical articles, whereas European scholars are more versatile with their methodological choices.

This chapter has implications for future research, especially for the European and North American intellectual capital and intangibles research communities, by demonstrating the strengths and weaknesses of the two major intellectual capital and intangibles research powerhouses, as well as by suggesting a way to progress the international intellectual capital and intangibles research community.

What is evident is that there have been two distinct bands of research evolving over the last two decades that have clearly defined demarcations: accounting for intellectual capital and managing intellectual capital. However, can we expect to continue to see more managerial articles published about intellectual capital and intangibles than we do accounting articles? This view is supported by Dumay and Guthrie (2019), who argue that intellectual capital and intangibles researchers, standard setters and policy-makers have long resolved the accounting problem for intellectual capital and intangibles, despite some researchers, such as Lev and Gu (2016), who still lament that accounting for intangibles has failed. Early intellectual capital and intangibles research advocated that accounting, based on the production of financial reports was deficient. As Cañibano and Sánchez (2009, p. 102) argue, this is because: 'firms feel a growing need to invest in intangibles on which the future of the company is based, but in most cases, those investments are not reflected in the balance sheet due to the existence of very restrictive accounting criteria for the recognition of assets and their valuation'.

Central to the concerns about accounting for intangibles was how to record them on the balance sheet, and regulators responded with regulations and standards, notably International Accounting Standard 38. Differing views on how to account for intangibles appear to be counterproductive, and, as Stolowy and Jeny-Cazavan (2001, p. 494) argue, the main concern was that the accounting treatment of intangibles was so diverse that the attempts to harmonise accounting in the late 1990s 'could result in failure in particular because of International Accounting Standard 38 which is in opposition to treatments adopted in several countries'. However, when implemented in 2005 in countries such as Australia and the United Kingdom, the so-called negative impacts of International Financial Reporting Standards and International Accounting Standard 38 did not materialise (Cheung et al., 2008).

Fast forward to 2019, and there does not appear to be much concern from regulators to change International Accounting Standard 38 because the Conceptual Framework for Financial Reporting (International Accounting Standards Board, 2018) has just revised the fundamental definitions of assets and liabilities. As the definitions of assets and liabilities for financial reporting have changed, it is unlikely that intangibles require rethinking (Dumay and Guthrie, 2019). What the accounting regulators seem to want is more description and narrative that help report users to understand what intangibles are and how they drive value creation in a company. As Paul George, Executive Director for Corporate Governance and Reporting at the Financial Reporting Council (2019), outlines:

> It is unrealistic to expect the value of a business to be fully represented in its balance sheet; there is always likely to be a gap between the balance sheet total and the market capitalisation of a company. The paper suggests several ideas for expanding the information provided, both quantitative and qualitative, to improve users' assessment of corporate value.

Accordingly, Dumay and Guthrie (2019, p. 2291) agree with Paul George and argue 'that current financial accounting regulations on the treatment of intellectual capital and intangibles is adequate, which is why there is so little pressure on accounting regulators to change how intangibles, and thus intellectual capital, is recognised on the balance sheet'. Additionally, there are currently no restrictions on companies producing extra commentary to comply with Paul George's suggestions, and companies can always use the International Financial Reporting Standards Management Commentary practice statement, released a decade ago to guide companies in providing any form of extra intangible and tangible information (International Accounting Standards Board, 2010).

In addition to the management commentary guidelines, there are a host of reporting frameworks available to companies, from intellectual capital statements (DATI, 2001; MERITUM, 2002), to integrated reports (International Integrated Reporting Council, 2013) and the new European Union Directive on non-financial and diversity reporting (European Union, 2014). However, despite the calls and the ample opportunities to disclose more about intangibles, many companies are reluctant to do so for fear of disclosing commercially sensitive information to their competitors (Schaper et al., 2017). Hence, companies are more concerned about managing their intellectual capital and intangibles than accounting and reporting.

CONCLUSION AND IMPLICATIONS

While we have presented evidence to argue that intellectual capital and intangibles research follows both management and accounting dimensions, we are not sure that is the case in practice. Even though Guthrie and Dumay (2015) identified a practice turn in intellectual capital research, it does not mean that researchers will always follow this turn. In a more recent work looking at more than 20 years of intellectual capital research, mainly in Europe, Guthrie et al. (forthcoming) compared intellectual capital accounting research in the periods 2000–2009 and 2010–2019, only to find that while some things were changing – such as intellectual capital research expanding into Asia and Africa, and an reincarnation of intellectual capital reporting in the guise of integrated reporting – the main corpus of intellectual capital accounting research topics and methodologies did not change much between those two periods. The only major change that Guthrie et al. (forthcoming) discovered was a change in geographical areas, with countries and regions such as Asia, Africa and the Middle East now starting to publish more research on intellectual capital accounting.

Thus, intellectual capital accounting research is truly becoming a global discipline. However, because research methodologies and topics remain the same, this led Guthrie et al. (forthcoming) to conclude, '*Plus ça change, plus c'est la même chose* [The more things change, the more they remain the same]'.

European and North American research seems well entrenched in its respective research patterns, even though there is an opportunity to further extend the research into new areas beyond just management and accounting. One notable feature of research steeped in empirical and positivist traditions is a general lack of critical scholarship. We mainly find critical scholarship in normative and commentary articles, of which we find very few in the literature from both Europe and North America. As Dumay et al. (2018) outline, for any form of intellectual capital research to have an impact it must address some of the more difficult, or wicked, problems of the world. Intellectual capital research with greater societal impact is now known as fifth-stage intellectual capital research, whereby intellectual capital research looks at the intellectual capital ecosystems of regions and countries, and how companies and organisations interact within the ecosystem, rather than how companies internally manage, measure and report their intellectual capital.

To increase the impact of intellectual capital and intangibles research, there needs to be a paradigm change from an ostensive view of research based on the empirical and positivist traditions, and even intellectual capital practice within an organisation, to thinking about how intellectual capital and intangibles research can make a difference. For example, Dumay and Guthrie (2019) argue that debate over whether or not intangibles should appear on the balance sheet is inconsequential to the average person on the street, and even accounting regulators are not overly concerned with such an academic debate.

What intellectual capital and intangibles researchers need to do is to take two steps backwards and think about how they can use what they know about IC and intangibles to add value to society. We are not arguing that intellectual capital and intangibles researchers should be ignoring the creation of monetary wealth through viable and well-functioning businesses, because all societies need robust and stable economies to progress and improve people's lives. However, addressing poverty is a double-edged sword, whereby people who gain affluence also start to crave the same trappings of affluence found today in industrialised countries. Thus, intellectual capital and intangibles researchers need to understand intellectual capital and intangibles of the planet as a whole, and not just the intellectual capital and intangibles of organisations.

NOTE

1. We acknowlege the limitations of the classifications of researchers as North American and European based on the university affiliation. At the same time, with the current state of academics with different nationalities working all over the world, this is the only objective approach available based on open data. While proceeding with research, academics follow the key performance indicators regarding research activities and publications of the universities they work at, which in their turn reflect national guidelines. This approach is also in line with Dumay et al. (2018), which also supports the idea that the focus on the geographical location of institutions producing publications reflects the differences between origin of the research.

   We also acknowledge a limitation that we focus only on North American and European research. Some international trends could be highlighted in future research by analysing trends in publications produced by authors representing Asia, Australia, emerging-market countries, and so on.

REFERENCES

Barker, R. (2015), 'Conservatism, prudence and the IASB's conceptual framework', *Accounting and Business Research*, 45 (4), 514–538.

Cañibano, L. and M.P. Sánchez (2009), 'Intangibles in universities: current challenges for measuring and reporting', *Journal of Human Resource Costing and Accounting*, 13 (2), 93–104.

Chaminade, C. and H. Roberts (2003), 'What it means is what it does: a comparative analysis of implementing Intellectual Capital in Norway and Spain', *European Accounting Review*, 12 (4), 733–751.

Cheung, E., Evans, E. and S. Wright (2008), 'The adoption of IFRS in Australia: the case of AASB 138 (IAS 38) Intangible Assets', *Australian Accounting Review*, 18 (3), 248–256.

Cuozzo, B., Dumay, J., Palmaccio, M. and R. Lombardi (2017), 'Intellectual capital disclosure: a structured literature review', *Journal of Intellectual Capital*, 18 (1), 9–28.

DATI (2001), *A Guide for Intellectual Capital Statements (English version)*, DTI Council, Danish Agency for Trade and Industry, Copenhagen.

de Villiers, C., Dumay, J. and W. Maroun (2019), 'Qualitative accounting research: dispelling myths and developing a new research agenda', *Accounting and Finance*, 59 (3), 1459–1487.

Dumay, J. (2016), 'A critical reflection on the future of intellectual capital: from reporting to disclosure', *Journal of Intellectual Capital*, 17 (1), 168–184.

Dumay, J., Bernardi, C., Guthrie, J. and P. Demartini (2016), 'Integrated reporting: a structured literature review', *Accounting Forum*, 40 (3), 166–185.

Dumay, J. and J. Guthrie (2019), 'Reflections on interdisciplinary critical intellectual capital accounting research', *Accounting, Auditing and Accountability Journal*, 32 (8), 2282–2306.

Dumay, J., Guthrie, J. and J. Rooney (2018), 'The critical path of intellectual capital', in J. Guthrie, J. Dumay, F. Ricceri and C. Nielsen (eds), *The Routledge Companion to Intellectual Capital: Frontiers of Research, Practice and Knowledge*, London: Routledge, pp. 21–39.

Dumay, J. and J. Rooney (2011), '"Measuring for managing?" An IC practice case study', *Journal of Intellectual Capital*, 12 (3), 344–355.

Eccles, R. and M. Krzus (2010), *One Report: Integrated Reporting for a Sustainable Strategy*, Hoboken, NJ: Wiley & Sons.

European Union (2014), 'DIRECTIVE 2014/95/EU', *Official Journal of the European Union*, 214 (330), 1–9.

Financial Reporting Council (2019), 'Consultation into improvements to the reporting of intangibles launched', accessed 12 May 2019 at https://www.frc.org.uk/news/february-2019/consultation-into-improvements-to-the-reporting-of.

Garanina, T., Hussinki, H., and J. Dumay (2021), 'Accounting for intangibles and intellectual capital: a literature review from 2000 to 2020', *Accounting & Finance*, published online.

Guthrie, J. and J. Dumay (2015), 'New frontiers in the use of intellectual capital in the public sector', *Journal of Intellectual Capital*, 16 (2), 258–266.

Guthrie, J., Dumay, J. and P.-C. Hsiao (forthcoming), 'A critical review of the intellectual capital accounting research literature: the past, present and future', *Critical Perspectives on Accounting*.

Guthrie, J., Ricceri, F. and J. Dumay (2012), 'Reflections and projections: a decade of intellectual capital accounting research', *British Accounting Review*, 44 (2), 68–92.

Harzing, A.-W. and S. Alakangas (2016), 'Google Scholar, Scopus and the Web of Science: a longitudinal and cross-disciplinary comparison', *Scientometrics*, 106 (2), 787–804.

Hussinki, H., Garanina, T., Dumay, J. and E. Steinhöfel (2020), 'Revisiting the intellectual capital research landscape – a systematic literature review', in P. Ordóñez de Pablos and L. Edvinsson (eds), *Intellectual Capital in the Digital Economy*, London: Routledge, pp. 279–292.

Hussinki, H., Ritala, P., Vanhala, M. and A. Kianto (2017), 'Intellectual capital, knowledge management practices and firm performance', *Journal of Intellectual Capital*, 18 (4), 904–922.

International Accounting Standards Board (IASB) (2010), *Management Commentary: A Framework for Presentation*, London: International Accounting Standards Board.

International Accounting Standards Board (IASB) (2018), *IFRS® Conceptual Framework Project Summary*, London: International Accounting Standards Board.

International Integrated Reporting Council (IIRC) (2013), *The International <IR> Framework*, London: International Integrated Reporting Council.

Latour, B. (1986), 'The powers of association', in J. Law (ed.), *Power, Action and Belief: A New Sociology of Knowledge?*, London: Routledge & Kegan Paul, pp. 264–280.

Lev, B. and F. Gu (2016), *The End of Accounting and the Path Forward for Investors and Managers*, Hoboken, NJ: Wiley & Sons.

Massaro, M., Dumay, J. and J. Guthrie (2016), 'On the shoulders of giants: undertaking a structured literature review in accounting', *Accounting, Auditing and Accountability Journal*, 29 (5), 767–801.

MERITUM (2002), *Guidelines for Managing and Reporting on Intangibles (Intellectual Capital Statements)*, Madrid: Vodafone Foundation.

Mouritsen, J. (2006), 'Problematising intellectual capital research: ostensive versus performative IC', *Accounting, Auditing and Accountability Journal*, 19 (6), 820–841.

Mouritsen, J., Larsen, H.T. and P.N.D. Bukh (2001), 'Intellectual capital and the "capable firm": narrating, visualising and numbering for managing knowledge', *Accounting, Organizations and Society*, 26 (7–8), 735–762.

Petty, R. and J. Guthrie (2000), 'Intellectual capital literature review: measurement, reporting and management', *Journal of Intellectual Capital*, 1 (2), 155–176.

Schaper, S., Nielsen, C. and R. Roslender (2017), 'Moving from irrelevant intellectual capital (IC) reporting to value-relevant IC disclosures: key learning points from the Danish experience', *Journal of Intellectual Capital*, 18 (1), 81–101.

Stolowy, H. and A. Jeny-Cazavan (2001), 'International accounting disharmony: the case of intangibles', *Accounting, Auditing and Accountability Journal*, 14 (4), 477–497.

5. Exploring the impact of intellectual capital narratives on corporate accountability

Alessandro Lai, Giulia Leoni and Riccardo Stacchezzini

INTRODUCTION

The relevance of intellectual capital (IC) narratives in corporate reporting is well acknowledged in IC research (Mouritsen et al., 2001a, 2001b, 2002, 2003; Dumay and Roslender, 2013; Dumay and Rooney, 2016). The increasing diffusion of integrated reporting (IR) and IC-related reporting frameworks, for example, the framework published by the World Intellectual Capital/Assets Initiative (WICI, 2016), may even expand the use of IC narratives to communicate the ways in which IC contributes to value creation (Abeysekera, 2013; de Villiers and Sharma, 2018). However, despite the 'emancipatory impact' associated with IC narratives (Dumay and Roslender, 2013), the way these narratives should be moulded to produce meaningful stories and facilitate dialogue with stakeholders has attracted limited research attention (Dumay, 2008). We fill this gap by outlining a methodological tool for testing the ability of IC narratives to address stakeholders' accountability expectations.

We develop the methodological tool by drawing on the 'functionalist approach' to narrative analysis depicted by the psychologist Jerome S. Bruner (1986, 1990, 1991). According to Bruner (1990), the function of narratives is to explain unexpected or anomalous events by recasting them in a story-based format that makes rare experiences seem safer or more familiar than they otherwise would. Those stories have specific narrative features – the so-called grammatical constituents in Bruner's (1990, p. 77) study – and can serve their function by solving problems, reducing tensions and resolving dilemmas. According to the accountability perspective, such stories address accountability challenges by enhancing dialogue between addressors (the providers of accountability) and addressees (the ones to whom accountability is provided) (Boland and Schultze, 1996). The methodological tool is useful to both academics and practitioners. Academics may draw on this tool to detect the potential of corporate reports to address accountability expectations; whereas practitioners may use it to test their ability to develop IC-related narratives that may address stakeholders' accountability expectations.

This chapter proceeds as follows. It first highlights the (growing) relevance of IC narratives in the context of corporate reporting. Drawing on prior critical/interpretative research on accountability, it then outlines the role of narratives in addressing stakeholders' accountability expectations. It also introduces Bruner's functionalist approach to narrative analysis. Next, it depicts the 'grammatical constituents' that allow (IC) narratives to enhance dialogue with stakeholders. The final section concludes by outlining some suggestions for those preparing IC narratives.

NARRATING INTELLECTUAL CAPITAL

The possibility of narrating IC is a matter of long-standing professional concern and academic research (Abhayawansa, 2014). Narratives offer an alternative way to measure and manage IC (Mouritsen et al., 2002), given their ability to help explain the complex nature of IC (Dumay and Cuganesan, 2011), and contribute to organisational change (Dumay, 2008). A pioneering example of IC reporting based on narratives derives from the 1997 project launched by the Danish Agency for Trade and Industry (DATI) (Mouritsen et al., 2002; Nielsen et al., 2017). The first guideline published by the DATI in 2000 emphasised the role of narratives in IC statements. The 'knowledge narrative' to be inserted in IC statements was intended to act as the narrative account of the ways that companies use their stock of knowledge resources to create products and services for customers. The knowledge narrative is complemented by 'management challenges' to explain the utilisation of four knowledge resources (employees, customers, processes and technology) for value creation.

Later, several initiatives used narratives to determine the manner in which IC drives value creation, such as the Meritum Project (2002), the IC Rating (2002), the Performance Prism (2002) and the DMSTI Danish Guidelines (2003). These initiatives highlighted the fundamental role of narratives in IC reporting, with important implications for the IC reports of public and private organisations worldwide. The attention on narratives is driven by their ability to elucidate the reasoning underlying an organisation's management and subsequent disclosure of IC (Dumay and Roslender, 2013), thereby offering an opportunity to explain how IC is managed and contributes to organisational development and value creation. However, while narratives have been considered throughout the evolution of IC research, attempts to grasp the full potential of narratives have developed only recently in research and practice, particularly during the so-called third stage of IC research (Guthrie et al., 2012). If we consider the three stages identified by Petty and Guthrie (2000), IC research from the late 1980s to the 1990s has increased awareness about IC and made it visible. This stage was fundamental in confirming the importance of IC. However, few empirical studies were conducted to identify methods to measure, disclose and manage IC (Petty and Guthrie, 2000). Such interest emerged only in the second stage of IC research development, from the early 2000s, when researchers started to define initial approaches and models for IC evaluation (Petty and Guthrie, 2000).

The second stage, which partially persists at present (Dumay and Garanina, 2013), has provided an extensive array of models to measure IC and to relate it to financial performance. This research is identified as ostensive research, which aims at generalising findings across organisations, and it contrasts with performative research, which focuses on practices within organisations (Mouritsen, 2006). Evidence from such ostensive research on IC and its effects on financial performance remains inconsistent (Guthrie et al., 2012), especially because of the lack of a generally accepted approach for IC measurement. However, within the wide range of IC frameworks that were developed during the second stage, some models were pivotal in highlighting the importance of narratives for explaining and understanding IC, such as the Meritum Project (2002) and the Danish Guidelines (2003). Narratives are defined as 'something close to the identity of the firm, and therefore presents some kind of *raison d'être* of its activities' (Mouritsen et al., 2002, p. 14), and they are increasingly employed to explain accounting numbers (Beattie, 2014). However, in this stage, the consideration of narratives was mainly focused on their ability to measure IC, often via content analysis, rather than on their ability to tell a story about the manner in which the organisation and its stakeholders create value. Conversely, by definition, 'narrative is the provision of meaningful explanations of why and how an organisation is concerned with managing its IC in addition to disclosing its IC measures' (Dumay, 2008, p. 519).

In the third stage, a more critical and performative consideration of IC practices has developed (Guthrie et al., 2012), including the understanding and use of narratives at their full potential. In this stage, IC has moved from being treated as an object that needs to be measured, to being a practice to be investigated and discussed through a bottom-up approach, thereby gathering insights from stakeholders within and outside the organisation. The intent is to consider more aspects than financial results and to focus on the organisational change that is attainable via IC. This third stage is expected to finally provide 'greater insights into how IC works rather than what IC is' (Dumay and Garanina, 2013, p. 21). As a result, narratives, rather than numbers, are seen as capturing the real meaning of IC and the response to the 'accountingisation' of the IC paradigm (Dumay and Roslender, 2013, p. 252). This quantification trend may result in IC being represented with a number that only accounting experts can understand, thereby excluding other members of the organisation from understanding IC and methods of IC management that create value within and outside the organisation (Dumay and Roslender, 2013).

As a result, both practice and research in the IC realm have delved into the potential of narratives to mobilise IC and escape the risk of accountingisation. With regard to practice initiatives, stronger attention to narratives in IC reporting is evident in the Intangible Reporting Framework published by the World Intellectual Capital/Assets Initiative (WICI, 2016), which suggests outlining a value creation story focused on intangibles. This story should outline three complementary issues: the company's activities and the value creation model; the intangibles and value creation from the past to the present; and the intangibles and value creation from the present to the future. The framework suggests incorporating key performance indicators to provide critical factors of value creation. Such indicators focused on intangible resources are intended to play a major role within the value creation story, providing objective evidence of performance trends.

Similarly, the International <IR> Framework published by the International Integrated Reporting Council (IIRC, 2013) also recognises the importance of narratives for mobilising IC. Although the framework does not focus only on IC, it identifies IC as one of the types of capital supporting value creation. IC and the other types of capital (financial, manufactured, human, social and relationship, and natural) should be interpreted as a stock of resources that companies increase, decrease and transform with their activities and outputs. The types are interdependent and in a continuous flow between each other. With its principles-based approach, the IIRC Framework allows organisations to flexibly mobilise IC elements while constructing their 'value creation story' via qualitative as well as quantitative indicators. The framework calls for narratives as an 'effective way to connect quantitative and qualitative information' (IIRC, 2013, p. 17), especially regarding the flow of capital types.

Within the IC research, one of the first efforts to identify the narrative features of IC statements is offered by Mouritsen et al. (2001b) in their analysis of IC statements of 17 Danish firms implementing the Danish Guidelines. The authors identify three recurring elements in the diverse narratives of IC statements: the knowledge narrative, which presents the story of the organisation and its resources; knowledge management challenges, which present the manager's actions to transform the knowledge resources; and the combination of numbers, narratives and visuals (Mouritsen et al., 2001b). Such a structure is found to be helpful in making the discussion of IC management more compelling and interesting in the IC statement: numbers are not enough, and narratives and visualisations reinforce the message (Mouritsen et al., 2001b). Further, Cuganesan et al. (2007) provide initial insights on the importance of narratives and discourses for IC evaluation and management. By means of a case study extending over four years on IC discourse production, tracing the actual practices of numerous discourse producers and consumers within an Australian public sector agency, Cuganesan et al. (2007) find that ambiguity in IC discourses, rather than codification, allows greater flexibility for discourse producers to translate discourse into practice. As a result, the narratives are found to be pivotal in providing flexibility and incentive to action within the organisation.

Another attempt to bring awareness to the relevance of narratives for evaluating IC is offered by Dumay (2008), who examines the use of narratives in IC disclosure and their impact on the organisation's social structure. Based on structuration theory, he discusses the importance of IC narratives and their ability to provide an understanding of the 'organisation's actions in relation to IC management, measurement and reporting and as a basis for explicating IC from the perspective of the organisation's actors who constructed the narrative' (Dumay, 2008, p. 519). By means of a case study, the author shows how narratives developed from telling stories to showcasing events enabled by IC in the future, thereby facilitating organisational change and dialogue among the actors who promoted that change. Narratives are found to enable the change because they produce new knowledge on IC that can be used by the organisation and its members to create (more) value (Dumay, 2008).

Delving into the power of narratives to provide insights on IC management, Dumay and Roslender (2013) explore how narratives can be used to understand and mobilise IC, thereby overcoming existing IC statements based on a 'management control' approach. They raise concerns about contemporary IC statements that follow traditional guidelines and only provide one-way communication, thereby excluding many members of the organisation from understanding IC and maintaining a controlling approach over them. Dumay and Roslender (2013) compare three examples of IC narratives from three different organisations, finding three different approaches to narratives. Only one organisation showed an innovative bottom-up approach to IC disclosure. In this organisation, IC disclosure is constructed via a constant dialogue with its members to understand how IC is developed within the organisation, and these 'stories' are used to mobilise the organisation's IC. With their findings, the authors underline the importance of moving beyond the 'accepted practice' (Dumay and Roslender, 2013, p. 265) around IC and developing new ways to disclose IC from within the organisation and the IC itself. They call for more attention to narrative and the need to develop new models and methods to delve into the narratives and understand their ability to mobilise IC.

NARRATIVES AND CORPORATE ACCOUNTABILITY: BRUNER'S 'FUNCTIONALIST APPROACH'

Critical scholars whose focus extends beyond highlighting the financial and nonfinancial nature of accountability content consider that a narrative mode of accountability, with its narratives and storytelling, 'is consistently undervalued and often suppressed' (Boland and Schultze, 1996, p. 62). Rather, calculative accountability is predominant in corporate reporting, based on the belief that 'numbers … speak for themselves, no interpretation needed, no narrative required, and the only story a "story of no story to tell"' (McKernan and McPhail, 2012, p. 179). Nevertheless, the International Accounting Standards Board (IASB) project on management commentary (IASB, 2010) and similar initiatives (for example, EFRAG, 2013) reveal an 'increasing reliance on narratives in the business reporting package' (Beattie, 2014, p. 121). Similarly, the IIRC project asks for reporting based on storytelling (Lai et al., 2018), as also indicated in the memorandum of understanding entered into by the IIRC and the IASB (IASB and IIRC, 2013).

Studies focused on procedural aspects of accountability (Messner, 2009, p. 922) attempt to link accountability content with the methods that addressors use in constructing relationships with addressees, such as involving them in dialogue or maintaining a distance from them (Roberts, 1991, 1996; Boland and Schultze, 1996). Roberts (1991) and McKernan and MacLullich (2004) ask that studies should be conducted to ascertain methods that would enrich the procedure through socialising forms of informal accountability, based on direct, personal interactions (Roberts, 1991, 1996).

Similarly, Boland and Schultze (1996) highlight a theoretical connection between the content and procedural dimensions of corporate accountability, arguing that the construction of corporate accountability relies on an addressor's modes of cognition. The literature shows that the narrative mode of cognition (Bruner, 1986) is the primary source for socialising forms of accountability, because the narrator constructs a meaningful dialogue with the addressee: '[N]arration as a mode of cognition is the principle [*sic*] occasion for socially constructing an accountable self and a world in which accountability is expected' (Boland and Schultze, 1996, p. 65). Accountors' storytelling ability influences whether they can establish a dialogue with accountees. The former must have narrative capacity, or 'ability to narrate their experience and that of others in making sense of the world' (Boland and Schultze, 1996, p. 64), if they desire to induce socialising effects, because this capacity enables narrators to choose and merge the elements of the story plot such that the story becomes plausible and conveys meaningful insights. Storytelling ability enables dialogue, because it allows and necessitates accountors to recognise others' needs. Bruner (1990) states that the purpose of a narrative is to explain noncanonical (unexpected or anomalous) events by re-presenting them in a story-based format, which leads to rare experiences seeming safer or more familiar than they otherwise would. By doing so, the narrative solves problems, reduces tensions and resolves dilemmas (Bruner, 1990). Moreover, Boland and Schultze (1996) consider that such a narrative yields socialising accountability effects. This is opposite to the paradigmatic form of cognition (Bruner, 1986) that is based on computing and presenting arguments, which is inadequate for establishing dialogue and, conversely, may create distance by individualising forms of accountability (Roberts, 1991, 1996).

In this regard, Bruner developed a 'functionalist approach' to narrative analysis (Bruner, 1986, 1990, 1991; Ignatow and Mihalcea, 2016) to examine whether narratives would enhance dialogue. The functionalist approach, which proposes that narrators' narrative mode of cognition and the resulting narrative representation must be interpreted together, instead of separately (Bruner, 1991, p. 5; see also Bruner, 1990; Boland and Schultze, 1996), highlights the narrators' interpretations of the events that they embed in the narrative, rather than the structural elements (Coghlan and Brydon-Miller, 2014). This type of analysis investigates the function of the narrative (cognition mode) in assisting individuals to make sense of their lives, particularly by re-presenting chaotic, unexpected and atypical events in a comprehensible story. To summarise, this approach to research could be used to test whether narratives facilitate dialogue and, specifically, to test whether IC narratives are able to deal with the accountability expectations of stakeholders. Bruner (1990) considers that the possibility of testing the potential of narratives depends on whether such narratives have specific 'grammatical constituents'. These features are explained in the next section, and examples are presented on how IC narratives can adopt them.

THE GRAMMATICAL CONSTITUENTS OF IC NARRATIVES

Narratives may enable dialogue with others in several ways. Bruner (1990, p. 77) argues that several narrative features – the 'grammatical constituents' that make a story 'tellable' – allow people to deal with the expectations and needs of others. In interpreting a narrative (cognition mode) and the manner in which it operates, researchers must interpret the story 'components' as 'functions' and not independent 'themes' or 'elements' (Bruner, 1990, p. 80), and thus investigate the reasons that narrators select and combine these components and the methods they use (Bruner, 1986). In 'The narrative construction of reality', Bruner (1991, p. 5) outlines the following ten narrative features, which are to be interpreted in the spirit of constructing an 'armature' on which a more systematic account might be constructed.

Narrative Diachronicity

A narrative reveals events occurring over time. A narrative 'is irreducibly durative' (Bruner, 1991, p. 6), since it offers a unique pattern of events. The time involved is not 'clock time', but 'human time', whose significance relies on the meaning assigned to the events that the narrator explicates. Narratives include a sequential order of events and mental states that involve human beings as characters or actors. Thus, IC narratives should explain the process through which IC influences value creation over time, particularly in the context of IR where companies are expected to explain their value creation process in the short, medium and long term (IIRC, 2013; Corbella et al., 2019).

Particularity

Particular happenings are narrated. They refer to unusual elements, which are also related to broader, more general types of human beings, things and events, among others. Narratives on IC should outline the IC resources, assets or states of being that concur to value creation and connect these elements to more general IC categories (for example, human, organisational or relational IC). Since IC elements are not fixed variables of a stable proposition of value creation (Mouritsen, 2006), narrators should strive to define and classify IC elements coherently within the context in which they produce the narrative. IR represents a fruitful context for highlighting how peculiar IC elements contribute to value creation (Stacchezzini et al., 2019).

Intentional State Entailment

The beliefs, desires, theories and values of actors are relevant aspects of a story. Even animals and objects are endowed with intentional states, and physical events affect the intentional states of human and nonhuman actors. Introducing such intentional states offers readers a basis for interpreting the reason behind the occurrence of events, rather than listing the specific reasons for such occurrences. Narratives on IC should detail the methods that organisational actors use in mobilising IC to create value. Further, IC elements may play a role as nonhuman actors that, in combination with other elements/actors, are able to contribute to value creation.

Hermeneutic Composability

The events considered in constructing the narrative must be involved in the context of the overall story, to 'provide an intuitively convincing account of the meaning of the text in the light of the constituent parts that make it up' (Bruner, 1991, p. 7). Thus, the parts of a narrative must be mobilised to 'serve as "functions" of the narrative structure as a whole' (Bruner, 1991, p. 8). Narratives on IC should be forged by considering the overall story to be communicated within the corporate reporting context. This means that narratives on IC should not be isolated in separate sections of a report; they should concur to the construction of the overall value creation story: explanations of how IC connects with other elements/ actors are fundamental to forging a coherent story and to depict the role that IC plays.

Canonicity and Breach

For being worthy of narration, a story must be about how an implicit canonical script has been breached, violated or deviated from in a manner that does violence to the 'legitimacy' of this script. A 'precipitating event' is then introduced and represents the exceptional. Then, the narrative should solve the mismatch between the exceptional and the ordinary. The narrators should be able to explain exceptional, noncanonical, unexpected or anomalous events by recasting them in a story-based format that makes the rare experiences seem safer or more familiar than they would otherwise. Breaches of the canonical are often highly conventional and strongly influenced by narrative traditions. However, the narrator may find new ways to go beyond conventional scripts, 'leading people to see human happenings in a fresh way' (Bruner, 1991, p. 12). The breach can be created by linguistic means or by introducing an event that delegitimises the status quo. In the context of corporate reporting, change in corporate governance or strategy may constitute 'precipitating events' for which explanation must be provided (Lai et al., 2017, 2018). Narratives on IC may help narrators to explain this change, and the company's actions for managing it, with the help of appropriate IC elements. In other words, narrators could explain an extraordinary event related to corporate governance or strategy change, but recast it as being under the control of the company's management, which is expected to deal with the extraordinary event by drawing on IC resources and capabilities.

Referentiality

The acceptability of a narrative does not rely on its accurate reflection of reality, 'else there would be no fiction' (Bruner, 1991, p. 13). Narrative 'truth' is judged by its verisimilitude rather than its verifiability (Bruner, 1991). Paradigmatic demonstrations of the process by which IC creates value are largely contested. For instance, Mouritsen (2009) rejects the possibility of an impeccable correspondence between IC and values, although they consider that IC measurements are useful to enhance the visibility of IC in action and help managers to intervene in organisational processes. In this vein, narratives on IC should be used to deploy a coherent explanation – rather than a demonstration – of the ways that IC elements contribute to value creation.

Genericness

The story should belong to a recognisable category of narratives (for instance, a genre). The genre facilitates the 'hermeneutic task of making sense of human happenings' (Bruner, 1991, p. 14), using language in a way that facilitates interpretation by restricting the boundaries of possible solutions. Genres are 'ways of telling that predispose us to use our minds and sensibilities in particular ways. ... As such, they may have quite as powerful an influence in shaping our modes of thought as they have in creating the realities that their plots depict' (Bruner, 1991, p. 15). IC elements have been largely categorised according to the following three forms of capital: human, organisational and relational (Stewart, 1997; Sveiby, 1997). Further, with the advent of IR, a new form of categorisation is used (Dumay, 2016): 'intellectual capital', 'human capital' and 'social and relationship capital' are the three types of capital defined by the International Integrated Reporting Framework (IIRC, 2013) that scholars and practitioners associate with IC. To develop a coherent narrative, narrators should clearly specify the categorisation used.

Normativeness

Since a breach presupposes a norm, and narratives rely on breaching conventional expectations, narratives are necessarily normative. In other words, narratives rely on cultural conventions; only when conventional expectations are breached does the ratio determined by conventions become unbalanced, and troubles emerge. Troubles provide storytelling with the engine. In the context of corporate reporting, normativeness is represented by business continuity through means of value creation. Corporate reports traditionally connect financial and manufactured assets with financial value creation, and management commentaries are developed accordingly. The expansion of nonfinancial reporting (Stolowy and Paugam, 2018) offers the ground for breaching this cultural convention, but narrators should explain how their nontangible assets (and intellectual ones in particular) are able to support value creation beyond financial categorisation.

Context Sensitivity and Negotiability

Narrators must be aware that each reader has personal background knowledge and sensitivity before reading the narrative. Readers take the teller's intentions into account. Hence, the narrative becomes an instrument for cultural negotiation. The context in which an IC narrative is produced should be considered in depth by narrators, given that 'IC is what it has come to be in the situation in hand … IC elements are mobilized and related to effects that themselves are invented in the network where IC is given meaning' (Mouritsen, 2006, p. 823). In a dialogical perspective, narratives on IC may foster shared views between narrators and readers on the role of IC in creating value (Stacchezzini et al., 2019).

Narrative Accrual

Narratives accrue and accruals eventually create something called 'culture', 'history' or 'tradition'. In other words, narratives can be connected to create greater stories. Accrual of narratives must be guided into larger-scale cultures, traditions or 'world versions', imposing a 'historical-causal entailment' (Bruner, 1991, p. 19). Once shared culturally, narrative accruals can achieve 'exteriority' and the power of constraint, creating 'a history, a tradition, a legal system, instruments assuring historical continuity if not legitimacy' (Bruner, 1991, p. 20).

Although IC is a malleable concept (Mouritsen, 2006), narratives on IC have obtained significant recognition in the corporate reporting context and hold a great possibility of further expanding (Dumay, 2016). However, the possibility of IC narratives obtaining larger legitimation is deemed to rely on different forms of reporting (for example, IR and sustainability reporting), rather than on dedicated IC reports (de Villiers and Sharma, 2018).

THE CONSTRUCTION OF IC NARRATIVES

The experience drawn from the IC narratives since the later decades of the 20th century, which enabled researchers (Petty and Guthrie, 2000) to codify three significant stages (see the previous section, on 'Narrating Intellectual Capital'), helps understand ways to use IC narratives to address stakeholders' accountability expectations. The directions identified in the literature express co-existing ways to deal with IC. Those stages, originally identified and observed in a diachronic perspective, may be considered in a new synchronic way, to take care of preparers' as well as readers' needs in preparing and using IC narratives. We recognise that the different paths suggested by researchers can help to identify three main themes of IC narratives and the related ways to mould accountability.

The first theme is related to 'IC visibility', where the aim of preparers is to increase awareness of IC and to make it visible; they are not concerned with detecting and investigating methods to measure, disclose and manage IC. A general, preliminary comprehension about IC helps introduce this meaningful asset to a large audience of stakeholders. The second theme deals with the opportunity to explain the 'IC role and value', in particular in specific organisations. Preparers must consider the need for deeper information about the nature, intentional rule, perspectives and value that IC has, together with the subjective involvement of management in using IC.

The third theme concerns 'IC functioning', namely, going beyond financial results and focusing on the organisational change attainable through IC by giving useful insights on the process by which IC works, rather than on what constitutes IC. Working from these premises, we investigate the manner in which the narrative features outlined by Bruner (1991) help preparers deal with these themes to improve the dialogue with readers and make IC stories more reliable to stakeholders. In proposing this view, we combine the results of a widely recognised study on IC narratives (Petty and Guthrie, 2000) with the assumptions about the 'grammatical constituents' of narratives (Bruner, 1991), namely, narrative features as outlined in the previous section.

For each of the three outlined themes, we suggest narrative features that appear to be significantly relevant for addressing stakeholders'

Table 5.1 Grammatical constituents and themes of IC narratives

	Themes		
Grammatical constituents	IC visibility	IC role and value	IC functioning
Narrative diachronicity	■	■	
Particularity		■	■
Intentional state entailment		■	■
Hermeneutic composability	■		
Canonicity and breach		■	■
Referentiality			■
Genericness	■		
Normativeness		■	
Context sensitivity		■	■
Narrative accrual	■		

accountability through IC narratives. These features are coloured in dark grey in Table 5.1.

The 'IC Visibility' Theme

The first theme is 'IC visibility'. This refers to the period when the relevance of IC in business was increasing, namely, the first stage discussed in the earlier section on 'Narrating Intellectual Capital'. At that time, IC narratives were mainly devoted to favouring and improving the awareness about IC, rather than measuring, disclosing and managing it. This purpose has not been completely fulfilled; it is still relevant to introduce IC narratives as a premise to explain the importance of IC in a broad sense and to make visible the significance of these types of assets in different situations.

This theme is deeply related to messages sent by the organisation according to readers' capability and interest, and does not involve offering complex reasoning about sophisticated assets that are difficult to understand or impossible to explain using complicated accounting patterns to a certain type of audience. The relevance and usefulness of IC in private or public sector organisations, for corporate managers and for policy-makers, should be revealed to make its use simple and detectable, to indicate the attention it needs and the related policies that, at the corporate level or at a broad level, are to be finalised.

Writing narratives for these assumed purposes requires the narrator to rely mainly on four of the constituents identified by Bruner (1991). First, narrators must consider carefully 'diachronicity' as a means to better reveal events over time. In particular, when the story told about IC must be generic and must present an overview of its role in a broad perspective, the use of diachronicity helps considerably in sustaining the discourse. Considering that in the past 30 years IC has become a dominant feature of life and of economic activity, as it is currently recognised, stories are helpful in introducing its presence to a stakeholder not much engaged in business processes. To be accountable to this type of stakeholder means that the discourse needs to be simplified, finding past reasons for legitimation as we seek legitimation in the present and the future through the lens of the past, which also occurs in qualified accounting contexts.

Combining 'diachronicity' with 'hermeneutic composability' would be useful. The latter reinforces the former: to narrate a new story, about aspects that the preparer should be accountable for towards stakeholders, requires basic knowledge, and the narrator must effectively include the past in this new story. Such a technique allows deeper comprehension of the context and improves the explanation of IC by relying on comprehensible (and sometimes known) facts that can support easy understanding. Moreover, IC narratives should be characterised by 'genericness' in the sense that referring to a recognisable genre facilitates their explanatory aim. Embedding the story to be told in a typology accepted by the literature or common practice enables readers or stakeholders to avoid mistakes and misunderstanding. In addition, it may enhance their knowledge about the matter to be detected and investigated.

Finally, for a preparer to be accountable they help the reader in contextualising the issue in a defined recognisable category. An IC narrative presenting these constituents must naturally add something more for the reader. Regardless of whether such narratives would be considered 'culture' or 'history' or 'tradition', this approach helps in creating greater stories that extend beyond any specific context. For this reason, the 'narrative accrual' feature, recognised by Bruner (1990) as one of the key constituents, easily fits with IC narratives.

The 'IC Role and Value' Theme

Another theme is about the 'IC role and value'. It refers to the second stage of the IC narratives where the relevance of IC was generalised across organisations. At first, this type of narrative was not always in tune with performative research aiming to ascertain practices within organisations (Mouritsen, 2006), and its impact on financial performance was initially inconsistent (Guthrie et al., 2012). Subsequently, the need to identify measures of IC – in particular, accounting measures – were highlighted

(Beattie, 2014). Considering that narratives have to provide meaningful explanations about the reasons that a company (and an organisation more generally) is concerned about managing its IC (Dumay, 2008) and the ways in which it does so – in addition to disclosing the nature, the intentional rule, the perspectives and the value that IC has – this theme has considerable significance currently. The theme must be dealt with in management commentaries and explanatory notes adding information to accounting reports, and in new forms of reporting extending beyond the limits of financial reporting – for example, in nonfinancial disclosure – which attempt to combine different types of reporting. In all these types of IC narratives, an adequate level of 'diachronicity' is recommended to embed the current story of IC in a broad stream of events that precede, explain and sometimes justify aspects of the past.

However, the key feature is to expand the amount of 'particularities' in explanations about IC, which is the main feature – the second in the list presented in the previous section – suggested as a 'grammatical constituent'. This feature is significant, owing to the necessity to set the narratives about IC on sound bases, full of details that cannot be taken for granted, but must be exposed and related with more general categories of concepts. The main reason for focusing on the role IC plays in an organisational context, and for understanding its value to that organisation, is to enrich the narrative with details that 'make the difference' and can be embedded into large concepts elaborated by practice and by the business and accounting literature.

However, these roles and these values do not count per se; should different people manage them, their roles and values would differ as well. Thus, in these types of narrative, we need to consider a further grammatical constituent: the 'intentional state entailment'. The actors of a story 'make the difference' according to their capability, wishes, values and knowledge. Their 'agentivity' (Bruner, 1990) is the first determinant to check whether IC can be used, supported, qualified and enhanced in an organisation. Moreover, their 'agentivity' lends credibility to the value assigned to IC, because it is related to the aims of people leveraging IC consciously and to the manner in which they would use IC to create value.

The settings in different organisations vary owing to their characteristics, especially in using and evaluating IC, which emerges from unique experiences. The differences among organisations depend on their agents (for example, managers and policy-makers) and on the intertwined stories of people working in their offices, thus determining the types of exceptional (or, at least, not ordinary) situations. To underline these differences and impart relevance to the various stories of these individuals, an important aim of an IC narrative is explaining IC value as it relates to them. The narrative must show how these peculiarities are typical of the different settings, while also recasting these in a known format to enhance overall comprehensibility, thus making these peculiar stories familiar. This highlights the importance of an IC narrative following these aims and drawing on 'canonicity and breach' as a further constituent.

In these IC narratives, norms have informed the capability of the preparers. This occurs not just because of the conventions related to the concepts that IC embraces, but also because of the context in which IC narratives are prepared: those of management commentaries, of notes to the financial reports and/or supplementary reports, especially in large or listed companies. These documents are intrinsically based on the norms supporting them and building the frame in which their concepts can be understood. Therefore, 'normativeness', as a further feature, is the framework within which IC narratives must be written. Conversely, it requires the boundaries to be breached to give sense to the exceptional IC characteristics that people have to manage. Recognising an appreciable value of IC means to be able, through narratives, to expose to stakeholders the non-ordinary relevance of IC assets that, in any case, should be understood within a known framework such as those elaborated by the accounting practice and literature. This explains why this form of accountability is a preconditional feature that a storyteller must consider while preparing an IC narrative.

Finally, preparers must consider that the dialogue they want to establish with their stakeholders depends also on the readers' knowledge, sensitivity and negotiability. This is the last feature to be considered in an IC narrative, giving evidence to the role and value of IC in a specific organisation, without forgetting its context made by different people. Addressing stakeholders' needs though IC narratives means being able to regulate 'context sensitivity and negotiability', by adjusting the narratives to the correct target audience and writing the right words, which would make the readers consider the preparer's intentions and combine them with their background knowledge. This cultural negotiation enhances the use of IC narratives as an instrument of accountability.

The 'IC Functioning' Theme

As a final theme, we consider 'IC functioning' as reflected by the third period of IC narratives. It requires going beyond the intimate intrinsic characteristics of IC and its financial value and instead focusing on the organisational change attainable through the IC. This approach requires building narratives to offer critical insights on how IC works rather than on what IC is (Mouritsen, 2006). This purpose can be easily linked to the more recent narratives embedded in the new reports debated by accounting practice and literature, which favour a new form of delivering accountability, in which nonfinancial issues become relevant to explain the results that an organisation is able to achieve and, finally, its value creation story (Beattie, 2014). The IR is just one of the more recent instruments proposed on the long path towards a new way of reporting in which narratives become relevant because they can offer a deeper comprehension of the role of IC in action in the specific organisations in which IC is used.

Dealing with this theme requires a great attention to 'particularity'; all types of narratives risk being too generic, able to be used in any situation and to develop a sort of boilerplate discourse, which may overlook intangible assets and how they work in the organisations where they are combined. Frequently, discourses about some parts of the organisations and their context, main aims, values and results can be copied and applied to other realities. If we begin examining a new document, as readers unaware of the object of the narrative, we are often unable to identify the organisation involved. This mistake must be avoided in an IC narrative, when the purpose is to examine IC in action. In this way, narratives will engage stakeholders, allowing them to perceive the potential of IC and improving the reliability of the story.

While writing these narratives, 'intentional state entailments' are to be considered carefully. If the IC works correctly, if IC can explain the difference between an organisation and its competitors, if IC is able to help organisations drive a change towards new patterns, if IC is the crucial asset through which a reliable recovery could begin and attain success, the main issue considered by the IC narrative preparers has to be the involvement of the organisational actors in those processes. The human intentions, thoughts, knowledge and behaviour make the difference not only in qualifying a certain type of IC or another, but also in explaining how human actors can mobilise the existing IC towards meeting new challenges and, finally, in explaining how the same IC characteristics change after the completion of these processes, owing to the agency of the actors involved.

In the case of IC, more than in the case of any other asset, the acceptability of a discourse on how IC works does not rely on its correct reference to reality. It cannot be verified *ex ante*, but it must be plausible and convincing. Therefore, 'referentiality', as a further feature of the narrative, helps avoid two opposite mistakes: to consider many parts of the story as taken for granted and thus not to explain them; or to try to present discourses that are quite unlikely. Rather, IC narratives should use coherent explanations, and be respectful of truth (and, hence, plausible and convincing) and of the reader in trying to show how IC elements enhance value creation in the organisational context.

Finally, in IC narratives about 'IC functioning', the teller should be fully aware that each stakeholder and reader has personal knowledge and sensitivity that they apply when reading the text; 'context sensitivity and negotiability' is the constituent that seems to be relevant in this case. Hence, the preparer of the narrative must develop the capability to drive the reader in accordance with the reader's own background, as though leading the reader towards new believable perspectives. It is a long and difficult journey that an advanced teller must face. Narratives, while becoming an instrument of cultural negotiations, become a way through which the preparers move stakeholders to make dialogue possible and comprehensible, and in some cases even interactive, thus enhancing their accountability towards the readers.

CONCLUSION

The analysis in this study allows us to design a framework that can help preparers and advisors (when they act as consultants of preparers) in constructing IC narratives. In this regard, preparers must clarify the information to be conveyed to better address stakeholders' accountability expectations, by choosing among a range of possible themes. The first theme aims to give a general view of IC ('IC visibility'); the second tries to explain the role and value of IC, by particularly considering a specific setting or organisation ('IC role and value'); the third offers a deeper insight about how IC works in an organisation or in any other context ('IC functioning'). Choosing one of these options is not easy; the boundaries between the various themes are not well defined, but present nuances and overlap. Moreover, the audience of the IC narratives is composed of a diverse panel of people with heterogeneous needs; satisfying a combination of readers is often not simple. Selecting a theme has a huge influence on the possibility of addressing – in a better or worse way – stakeholders' accountability needs. Hence, it requires the narrator to carefully screen readers' needs and identify aspects that really matter to them.

Conversely, the framework suggests how IC narrative preparers could be more effective when narrating a selected theme. Based on the analysis of the 'grammatical constituents' proposed by Bruner (1990, 1991), we presented the features that appear more relevant for addressing stakeholders' accountability through the IC narratives. Although the other features that Bruner identified are important, those we suggest can be considered particularly 'in tune' with the themes that IC narratives try to deal with as the constituents of a story that must be considered 'tellable'. Therefore, when IC narratives are more 'generic' ('IC visibility'), the selected features try to emphasise the reliability of the story for an audience that needs to improve its IC literacy.

When the theme refers to specific technical IC issues ('IC role and value'), the features must help in explaining, and making more familiar, the significance IC has in a setting, the commitment of the organisation agents in using it, and the IC details that 'make the difference' with other contexts, considering the readers' knowledge, sensitivity and negotiability. Finally, when the theme requires the narrator to explain how IC is used in organisations ('IC functioning'), the main features of the IC narrative must help the story be plausible and convincing, using coherent explanations, to enable a dialogue with stakeholders about the interaction of the IC in that context.

We believe the use of the framework is not limited to preparers: it can be fruitfully employed by scholars, who – as the current literature suggests – are now extensively engaged in exploring the role of different types of narratives and detecting whether preparers are able to address stakeholders' accountability expectations through IC narratives. To achieve this purpose, the framework is helpful in making the scholars think about coherence in the narratives they investigate.

First, researchers must check the coherence between the selected theme of the IC story and the audience the preparers would like to satisfy. Although scholars should carefully consider the document (for example, management commentary, financial statement, sustainability report, integrated report) that the IC narrative intends to contribute, they should also examine the readers' expectations regarding that document, even considering the different types of stakeholders composing the audience.

In addition, scholars have the opportunity to detect, in an IC narrative, the coherence between the selected theme and the main features they can identify in the investigated story. Narratives that are far from presenting some of the 'constituents' discussed in this study, especially those highlighted in Table 5.1, would be less effective in satisfying accountability needs.

In tune with the functionalistic approach we selected, scholars should interpret the 'components' of an IC narrative as 'functions' of this story rather than autonomous 'themes' or 'elements' (Bruner, 1990, p. 80), thus investigating the reasons that narrators select and combine these components to be more effective in achieving their aims and the process they use towards this end.

Finally, the framework may offer some insights to the ongoing debate that preparers, users, academics, standard-setters and regulators are facing about the role of new reporting instruments, especially those regarding nonfinancial information, or integrated reporting. Since the information provided in these reports is mainly principles-based, considerable scope exists to have more detailed requirements, if we agree that a functionalistic approach may offer new ways of meeting the stakeholders' accountability needs.

ACKNOWLEDGEMENTS

The authors gratefully thank John Dumay for the insightful comments provided on a prior version of this chapter. While the research is the result of a joint effort of the authors, the individual contributions are as follows: Alessandro Lai wrote the section on 'The Construction of IC Narratives' and the 'Conclusion'; Giulia Leoni wrote 'Narrating Intellectual Capital'; Riccardo Stacchezzini wrote the 'Introduction', 'Narratives and Corporate Accountability: Bruner's "Functionalist Approach"' and 'The Grammatical Constituents of IC Narratives'.

REFERENCES

Abeysekera, I. (2013), 'A template for integrated reporting', *Journal of Intellectual Capital*, 14 (2), 227–245.

Abhayawansa, S.A. (2014), 'A review of guidelines and frameworks on external reporting of intellectual capital', *Journal of Intellectual Capital*, 15 (1), 100–141.

Beattie, V. (2014), 'Accounting narratives and the narrative turn in accounting research: issues, theory, methodology, methods and a research framework', *British Accounting Review*, 46 (2), 111–134.

Boland, R. and U. Schultze (1996), 'Narrating accountability: cognition and the production of the accountable self', in R. Munro and J. Mouritsen (eds), *Accountability: Power, Ethos and the Technologies of Managing*, London: International Thomson Business Press, pp. 62–82.

Bruner, J.S. (1986), 'Actual minds, possible world', The Jerusalem–Harvard Lectures, Cambridge, MA: Harvard University Press.

Bruner, J.S. (1990), *Acts of Meaning*, Cambridge, MA: Harvard University Press.

Bruner, J.S. (1991), 'The narrative construction of reality', *Critical Inquiry*, 18 (1), 1–21.

Coghlan, D. and M. Brydon-Miller (2014), *The SAGE Encyclopedia of Action Research*, Thousand Oaks, CA: SAGE.

Corbella, S., Florio, C., Sproviero, A.F. and R. Stacchezzini (2019), 'Integrated reporting and the performativity of intellectual capital', *Journal of Management and Governance*, 23 (2), 459–483.

Cuganesan, S., Boedker, C. and J. Guthrie (2007), 'Enrolling discourse consumers to affect material intellectual capital practice', *Accounting, Auditing and Accountability Journal*, 20 (6), 883–911.

de Villiers, C. and U. Sharma (2018), 'A critical reflection on the future of financial, intellectual capital, sustainability and integrated reporting', *Critical Perspectives on Accounting*, accessed 5 September 2019 at https://doi.org/10.1016/j.cpa.2017.05.003.

Dumay, J.C. (2008), 'Narrative disclosure of intellectual capital: a "structurational" analysis', *Management Research News*, 31 (7), 518–537.

Dumay, J.C. (2016), 'A critical reflection on the future of intellectual capital: from reporting to disclosure', *Journal of Intellectual Capital*, 17 (1), 168–184.
Dumay, J.C. and S. Cuganesan (2011), 'Making sense of intellectual capital complexity: measuring through narrative', *Journal of Human Resource Costing and Accounting*, 15 (1), 24–49.
Dumay, J.C. and T. Garanina (2013), 'Intellectual capital research: a critical examination of the third stage', *Journal of Intellectual Capital*, 14 (1), 10–25.
Dumay, J.C. and J. Rooney (2016), 'Numbers versus narrative: an examination of a controversy', *Financial Accountability and Management*, 32 (2), 202–231.
Dumay, J.C. and R. Roslender (2013), 'Utilising narrative to improve the relevance of intellectual capital', *Journal of Accounting and Organizational Change*, 9 (3), 248–279.
EFRAG (2013), 'The role of the business model in financial reporting', research paper, European Financial Reporting Advisory Group, Bruxelles, accessed 10 July 2018 at www.efrag.org/files/EFRAG%20Output/131218_Business_Model_Research_Paper.pdf.
Guthrie, J., Ricceri, F. and J. Dumay (2012), 'Reflections and projections: a decade of intellectual capital accounting research', *British Accounting Review*, 44 (2), 68–82.
IASB and IIRC (2013), *Memorandum of Understanding – Integrated Corporate Reporting*, accessed 5 September 2019 at https://integratedreporting.org/wp-content/uploads/2014/01/MoU-IIRC-SASB-Final.pdf.
Ignatow, G. and R. Mihalcea (2016), *Text Mining: A Guidebook for the Social Sciences*, Thousand Oaks, CA: SAGE.
International Accounting Standards Board (IASB) (2010), *IFRS Practice Statements, Management Commentary. A Framework for Presentation*, accessed 5 September 2019 at https://service.betterregulation.com/sites/default/files/upload/2019-03/ifrspracticestatement1_130.pdf.
International Integrated Reporting Council (IIRC) (2013), *International Integrated Reporting Framework*, accessed 5 September 2019 at https://integratedreporting.org/wp-content/uploads/2015/03/13-12-08-THE-INTERNATIONAL-IR-FRAMEWORK-2-1.pdf.
Lai, A., Melloni, G. and R. Stacchezzini (2017), 'What does materiality mean to integrated reporting preparers? An empirical exploration', *Meditari Accountancy Research*, 25 (4), 533–552.
Lai, A., Melloni, G. and R. Stacchezzini (2018), 'Integrated reporting and narrative accountability: the role of preparers', *Accounting, Auditing and Accountability Journal*, 31 (5), 1381–1405.
McKernan, J.F. and K. MacLullich (2004), 'Accounting, love and justice', *Accounting, Auditing and Accountability Journal*, 17 (3), 327–360.
McKernan, J.F. and K. McPhail (2012), 'Editorial – Accountability and accounterability', *Critical Perspectives on Accounting*, 23, 177–182.
Messner, M. (2009), 'The limits of accountability', *Accounting, Organizations and Society*, 34 (8), 918–938.
Mouritsen, J. (2006), 'Problematising intellectual capital research: ostensive versus performative IC', *Accounting, Auditing and Accountability Journal*, 19 (6), 820–841.
Mouritsen, J. (2009), 'Classification, measurement and the ontology of intellectual capital entities', *Journal of Human Resource Costing and Accounting*, 13 (2), 154–162.
Mouritsen, J., Bukh, P.N., Flagstad, K., Thorbjørnsen, S., Johansen, M.R., et al. (2003), *Intellectual Capital Statements – The New Guideline*, Copenhagen: Danish Ministry of Science, Technology and Innovation.
Mouritsen, J., Bukh, P.N., Larsen, H.T. and M.R. Johansen (2002), 'Developing and managing knowledge through intellectual capital statements', *Journal of Intellectual Capital*, 3 (1), 10–29.
Mouritsen, J., Johansen, M.R., Larsen, H.T. and P.N. Bukh (2001a), 'Reading an intellectual capital statement: describing and prescribing knowledge management strategies', *Journal of Intellectual Capital*, 2 (4), 359–383.
Mouritsen, J., Larsen, H.T. and P.N. Bukh (2001b), 'Intellectual capital and the "capable firm": narrating, visualising and numbering for managing knowledge', *Accounting, Organizations and Society*, 26 (7–8), 735–762.

Nielsen, C., Roslender, R. and S. Schaper (2017), 'Explaining the demise of the intellectual capital statement in Denmark', *Accounting, Auditing and Accountability Journal*, 30 (1), 38–64.

Petty, R., and J. Guthrie (2000), 'Intellectual capital literature review: measurement, reporting and management', *Journal of Intellectual Capital*, 1 (2), 155–176.

Roberts, J. (1991), 'The possibilities of accountability', *Accounting, Organizations and Society*, 16 (4), 355–368.

Roberts, J. (1996), 'From discipline to dialogue: individualizing and socializing forms of accountability', in R. Munro and J. Mouritsen (eds), *Accountability: Power, Ethos and the Technologies of Managing*, London: International Thomson Business Press, pp. 40–61.

Stacchezzini, R., Florio, C., Sproviero, A.F. and S. Corbella (2019), 'An intellectual capital ontology in an integrated reporting context', *Journal of Intellectual Capital*, 20 (1), 83–99.

Stewart, T. (1997), *Intellectual Capital: The New Wealth of Organizations*, London: Nicholas Brealey.

Stolowy, H. and L. Paugam (2018), 'The expansion of non-financial reporting: an exploratory study', *Accounting and Business Research*, 48 (5), 525–548.

Sveiby, K.E. (1997), *The New Organizational Wealth: Managing and Measuring Knowledge-Based Assets*, San Francisco, CA: Berrett-Koehler Publishers.

World Intellectual Capital/Assets Initiative (WICI) (2016), 'WICI intangibles reporting framework. Version 1.0', accessed 10 July 2018 at http://www.wici-global.com/wirf/WICI_Intangibles_Reporting_Framework_v1.0.pdf.

6. Deductive versus inductive content analysis: a methodological research note to disclosures studies in intellectual capital research

Gunnar Rimmel and Michela Cordazzo

INTRODUCTION

Since the mid-1990s, corporations' dissemination of intellectual capital information and disclosures for investor relations purposes have dramatically increased (Rimmel, 2003). During the last decades, globalization has resulted in the emergence of global capital markets and an increased number of international listings. However, it has been hypothesized that accounting information is, although probably still the most important form of information, insufficient for investors and analysts when they are seeking to value companies. Organizational intangible resources – the company's soft data such as human resources, know-how, intellectual property rights, manufacturing procedures or organizational structure – are important pieces of information for analysts when valuing companies (Nielsen et al., 2015). This kind of information on corporate intellectual capital is often issued as voluntary disclosures. Voluntary disclosure is any information released beyond mandatory disclosure. Mandatory disclosure involves information released according to institutional regulations and standards. Voluntary disclosures are expected to lower the cost of equity capital because increased disclosure reduces information asymmetry, and to enhance stock market liquidity by increasing the demand for a company's stocks. This, in turn, may facilitate a more precise valuation of the company (Baboukardos and Rimmel, 2016).

A growing area in accounting research is studying the amount, content and effect of corporate disclosures. Corporate disclosure is a deliberate release of financial and non-financial information, whether numerical or qualitative, mandatory or voluntary, via formal or informal channels (Gibbins et al., 1990). Investors need even narrated non-financial voluntary information that goes beyond pure financial information (IIRC, 2015). A large number of disclosure studies apply content analysis methodologies to classify disclosures according to several classifications based on prior research (Hassan and Marston, 2010).

In recent years the concept of intellectual capital (IC) has become a much discussed topic among company managers, accounting practitioners and researchers. In the corporate world, IC refers to the knowledge, skills and experience of a company's employees as well as the company's research and development (R&D) activities, routines, procedures, systems, intellectual property and external relationships (IIRC, 2015; RICARDIS, 2006; Meritum, 2002). It is the unique combination of these different IC elements that also determine a company's profitability and competitive advantage (IIRC, 2015; Boedker et al., 2008; Beattie and Pratt, 2002). At the same time as the interest in IC has increased, so has the voluntary disclosure of information. In the early days of the IC movement, individual corporate efforts drove the interest in reporting IC (Rimmel, 2003).

This interest has resulted in numerous disclosure studies focused on examining the determinants of voluntary disclosures and their impact on the capital market (Nielsen et al., 2015; Beattie and Thomson, 2007; Rimmel, 2003). Healy and Palepu's (2001) review of empirical disclosure literature illuminates the problems and limitations of studies that are measuring the extent of voluntary disclosure. Conventionally, many empirical disclosure studies apply a pre-conceptualized and pre-composed disclosure index (Beattie and Thomson, 2007; Beattie et al., 2004). Pre-conceptualized and pre-composed disclosure indexes include previous research on disclosure, which means that in many cases categories and items of disclosures scoreboards are identical (for example, Bukh et al., 2005; Cordazzo, 2007; Nielsen et al., 2015; Rimmel, 2018).

Content analysis is used in many accounting studies and has a long history in other disciplines including psychology, linguistics and mass communication research (Beattie and Thomson, 2007; Beattie et al., 2004). Although content analysis is widely accepted in accounting research, little has been published on how to apply the method. The number of methodological papers concerning content analysis in accounting research is diminutive. To our knowledge, there is no disclosure study available that makes a significant attempt to resolve the problems and limitations of voluntary disclosure studies as identified by Healy and Palepu (2001) and Beattie and Thomson (2007).

The general intent of this chapter is to widen the scope of intellectual capital research in two key directions. First, this chapter contrasts the common strand of deductive content analysis in intellectual capital disclosure research by introducing an inductive approach. Second, it illustrates specific issues that arise in using either deductive or inductive content analysis. This chapter outlines a general approach for qualitative data analysis, providing details about the assumptions and procedures used in deductive and inductive content analysis.

The empirical material stems from the annual report of a Swedish information technology company that has already been studied in the mid-1990s when the Skandia Navigator was mentioned as one of the leading intellectual capital reporting tools (Rimmel, 2003). The annual report was used to illustrate methodological differences between deductive and inductive approaches in relation to the content of intellectual capital. This chapter illustrates an intellectual capital disclosure index based on the process of generating items, lists and categories during inductive content analysis. The purpose of this chapter is to illustrate an alternative approach to the existing strand of intellectual capital studies using deductive content analysis.

The remainder of this chapter is structured as follows. The following section describes a general background on content analysis. Subsequently, in the section on content analysis as a methodological choice, we illustrate elements of inductive and deductive content analysis based on methodological and theoretical knowledge. Thereafter, we outline IC frameworks that adopt a deductive method for content analysis. This is followed by a systematic review of the assumptions and procedures made when conducting inductive content analysis. Through describing the different stages and considerations made to code and generate categories from raw data, we outline how to use an inductive approach to content analysis studies. We discuss the process of inductive coding and assessing trustworthiness, as well as implications on writing the findings. Finally, in the conclusions we argue that inductive content analysis could be a different, valuable method complementing the existing stream of deductive intellectual capital research, particularly as it has the potential to increase methodological transparency in disclosure studies, and could facilitate replication and comparison.

BACKGROUND ON CONTENT ANALYSIS

Over the last decades, there have been continual developments in accounting research of conducting disclosure studies that are based on a content analysis methodology (Rimmel, 2018; Beattie and Thomson, 2007). Content analysis is a method of analysing written, verbal or visual communication messages to identify signals in blocks of text and convert them to numerical values. This conversion from text to numbers can be used to produce replicable findings that enable analysis of the quantity of information items in text (Dey, 1993). Content analysis has developed as a method for analysing texts in hermeneutic contexts as well as for comparing content in newspapers, political speeches and magazines (Mayring, 2000). The procedures of the methodological approach have been refined and broadened into interdisciplinary research and this method is currently widely applied in disciplines such as communication, sociology, psychology, sociology, history and arts as well as accounting research (Neuendorf, 2002).

Therefore, content analysis has become recognized as a methodological approach for analysing texts. According to Mayring (2000), content analysis wants to preserve the advantages of quantitative analysis for a more qualitative text interpretation. Usually, content analysis follows procedures to refine and aggregate words into fewer categories that represent similar content. The underlying assumption in content analysis methodology is that the aggregation of words, sentences or phrases into the same category share the same meaning (Beattie and Thomson, 2007; Milne and Adler, 1999; Beattie et al., 2004). According to Krippendorff (2012), the intention with content analysis as a research method is to apply systematic and objective means to describe and quantify phenomena. This enables researchers to obtain new insights and knowledge by making replicable interpretations from text. Researchers that conduct content analysis will get a condensed and eclectic picture through aggregated categories and sub-categories. Consequently, the derived picture can be used to build up a model, which contributes to theoretical knowledge about the phenomenon.

Although content analysis has been widely accepted as a research method in accounting research and many other disciplines, it has been criticized by both quantitative and qualitative researchers. On the one hand, quantitative researchers argue that content analysis should be regarded as a simplistic technique that does not live up to the objective rigour of statistical analysis (Dey, 1993). On the other hand, qualitative researchers argue that content analysis is not qualitative enough in its nature, as it might be possible to achieve results by simply applying quantitative methods if the expertise of analysis is missing (Neuendorf, 2002).

Despite criticism of both quantitative and qualitative researchers, content analysis has become established as a method among accounting researchers that conduct disclosure studies, including on intellectual capital. Content analysis offers accounting researchers many benefits, as it is an easy-to-comprehend, content-sensitive method that offers a large degree of flexibility regarding research design (Guthrie et al., 2004).

CONTENT ANALYSIS AS A METHODOLOGICAL CHOICE

When considering content analysis as the main methodological technique for conducting a study, there are many avenues for researchers to choose from. One of the most commonly used forms of content analysis is based on a pre-established and pre-conceptualized frame of categories (Krippendorff, 2012). Such deductive forms of content analysis have traditionally been used in accounting research on the content of disclosures made by corporations (Rimmel, 2003). Focusing on the analysis of IC disclosures in corporate reports, accounting researchers have used a pre-established set of categories for their IC disclosure checklists derived from earlier studies in this field (for example, Rimmel, 2003; Bukh et al., 2005; Cordazzo, 2007; Nielsen et al., 2015; Rimmel, 2018), which in turn have been developed from the stream of disclosure studies in accounting research that studied related issues in annual reports.

However, the deductive approach has a disadvantage in the sense that it is impossible in practice to create a predefined set of categories that does not involve elements of interpretation from the researcher's side (Beattie and Thomson, 2007). Thus, using a set of categories based on the previous theories and the researcher's interpretation might raise the risk of there being a mismatch between empirical data and the categories. Moreover, it is necessary to take into account that disclosure checklists from prior research might not capture all the variety of new features of modern intellectual capital areas (for example, influences from the integrated reporting framework). As such, disclosure checklists focusing on intellectual capital should be developed further to capture recent development of intellectual capital practice.

This gap within deductive approaches to content analysis could be avoided by pursuing an alternative approach within the methodology of content analysis, namely, inductive category development (Mayring, 2000). Employing this type of content analysis requires researchers to be immersed in empirical data without using preconceived categories, consequently allowing categories to emerge from the data (Krippendorff, 2012).

In order to elaborate upon the differences between deductive and inductive content analysis, a concise review on the processes is represented in terms of the main phases of: preparation, operationalization, analysis and interpretation of results (see Figure 6.1). However, there are no systematic rules for analysing data in content analysis. The generic feature of all content analysis is that the many words of text are classified into much smaller content categories that contain varying numbers of

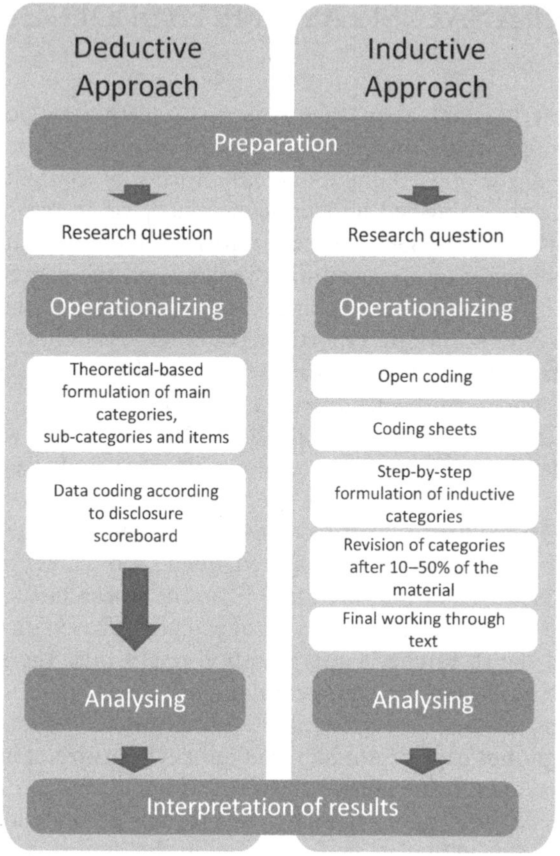

Figure 6.1 Content analysis process by deductive and inductive approach

information items. The different steps in Figure 6.1 will not be explained with greatest detail within this short overview. Both deductive and inductive content analysis start with a preparation phase, conducting a literature review to formulate the research question (Guthrie et al., 2004). Deductive and inductive content analysis differ in the way they operationalize and analyse the data.

Deductive content analysis is generally theoretical, based on prior studies and literature reviews (Guthrie et al., 2004). In many studies, deductive content analysis has been applied to retest results of existing studies in a new context (Beattie and Thomson, 2007). Once the option for conducting a deductive content analysis is selected, a disclosure scoreboard has to be developed in order to code the data according to the categories, sub-categories and specific information items. Milne and Adler (1999) showed that when the number of content categories in a disclosure scoreboard increases, the potential for coding errors increases. Despite this problem, too few coding categories might increase the likelihood of random agreement in coding decisions. This would cause another problem, as it may result in overestimation within categories and consequently adversely affect reliability (Milne and Adler, 1999). As soon as the disclosure scoreboard has been developed, the entire data has to be coded using the identified categories (Beattie and Thomson, 2007). Only data that fits into the items that are built into the scoreboard is included. This is a limitation, as content that might not fit the items on the scoreboard is excluded.

This problem does not arise if the researcher adopts an inductive approach. As this approach does not develop categories and items for a disclosure scoreboard beforehand, it allows open coding. Open coding derives categories through the content of the data. During open coding, notes are made while reading data. Written material is read through again, and as many notes as necessary are taken to describe all aspects of the content (Mayring, 2000). The notes are transferred on to a coding sheet and categories are freely generated at this stage. After the process of open coding, the lists of categories are grouped and aggregated into main and sub-categories by collapsing those that are similar or dissimilar. Creating categories through inductive content analysis implies that researchers have to interpret the data to make a decision about what items belong to which category.

According to Milne and Adler (1999), coding needs to be reliable in terms of decisions and rules on categories, to achieve consistent coding decisions across time and researchers, which enhances the reliability of the study. This applies to both deductive and inductive content analysis. Therefore, reliability can be enhanced by using multiple coders at different times to reveal inconsistencies in coding.

THE PROPOSAL OF IC FRAMEWORKS WITH A DEDUCTIVE METHOD

The deductive method in content analysis is the most popular research approach in understanding IC information. The reviews of IC literature suggest different motivations for and contributions to the application of this approach (Guthrie et al., 2004; Dumay and Cai, 2014, 2015), which primarily depend on the methodology and the environment for investigating IC disclosures.

We have noticed that the frameworks based on a deductive method in IC literature are classifiable into four main levels of development. A first level concerns the frameworks defined as an 'original proposal' because they do not refer to any previous IC framework; while a second level is about those offering an important revision of a framework classified in the first level.

The IC frameworks by Bontis (1998), Guthrie and Petty (2000), Brennan (2001), Guthrie et al. (2004) and Abeysekera and Guthrie (2005) are classified as 'original proposals'. Bontis (1998) develops a framework for managing and measuring the knowledge-based assets, which were perceived by scholars and managers as the new wealth of organization in the third millennium (Brooking, 1996; Edvinsson and Sullivan, 1996; Stewart, 1997; Sveiby, 1997). A similar approach, but more focused on the models for presenting and measuring IC in annual reports, is proposed by Guthrie and Petty (2000). The main purpose of this framework is to improve business reporting practices by addressing the importance of IC information and its determinants. Given its purpose, it has been extensively applied in IC literature for developing further research approaches of analysis with a deductive method.

Even though the frameworks by Brennan (2001), Guthrie et al. (2004) and Abeysekera and Guthrie (2005) are not frequently used in IC literature, they are an 'original proposal' containing some new key elements. They introduce a detailed application of methodologies for reporting IC in annual reports (Brennan, 2001), a critical perspective on the use of content analysis in examining IC (Guthrie et al., 2004) and a framework for analysing the dissemination of IC information in emerging markets (Abeysekera and Guthrie, 2005).

Li et al. (2008) also propose an 'original proposal'. This study is original based on the development of an IC framework solely addressing the influence of the several dimensions of corporate governance structure on IC information. There are no other examples of frameworks with this purpose in the IC literature, and this justifies its qualification in the first level.

The most common IC framework classified in the second level is by Bukh et al. (2005), which builds on Guthrie and Petty (2000). It addresses several dimensions of IC disclosure, both voluntary and mandatory, which enhance the use of a disclosure index for measuring the IC information-related item of the framework. After that, the IC disclosure is associated to some firm-specific determinants that influence the disclosure of IC information in IPOs. This framework has been widely used in IC literature as it allows some changes in several manners. Some studies apply several adaptations by addressing the different perspectives of investment decisions in financial markets included in analyst reports, which require diverse additional items in the framework (García-Meca et al., 2005; García-Meca and Martínez, 2007). Other studies propose some revisions due to the requirements of financial markets for the preparation of initial public offerings (IPOs) in a particular activity segment, which affect IC disclosure and its measurement (Cordazzo, 2007; Cordazzo and Vergauwen, 2012), or a more detailed investigation of the firm-specific characteristics affecting IC disclosure in IPOs (Singh and Van der Zahn, 2008).

Bozzolan et al. (2003) extend the framework by Guthrie and Petty (2000), without changing its structure and items but by emphasizing its use in the different phases of the content analysis method. This is a first attempt to apply this method in a more reliable and valid manner within the IC research field; as such, it is a good example of application of an IC framework according to the rules of the content analysis method. Some studies apply this framework but without any or a partial change to its methodology (Vandemaele et al., 2005; Bozzolan et al., 2006).

The use of more frameworks in the third and fourth levels is not always supported by a clear justification. The third level combines two frameworks, where the former always refers to Guthrie and Petty (2000) and the latter to Bontis (1998), Bozzolan et al. (2003), Guthrie et al. (2004) or Abeysekera and Guthrie (2005). These combinations are mainly connected to a specific activity sector (Cerbioni and Parbonetti, 2007) and country (Oliveras et al., 2008; Striukova et al., 2008; Brüggen et al., 2009), or are without any explanation (Muttakin et al., 2015). They do not provide any particular change to the IC methodology of analysis and measurement proposed by the previous frameworks.

Those in the fourth level are a mixture of several frameworks referring to the first and second levels. It is difficult indeed to understand whether their main contribution is associated with the purpose of investigating the IC disclosure practices in annual reports, or with representing a new approach to the measurement and analysis of IC information (Abeysekera, 2008; Sonnier, 2008; Singh and Kansal, 2011; Vafaei et al., 2011; Ott et al., 2014; Abhayawansa and Guthrie, 2016). They propose articulated and detailed quantitative analysis and measurement tools of IC, which may show bias if the primary purpose of investigating the IC practices in annual reports is to propose a model for managing the resources of a firm denoting intangible connotations. Further, the combination of several frameworks based on slightly different methodologies hampers the interpretation and comparability of IC disclosures, as each methodology relies on a different conceptualization of IC (Beattie and Thomson, 2007).

CONDUCTING INDUCTIVE CONTENT ANALYSIS

The key difference between deductive and inductive content analysis is whether to apply a pre-established and pre-conceptualized frame of categories in a disclosure scoreboard, or to establish a disclosure scoreboard through inductive inquiry. Pursuing an inductive approach in content analysis does not mean that the researcher will not address previous theories and research. However, in comparison to a deductive approach, the research conducted in an inductive study is not driven by the chosen frame of existing categories in prior research. In other words, the research instrument – the coding sheet that establishes the disclosure scoreboard – emerges during the data analysis process and is not pre-conceptualized based on previous research as in the deductive approach.

According to Mayring (2000), inductive content analysis methodologically follows a step-wise logic of inquiry. Operationalizing inductive content analysis requires that the researcher uses open coding to create categories, revise categories and analyse the results. Open coding means that notes are written in the text while reading it, as well as highlighting words and information items. These notes have to be transferred to a coding sheet to allow systematic scrutiny. The written material is read through again, and as many notes as necessary are written down on the margins to describe all aspects of the content (Hsieh and Shannon, 2005). The notes are collected from the margins and transferred onto the coding sheets, and categories are freely generated at this stage (Krippendorff, 2012).

The next step of inductive content analysis is the determination of criteria for category selection. After open coding, the lists of items should be grouped into categories under higher-order headings. For example, the focus could be on human resource disclosures within intellectual capital information in annual reports (see Figure 6.2). Reading a corporate annual report could give an indication that the annual report might contain a certain structure, main themes or headings about human resources, which could be treated as a step in the formulation of inductive categories. The content of an annual report is often structured in a way where the main themes are shown on a sidebar or at the top of a page, or within a table of contents; these could be themes to represent main categories in a coding sheet. However, when all notes of items on human resources are documented and transferred to the coding sheet, it might appear that a number of items belong to a category that was not explicitly presented as a theme in the annual report.

Grouping data works to reduce the number of sub-categories by collapsing those that are similar or dissimilar into broader generic categories,

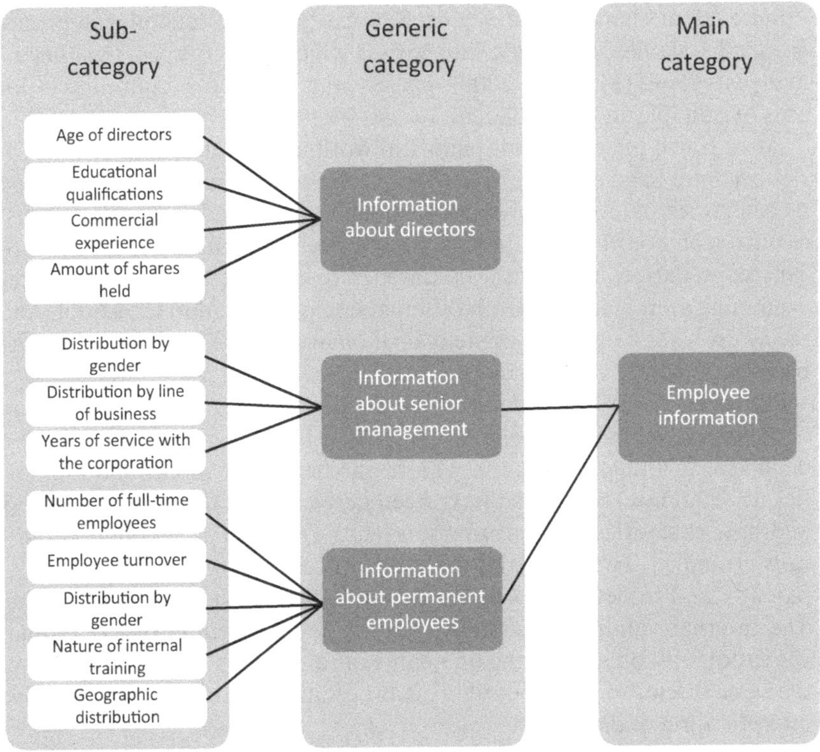

Figure 6.2 Inductively developed category and information items

and at the highest order, collapsing into main categories. When formulating categories by inductive content analysis, the researcher can derive a decision, through interpretation, as to which things to put in the same category (Dey, 1993). The formulation of inductive categories involves a process of developing the disclosure scoreboard parallel with the empirical investigation of annual report content. Categories might be generated directly from the structure of the annual report. An important issue that may arise during the process of creating categories is the interpretation of synonyms. Different companies might refer to the main categories of intellectual capital differently (Rimmel, 2003). For example, categories intended to present a company's financial information might be called 'financial data', 'financial performance', 'financial information', and so on. In this case, the researcher has to employ their own judgement in order to collapse these categories into one. The abstraction in inductive content analysis means formulating a general description of the research topic by generating main categories. Each main category is named using content-characteristic words. Sub-categories with similar items are grouped together as generic categories, which are grouped together as main categories (Mayring, 2000). The abstraction process continues as far as is reasonable and possible.

After 10–50 per cent of the empirical work, the number of main categories becomes fixed and can be used for the rest of the sample. The revision of categories involves a process of matching empirically developed disclosure scoreboards, with the list of items derived from the coding sheets. This compilation enables the researcher to refine the scoreboard after examining annual reports from different companies within the sample and seeing to what extent the content of human resource disclosures differs between a sample of companies.

Trustworthiness and validity are common measures of quality of any qualitative research and content analysis, regardless of whether it is of a deductive or inductive nature. The researcher needs to elucidate in sufficient detail how the results have been derived from the analysis process and how categories and information items are conceptually and empirically grounded. Therefore, the analysing process has to be explained transparently and in detail in order to facilitate the transferability of results. The internal validity of content analysis can be demonstrated though validation of scores by letting of a panel of researchers code data applying the same disclosure scoreboard. This procedure will reduce the subjective interpretation of data by the researchers.

DISCUSSION

At the beginning of this chapter, it was stated that the general intent was to widen the scope of intellectual capital research in two key directions. Currently, intellectual capital disclosure research commonly applies deductive content analysis. This chapter has deliberately tried to open up the prevailing path of intellectual capital disclosure research by introducing an inductive approach. This intent should not be misunderstood as a disavowal of deductive intellectual capital disclosure research in favour of the inductive content analysis method. Both methods have their advantages and disadvantages.

However, by conducting a content analysis of annual reports' intellectual capital disclosure using an inductive category development approach, categories are allowed to stem directly from the content. In comparison to the deductive approach previously used in intellectual capital disclosure research (for example, Bukh et al., 2005), the outcome of the inductive approach is a larger number of main categories and sub-categories with more detailed information items. According to Beattie and Thomson (2007), increased numbers of categories lead to increased understanding of the content, on the one hand, and to decreased comparability, on the other hand. The inductive approach and increased number of categories could be advantageous for contributing to a deeper understanding of intellectual capital disclosures in annual reports.

Beattie and Thomson (2007) address a critique to content analytic studies that only capture the presence of one type of information in the document and do not take the volume of information into account. This assumption is based on the fundamental idea of content analysis, where the importance of a certain item of information is mirrored by the number of times the information is disclosed (Krippendorff, 2012). As highlighted by Beattie and Jones (2001), repetition is a communication strategy employed by companies for emphasizing the importance of certain messages. Occurrences are therefore essential for content analysis and interpretation. Inductive category development allows the study to capture the volume of information by recording all small items of information that are presented under each category.

An inductive approach offers a possibility to find those informational items in the annual reports that are not expected to be found, differently from the deductive approach. In consequence, there might be less risk of missing some important disclosure items on companies' intellectual capital. However, inductive content analysis does not proceed in a linear manner, and is more complex and difficult than deductive analysis because it is less standardized and rigid. There are no simple or ready-made guidelines for instant data analysis in inductive content analysis. Each inquiry is distinctive, and the results depend on the skills, insights, analytic abilities and style of the investigator. The empirical material is generally not linear and may contain elements relating to several categories. This is an issue for the researcher to interpret, judge and resolve. Therefore, a great challenge of content analysis is the flexibility of the method applied; unlike quantitative methods, there is no 'right' way of conducting content analysis.

Deductive content analysis bears the strength of better comparability with previous disclosure studies through the application of partial or identical disclosure scoreboard items. Increased number of categories and items in a disclosure scoreboard can also lead to a decreased comparability of the study's results with other studies' results. To moderate such conflict between decreased comparability of data and increased understanding of data, the prior methodological research suggests involving more coders and extending the research on a longitudinal basis (Beattie and Thomson, 2007).

This chapter shows an alternative avenue for disclosure studies to take by illustrating that inductive content analysis may increase methodological transparency in disclosure studies and could facilitate replication and comparison. Researchers often wish for more detailed instructions on how to carry out content analysis. Qualitative data analysis software has improved considerably during recent years, and can facilitate the analysis of deductive and inductive content analysis. However, parts of the research process will remain dependent on researchers' actions, insights and interpretations based on the empirical material.

REFERENCES

Abeysekera, I. (2008), 'Intellectual capital disclosure trends: Singapore and Sri Lanka', *Journal of Intellectual Capital*, 9 (4), 723–737.

Abeysekera, I. and J. Guthrie (2005), 'An empirical investigation of annual reporting trends of intellectual capital in Sri Lanka', *Critical Perspectives on Accounting*, 16 (3), 151–163.

Abhayawansa, S. and J. Guthrie (2016), 'Drivers and semantic properties of intellectual capital information in sell-side analysts' reports', *Journal of Accounting and Organizational Change*, 12 (4), 434–471.

Baboukardos, D. and G. Rimmel (2016), 'Relevance of accounting information under an integrated reporting approach: A research note', *Journal of Accounting and Public Policy*, 35 (4), 437–452.

Beattie, V. and M.J. Jones (2001), 'A six-country comparison of the use of graphs in annual reports', *International Journal of Accounting*, 36, 195–222.

Beattie, V., McInnes, B. and S. Fearnley (2004), 'A methodology for analysing and evaluating narratives in annual reports: A comprehensive descriptive profile and metrics for disclosure quality attributes', *Accounting Forum*, 28 (3), 205–236.

Beattie, V. and K. Pratt (2002), *Voluntary Annual Report Disclosures: What Users Want*, Glasgow: Institute of Chartered Accountants of Scotland.

Beattie, V. and S. Thomson (2007), 'Lifting the lid on the use of content analysis to investigate intellectual capital disclosures in corporate annual reports', *Accounting Forum*, 31 (2), 129–163.

Boedker, C., Mouritsen, J. and J. Guthrie (2008), 'Enhanced business reporting: International trends and possible policy directions', *Journal of Human Resource Costing and Accounting*, 12 (1), 14–25.

Bontis, N. (1998), 'Intellectual capital: An exploratory study that develops measures and models', *Management Decision*, 36 (2), 63–76.

Bozzolan, S., Favotto, F. and F. Ricceri (2003), 'Italian annual intellectual capital disclosure: An empirical analysis', *Journal of Intellectual Capital*, 4 (4), 543–558.

Bozzolan, S., O'Regan, P. and F. Ricceri (2006), 'Intellectual capital disclosure (ICD). A comparison of Italy and the UK', *Journal of Human Resource Costing and Accounting*, 10 (2), 92–113.

Brennan, N. (2001), 'Reporting intellectual capital in annual reports: Evidence from Ireland', *Accounting, Auditing and Accountability Journal*, 14 (4), 423–436.

Brooking, A. (1996), *Intellectual Capital: Core Asset for the Third Millennium*, London: International Thomson Business Press.

Brüggen, A., Vergauwen, P. and M. Dao (2009), 'Determinants of intellectual capital disclosure: Evidence from Australia', *Management Decision*, 47 (2), 233–245.

Bukh, P.N., Nielsen, C., Mouritsen, J. and P. Gormsen (2005), 'Disclosure of information on intellectual capital indicators in Danish IPO prospectuses', *Accounting, Auditing and Accountability Journal*, 18 (6), 713–732.

Cerbioni, F. and A. Parbonetti (2007), 'Exploring the effects of corporate governance on intellectual capital disclosure: An analysis of European biotechnology companies', *European Accounting Review*, 16 (4), 791–826.

Cordazzo, M. (2007), 'Intangibles and Italian IPO prospectuses: A disclosure analysis', *Journal of Intellectual Capital*, 8 (2), 288–305.

Cordazzo, M. and P.G. Vergauwen (2012), 'Intellectual capital disclosure in the UK biotechnology IPO prospectuses', *Journal of Human Resource Costing and Accounting*, 16 (1), 4–19.

Dey, I. (1993), *Qualitative Data Analysis: A User-Friendly Guide for Social Scientists*, London: Routledge.

Dumay, J. and L. Cai (2014), 'A review and critique of content analysis as a methodology for inquiring into IC disclosure', *Journal of Intellectual Capital*, 15 (2), 264–290.

Dumay, J. and L. Cai (2015), 'Using content analysis as a research methodology for investigating intellectual capital disclosure: A critique', *Journal of Intellectual Capital*, 16 (1), 121–155.

Edvinsson, L. and P. Sullivan (1996), 'Developing a model for managing intellectual capital', *European Management Journal*, 14 (4), 356–364.

García-Meca, E. and I. Martínez (2007), 'The use of intellectual capital information in investment decisions: An empirical study using analyst reports', *International Journal of Accounting*, 42 (1), 57–81.

García-Meca, E., Parra, I., Larrán, M. and I. Martínez (2005), 'The explanatory factors of intellectual capital disclosure to financial analysts', *European Accounting Review*, 14 (1), 63–94.

Gibbins, M., Richardson, A. and J. Waterhouse (1990), 'The management of corporate financial disclosure: Opportunism, ritualism, policies and processes', *Journal of Accounting Research*, 28 (1), 121–143.

Guthrie, J. and R. Petty (2000), 'Intellectual capital: Australian annual reporting practices', *Journal of Intellectual Capital*, 1 (3), 241–251.

Guthrie, J., Yongvanich, K. and F. Ricceri (2004), 'Using content analysis as a research method to inquire into intellectual capital reporting', *Journal of Intellectual Capital*, 5 (2), 282–293.

Hassan, O. and C.L. Marston (2010), 'Disclosure measurement in the empirical accounting literature – A review article', *SSRN eLibrary*.

Healy, P.M. and K.G. Palepu (2001), 'Information asymmetry, corporate disclosure, and the capital market: A review of the empirical disclosure literature', *Journal of Accounting and Economics*, 31 (1–3), 405–440.

Hsieh, H-F. and S.E. Shannon (2005), 'Three approaches to qualitative content analysis', *Qualitative Health Research*, 15 (9), 1277–1288.

International Integrated Reporting Council (IIRC) (2015), *Creating Value, Integrated Reporting <IR> and Investor Benefits*, accessed 12 September 2018 at www.integratedreporting.org/wpcontent/uploads/2016/01/1323_CreatingValue_No3_8a-1.pdf.

Krippendorff, K. (2012), *Content Analysis: An Introduction to its Methodology* (3rd edn), New York: SAGE.

Li, J., Pike, R. and R. Haniffa (2008), 'Intellectual capital disclosure and corporate governance structure in UK firms', *Accounting and Business Research*, 38 (2), 137–159.

Mayring, P. (2000), 'Qualitative content analysis', *Forum: Qualitative Social Research*, 1 (2), Art 20. http://nbn-resolving.de/urn:nbn:de:0114-fqs0002204.

Meritum (2002), *Measuring Intangibles to Understand and Improve Innovation Management*, Target Socio-Economic Research, Brussels: European Commission.

Milne, M. and R. Adler (1999), 'Exploring the reliability of social and environmental disclosures content analysis', *Accounting, Auditing and Accountability Journal*, 12 (2), 237–256.

Muttakin, M.B., Khan, A. and A.R. Belal (2015), 'Intellectual capital disclosures and corporate governance: An empirical examination', *Advances in Accounting, Incorporating Advances in International Accounting*, 31, 219–227.
Neuendorf, K.A. (2002), *The Content Analysis Guidebook*, Thousand Oaks, CA: SAGE.
Nielsen, C., Rimmel, G. and T. Yosano (2015), 'Outperforming markets: IC and the long-term performance of Japanese IPOs', *Accounting Forum*, 39 (2), 83–96.
Oliveras, E., Gowthorpe, C., Kasperskaya, Y. and J. Perramon (2008), 'Reporting intellectual capital in Spain', *Corporate Communications: An International Journal*, 13 (2), 168–181.
Ott, C., Schmidt, U. and T. Guenther (2014), 'Information dissemination on intellectual capital in mergers and acquisitions: Purchase price allocations, press releases and business press', *Accounting and Business Research*, 44 (3), 280–314.
RICARDIS (2006), *Reporting Intellectual Capital to Augment Research, Development and Innovation in SMEs*, Report to the Commission of the High Level Expert Group on RICARDIS, Directorate-General for Research, EUR 22095 EN.
Rimmel, G. (2003), 'Human resource disclosures: A comparative study of annual reporting practice about information, providers and users in two corporations', Doctoral dissertation, Göteborg University, Sweden.
Rimmel, G. (2018), 'Chapter 3 – Human capital disclosures in Swedish state-owned enterprises – A comparison of integrated reporting versus traditional reporting', in Susanne Arvidsson (ed.), *Challenges in Managing Sustainable Business*, London: Palgrave Macmillan, pp. 55–75.
Singh, I. and M. Van der Zahn (2008), 'Determinants of intellectual capital disclosure in prospectuses of initial public offerings', *Accounting and Business Research*, 38 (5), 409–443.
Singh, S. and M. Kansal (2011), 'Voluntary disclosures of intellectual capital: An empirical analysis', *Journal of Intellectual Capital*, 12 (2), 301–318.
Sonnier, B.M. (2008), 'Intellectual capital disclosure: High-tech versus traditional sector companies', *Journal of Intellectual Capital*, 9 (4), 705–722.
Stewart, T. (1997), *Intellectual Capital: The New Wealth of Nations*, New York: Doubleday Dell Publishing Group.
Striukova, L., Unerman, J. and J. Guthrie (2008), 'Corporate reporting of intellectual capital: Evidence from UK companies', *British Accounting Review*, 40 (4), 297–313.
Sveiby, K.E. (1997), *The New Organizational Wealth: Managing and Measuring Knowledge-Based Assets*, San Francisco, CA: Berrett-Koehler Publishers.
Vafaei, A., Taylor, D.W. and A. Kamran (2011), 'The value relevance of intellectual capital disclosures', *Journal of Intellectual Capital*, 12 (3), 407–429.
Vandemaele, S.N., Vergauwen, P.G. and A.J. Smits (2005), 'Intellectual capital disclosure in The Netherlands, Sweden and the UK: A longitudinal and comparative study', *Journal of Intellectual Capital*, 6 (3), 417–426.

7. Assessing the value relevance of intellectual capital disclosure: are price-level models effective?

Lorenzo Simoni and Francesco Giunta

INTRODUCTION TO THE VALUE RELEVANCE OF INTELLECTUAL CAPITAL

Increasing importance has been attributed to intangibles and intellectual capital (IC) to explain a company's market value, which has led many accounting scholars to investigate IC disclosure practices (see Petty and Guthrie, 2000). Given their attributes, IC elements are usually described through narrative reporting (Holland, 2004; Mouritsen, 2004). Among the different strands of research that deal with the consequences of IC disclosure, a specific approach aims to assess IC value relevance. In the accounting field, the concept of value relevance is related to the capability of a piece of information to make a difference in an investment decision (FASB, 1984; IASB, 2010b). To assess the value relevance of a piece of information, accounting studies usually determine whether the disclosure of that item is significantly associated with a company's share price. These criteria represent the operationalization of the value relevance concept. In fact, a piece of information is deemed to impact upon share prices only if that information is valued by investors in their decision processes (Barth et al., 2001).

Statistical models are used to test for the presence of a significant association between the disclosure of an item and share price. Those models are derived from the model developed by Ohlson (1995) and subsequent extensions (Feltham and Ohlson, 1995, 1996; Ohlson, 1999, 2000). In the original model developed by Ohlson (1995), which is a price-level model, the price of a stock is expressed as a linear function of its book value and earnings.

In the IC domain, price-level models can be used to measure the value relevance of intangibles. IC disclosure is usually assessed by means of manually built disclosure indexes that capture the presence or absence of IC elements in companies' reports. The variables that measure IC disclosure are then used as independent variables in a price-level model to evaluate whether they are related to stock prices.

This chapter reviews existing literature investigating IC value relevance by means of price-level models. The review discusses the main methodological issues in IC value relevance literature and their advantages and disadvantages. The chapter briefly summarizes the results of IC value relevance studies. IC disclosure value relevance research mainly consists of two phases: the assessment of IC disclosure levels through a structured content analysis, which draws upon one or more IC framework(s) the use of a statistical model based on the model developed by Ohlson (1995) to assess the relationship between IC disclosure level and stock prices. Most of the studies that apply this methodology show a positive and significant relationship between IC disclosure and stock prices. These findings support the view that investors value information about intangibles.

At the same time, IC value relevance studies have some limitations. The use of content analysis to investigate IC disclosure has been criticized in terms of coding reliability and transparency issues (Beattie and Thomson, 2007). Another limitation is related to the fact that the different frameworks and IC definitions that have been used by researchers so far do not take into account the concept of connectivity capital (Habersam and Piber, 2003; Bjurström and Roberts, 2007) and the different value generation models that characterize companies (Hamel, 2000). Moreover, price-level models are characterized by intrinsic limitations, namely, the assumption of efficient capital markets.

However, several scholars in the field of IC reporting have identified possible ways to improve IC content analysis and the examination of the consequences of IC disclosure. Some contributions illustrate how reliability of content analysis can be improved (for example, Beattie and Thomson, 2007), while others advocate for the inclusion of qualitative aspects of disclosure in disclosure indexes (for example, Beretta and Bozzolan, 2008). Some authors suggest the use of the concept of business models to assess IC in relation to value creation processes (Bini et al., 2016). Finally, some studies use alternative approaches to price-level models to assess the value relevance of IC (Hope, 2003; Vanstraelen et al., 2003; Dhaliwal et al., 2012; Premti et al., 2017).

THE RISE OF INTELLECTUAL CAPITAL AS A PREDICTOR OF FIRM VALUE

In modern economies, companies' success is largely based on intangible elements – such as knowledge, skills, relationships, information, intellectual property and experience – that can be put to use to create wealth

(Edvinsson and Malone, 1997; Ittner et al., 1997; OECD, 1999; Bontis, 2001). All these elements form a company's IC (Stewart, 1997).

The importance attributed to IC in value creation has led investors to demand more and more information about intangible resources (Eccles and Mavrinac, 1995; Holland and Johanson, 2003; Alwert et al., 2009). For this reason, standard-setters and professional bodies have made significant effort to support the disclosure of non-financial information. In the United States, the American Institute of Certified Public Accountants edited the report titled *Improving Business Reporting – A Customer Focus* (AICPA, 1994). The document recommends the disclosure of non-financial information in the annual report in order to improve the overall quality of corporate reporting. Following that initiative, the Financial Accounting Standards Board (FASB, 2001) advocated disclosing non-financial items that can improve understandings of companies' critical success factors. The Canadian Institute of Chartered Accountants (CICA) has launched different initiatives to explore the role of non-financial items in corporate reporting. In Europe, the Institute of Chartered Accountants of England and Wales (ICAEW) has started discussing the opportunity for firms to communicate information about their intangible resources and strategies.

In response to the demand for non-financial information, companies have started to include information about their IC in the documents they publish. In some cases, IC statements or reports have been used to convey this kind of information (Brooking, 1997; Edvinsson, 1997; Edvinsson and Malone, 1997; Roos et al., 1997; Stewart, 1997; Sveiby, 1997; Petty and Guthrie, 2000). In other cases, information about IC has been included in the narrative part of the annual report. The use of narrative reporting for intangibles is related to the nature of the information that is conveyed. Since knowledge 'does not consist of separable "assets" that can be captured … by accounting rules' (Mouritsen et al., 2001, p. 740), IC statements use narrative to describe those activities that allow managers to manage knowledge. In this context, disclosure helps information users better understand how knowledge contributes to the definition of a product or a service that has a value to customers (Mouritsen, 2004).

Numbers can support IC disclosure. Many companies have started developing their own sets of non-financial indicators (Arvidsson, 2003). These two dimensions together define IC communication. Indicators measure the outcome of knowledge management activities, while narrative information explains how those activities are supposed to generate value (Mouritsen et al., 2001).

THE MAIN STAGES OF IC RESEARCH AND IC VALUE RELEVANCE STUDIES

As IC is widely recognized as the primary source of value, it has become a prominent topic in accounting and management research (Petty and Guthrie, 2000). IC research has passed through different stages (Petty and Guthrie, 2000; Dumay and Garanina, 2013). In the first stage, scholars used theories to define IC and raise awareness of the concept (Dumay, 2012). At this stage, however, empirical studies were still scarce.

In the second stage, researchers developed approaches to measure, manage and report IC (Petty and Guthrie, 2000; Guthrie et al., 2007; Ricceri, 2008). In this phase, empirical studies on the intensity and content of IC disclosure began to flourish. Many authors applied IC management and reporting approaches developed in this phase to assess how IC affects companies' performance. The third stage focused on the investigation of IC management and implementation inside organizations, following a bottom-up approach (Guthrie et al., 2012; Dumay and Garanina, 2013).

One of the most important areas in IC empirical examination within the second phase of IC research is represented by the investigation of the ability of IC to predict market values. In the accounting field, the strand of research that examines the association of IC with market values is part of the literature on 'value relevance'. According to the International Accounting Standards Board (IASB) Framework for Financial Reporting (IASB, 2010b), information is only relevant if it is 'capable of making a difference in the decisions made by users' even if 'some users choose not to take advantage of it or are already aware of it from other sources' (ibid., Chapter 3: Qualitative characteristics of useful financial information, QC6, p. A27). Similarly, the FASB (1984) defines an item as relevant when it makes a difference to financial statement users' decisions (SFAC No. 5). Barth (2000, p. 10) states that 'investors are primarily interested in information that can help them assess the value of the firm for purposes of making informed investment choices'. The researchers' focus is on investors as they represent a large class of financial statement users. The IASB also agrees that investors are the primary users of financial statements (IASB, 2010a, Conceptual Framework for Financial Reporting, Chapter 1: The objective of general purpose financial reporting, OB2, p. A21).

To evaluate the role that a piece of information plays in investment decisions, value relevance studies usually verify whether an amount acts as a predictor of equity market values (Barth et al., 2001). This approach is based on the assumption that capital markets are efficient and unbiased (Fama, 1970, 1991). In this setting, changes in security prices will reflect the flow of information available to the market (Ball and Brown, 1968).

Scholars have used a few models to investigate the value relevance of an item. The model developed by Ohlson (1995), with its extensions and refinements (Feltham and Ohlson, 1995, 1996; Ohlson, 1999, 2000; Stober, 1999; Barth et al., 2001) is one of the most used. The Ohlson (1995) model expresses the market value as a linear function of earnings, book value of equity and other information. The variable related to other information represents all the useful information that is not captured by the accounting standards.

In a general form, the basic expression of the model can be formulated as follows:

$$MV_{it} = \alpha + \beta_1 BV_{it} + \beta_2 NI_{it} + \beta_3 OI_{it} + \varepsilon \quad (7.1)$$

where:
MV_{it} = market value for company i at time t
BV_{it} = book value of equity for company i at time t
NI_{it} = net income for company i at time t
OI_{it} = other information for company i at time t

In many cases, the three basic variables of the model are scaled by the number of shares. This operation leads to the expression of a company's share price as the linear function of its book value per share and its earnings per share. For this reason, the models based on the Ohlson (1995) model are called price-level models.

Price-level models have been extensively used in the literature to investigate the value relevance of different kinds of non-financial items. Researchers usually build a variable that captures the intensity of a non-financial item. That variable is used as part of the other information in the model. Following this approach, Amir and Lev (1996) have measured the value relevance of two non-financial measures that are supposed to be key determinants of firm value in the wireless and telecommunications industry, population size and market penetration, calculated as the ratio between subscriptions and population size. The results of their study show that both the indexes are positively and significantly associated with market value. Thus, the authors conclude that those non-financial measures are value relevant. Clarkson et al. (2004) have used the Ohlson model to evaluate the value relevance of commitment towards environmental safeguards. A specific measure of environmental commitment is developed in the study. The authors find the measure to be value relevant for companies with low pollution levels.

Other studies on the value relevance of intangibles specifically focus on brand value (Barth et al., 1998; Barth and Clinch, 1998;

Seethamraju, 2003), advertising expenses (Chauvin and Hirschey, 1993), research and development (R&D) disclosure (Hirschey, 1982; Doukas and Switzer, 1992; Lev and Sougiannis, 1996; Ballester et al., 2003), patents (Griliches, 1981; Austin, 1993), customer satisfaction measures (Ittner and Larcker, 1998), and customer franchise value (Bonacchi et al., 2015).

While all those studies focus on specific non-financial measures, price-level models have also been used to assess the relevance of IC disclosure. In this case, IC is considered a concept that addresses all the different kinds of intangibles that can be found in a company. Thus, studies that address the value relevance of IC narratives attempt to measure disclosures about intangibles with reference to one of the conceptual frameworks that try to define IC.

RESEARCH DESIGN OF IC VALUE RELEVANCE STUDIES

The investigation of IC value relevance empirically supports the hypothesis that investors consider IC in their valuations. Thus, the assessment of IC value relevance can be positioned among the empirical studies that characterize the second phase of IC literature (Dumay and Garanina, 2013).

Two common traits can be found in the different empirical works that aim to measure IC value relevance:

1. The assessment of IC disclosure;
2. The use of a statistic model to test the association between IC and share price.

The first step is necessary to measure different intensity levels in IC disclosure. Once a measure of IC disclosure has been built, it is possible to test for the presence of a statistic association between IC and market values using a price-level model (see Barth et al., 2001). A schematic representation of these two steps of IC assessment is shown in Figure 7.1.

Assessing IC Disclosure

The assessment of IC disclosure aims to capture the different levels of IC intensity across the companies that are investigated. Scholars usually assess IC disclosure by means of a content analysis of the narrative sections of the annual report (see Guthrie et al., 2004). Some studies examine sources of information not included in the annual report (ibid.). This

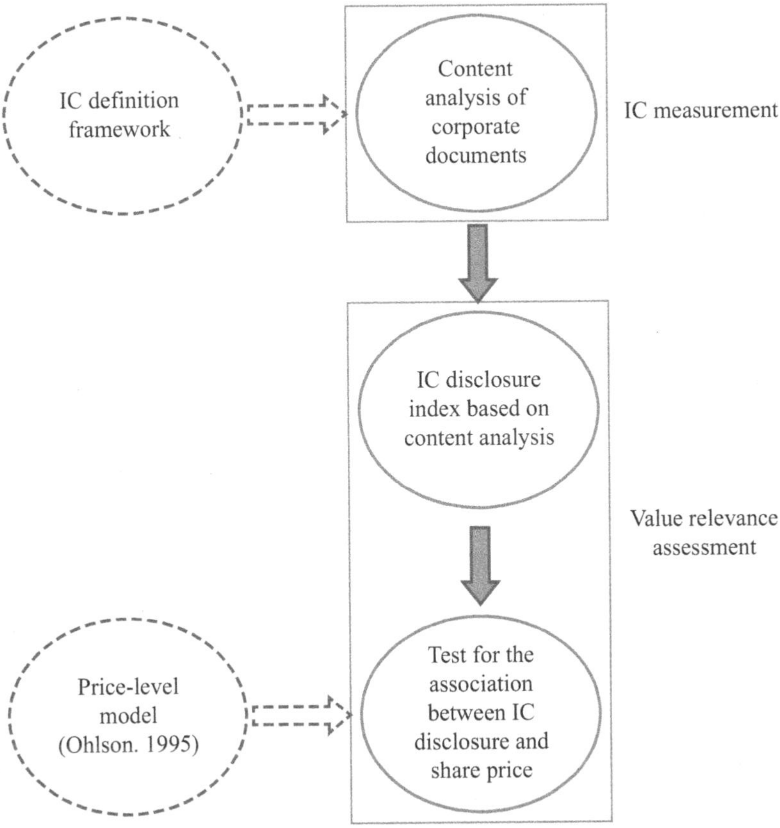

Figure 7.1 *The steps of IC disclosure value relevance assessment*

methodology has been widely used in business studies to assess corporate disclosure in general (Bukh et al., 2005; Rimmel et al., 2009; Bryman and Bell, 2015) and IC disclosure (Guthrie and Petty, 2000; Abeysekera and Guthrie, 2002; Bontis, 2003).

The analysis usually refers to one of the existing frameworks that define IC and its constitutive elements. Many researchers (Guthrie and Petty, 2000; Brennan, 2001; Bozzolan et al., 2003) refer to the framework elaborated by Sveiby (1997). Sveiby's framework categorizes intangibles in three broad categories: organizational capital, relational capital and human capital.

Another well-known framework is proposed by Bontis (2003), which draws upon the classification of the World Congress on Intellectual Capital to identify 38 items. In this case, items are also grouped in the three main categories of organizational, relational and human capital. Other classifications include those developed by Abeysekera (2007) and Sanchez et al. (2000). In developing his framework, Abeysekera (2007) draws upon Sveiby's framework (1997) and its adaptation by Guthrie and Petty (2000). The framework features 45 items and considers three different types of disclosure (narrative, visual and numeric). The 45 items are divided into the same three categories as Sveiby's (1997) model. Also, Sanchez et al. (2000) have drawn inspiration from Sveiby (1997) to develop a set of 101 items that are organized into the three categories.

Despite the presence of many sources of information, the annual report is the most frequently analysed document by researchers (see Guthrie et al., 2004). Annual reports, in fact, represent the primary source of information for stakeholders (Knutson, 1992; Botosan, 1997; AIMR, 2002). Empirical evidence shows a positive correlation between the amount of information disclosed in a company's annual report and the quantity of information conveyed through other channels by the same company, such as 'one-to-one' interviews with analysts or press releases (Lang and Lundholm, 1993; Botosan and Plumlee, 2002). Therefore, the company's disclosure through the annual report is considered as a proxy for the disclosure provided through all the other channels.

Using Statistic Models to Test the Association between IC and Share Price

Once the content analysis has been conducted, an IC disclosure index is built. IC disclosure indexes take the form of scope indexes (see Urquiza et al., 2009): indexes that measure how many items are disclosed out of a predetermined list of items. In the case of IC, researchers usually build a disclosure index based on the framework that has been chosen for the content analysis. IC disclosure indexes are calculated as the number of items in the framework that are disclosed divided by the total number of items in the framework. The formula is the following:

$$ICdisclosure = \frac{Number\ of\ elements\ disclosed}{Number\ of\ items\ in\ the\ IC\ framework}$$

In some cases (for example, Abeysekera, 2011), the author makes a distinction between the types of information. An element can be assigned a different score when narrative information about that element is supported by numbers and/or visual representations.

In order to assess the value relevance of IC narrative information, the disclosure index is included as an independent variable in the regression of the general Ohlson (1995) model. Control variables are added in order to take into account the effects of other factors on both disclosure and market value. Those factors include the company's size, leverage and industry effects. Different proxies for size and leverage have been used in the literature.

Usually, proxies for size are represented by total assets (Seetharaman et al., 2002; Baboukardos and Rimmel, 2016) and revenues (Abeysekera, 2011). The ratio between total liabilities and total assets (Baboukardos and Rimmel, 2016), and the ratio between total liabilities and shareholders' equity (Omar, 2008; Anam et al., 2011), are used as proxies for the company's leverage. IC disclosure is considered part of the 'other information' that is recalled in the general model. The equation (7.1) thus becomes:

$$MV_{it} = \alpha + \beta_1\, BV_{it} + \beta_2\, NI_{it} + \beta_3\, ICdisclosure_{it} + Controls_{it} + \varepsilon \qquad (7.2)$$

where:
MV_{it} = market value for company *i* at time *t*
BV_{it} = book value for equity of company *i* at time *t*
NI_{it} = net income for company *i* at time *t*
$ICdisclosure_{it}$ = IC disclosure index built through the content analysis for company *i* at time *t*
$Controls_{it}$ = control variables for company *i* at time *t*.

The aim of the research is to assess whether there is a significant relationship between the IC disclosure index and the share price. The presence of such a relationship would be a sign that investors value IC narrative in their investment decision processes.

THE APPLICATION OF PRICE-LEVEL MODELS TO IC: MAIN FINDINGS

The first studies to apply this methodology to assess the value relevance of IC disclosure were published around 2011. Different authors have run the same kind of analysis using different frameworks for content analysis and examined companies in different settings. Some studies focus on one country, while others consider different countries and make a comparison.

Abeysekera (2011) has investigated the value relevance of IC disclosures in the annual report of companies in Sri Lanka. The same companies are examined in two different periods: a period of peace and a period when the country was affected by a civil war. The author has built a disclosure index made of 45 items based on the framework developed in a previous study (Abeysekera, 2007). The relationship between this index and market prices has then been tested. His findings show that IC disclosure is not relevant in the period of civil war, but it is valued by investors in the truce period.

Anam et al. (2011) have used content analysis to measure IC disclosure of Malaysian companies. The index draws upon the framework of Sanchez et al. (2000) and it is made up of 101 items. Their findings reveal that IC disclosures in the annual reports of Malaysian companies are value relevant.

Similarly, in a study by Vafaei et al. (2011), IC disclosure level is assessed using a content analysis to detect the presence of 38 items. The items are derived from the framework of Brüggen et al. (2009). The study investigates companies from different countries, namely Britain, Australia, Hong Kong and Singapore. The results indicate that IC disclosure has a significant relationship with share price only in Britain and Australia and only for those companies that operate in non-traditional industries, which are supposed to have a greater intangibles intensity. The findings of this study suggest that national culture influences investors' use of IC information. Moreover, the branch of industry has an impact on the relationship between IC disclosure and share prices. This result is not surprising, since non-financial reporting practices of companies that operate in technology-intensive industries may differ significantly from companies that operate in traditional industries (Gu and Li, 2003; Oliveira et al., 2006). Uyar and Kilic (2012) have replicated this type of study in Turkish companies. They use a list of 96 items to measure IC and show that IC disclosure is value relevant.

Gamerschlag (2013) has examined the impact of human capital disclosure on share prices in Germany using a framework by Moller et al. (2011). They develop a list of 27 keywords that should reflect IC elements. The study does not consider IC as a whole, but only one of its main dimensions. The analysis yields a positive and significant association between human capital disclosure and market prices.

The findings of the studies on the value relevance of IC disclosure indicate that IC disclosure generally has a positive and significant relationship with share prices. This result suggests that investors value IC in their investment decisions, and supports the view that improved disclosure of intangibles may provide users with information that complements financial measures. Results of existing studies also show how the importance attributed to IC by investors is influenced by contingent factors, such as industry or country characteristics.

ADVANTAGES AND DISADVANTAGES OF IC DISCLOSURE VALUE RELEVANCE STUDIES

Price-level models represent a useful empirical investigation tool for the assessment of IC disclosure value relevance. This approach allows researchers to verify whether investors value IC narrative disclosure and offers empirical evidence about the consequences of different levels of IC disclosure. At the same time, this approach suffers from some limitations. The limitations of this method depend on the use of content analysis, the conceptual frameworks that are used to measure IC and, to some extent, the assumptions at the basis of the Ohlson model. This section deals with the main advantages and disadvantages of such an approach and possible further developments of this strand of research.

The Usefulness of Examining IC Value Relevance

While IC is considered the primary source of value in modern economies and its disclosure is deemed to have a primary role in offering valuable information to investors and stakeholders, value relevance studies provide empirical evidence that supports this view. IC value relevance studies draw upon the most important and widely used IC frameworks to assess disclosure. Most studies show that investors take into account the constitutive elements of the main frameworks developed by researchers (for example, Sveiby, 1997; Sanchez et al., 2000; Abeysekera, 2007; Brüggen et al., 2009). The findings also suggest that the frameworks used in the IC value relevance literature can be effective tools to structure IC disclosure.

Research on the value relevance of IC disclosure also broadens the literature on the value relevance of intangibles. In fact, many studies have reported the value relevance of different non-financial items, such as R&D (Hirschey, 1982; Doukas and Switzer, 1992; Lev and Sougiannis, 1996; Ballester et al., 2003), brands (Barth et al., 1998; Barth and Clinch, 1998; Seethamraju, 2003), customer-related measures (Bonacchi et al., 2015) or sustainability information (Carnevale and Mazzucca, 2014). The investigation of IC narrative adds a new perspective to the investigation of the relevance of non-financial disclosures.

The Limitations of IC Value Relevance Studies

Research on IC value relevance faces three main methodological issues and limitations:

1. the use of content analysis to measure IC disclosure;
2. the way IC disclosure indexes are built; and
3. the assumptions at the basis of price-level models.

Using content analysis to measure IC disclosure

The content analysis techniques used by accounting scholars to date show some critical aspects related to the level of reliability and to the use of previously defined IC theoretical frameworks. The reliability issue is grounded in the degree of subjectivity that characterizes the coding procedure (Deegan and Rankin, 1996; Frost and Wilmshurst, 2000). Beattie and Thomson (2007) identify some crucial aspects of IC content analysis which may affect coding reliability: concept boundary problems, the lack of transparency by the authors and the different unit of analysis chosen by researchers.

The concept boundary issue may arise when the researcher decides on the classification of a description to one of the IC elements identified by a framework (Steenkamp and Northcott, 2007). This decision is affected by the reader's subjectivity. For this reason, coding categories and coding rules must be carefully defined and specified by researchers. In order to demonstrate procedure reliability, the use of multiple coders is recommended (Beattie and Thomson, 2007). Having different researchers, who read the same text and obtain similar results, can increase the reliability of the coding procedure and help to overcome this limitation.

Here the second problem emerges: transparency by researchers. Many authors, who investigate IC narrative by means of content analysis, do not clearly provide definitions of the categories used and do not address the problem of coding reliability (Anam et al., 2011). In some cases (Abeysekera, 2011), researchers declare that multiple coders have undertaken content analysis of the documents, but do not show the results of reliability tests. One of the few exceptions is the work by Bozzolan et al. (2003).

The different units of analysis used by researchers represents another major problem in IC content analysis. Possible units of analysis in IC disclosure investigation are words (Vafaei et al., 2011; Gamerschlag, 2013), sentences (Bozzolan et al., 2003) and text-units (Beattie et al., 2004). In some studies (Anam et al., 2011), the unit of analysis is not well specified. In other cases, authors take into account not only narrative parts, but also visual representations (Abeysekera, 2011). The different choices may hinder comparability of different studies.

IC theoretical frameworks also pose a challenge for content analysis. Researchers usually draw upon established frameworks to define IC elements and then make a list of items out of this definition process. IC disclosure is assessed on the basis of the presence or absence of descriptions related to each of the elements identified. This method allows researchers to ground their empirical investigation in a theoretical framework. At the same time, this method has some limitations. The use of different frameworks for disclosure assessment decreases comparability among the findings of different studies.

In addition, the most well-known frameworks refer to the three main categories of IC, namely human, structural and relational capital. This classification does not take into account a new emerging dimension of IC, the so-called 'connectivity capital' (Habersam and Piber, 2003; Bjurström and Roberts, 2007). The connectivity capital acts as the element that links the other three types of IC (Habersam and Piber, 2003). So far, researchers in the field of IC have not taken into account this fourth dimension in the assessment of IC disclosure. This can be viewed as a limitation, since the interaction between the different types of capital is a crucial aspect of value creation (Taug, 2004; IIRC, 2013).

Following a top-down approach, IC disclosure assessment is based on a predefined framework, which is taken as a reference for all the companies in the study. Applying lists of items that are derived from an IC framework, scholars implicitly assume that all the items have the same importance for all the companies under scrutiny. This assumption is not realistic. In fact, each company relies on a different set of intangible resources (Hamel, 2000; Amit and Zott, 2001). Even within a single industry, companies very often base their competitive advantage on different business concepts (Hamel, 2000).

According to this view, intangible resources alone cannot provide a company with a strong and sustainable competitive advantage (Bukh, 2003). The unique value of a company lies in the way those intangible resources are managed and combined, that is, a company's business model (BM) (Bukh, 2003; Nielsen, 2010; Nielsen and Bukh, 2011). The BM describes how a company combines its know-how and resources to deliver the value proposition (Casadesus-Masanell and Ricart, 2010). Companies with different BMs have different value generation models and different value drivers.

Some scholars maintain that, in order for IC disclosure to be meaningful, IC information should be disclosed within the framework represented by the company's BM (Bukh, 2003; Bini et al., 2016). BM disclosure is supposed to provide context for non-financial information in general, and IC in particular (Holland, 2004; Beattie and Smith, 2013; FRC, 2014; EC, 2017). In other words, investors are able to understand the importance of intangible resources for a company only if they know what the BM is.

In this respect, IC can be viewed as having two components: a 'static' component and a 'dynamic' one. The former is represented by stocks of intangible resources. The latter aspect is related to the activities aimed at allocating existing resources and acquiring new ones (Meritum Report, 2002; Beattie and Thomson, 2007; Chiucchi, 2013). Knowing a company's BM allows researchers to take into account the dynamic dimension of IC (Nielsen et al., 2009). The BM itself can be considered as an aspect of the fourth dimension of IC, namely the connectivity capital (Bini et al., 2016). At the same time, BM communication contributes to IC generation (Osterwalder et al., 2005; Bini et al., 2016). To the knowledge of the authors, only Bini et al. (2016) have assessed companies' IC disclosure 'in action', based on the framework provided by the BM.

Dumay and Garanina (2013) criticize the heavy use of theoretical frameworks in the second stage of IC research, and point out the limitations of IC investigations undertaken on the basis of a predefined framework, which does not take into account the different value generation models that characterize companies. This scepticism derives from the use of theories that are not empirically proven. The extensive use of existing frameworks and models is directly related to their popularity. This may represent a potential obstacle to the third stage of IC research, as scholars may find it easier to use already existing frameworks.

Building IC disclosure indexes

The second main limitation of studies that deal with IC disclosure value relevance refers to the disclosure indexes that are used by scholars to assess IC disclosure, specifically scope indexes that capture how many of the elements in a predefined list are disclosed. Each item is assigned a score equal to 1 if disclosed, 0 otherwise. The implicit assumption is that the quantity of disclosure reflects its quality (Botosan, 1997; Lang and Lundholm, 2000). Disclosure quality is a complex concept that is related to several different aspects (Beattie et al., 2004). When researchers assign the same score to each component, they are not taking into account some aspects that can determine disclosure quality. First, all elements are assigned the same value; however, some intangibles may be more valuable than others for a certain company. Again, the different value creation models that characterize different companies are ignored. In addition to this, pieces of text are coded only on the basis of the topic. Characteristics such as time orientation, financial orientation and extension of disclosure – the amount of information disclosed for each item – are not considered (Beattie et al., 2004).

The assumptions behind price-level models

The third main limitation is related to the assumptions behind price-level models that are derived from Ohlson's (1995) work. This limitation characterizes not only IC research, but all value relevance studies that rely on share price dynamics in financial accounting.

Price-level models assume that financial markets are efficient: market prices reflect all publicly available information (Fama, 1970). This assumption has been widely criticized by different authors in the fields of accounting and finance (see Shleifer and Vishny, 1997; Koonce, 2001; Farmer et al., 2012). The Ohlson (1995) model also imposes a particular structure on the abnormal earnings process and other information. For these reasons, some authors claim that the models derived from the one developed by Ohlson (1995) are built on unrealistic assumptions (Kothari, 2001).

Another feature that has been criticized is the linearity of the relationship between share prices and the two main variables, namely the book value and earnings. In his extensive review of capital markets literature in accounting, Kothari (2001) explains that some authors have tested Ohlson's (1995) linear valuation model using different approaches (Myers, 1999; Hand and Landsman, 1998, 1999). Their findings are not consistent with the linear information dynamics. The author also addresses the issue of the autoregressive structure of Ohlson's (1995) model when he states: 'While an autoregressive process in residual income as a parsimonious description is economically intuitive, there is nothing in economic theory to suggest that all firms' residual earnings will follow an autoregressive process at all stages in their life cycle' (Kothari, 2001, p. 181).

IMPROVING IC DISCLOSURE VALUE RELEVANCE ASSESSMENT: AVENUES FOR FUTURE RESEARCH

The previous section has discussed the main limitations of IC disclosure value relevance studies. The present section discusses possible ways to refine and improve IC disclosure value relevance assessment. These suggestions for future research are based on prior literature; in particular, work that has tried to overcome the above-mentioned methodological limitations.

Content Analysis of IC Narrative: Potential Developments

As previously discussed, a major problem of the application of content analysis to study IC narratives is represented by the lack of transparency about the coding procedure (Beattie and Thomson, 2007). In order for the results of the content analysis to be reliable, the researchers should clearly define the coding categories. Sound examples of the coding procedure should be provided. Multiple coders are necessary in order to reduce subjectivity (Beattie and Thomson, 2007).

Consistency in the results obtained by different coders should be demonstrated. In this respect, agreement levels based on measures such as Scott's pi (Krippendorff, 1980) can be reported. The choice of the unit of analysis should be disclosed and justified as well (Beattie and Thomson, 2007). An example of a detailed description of IC content analysis procedure can be found in Bozzolan et al. (2003). In the section dedicated to methodology, the authors address the issue of coding reliability. They provide explanatory notes and examples for each coding category. Multiple coders who analysed the same reports at different points in time have been used, and Krippendorff's alpha coefficient has been calculated to account for reproducibility. The coefficients are reported in the paper.

Another crucial aspect is the development of the list of items that is used to assess disclosure. The items are usually drawn from popular IC frameworks (Dumay and Garanina, 2013). Each item is coded as present or absent. This choice does not allow researchers to take into account the relationships among different IC elements and the different value creation models. Drawing from the research in the field of social and environmental disclosure (Toms, 2002; Hasseldine et al., 2005), Guthrie and Abeysekera (2006) propose to combine content analysis with other methods to overcome this limitation and draw a hierarchy of the IC items. In particular, surveys and semi-structured interviews may help define what aspects of IC are considered the most important for a company. Once the crucial aspects have been defined, it is possible to weigh the different items on the basis of the hierarchy that develops from the interviews (Abeysekera and Guthrie, 2004a, 2004b, 2005).

A further refinement of IC disclosure assessment is represented by the use of the BM as a framework for non-financial disclosure (Bukh, 2003; Nielsen et al., 2009; Bini et al., 2016). As the BM offers a simplified representation of the company's activities and value generation model (Nielsen, 2010), it also allows a better understanding of the role of different intangible resources in value generation. Future studies could assess IC disclosure taking into account the different BM configurations. This could be done by applying a framework for BM disclosure in content analysis. Bini et al. (2016) assess the ways companies make use of BM disclosure to highlight the contribution of IC to value creation. To analyse a company's IC disclosure, the authors use the BM ontology developed by Osterwalder et al. (2005).

Future studies may also consider the opportunity to classify companies according to their BM configuration using one of the existing frameworks. Taran et al. (2016) have developed a taxonomy of BM. This taxonomy is based on an extensive analysis of potential definitions of BM presented in the literature and has produced 71 configurations of BM. The taxonomy focuses on value drivers, that is, all the factors that contribute to the achievement of a company's unique competitive advantage.

Classifying companies on the basis of the BM allows researchers to identify the main value drivers of each company (Nielsen et al., 2017). As this kind of classification scheme offers a picture of the main factors that generate value, researchers might weigh IC items disclosed by companies on the basis of their role in the value creation process.

Including Qualitative Aspects in IC Disclosure Indexes

The second critical aspect of the measurement of IC disclosure value relevance is related to a disclosure index that goes beyond the scope of disclosure. This concern emerges from the different levels of importance assigned to different disclosure by companies (Coy et al., 2001; Ryan et al., 2002). Several authors have tried to build disclosure indexes with the aim to include qualitative features of disclosure. To tell 'general rhetoric' disclosure from 'specific endeavour', Toms (2002) and Hasseldine et al. (2005) have built disclosure indexes for social and environmental disclosures that address the degree of specification of information disclosed. The authors assign greater scores to companies that disclose information about specific policies, targets and results, respectively.

Beattie et al. (2004) propose a measure that takes into account not only the amount, but also the spread of disclosure among the different topics identified. Beretta and Bozzolan (2008) have tried to capture both the quantity and the quality of forward-looking information by resorting to two indexes: a relative quality index and a richness index. The former is based on the difference between actual and expected disclosure amounts. The difference is assessed using a standardized residual from an OLS regression, where size and industry are independent variables. The richness index takes into account many aspects: the coverage and the dispersion of disclosure, the type and economic sign of a measure, and the outlook profile (actual state of the business, management's expectations, planned actions, actions already taken). The disclosure quality index is calculated as the average between the two indexes.

Finally, some authors have tried to take presentation format into account. In their work on performance indicator disclosure, Bini et al. (2017) identify six presentation attributes: data source (reconciliation with financial statements), the presence of amount from the previous year, peer or sector benchmarks, the presence of graphs, an explicit link to strategic aims and the quantification of future targets.

Future studies that address the value relevance of IC disclosure should pay greater attention to qualitative aspects of the disclosure index. Richness and forward-looking orientation of disclosure (Beretta and Bozzolan, 2008), spread among different sub-topics (Beattie et al., 2004) and presentation formats (Bini et al., 2017), could be applied to IC disclosure assessment. The indexes proposed by Beretta and Bozzolan (2008) and Beattie et al. (2004) are designed for narrative and can be easily adapted to IC disclosure. While not all the presentation features identified by Bini et al. (2017) can be used to assess narrative, some aspects could be adapted to IC disclosure investigation. In particular, the presence of graphs or tables can be considered. In fact, visual representations can support disclosure by providing an immediate understanding of the relationship between intangible elements (Beattie and Jones, 1992, 2008). Thus, IC disclosure assessment could take into account the presence of visual representations of IC, as in the case of Abeysekera (2011). The communication of future targets can also be adapted to IC. In this perspective, the presence of forward-looking information should be considered, such as in Beretta and Bozzolan (2008).

As already emphasized in the discussion about coding procedures in content analysis, the assessment of IC disclosure should take into account a company's underlying BM (Bini et al., 2016). Therefore, the IC disclosure index could consider the role of each element in value generation. A hierarchy of IC elements could be developed for each company according to its BM configuration (Taran et al., 2016; Nielsen et al., 2017). Then, different scores can be attributed to the items on the basis of the BM.

Assessing IC Value Relevance: The Role of Financial Analysts

The limitations that affect price-level models may lead to the adoption of different approaches to evaluate the importance of a piece of information in investment decisions. An alternative way to examine the relevance of an item is to look at sell-side financial analysts. Financial analysts are considered the best proxy for investors, as they are qualified individuals who make investment recommendations on the basis of a formalized company valuation process (Anderson, 1988).

Three types of analyses can be run in order to understand whether IC disclosure impinges on financial analysts' decision-making processes: the examination of the contents included in analyst reports by means of a comparative approach (Previts et al., 1994; Breton and Taffler, 2001;

Premti et al., 2017); case studies and interviews with analysts (Johansson, 2007; Sakakibara et al., 2010; Bukh and Nielsen, 2011); and the assessment of a relationship between disclosure levels and analyst forecast errors (Lang and Lundholm, 1996; Hope, 2003; Vanstraelen et al., 2003; Dhaliwal et al., 2012).

Some scholars have investigated the use of IC information by analysts by means of the examination of analyst reports (Flöstrand, 2006; García-Meca and Martínez, 2007; Nielsen, 2008; Abhayawansa and Guthrie, 2014). This research shows mixed results. Flöstrand (2006) and Abhayawansa and Guthrie (2014) find that analysts make extensive use of IC information. García-Meca and Martínez (2007) find that only some kinds of IC information are used by analysts, and firm profitability and growth opportunities affect analysts' behaviour. Finally, Nielsen (2008) finds that the amount of information about IC in analyst reports is low.

Abhayawansa (2011) has tried to develop a framework for content analysis of analyst reports. He recommends considering only initial coverage reports, and provides a categorization scheme that considers different aspects of disclosure (topic, type of information, time orientation, news-tenor). A detailed description of the coding categories and the procedure and multiple coders are also suggested to ensure reliability. Sakakibara et al. (2010) and Bukh and Nielsen (2011) use case studies and interviews with analysts to investigate the usefulness of IC information. Sakakibara et al. (2010) interview analysts with a focus on IC. Bukh and Nielsen (2011) conduct a case study on a single company. They interview analysts who follow the company, the senior managers of the company and the fund managers who represent major stockholders. The interview topics include, but are not limited to, IC. Both studies show that analysts have an interest in IC elements. At the same time, both studies support the view that non-financial disclosure in the annual report does not provide analysts with sufficient information about intangibles. Thus, other channels become fundamental tools to convey IC information.

The third approach aims at assessing the effects of disclosure on analyst forecasting. The only study that examines the effects of IC disclosure on analyst forecasts is the work by Hsu and Chang (2011). The authors measure the impact of IC disclosure on analyst forecast errors and dispersion for companies operating in the high-tech industry in Taiwan.

Forecast error is defined as the absolute difference between actual future earnings and mean analyst forecast of earnings for a year, deflated by the stock price at the beginning of the same year. Forecast dispersion is defined as the standard deviation of forecast, deflated by the stock price at the beginning of the year. The results of the study show that a higher amount of IC disclosure is associated with lower forecast errors and lower dispersion.

The research methods that involve financial analysts suffer from some of the limitations of the methods discussed in the main section. The analysis of the impact of IC disclosure on analyst forecasts requires the development of an IC index, which is problematic in similar ways to the content analysis of annual reports, namely in terms of coding category boundary issues, reliability issues and transparency issues.

However, these methods can be used to reinforce the value relevance analyses based on price-level models. Price-level models can be complemented by the investigation of analyst perceptions or analyst forecasts. Future studies may combine different methods to obtain stronger and more reliable results.

CONCLUSIONS

This chapter examined the use of price-level models, derived from the Ohlson (1995) model, for assessing the relevance of IC disclosure. Studies that rely on this method can be considered as a part of the second phase of IC investigation (Dumay and Garanina, 2013), since they apply existing frameworks to empirically investigate IC.

As IC is believed to represent the main source of value creation for companies, the disclosure of information about IC elements is supposed to be of value to investors. Most of the empirical studies that apply the framework described here to assess IC value relevance have found a positive and significant impact of IC disclosure on share prices. These results support the view that investors use IC information in their valuation processes. Thus, this strand of research contributes to the literature on IC. It also strengthens previous literature, which claims that financial measures alone are no longer able to explain and measure the value of a stock (for example, Amir and Lev, 1996; Francis and Schipper, 1999; Lev and Zarowin, 1999).

While this kind of study can add value to IC empirical research, much has to be done to complete the transition from the second to the third stage of IC investigation. In the third stage, researchers go into the organizations in order to assess how intangible resources generate value. Nevertheless, Dumay and Garanina (2013) identify a potential 'evolutionary trap' in IC research. This trap relates to the fact that scholars argue that IC is the main driver of a company's value on the basis of a number of assumptions, some of which can be contested.

The assumptions that can be questioned in IC value relevance assessment relate to the validity of the different frameworks used to gauge IC disclosure in corporate documents and the efficiency of capital markets. Other issues that represent limitations of this method are the reliability and the transparency of content analysis (see Beattie and Thomson, 2007), and the development of a proper IC disclosure index. Disclosure indexes, in fact, should include not only quantitative but also qualitative aspects of disclosure (Beattie et al., 2004; Hasseldine et al., 2005; Beretta and Bozzolan, 2008).

We have proposed some possible solutions to these problems, which can be considered for future research. First of all, in order to ensure reliability of the content analysis, coding categories and procedures need to be reported and explained (Beattie and Thomson, 2007). Other methods, such as semi-structured interviews, could be adopted to complement content analysis in IC disclosure assessment (Guthrie and Abeysekera, 2006).

Future studies could assess disclosure of intangibles taking into account the different role played by different intangible resources in the value creation process. In this way, research should focus on the BM that characterizes each company, as IC and BM disclosure are intertwined (Nielsen et al., 2009; Bini et al., 2016). In this respect, IC items could be classified according to their relationship with some BM classification schemes, such as the framework proposed by Osterwalder et al. (2005) or the Five-V framework (Taran et al., 2016; Nielsen et al., 2017). The latter framework can be used to define the company's BM configuration (Taran et al., 2016; Nielsen et al., 2017) and examine disclosure in light of the different value generation processes that characterize each configuration.

Third, the development of disclosure indexes should take into account qualitative aspects of disclosure. Possible solutions are represented by the different weight assigned to the disclosed items on the basis of attributes such as coverage, tone, forward-looking orientation (Beretta and Bozzolan, 2008), sub-topics covered (Beattie et al., 2004), and presentation format (Bini et al., 2017).

Finally, other approaches could be used to investigate the value relevance of IC disclosures. In accounting studies, financial analysts are considered the main proxy for investors. Analysts make investment recommendations on the basis of formalized decision processes that rely on a structured information search (Anderson, 1988). For this reason, many studies focus on financial analysts to assess whether a piece of information is useful (Kelly and Ljungqvist, 2012; Brown et al., 2015). In this respect, financial analysts' forecasts could be examined in order to verify whether better IC disclosure can reduce analyst forecast errors (Hsu and Chang, 2011). The investigation of analyst reports (García-Meca and Martínez, 2007; Nielsen, 2008) and interviews with analysts (Sakakibara et al., 2010; Bukh and Nielsen, 2011) can be used to strengthen this kind of analysis.

REFERENCES

Abeysekera, I. (2007), 'Intellectual capital reporting differences between a developing and developed nation', *Journal of Intellectual Capital*, 8 (2), 329–345.

Abeysekera, I. (2011), 'The relation of intellectual capital disclosure strategies and market value in two political settings', *Journal of Intellectual Capital*, 12 (2), 319–338.

Abeysekera, I. and J. Guthrie (2002), 'An updated review of literature on intellectual capital reporting', accessed 13 February 2020 at https://papers.ssrn.com/sol3/papers.cfm?abstract_id=1362158.

Abeysekera, I. and J. Guthrie (2004a), 'How is intellectual capital being reporting in a developing nation?', *Research in Accounting in Emerging Economies*, 2, 149–165.

Abeysekera, I. and J. Guthrie (2004b), 'Human capital reporting in a developing nation: an analysis of practice', *British Accounting Review*, 36 (3), 251–268.

Abeysekera, I. and J. Guthrie (2005), 'An empirical investigation of annual reporting trends of intellectual capital in Sri Lanka', *Critical Perspectives on Accounting*, 16 (3), 151–163.

Abhayawansa, S. (2011), 'A methodology for investigating intellectual capital information in analyst reports', *Journal of Intellectual Capital*, 12 (3), 446–476.

Abhayawansa, S. and J. Guthrie (2014), 'Importance of intellectual capital information: a study of Australian analyst reports', *Australian Accounting Review*, 24 (1), 66–83.

AIMR (2002), *What Analysts and Investors Want*, Investor Relations Guide.

Alwert, K., Bornemann, M. and M. Will (2009), 'Does intellectual capital reporting matter to financial analysts?', *Journal of Intellectual Capital*, 10 (3), 354–368.

American Institute of Certified Public Accountants (AICPA) (1994), *Improving Business Reporting – A Customer Focus*, Special Committee on Financial Reporting, New York: AICPA.

Amir, E. and B. Lev (1996), 'Value-relevance of nonfinancial information: the wireless communications industry', *Journal of Accounting and Economics*, 22 (1–3), 3–30.

Amit, R. and C. Zott (2001), 'Value creation in e-business', *Strategic Management Journal*, 22 (6–7), 493–520.

Anam, O.A., Fatima, A.H. and A.R.H. Majdi (2011), 'Effects of intellectual capital information disclosed in annual reports on market capitalization', *Journal of Human Resource Costing and Accounting*, 15 (2), 85–101.

Anderson, M.J. (1988), 'A comparative analysis of information search and evaluation behaviour of professional and non-professional financial analysts', *Accounting, Organizations and Society*, 13 (5), 431–446.

Arvidsson, S. (2003), 'The extent of disclosure on intangibles in annual reports', paper presented at the 4th Annual SNEE Congress in Mölle.

Austin, D.H. (1993), 'An event-study approach to measuring innovative output: the case of biotechnology', *American Economic Review*, 83 (2), 253–258.

Baboukardos, D. and G. Rimmel (2016), 'Value relevance of accounting information under an integrated reporting approach: a research note', *Journal of Accounting and Public Policy*, 35, 437–452.

Ball, R. and P. Brown (1968), 'An empirical evaluation of accounting income numbers', *Journal of Accounting Research*, 6 (2), 159–178.

Ballester, M., Garcia-Ayuso, M. and J. Livnat (2003), 'The economic value of the R&D intangible asset', *European Accounting Review*, 12 (4), 605–633.

Barth, M.E. (2000), 'Valuation-based accounting research: implications for financial reporting and opportunities for future research', *Accounting and Finance*, 40 (1), 7–32.

Barth, M.E., Beaver, W.H. and W.R. Landsman (1998), 'Relative valuation roles of equity book value and net income as a function of financial health', *Journal of Accounting and Economics*, 25 (1), 1–34.

Barth, M.E., Beaver, W.H. and W.R. Landsman (2001), 'The relevance of the value relevance literature for financial accounting standard setting: another view', *Journal of Accounting and Economics*, 31 (1–3), 77–104.

Barth, M.E. and G. Clinch (1998), 'Revalued financial, tangible, and intangible assets: associations with share prices and non-market-based value estimates', *Journal of Accounting Research*, 36, 199–233.

Beattie, V. and M.J. Jones (1992), 'The use and abuse of graphs in annual reports: theoretical framework and empirical study', *Accounting and Business Research*, 22 (88), 291–303.

Beattie, V. and M.J. Jones (2008), 'Corporate reporting using graphs: a review and synthesis', *Journal of Accounting Literature*, 27, 71–110.

Beattie, V., McInnes, B. and S. Fearnley (2004), 'A methodology for analysing and evaluating narratives in annual reports: a comprehensive descriptive profile and metrics for disclosure quality attributes', *Accounting Forum*, 28 (3), 205–236.

Beattie, V. and S.J. Smith (2013), 'Value creation and business models: refocusing the intellectual capital debate', *British Accounting Review*, 45 (4), 243–254.

Beattie, V. and S.J. Thomson (2007), 'Lifting the lid on the use of content analysis to investigate intellectual capital disclosures', *Accounting Forum*, 31 (2), 129–163.

Beretta, S. and S. Bozzolan (2008), 'Quality versus quantity: the case of forward-looking disclosure', *Journal of Accounting, Auditing and Finance*, 23 (3), 333–376.

Bini, L., Dainelli, F. and F. Giunta (2016), 'Business model disclosure in the Strategic Report: entangling intellectual capital in value creation process', *Journal of Intellectual Capital*, 17 (1), 83–102.

Bini, L., Dainelli, F. and F. Giunta (2017), 'Is a loosely specified regulatory intervention effective in disciplining management commentary? The case of performance indicator disclosure', *Journal of Management and Governance*, 21 (1), 63–91.

Bjurström, E. and H. Roberts (2007), 'The principle of connectivity: networked assets, strategic capabilities and bundled outcomes', in Cristina Chaminade and Bino Catasús (eds), *Intellectual Capital Revisited: Paradoxes in the Knowledge Intensive Organization*, Cheltenham, UK and Northampton, MA, USA: Edward Elgar Publishing, pp. 45–60.

Bonacchi, M., Kolev, K. and B. Lev (2015), 'Customer franchise – a hidden, yet crucial, asset', *Contemporary Accounting Research*, 32 (3), 1024–1049.

Bontis, N. (2001), 'Assessing knowledge assets: a review of the models used to measure intellectual capital', *International Journal of Management Reviews*, 3 (1), 41–60.

Bontis, N. (2003), 'Intellectual capital disclosure in Canadian corporations', *Journal of Intellectual Capital*, 7 (1), 9–20.

Botosan, C.A. (1997), 'Disclosure level and the cost of equity capital', *Accounting Review*, 72, 323–349.

Botosan, C.A. and M.A. Plumlee (2002), 'A re-examination of disclosure level and the expected cost of equity capital', *Journal of Accounting Research*, 40 (1), 21–40.

Bozzolan, S., Favotto, F. and F. Ricceri (2003), 'Italian annual intellectual capital disclosure: an empirical analysis', *Journal of Intellectual Capital*, 4 (4), 543–558.

Brooking, A. (1997), 'The management of intellectual capital', *Long Range Planning*, 30 (3), 364–365.

Brennan, N. (2001), 'Reporting intellectual capital in annual reports: evidence from Ireland', *Accounting, Auditing and Accountability Journal*, 14 (4), 423–436.

Breton, G. and R.J. Taffler (2001), 'Accounting information and analyst stock recommendation decisions: a content analysis approach', *Accounting and Business Research*, 31 (2), 91–101.

Brown, L.D., Call, A.C., Clement, M.B. and N.Y. Sharp (2015), 'Inside the "black box" of sell-side financial analysts', *Journal of Accounting Research*, 53 (1), 1–47.

Brüggen, A., Vergauwen, P. and M. Dao (2009), 'Determinants of intellectual capital disclosure: evidence from Australia', *Management Decision*, 47, 233–245.

Bryman, A. and E. Bell (2015), *Business Research Methods*, New York: Oxford University Press.

Bukh, P.N. (2003), 'The relevance of intellectual capital disclosure: a paradox?', *Accounting, Auditing and Accountability Journal*, 16 (1), 49–56.

Bukh, P.N. and C. Nielsen (2011), 'The supply and demand for strategic information: a case study of a large medical device company', *Journal of Human Resource Costing and Accounting*, 15 (1), 50–77.

Bukh, P.N., Nielsen, C., Gormsen, P. and J. Mouritsen (2005), 'Disclosure of information on intellectual capital in Danish IPO prospectuses', *Accounting, Auditing and Accountability Journal*, 18 (6), 713–732.

Carnevale, C. and M. Mazzucca (2014), 'Sustainability report and bank valuation: evidence from European stock markets', *Business Ethics: A European Review*, 23 (1), 69–90.

Casadesus-Masanell, R. and J.E. Ricart (2010), 'From strategy to business models and onto tactics', *Long Range Planning*, 43 (2–3), 195–215.

Chauvin, K.W. and M. Hirschey (1993), 'Advertising, R&D expenditures and the market value of the firm', *Financial Management*, 22 (4), 128–140.

Chiucchi, M.S. (2013), 'Intellectual capital accounting in action: enhancing learning through interventionist research', *Journal of Intellectual Capital*, 14 (1), 48–68.

Clarkson, P., Li, Y. and G.D. Richardson (2004), 'The market valuation of environmental capital expenditures by pulp and paper companies', *Accounting Review*, 79 (2), 329–353.

Coy, D., Fisher, M. and T. Gordon (2001), 'Public accountability: a new paradigm for college and university annual reports', *Critical Perspectives on Accounting*, 12 (1), 1–31.

Deegan, C. and M. Rankin (1996), 'Do Australian companies report environmental news objectively? An analysis of environmental disclosures by firms prosecuted successfully by the Environmental Protection Authority', *Accounting, Auditing and Accountability Journal*, 9 (2), 52–69.

Dhaliwal, D.S., Radhakrishnan, S., Tsang, A. and Y.G. Yang (2012), 'Nonfinancial disclosure and analyst forecast accuracy: international evidence on corporate social responsibility disclosure', *Accounting Review*, 87 (3), 723–759.

Doukas, J. and L. Switzer (1992), 'The stock market's valuation of R&D spending and market concentration', *Journal of Economics and Business*, 44 (2), 95–114.

Dumay, J.C. (2012), 'Grand theories as barriers to using IC concepts', *Journal of Intellectual Capital*, 13 (1), 4–15.

Dumay, J. and T. Garanina (2013), 'Intellectual capital research: a critical examination of the third stage', *Journal of Intellectual Capital*, 14 (1), 10–25.

Eccles, R.G. and S.C. Mavrinac (1995), 'Improving the corporate disclosure process', *Sloan Management Review*, 36 (4), 11–25.

Edvinsson, L. (1997), 'Developing intellectual capital at Skandia', *Long Range Planning*, 30 (3), 366–373.

Edvinsson, L. and M.S. Malone (1997), *Intellectual Capital: Realizing your Company's True Value by Finding its Hidden Brainpower*, New York: Harper Business.

European Commission (EC) (2017), Guidelines on non-financial information (methodology for reporting non-financial information) (2017/C 215/01).

Fama, E.F. (1970), 'Efficient capital markets: a review of theory and empirical work', *Journal of Finance*, 25 (2), 383–417.

Fama, E.F. (1991), 'Efficient capital markets: II', *Journal of Finance*, 46 (5), 1575–1617.

Farmer, J.D., Gallegati, M., Hommes, C., Kirman, A., Ormerod, P., et al. (2012), 'A complex systems approach to constructing better models for managing financial markets and the economy', *European Physical Journal Special Topics*, 214 (1), 295–324.

Feltham, G.A. and J.A. Ohlson (1995), 'Valuation and clean surplus accounting for operating and financial activities', *Contemporary Accounting Research*, 11 (2), 689–731.

Feltham, G.A. and J.A. Ohlson (1996), 'Uncertainty resolution and the theory of depreciation measurement', *Journal of Accounting Research*, 34 (2), 209–234.

Financial Accounting Standards Board (FASB) (1984), 'Statement of Financial Accounting Concepts No. 5, Recognition and measurement in financial statements of business enterprises', Stamford, CT: FASB.

Financial Accounting Standards Board (FASB) (2001), 'Statement of Financial Accounting Standard No. 142, Goodwill and intangible assets', Stamford, CT: FASB.

Flöstrand, P. (2006), 'The sell side – observations on intellectual capital indicators', *Journal of Intellectual Capital*, 7 (4), 457–473.

Francis, J. and K. Schipper (1999), 'Have financial statements lost their relevance?', *Journal of Accounting Research*, 37 (2), 319–352.

FRC (2014), 'Guidance on the strategic report', Financial Reporting Council, London, accessed 13 February 2020 at www.frc.org.uk/Our-Work/Publications/Accounting-and-Reporting-Policy/Guidance-on-the-Strategic-Report.pdf.

Frost, G. and T. Wilmshurst (2000), 'The adoption of environment related management accounting: an analysis of corporate environment sensitivity', *Accounting Forum*, 24 (4), 344–365.

Gamerschlag, R. (2013), 'Value relevance of human capital information', *Journal of Intellectual Capital*, 14 (2), 325–345.

García-Meca, E. and I. Martínez (2007), 'The use of intellectual capital information in investment decisions: an empirical study using analyst reports', *International Journal of Accounting*, 42 (1), 57–81.

Griliches, Z. (1981), 'Market value, R&D, and patents', *Economics Letters*, 7 (2), 183–187.

Gu, F. and J.Q. Li (2003), 'Disclosure of innovation activities by high-technology firms', *Asia-Pacific Journal of Accounting and Economics*, 10 (2), 143–172.

Guthrie, J. and I. Abeysekera (2006), 'Content analysis of social, environmental reporting: what is new?', *Journal of Human Resource Costing and Accounting*, 10 (2), 114–126.

Guthrie, J. and R. Petty (2000), 'Intellectual capital: Australian annual reporting practices', *Journal of Intellectual Capital*, 1 (3), 241–251.

Guthrie, J., Petty, R. and F. Ricceri (2007), *Intellectual Capital Reporting: Lessons from Hong Kong and Australia*, Edinburgh: Institute of Chartered Accountants of Scotland (ICAS).

Guthrie, J., Petty, R., Yongvanich, K. and F. Ricceri (2004), 'Using content analysis as a research method to inquire into intellectual capital reporting', *Journal of Intellectual Capital*, 5 (2), 282–293.

Guthrie, J., Ricceri, F. and J. Dumay (2012), 'Reflections and projections: a decade of intellectual capital accounting research', *British Accounting Review*, 44 (2), 68–82.

Habersam, M. and M. Piber (2003), 'Exploring intellectual capital in hospitals: two qualitative case studies in Italy and Austria', *European Accounting Review*, 12 (4), 753–779.

Hamel, G. (2000), *Leading the Revolution*, Boston, MA: Harvard Business School Press.

Hand, J. and W. Landsman (1998), 'Testing the Ohlson model: v or not v, that is the question', Working paper, University of North Carolina.

Hand, J. and W. Landsman (1999), 'The pricing of dividends in equity valuation', Working paper, University of North Carolina.

Hasseldine, J., Salama, A.I. and J.S. Toms (2005), 'Quantity versus quality: the impact of environmental disclosures on the reputations of UK Plcs', *British Accounting Review*, 37 (2), 231–248.

Hirschey, M. (1982), 'Intangible capital aspects of advertising and R&D expenditures', *Journal of Industrial Economics*, 30 (4), 375–390.

Holland, J. (2004), *Corporate Intangibles, Value Relevance, and Disclosure Content*, Edinburgh: Institute of Chartered Accountants of Scotland (ICAS).

Holland, J. and U. Johanson (2003), 'Value-relevant information on corporate intangibles – creation, use, and barriers in capital markets – "between a rock and a hard place"', *Journal of Intellectual Capital*, 4 (4), 465–486.

Hope, O. (2003), 'Disclosure practices, enforcement of accounting standards, and analysts' forecast accuracy: an international study', *Journal of Accounting Research*, 41, 235–272.

Hsu, W.H. and Y.L. Chang (2011), 'Intellectual capital and analyst forecast: evidence from the high-tech industry in Taiwan', *Applied Financial Economics*, 21 (15), 1135–1143.

IASB (2010a), *Conceptual Framework for Financial Reporting*, London: IASB.

IASB (2010b), *Management Commentary. A Framework for Presentation*, International Accounting Standards Board (IASB), accessed 14 September 2017 at http://www.ifrs.org/issued-standards/management-commentary-practice- statement/.

IIRC (2013), *The Integrated IR Framework*, International Integrated Reporting Council, London, accessed 13 February 2020 at www.theiirc.org.

Ittner, C.D. and D.F. Larcker (1998), 'Are nonfinancial measures leading indicators of financial performance? An analysis of customer satisfaction', *Journal of Accounting Research*, 36, 1–35.

Ittner, C.D., Larcker, D.F. and M.V. Rajan (1997), 'The choice of performance measures in annual bonus contracts', *Accounting Review*, 72 (2), 231–255.

Johansson, J. (2007), 'Sell-side analysts' creation of value – key roles and relational capital', *Journal of Human Resource Costing and Accounting*, 11 (1), 30–52.

Kelly, B. and A. Ljungqvist (2012), 'Testing asymmetric-information asset pricing models', *Review of Financial Studies*, 25, 1366–1413.

Knutson, P. (1992), *Financial Reporting in the 1990's and Beyond*, AIMR.

Koonce, L. (2001), 'Inefficient markets: an introduction to behavioral finance', *Accounting Review*, 76 (3), 461.

Kothari, S.P. (2001), 'Capital markets research in accounting', *Journal of Accounting and Economics*, 31 (1–3), 105–231.

Krippendorff, K. (1980), *Content Analysis: An Introduction to its Methodology*, Beverley Hills, CA: SAGE Publications.

Lang, M. and R. Lundholm (1993), 'Cross-sectional determinants of analysts ratings of corporate disclosures', *Journal of Accounting Research*, 31 (2), 246–271.

Lang, M. and R. Lundholm (1996), 'Corporate disclosure policy and analyst behavior', *Accounting Review*, 71 (4), 467–493.

Lang, M. and R. Lundholm (2000), 'Voluntary disclosure and equity offerings: reducing information asymmetry or hyping the stock?', *Contemporary Accounting Research*, 17 (4), 623662.

Lev, B. and T. Sougiannis (1996), 'The capitalization, amortization, and value-relevance of R&D', *Journal of Accounting and Economics*, 21 (1), 107–138.

Lev, B. and P. Zarowin (1999), 'The boundaries of financial reporting and how to extend them', *Journal of Accounting Research*, 37 (2), 353–385.

Meritum Report (2002), 'Guidelines for managing and reporting on intangibles', Madrid.

Moller, K., Gamerschlag, R. and F. Gunther (2011), 'Determinants and effects of human capital reporting and controlling', *Journal of Management Control*, 22 (3), 311–334.

Mouritsen, J. (2004), 'Measuring and intervening: how do we theorise intellectual capital management?', *Journal of Intellectual Capital*, 5 (2), 257–267.

Mouritsen, J., Larsen, H.T. and P.N. Bukh (2001), 'Intellectual capital and the "capable firm": narrating, visualising and numbering for managing knowledge', *Accounting, Organizations and Society*, 26 (7–8), 735–762.

Myers, J. (1999), 'Implementing residual income valuation with linear information dynamics', *Accounting Review*, 74, 1–28.

Nielsen, C. (2008), 'A content analysis of analyst research: health care through the eyes of analysts', *Journal of Health Care Finance*, 34 (3), 66–90.

Nielsen, C. (2010), 'Conceptualizing, analyzing and communicating the business model', Working Paper Series, accessed 13 February 2020 at https://www.researchgate.net/profile/Christian_Nielsen3/publication/228842227_Conceptualizing_Analyzing_and_Communicating_the_Business_Model/links/02e7e5214f40525653000000.pdf.

Nielsen, C. and P.N. Bukh (2011), 'What constitutes a business model: the perception of financial analysts', *International Journal of Learning and Intellectual Capital*, 8 (3), 256–271.

Nielsen, C., Lund, M. and P. Thomsen (2017), 'Killing the balanced scorecard to improve internal disclosure', *Journal of Intellectual Capital*, 18 (1), 45–62.

Nielsen, C., Roslender, R. and P.N. Bukh (2009), 'Intellectual capital reporting: can a strategy perspective solve accounting problems?', in M.D. Lytras (ed.), *Knowledge Ecology in Global Business: Managing Intellectual Capital*, Hershey, PA: Information Science Reference, pp. 174–191.

Ohlson, J.A. (1995), 'Earnings, book values, and dividends in equity valuation', *Contemporary Accounting Research*, 11 (2), 661–687.

Ohlson, J.A. (1999), 'On transitory earnings', *Review of Accounting Studies*, 4 (3–4), 145–162.

Ohlson, J.A. (2000), 'Residual income valuation: the problems', Working paper, New York University.

Oliveira, L., Rodrigues, L.L. and R. Craig (2006), 'Firm-specific determinants of intangibles reporting: evidence from the Portuguese stock market', *Journal of Human Resource Costing and Accounting*, 10 (1), 11–33.

Omar, I.H.J. (2008), 'Voluntary intellectual capital disclosure: evidence from Bahrain', Working paper, University of Bahrain.

Organisation for Economic Co-operation and Development (OECD) (1999), 'Guidelines and instructions for OECD Symposium', International Symposium Measuring Reporting Intellectual Capital: Experiences, Issues, and Prospects, June, Amsterdam, OECD, Paris.

Osterwalder, A., Pigneur, Y. and C.L. Tucci (2005), 'Clarifying business models: origins, present, and future of the concept', *Communications of the Association for Information Systems*, 16 (1), 1–25.

Petty, R. and J. Guthrie (2000), 'Intellectual capital literature review: measurement, reporting and management', *Journal of Intellectual Capital*, 1 (2), 155–176.

Premti, A., Garcia-Feijoo, L. and J. Madura (2017), 'Information content of analyst recommendations in the banking industry', *International Review of Financial Analysis*, 49, 35–47.

Previts, G.J., Bricker, R.J., Robinson, T.R. and S.J. Young (1994), 'A content analysis of sell-side financial analyst company reports', *Accounting Horizons*, 8 (2), 55–70.

Ricceri, F. (2008), *Intellectual Capital and Knowledge Management: Strategic Management of Knowledge Resources*, Abingdon: Routledge.

Rimmel, G., Nielsen, C. and T. Yosano (2009), 'Intellectual capital disclosures in Japanese IPO prospectuses', *Journal of Human Resource Costing and Accounting*, 13 (4), 316–337.

Roos, J., Edvinsson, L. and N.C. Dragonetti (1997), *Intellectual Capital: Navigating the New Business Landscape*, London: Springer.

Ryan, C., Stanley, T. and M. Nelson (2002), 'Accountability disclosures by Queensland Local Government Councils: 1997–1999', *Financial Accountability and Management*, 18 (3), 261–289.

Sakakibara, S., Hansson, B., Yosano, T. and H. Kozumi (2010), 'Analysts' perceptions of intellectual capital information', *Australian Accounting Review*, 20 (3), 274–285.

Sanchez, P., Canibano, L., Covarsi, M.G., Chaminade, C., Olea, M., et al. (2000), 'Guidelines for the measurement and disclosure of intangibles', Working paper, Seville: MERITUM Project.

Seethamraju, C. (2003), 'The value relevance of trademarks', in J. Hand and B. Lev (eds), *Intangible Assets: Values, Measures, and Risks*, Oxford: Oxford University Press, pp. 228–247.

Seetharaman, A., Gul, F.A. and S.G. Lynn (2002), 'Litigation risk and audit fees: evidence from UK firms cross-listed on US markets', *Journal of Accounting and Economics*, 33 (1), 91–115.

Shleifer, A. and R.W. Vishny (1997), 'The limits of arbitrage', *Journal of Finance*, 52 (1), 35–55.

Steenkamp, N. and D. Northcott (2007), 'Content analysis in accounting research: the practical challenges', *Australian Accounting Review*, 17 (43), 12–25.

Stewart, T. (1997), *The New Wealth of Organizations*, London: Nicholas Brealey.

Stober, T.L. (1999), 'Empirical applications of the Ohlson [1995] and Feltham and Ohlson [1995, 1996] valuation models', *Managerial Finance*, 25 (12), 3–16.

Sveiby, K.E. (1997), *The New Organizational Wealth: Managing and Measuring Knowledge-Based Assets*, New York: Berrett-Koehler Publishers.

Taran, Y., Nielsen, C., Montemari, M., Thomsen, P. and F. Paolone (2016), 'Business model configurations: a five-V framework to map out potential innovation routes', *European Journal of Innovation Management*, 19 (4), 492–527.

Taug, J. (2004), 'Intangibles and capital conversion in complex organizations', PhD dissertation, Fielding Graduate Institute, USA.

Toms, J.S. (2002), 'Firm resources, quality signals and the determinants of corporate environmental reputation: some UK evidence', *British Accounting Review*, 34 (3), 257–282.

Urquiza, F.B., Navarro, M.C.A. and M. Trombetta (2009), 'Disclosure indices design: does it make a difference?', *Revista de Contabilidad*, 12 (2), 253–277.
Uyar, A. and M. Kilic (2012), 'Value relevance of voluntary disclosure: evidence from Turkish firms', *Journal of Intellectual Capital*, 13 (3), 363–376.
Vafaei, A., Taylor, D. and K. Ahmed (2011), 'The value relevance of intellectual capital disclosures', *Journal of Intellectual Capital*, 12 (3), 407–429.
Vanstraelen, A., Zarzeski, M.T. and S.W.G. Robb (2003), 'Corporate nonfinancial disclosure practices and financial analyst forecast ability across three European countries', *Journal of International Financial Management and Accounting*, 14 (3), 249–278.

PART II

VISUAL METHODOLOGIES

8. Research methodologies for intellectual capital visual representations

Jan Michalak

INTRODUCTION

The visualisation of intellectual capital (IC) through diagrams, graphs, pictures and photographs has been important for understanding, managing and reporting on IC since the onset of the IC debate, prompted by the Skandia Navigator model published as early as 1994 in the supplement to the Skandia annual report (Edvinsson and Malone, 1997, pp. 52–53). Davison (2014) argues that the exploration of visuals has the potential for advancing the development of IC studies, because they:

1. are ubiquitous;
2. are multifaceted, carry complex and co-existing messages and are open to rich and varied interpretation;
3. have interwoven roles as incremental information and impression management (or representation and construction);
4. have a special place in memory and cognition; and
5. have emotional power.

Based on these characteristics, IC has the ability to facilitate transformation from invisibility or nothingness into visibility or somethingness (Mouritsen et al., 2001). With the increasing scope of their application both in traditional communication channels (annual reports, company presentations) and through more modern modes (social media), IC visualisations have emerged as a vital field of study. The methods for investigating the visual presentations of intellectual capital help answer some of the core questions asked by researchers: How does IC work in firms? What is IC composed of? How is IC related to value? (Mouritsen, 2006, p. 823). A key benefit of revisiting visual research methodologies is that they assist researchers and organisations in producing a more thorough representation of how IC functions in firms and, thereby, contribute to answering the above questions.

Despite this, studies on the graphic presentation of intellectual capital are still limited compared with the extensive research into the narrative and numerical representations of intellectual capital (Campbell and Rahman, 2010). This gap can be partly attributed to the lack of theoretical framework through which a detailed analysis of the modus operandi of the visual image could be built (Mitchell, 1994; Roque, 2005). Another reason may be limited knowledge of management researchers on methodologies for intellectual capital visual representations. Bell and Davison (2013) point out that handbooks discussing such methods in the field of management were published relatively recently (for example, Banks, 2007; Warren, 2009; Margolis and Pauwels, 2011). This chapter has been prepared to contribute to this area of IC scholarship.

The chapter is organised as follows. The next section discusses the importance of visualising IC and various methods that are used to this end, including classification trees, histograms, balanced scorecards, value creation maps, the IC Navigator and the method developed by Cuganesan and Dumay (2009). The following section describes the use of visual rhetoric in IC studies. The chapter then focuses on impression management studies on IC visualisation, including those utilising the graph discrepancy index proposed by Tufte (1983). The chapter concludes with a discussion of the advantages and disadvantages of methods for studying the visualisations of intellectual capital and of their relationships with other IC research methods. It also indicates three concrete areas within IC visualisation that are worthwhile considering as future research trajectories.

IC VISUALISATION METHODS

In recent decades, organisations have realised the increasing importance of intellectual capital (see, for example, Teece, 1998; Blair and Wallman, 2001; Lev, 2004; Guthrie et al., 2012). As IC resources are intangible and therefore hard to identify, understand, describe, measure, manage and communicate to stakeholders, academia and managers use various techniques to visualise intellectual capital and its components. Findings in contemporary experimental psychology indicate several advantages associated with information visualisation. First, it reduces the amount of time needed to analyse the data (Tversky, 1974). Second, pictures are a simple way of delivering complex messages (Anderson, 1980). Third, a lucid visual structure facilitates proper understanding of information (Spoehr and Lehmkuhle, 1982).

Skandia is one of the companies that have pioneered the use of the intellectual capital concept for management and dialogue with stakeholders (Edvinsson and Malone, 1997), including the frequent application of images to enhance the supplements to its annual financial statements.

Two visualisations of Skandia's intellectual capital that have been widely publicised through these supplements are Skandia's Forms of Capital (Figure 8.1) and Skandia's Navigator (Figure 8.2).

The first visualisation is a relatively simple structural diagram showing the components of market capital and the hierarchical dependencies between them. Diagrams have also been used to depict other variants of intellectual capital structure (for example, the tripartite model; see Guthrie and Petty, 2000) or to present more in detail the sub-elements of a given type of intellectual capital (Henry, 2013).

The second visualisation, Skandia's Navigator diagram, is less explicit and more open to competing interpretations. Mouritsen et al. (2001) have observed that 'the sketch is ambiguous, as is not really obvious whether to be read from the top or from the bottom. The navigator is another sketch which "provides a more balanced, overall picture of operations – a balance between the past (financial focus), the present (customer focus, process focus and human focus) and the future (renewal and development)" (Skandia, 1988, p. 5)'. It is a sketch that promises a new business-planning mode where future planning is integrated with the concerns of yesterday and today. The metaphor of the dolphin with its intelligence, sensitivity

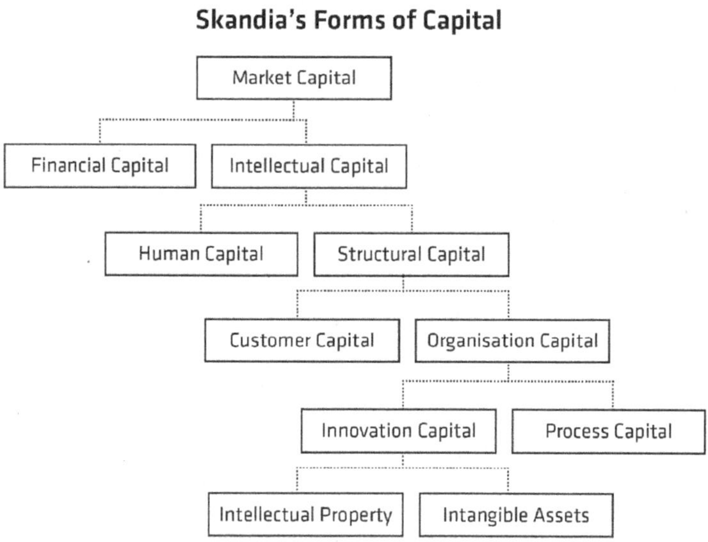

Source: Adapted from Skandia (1995).

Figure 8.1 Skandia's forms of capital

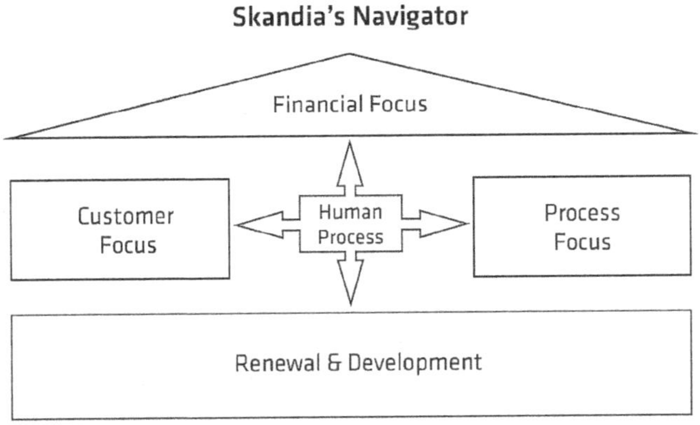

Source: Adapted from Skandia (1995).

Figure 8.2 Skandia's Navigator

and versatility supports this software being named after this mammal (Mouritsen et al., 2001).

The observation well illustrates the fact that diagrams can be understood in a broad and ambiguous way. Diagrams and other types of graphic visualisations facilitating the use of metaphors and other rhetorical figures are presented in the visual rhetoric section.

In order to be able to visualise intellectual capital, particularly the way its components create value, firm managers and scholars have developed a range of methods such as strategy maps (Kaplan and Norton, 2000, 2004), value creation maps (Marr et al., 2004), the IC Navigator (Fernstrom et al., 2004; Burton et al., 2013), social network diagrams, graphs, dashboards and even methods using plain pictures.

The authors of the strategy maps method argue that the only way to determine the value of intangible assets is to assess their impact on critical business processes: 'Even though intangible assets have become major sources of competitive advantage, no tools existed to describe them and the value they can create. The main difficulty is that the value of intangible assets depends on their organizational context and a company's strategy' (Kaplan and Norton, 2000, p. 169).

They also stress that the organisation-wide understanding of the adopted strategy is crucial to successful execution and that strategy maps can improve this understanding, 'including the crucial but perplexing processes by which intangible assets will be converted into tangible outcomes' (Kaplan and Norton, 2000, p. 167). However, Norreklit (2000) criticised both the balanced scorecard and the strategy maps, especially questioning the reliability of maps of causal relationships. She has also observed that placing processes and their efficiency in the centre of strategy maps reduces the utility of strategy maps as a means of intellectual capital visualisation.

Another method for visualising IC is value creation maps proposed by Marr et al. (2004), according to whom managers using the maps should first identify the 'key value drivers' (knowledge assets that include the brand, know-how, organisational culture) and only then determine the direct and indirect dependencies between the key value drivers. The direct and indirect dependencies show relationships between organisational assets and strategy objectives, and between organisational assets, respectively. At the third stage, managers should determine whether the importance of the relationships between various organisational resources and between the identified value drivers is moderate or high. The last step involves the visualisation of value drivers as ellipses connected by arrows representing their relationships, with the size of an arrow indicating whether the importance of a relationship is deemed moderate or high.

The IC Navigator proposed by Fernstrom et al. (2004) is built on a similar concept. It, too, involves the identification of key organisational resources (including IC) by managers during workshops and individual interviews, but differs from value creation maps in that managers are requested to assess the relative importance of organisational resources for value creation, as well as the salience of interactions between resources. The IC Navigator diagram consists of circles and arrows. The size of the circle is selected to visualise the weight of an IC element for the value creation process, while the width of the arrow is a measure of the importance of transforming one resource into another.

Another sophisticated approach to IC visualisation has been developed by Cuganesan and Dumay (2009), who have proposed a two-step procedure to visualising IC. The first step involves interviews with managers in order to establish which IC components are crucial to organisational processes in their firm. In the second step, employees are asked to give at least one narrative answer to each of five questions exploring their experiences of work life. The answers are then analysed using complementary software. The software generates scatter diagrams that visualise the identified inter-dependencies and associations between IC components and thereby their structure in the organisation. Finally, maps similar to value creation maps and the IC Navigator are created. The connections between indicators representing particular IC components have double-headed arrows to mark that the nature of the connections is associative rather than causal.

Social network graphs are a visualisation method that help investigate and improve IC components deriving from social and relational capital. The graphs are constructed as knowledge maps that are instrumental in understanding and improving knowledge flows in the organisation (Liebowitz, 2005). They are also useful for predicting the likely evolution of the graphed network. A social network graph consists of nodes and interconnecting lines. The nodes stand for individuals or organisations, and the lines for the relationships between them, for example, similarities, social relations, interactions and flows (Borgatti et al., 2009). Similarities may include shared location in time and space, membership of the same clubs, participation in the same events, the same gender, and shared attitudes toward other people or ideas. Social relations encompass the degree of kinship, affections (likes, hates), friendships, other kinds of relations (rivalry, friendship) and cognitive relations (knowing about something or perceptions). As for interactions, these include talks, meetings, aids and harms. Flows may relate to information, beliefs and resources. Much of the social network research is focused on capturing how these different kinds of ties affect each other. In investigating IC with social network graphs, the analysis of the network structure is crucial. It is important to remember that the nodes in the centre of the network play a more influential role than those on its edges. In the case of enterprises, the central position of the organisation in the network is a predictor of its superior financial performance (Shipilov and Li, 2008) as well as its ability to innovate (Powell et al., 1996). Some types of network structures are more efficient in delivering their message than others.

Other forms of IC visualisation include graphs (Kok, 2007), dashboards (Marr et al., 2004; Mention and Bontis, 2013) and pictures (Davison, 2010). The graphs are a way to visualise the indices characterising IC elements and their performance. IC dashboards display multiple indicators on a single screen for all information to be monitored at a glance. They are provided with a functionality that allows the top-down (and bottom-up) exploration of the data, as well as changing display modes, selecting data and asking queries. The IC benchmarking functionality is instrumental in revealing the structure, pattern and trends in IC elements and their performance. The advantage of IC dashboards lies in their ability to promptly and effectively provide the users with up-to-date, specific information about different IC elements and their changes in time and space (Mention and Bontis, 2013).

Recent years have seen a rise in the use of the value creation process diagram created by the International Integrated Reporting Council (IIRC) (see Figure 8.3). The diagram shows how six types of input capital (including IC) turn into six kinds of outcomes through a process carried out by the organisation based on its business model comprising business activities and outputs (products, services, by-products and waste). The diagram is notable because it is widely used in integrated reporting discussions, and

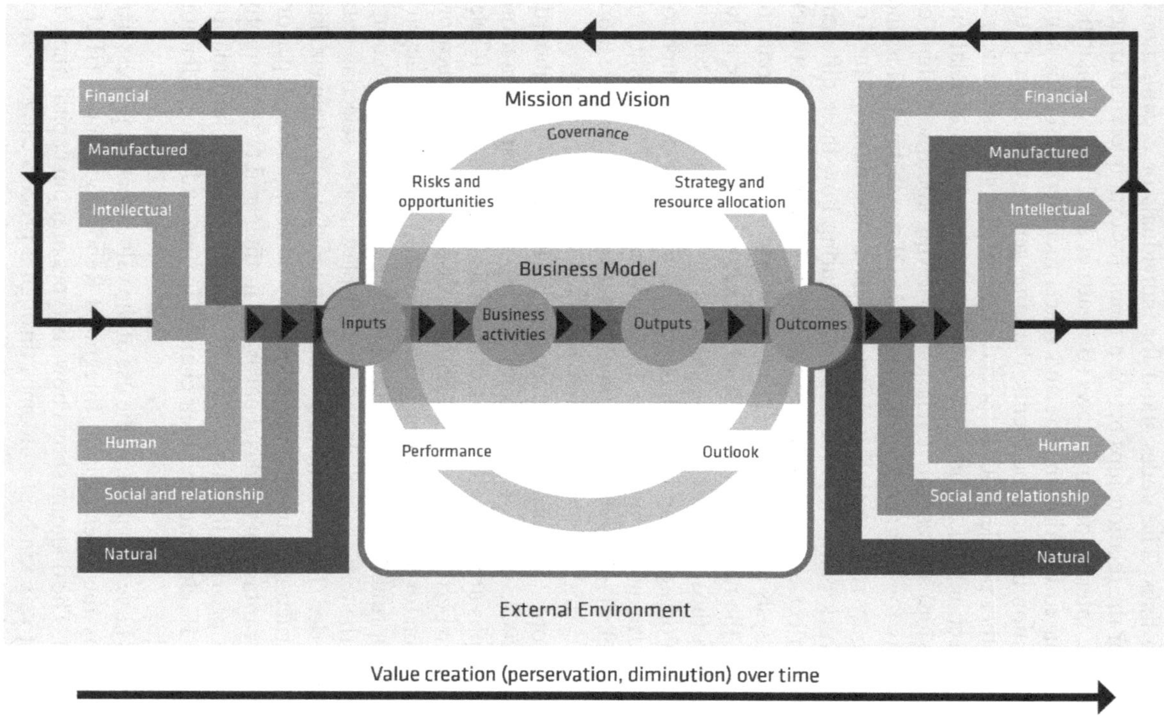

Source: IIRC (2013, p. 13).

Figure 8.3 IIRC value creation process diagram

influences the diagrams of value creation processes and IC employed by firms publishing their integrated reports (Sukhari and De Villiers, 2019; Barnabè et al., 2019).

Summing up, a whole range of IC visualisation methods exist that organisations and researchers can use to make sense of the complex relationships between IC components and thus reduce the ambiguity surrounding value creation. IC visualisations help analyse, discuss and explain how organisational IC works and how it can be developed and managed. Despite a substantial number of IC visualisation guidelines, there still seems to be a need for a critical and performative analysis of IC visualisation practices in action (Dumay et al., 2018).

IC VISUALISATIONS AND VISUAL RHETORIC STUDIES

As mentioned in the introduction, one of the main challenges in studies on visuals is a lack of general theory to draw on. Among the available theoretical approaches, visual rhetoric is most often used (Bernardi et al., 2002; Davison, 2008, 2010, 2014; Fu, 2015; De Groot et al., 2016).

Danesi (2017) has defined visual rhetoric (VR) as a:

> field of inquiry aiming to analyse all kinds of visual images and texts as rhetorical structures. VR is an offshoot of both visual semiotics, or the study of the meanings of visual signs in cultural contexts; and of the psychology of visual thinking, as opposed to verbal thinking – defined as the capacity to extract meaning from visual images.

Visual rhetoric employs the techniques of semiotics and rhetorical analysis. The focus of semiotics is on signs: all kinds of messages that convey meaning. Rhetorical analysis examines the structure and uses of figurative language (metaphors, metonymy, paradoxes, anaphors, irony and so on). The essential difference between visual rhetoric and 'traditional rhetoric' lies in the type of objects they analyse. Compared with traditional rhetoric, which focuses on texts, visual rhetoric is a means of performing critical analysis of visual messages, such as paintings, movies, ads, posters and films. Visual rhetoric scholars analyse the structure of an image (its language or visual representation) in terms of its influence or persuasive force and the rhetorical consequences embodied in answers to the following questions: Who is persuaded? How? To what end? Danesi (2017) states that 'the key insight of VR is that connotation is anchored in rhetorical structure, that is, in cognitive-associative processes such as metaphor and allusion, which are imprinted not only in verbal expressions but also in visual images'.

The basic method of visual rhetoric, traceable back to Barthes's (1964) pivotal article 'The rhetoric of the image', is to unravel the connotative meanings of visual images. In the article, Barthes separated the visual image into 'linguistic' and 'iconic' elements and concluded that the codes of the reception were not anarchic but depended on knowledge levels, which might be practical, national, cultural or aesthetic, and on attitudes. In analysing an advertisement for Panzani pasta, he noted five main connotations:

1. Freshness and domesticity – a connotation built on the half-open bag and the fresh vegetables.
2. 'Italianicity' – a connotation carried by tri-coloured hues.
3. Plentifulness – a connotation evoked by full culinary service.
4. Artistic convention of 'still-life' – a connotation recalled by the composition of the image resembling those of master paintings.
5. Advertising medium – a connotation given by the packaging labels and the caption.

The relatively extensive use of visual rhetoric in IC research is quite understandable, given that photographs are among the most common visuals used in easily available annual reports. Their number has been rising over time (Davison and Skerratt, 2007; Campbell and Rahman, 2010).

Davison (2010, 2014) used a visual rhetoric analysis of IC, based on Barthes's approach. One of her investigations involved the analysis of the photos of top managers at Thomson Reuters and Virgin Group included in the annual reports and other communications. Davison concluded that the widely available photos had the potential of conveying messages about leadership and the associated intellectual, symbolic and social intangibles. Accordingly, studying the pictures of chief executive officers (CEOs) can be useful for several reasons. First, leadership is a critical criterion in evaluating a firm's potential and its future performance. Today's top managers are celebrities who play a crucial role in creating and communicating the intellectual capital of their companies (Rindova et al., 2006). Business leaders such as Elon Musk, Richard Branson and Mark Zuckerberg are carefully listened to and watched, and their statements have an enormous impact on the image of the company in the eyes of investors and other stakeholders. Second, as IC communication shows a tendency to disregard intangibles, such as leadership, they are absent from annual reports. Davison (2010, p. 179) has observed that, 'Portraits of business leaders and their associated [in]tangibles are everywhere in business communication and increasingly in society generally, as the power of the image continues to grow, or perhaps paradoxically revert to its primitive pride of place.' The observation has recently become even more valid, with organisations increasingly focusing on media, such as Facebook, YouTube and Instagram, to communicate with their stakeholders.

Davison (2010) analysed top managers' photographs in annual reports with respect to four types of codes: physical, dress, interpersonal and spatial. Most photographs analysed were passport-style pictures presenting the manager's face and shoulders. The main physical codes (physical characteristics) included gender, age and ethnic origin. They may be perceived as hints of a CEO's leadership and risk aversion profiles. Dress codes are similarly significant signals in social communication representing social and professional status and wealth. Moreover, dress codes convey rich messages of a person's (in the case of Davison's study, business celebrities) authority, approachability and leadership style.

Interpersonal codes evoke emotions and can be communicated through facial expressions and body language. For example, innovativeness and creativity can be communicated through thoughtful facial expressions and poses (Brilliant, 1991). An example of such a pose can be found in Steve Jobs's picture in his biography by Walter Isaacson. Motivation and communication skills can be effectively suggested through outgoing gestures of the hands. The iconic elements of photos of CEOs include smiles, which traditionally communicate self-confidence and leadership qualities. Where two or more persons are shown in a picture, interpersonal codes can reveal themselves through their positions, looks and gestures. Spatial codes are communicated by the use of space (the composition of the picture) and physical artefacts, some of which – for example chairs, tables, mirrors and light sources (candles, bulbs, reflectors) – carry wide and nuanced messages. The physical artefacts with which business leaders are frequently depicted with are selected to symbolise their business; for instance, an aeroplane (Richard Branson), computer or a smartphone (Steve Jobs), or a screen (Peter Job).

Research methodologies applied to IC visuals (mostly human capital) are also used to examine gender stereotypes (Benschop and Meihuizen, 2002), gender diversity (Bernardi et al., 2002; Bujaki and McConomy, 2010) and cultural differences (De Groot et al., 2011; Fu, 2015). Fu (2015) used the codes explored by Davison (2010) to study the portraits of business leaders in corporate reports in the United Kingdom (UK), mainland China and Hong Kong. His dissertation revealed similarities between interpersonal codes, as well as some differences in dress codes and spatial codes; for example, in mainland China, dress codes were more formal and photos more frequently featured plain backgrounds.

In her other study, Davison (2014) examined pictures illustrating the selected 'soft' IC components ('brainpower', 'strategy', 'shareholder value', 'transformation', 'customers') and their interrelations in the annual reports of four firms (BAT, Gallaher, Shire Pharmaceuticals, WPP).

Her analysis of the 'soft' IC components, in terms of the rhetoric figure of repetition, resulted in the determination of four types of visual repetition: identity, similarity, accumulation and series. Identity is 'pure repetition where the repeated elements are identical – not only the shapes/colours/style, but also the people/places/things' (Davison, 2014, p. 26). According to Durand (1987), identity can help attach the connotations of fantasy and hallucination, as well as enabling the transformation of the ordinary into the extraordinary.

Similarity is a product of repetition and variation. Visual information frequently employs repetition to encourage visual reasoning involving comparison and the analysis of similarities, differences and alternatives (Tufte, 1990). Accumulation is a form of repetition where objects are often chaotically arranged and crowded together. Davison (2014) indicates that accumulation can evoke the connotations of pleasure, exuberance and obsession.

The last type of repetition is series. In the case of series, repetition is linked with time to add a temporal and narrative dimension to visuals (pictures and photographs). Series may convey various connotations depending on the number, type and repetition time intervals in the series. Davison (2014) found different types of repetition in the parts of company reports relating to the 'soft' IC components. In the Gallaher annual report, the description of the strategy was enhanced by a picture of cigarette packets on the chessboard. The picture delivers multiple messages at the symbolic level. The game of chess is associated with strategy and competition. Packets of cigarettes as chess pieces emphasise the importance of strategy and brands as the centrepieces of Gallaher intellectual capital. Also, because of the similarity of the objects, the picture uses a figure of repetition. Cigarette packets are identical in shape, colour and style, but differ in size. Davison (2014) established that identity (a type of repetition) was also present in the Shire Pharmaceuticals graphic (a scientific dot matrix conveying the symbol of research and development) that was displayed on the title page of the corporate annual report. Similar graphics depicting brands of companies owned by Shire Pharmaceuticals offer an example of using series from year to year.

One advantage of using visual rhetoric in IC studies is that it allows for an in-depth analysis of messages contained in IC visualisations. Davison's (2014) research has confirmed that IC visualisations use a variety of rhetorical figures. Visual rhetoric methodology can also be applied to study other types of communication (internal and external IC presentations) or used in combination with other research methods, such as interviews and participatory observation. However, visual rhetoric presents some limitations; for example, outcomes are largely dependent on the researcher's interpretation. Results from such analysis would certainly be more convincing if the method also allowed for the perspective of IC visuals' recipients and authors.

IC VISUALISATION AND IMPRESSION MANAGEMENT

The concept of impression management derives from social psychology. Introduced by Goffman in 1959, it initially focused on the behaviour of individuals. At its simplest, the concept describes the process of influencing individuals' perceptions of other people (Leary and Kowalski, 1990). Impression management in corporate reporting and IC communication is intended to boost the image of the organisation and its management (Beattie and Jones, 2000b; Clatworthy and Jones, 2006). For this reason, it is frequently criticised for encouraging opportunistic disclosure practices (Guillamon-Saorin et al., 2012) and potentially impairing reporting quality (Leung et al., 2015).

Merkl-Davies and Brennan (2007) identified two main impression management strategies in corporate narrative documents: attribution and concealment, which are further broken down into the obfuscation of bad new news and the emphasis of good news. Finally, they ascertained the existence of seven types of impression management strategies, namely:

1. reading ease manipulation;
2. rhetorical manipulation;
3. thematic manipulation;
4. visual and structural manipulation;
5. performance comparisons;
6. choice of earnings number; and
7. attribution of performance.

Reading ease manipulation refers to the use of syntactical complexity to make the narrative of corporate documents difficult to comprehend and to 'bury' the bad news. Typical instruments for detecting syntactical complexity are readability indices, where high values suggest an attempt at obfuscation. In the case of visuals, reading ease manipulation or, rather, comprehension ease manipulation, can be achieved through overly complicated graphs or diagrams that are difficult to analyse.

Rhetorical manipulation involves the use of persuasive language, including rhetorical figures. As stated in the previous section, rhetorical figures are not solely the domain of words. Pictures are also useful as a means of persuading the audience and showing top managers (perceived as key IC elements) in a positive light (Davison, 2010).

Thematic manipulation aims to conceal information either by not revealing bad news or by presenting it as good news. It is used by managers to present themselves and the performance of their firms in the best possible light. In order to induce the optimism bias, an overly positive tone (more positive than negative words or themes) is used. In the early research into thematic manipulation, tone was assessed by the researcher based on the message content (see Loughran and McDonald, 2015). Recently it has become possible to automate the tone assessment process. Today, it involves the use of word dictionaries with a positive and negative emotional charge, algorithms based on dictionaries and the assumption that the tone is fixed in the area of lexically related words (Valitutti et al., 2004), the methods of clustering related words (Hatzivassiloglou et al., 2009) and machine learning algorithms. The thematic manipulation of visual IC information is closely related to the structural manipulation strategy. Both strategies use graphs, diagrams and pictures that selectively highlight handpicked IC information.

The instrument of visual and structural manipulation is the presentation of biased information. Merkl-Davies and Brennan (2007) have identified four subtypes of this strategy: repetition, reinforcement, visual emphasis, and order or location of information. In the case of narrative information, visual emphasis consists of foregrounding some element by highlighting the text, using boldface, colour or different typeface, or by adding visuals such as graphs or pictures that catch readers' attention or evoke positive emotions. Visual emphasis applied to visual information makes use of bolded lines, contrasting colours or the 'magnifying glass' effect that enlarges some part of the diagram.

The last subtype of visual and structural manipulation is ordering and physical location. It comes down to abusing the proper text layout, which requires that the most important information be placed at the beginning or end of the text. In the case of visual information, physical location manipulation can be performed by placing information in the upper left part of the picture or its centre.

IC performance comparisons based on the impression management strategy typically use comparative (benchmark) data from periods when trends in organisational IC performance were favourable (and easy to spot), or juxtaposition with less successful organisations. In the case of visual performance comparisons, graphs comparing organisational IC performance now and in the past, or with other firms, are used.

Some firms use a similar strategy when presenting their earnings or other performance figures; the most favourable indicators are brought to the fore, while those pointing to poor performance are concealed. The strategy can be enhanced by the selective use of graphical information and graph distortion, discussed below.

The last of the impression management strategies identified by Merkl-Davies and Brennan (2007) is performance attribution. It consists in managers ascribing their high performance to internal factors (such as managers' competence) and blaming poor performance on external factors (such as events beyond management control). This strategy is more common for narratives because visual information is less susceptible to such manipulation.

Having examined intellectual capital narratives in integrated reports, Melloni (2015) noted that most IC disclosures were focused on relational capital, and that IC narratives were much more optimistic compared with other narratives. She also found a significant association between the positive tone of a company's IC disclosures and its declining performance, bigger size and a higher level of intangibles. The results led her to conclude that IC information had been used in the integrated reports as an impression management strategy.

Studies investigating impression management of visuals are less frequent than those dealing with narratives, although the potential for such studies is considerable. For example, Davison (2010) claims that 'visual portraits of business leaders constitute an important form of impression management, perception management, or even "intangibles management", whether disseminated as voluntary disclosures in annual reports or whether circulated more widely in the media'. She also argues that such visualisations should primarily create the impression of credibility among investors, customers and other stakeholders.

Studies from other disciplines have shown that visual aids are used for effective impression management. In a world dominated by social media, visuals seem to be more persuasive than other tools of communication. Siibak (2009) observed significant differences in the aesthetic, emotional, self-reflecting and aesthetic-symbolical aspects of photographs that male and female teenagers post to social media to create visual self-value. She also noted that teenagers' visual impression management in social media was guided by the expectations of other teenagers in the reference group. Clarke (2011) analysed visual aids used by entrepreneurs in impression management to influence their stakeholders and potential investors. The range of visual symbols he identified included settings (office furniture, office space, office arrangements, external surroundings), props (pictures, displays of prototypes, framed patents and historical documents, luxury vehicles), dresses, expressive body and facial movements. The results of Clarke's study suggest that entrepreneurs intentionally use visual symbols to win acceptance of their ventures. He also noted that the more experienced and more successful entrepreneurs were more effective in managing and manipulating visual symbols and, thus, acquiring stakeholder support.

The advantage of graphs as the instrument of impression management is that they deliver IC information in a way that allows trends, patterns and information anomalies to be captured by taking advantage of a natural property of the human brain: spatial intelligence (see Beattie and Jones, 2000a). The users of IC graphs should, however, be aware that they can be prepared and presented in a way that suggests a given quantity increases (decreases) at a faster (slower) rate than it really does. Tufte (1983) called this phenomenon graph distortion.

There are many ways in which graphs and other visual aids can be distorted to deliver the desired message to IC information users. One involves a careful selection of information to be presented in graphs, which tend to attract more attention from the audience. For instance, the management may decide to create a more positive picture of the company's IC elements and IC performance by presenting graphically only those IC items (or IC performance metrics) that have changed in line with the board's and stakeholders' expectations. Stakeholders' impressions can also be manipulated by breaching the principle of proportionality and mapping the growth dynamics of some value inconsistently with the actual data. Leach (1988) was among the first researchers to identify such techniques, observing that, although between 1982 and 1986 Asda-MFI's profit increased by 136 per cent, the graph pointed to an increase of 330 per cent.

Tufte (1983) proposed measuring the degree of graph disruption with an indicator that he called the 'lie factor'. Refined and renamed the graph discrepancy index (GDI) by Taylor and Anderson (1986), it was popularised as a tool of accounting research by Beattie and Jones (1992). The graph discrepancy index is calculated as follows:

$$Graph\ Discrepancy\ Index = \left(\frac{a}{b} - 1\right) \times 100\%$$

where:

a = percentage change of column height (in centimetres) depicted in the graph;

b = percentage change in data.

A zero value of the GDI means that the trend plot and the data are consistent with each other. Negative or positive values of the GDI indicate that the plot is exaggerated or understated, respectively. Beattie and Jones (1992) also proposed adopting a 5 per cent GDI as a threshold for identifying significantly inconsistent annual report charts.

The results of their research revealed many more cases of overestimated trends than of trends that were considerably underestimated. Jones et al. (2020) found that concealing negative information (not presenting it graphically) was used by public banks to manage impression more often than favourable distortions or comparisons.

The graph discrepancy index has several, mostly technical, limitations. First, it can only be applied to some types of graphs, such as columns, lines, bars, but not to pie charts or radar charts. Second, because of the risk of inconsistencies in interactive graphs (which are HTML files) related to browser settings, only graphs in printed documents or pdf files can be assessed with it.

To date, impression management research in the IC area has predominantly focused on the use of narratives. Results have confirmed the common use of various impression management techniques that Merkl-Davies and Brennan (2007) have broadly divided into concealment and attribution. The main area explored by studies on visuals has been the use of business leaders' portraits in impression management. Impression management has also been explored in relation to the selective use of graphs and graph distortion techniques. Studies in other fields (Clarke, 2011) have also provided evidence that visual messages (delivered through clothing, office equipment, documents, body and facial movements) play an important role in attracting and managing the impressions of stakeholders.

There is, however, a notable lack of holistic studies evaluating the application of numbers (that is, classification shifting), narratives and visuals as the instruments of impression management simultaneously. Such studies could use the video recordings of annual shareholder meetings, IC presentations for potential investors and the participatory observation of organisational meetings on IC development.

CONCLUSIONS AND TRAJECTORIES FOR FURTHER RESEARCH

Studies of IC visualisations are still relatively sparse, especially when compared with studies of IC narratives and other types of IC quantification methods. However, as visuals are increasingly used to assist readers in understanding, communicating and managing IC, this type of communication is likely to attract more interest from researchers in the future.

The clearest benefit of the visual research methodologies explored in this chapter relates to their contribution to a more thorough debate on IC functioning in organisations, which can help answer the three questions raised by Mouritsen (2006) that were highlighted in the introduction. The most common line of research in IC focuses on visualisation methods, such as models like the Skandia Navigator, value creation maps (Marr et al., 2004), the IC Navigator (Fernstrom et al., 2004) and social network diagrams and their use by managers in charge of IC resources. All of the mentioned methods illustrate, in their own way, the composition and functioning of organisational IC, thus responding to the first two questions raised by Mouritsen (2006). Second, some of these methods – the value creation maps, the method developed by Cuganesan and Dumay (2009) and performance dashboards – have the potential for answering Mouritsen's (2006) third question about the relationship between IC and value. Critical and performative analyses of IC visualisations in action, the third phase of IC research according to Dumay et al. (2018), are essential for capturing the deeper explanation of how IC relates to value creation processes.

A useful tool of IC research appears to be social network graphs, which show information flows and the relations between organisation members, thus providing an insight into how knowledge and innovation are created and disseminated. One has to realise, however, that the visual presentation of relationships between IC elements is vulnerable to oversimplification as well as to the visual clutter phenomenon, which involves the risk of a graphic presentation losing of some of its inherent advantages such as the ease of comprehension, analysis, memorising and recollection. For example, many visualisations of the value creation process in the integrated reports use the integrated reporting guidelines' template to show the process as the transformation of six capitals input (on the left) into six capitals output (on the right) (Michalak et al., 2017). The 'IIRC's linear accounting framework' has been criticised by Tweedie et al. (2018) as ill-suited for modelling complex inter-dependencies in the value creation process that are relevant to shareholders and other stakeholders.

Studying IC visualisations facilitates better understanding how IC is communicated to stakeholders (investors, employees, customers). Moreover, it offers a more comprehensive picture of IC because it considers aspects such as the images and perceptions of business leaders and the 'soft' components (including brainpower and transformation), and their impact on value creation, that many other research approaches overlook.

Visual rhetoric is a common theoretical underpinning of IC visualisation studies, which examine visual signs by means of rhetorical figures such as repetitions and metaphors. This technique is instrumental in decoding multifaceted, complex and co-existing messages delivered via IC visuals, such as the pictures of top managers and customers. The exploration of physical, dress, interpersonal and spatial codes enables better comprehension of messages about leadership and associated intellectual, symbolic and social intangibles created by top management. In addition to advantages, visual rhetoric research also has certain limitations; namely, its outcomes largely depend on the researcher's interpretation. This weakness may be rectified by including the perspectives of users and preparers of IC visuals in the scope of visual rhetoric research.

Another interesting object of IC visualisation studies is impression management. Although the focus of impression management studies is on narratives, they increasingly pay more attention to visuals, such as pictures, diagrams and graphs, that are increasingly popular as a means of influencing IC information users. The strength of a graph as an impression management tool lies in the possibility of selecting information and the period to be presented, and in designing a graph so that it creates the illusion that some quantity grows (decreases) faster (more slowly) than it really does. Specific codes and rhetorical figures built into top managers' pictures or entrepreneurs' presentations are to evoke the impression of credibility among investors, customers and other stakeholders. The downside of the research in visual impression management is that some of the applied techniques (for example, the graph distortion index) may not be practical when applied to dynamic graphs presented on webpages or in other electronic documents, which limits their use to traditional printed visuals.

A research method that IC studies could benefit from, but which has not yet been used in this field, is eye-tracking. By recording and analysing eye shifts between particular elements of a image, this method provides an insight into decision-making processes taking place in the viewer's mind, thus making it easier to identify how they unfold and how they vary depending on the task to be done and the pressure of time (Orquin and Loose, 2013).

The review presented in this chapter points to a number of gaps in the existing literature and indicates key areas for future studies on IC visualisations. The first suggestion here is to extend the range of stakeholders included in studies of the use of IC visualisations, including employees, shareholders and other stakeholders. The participation of new stakeholders and the use of techniques such as in-depth interviews, focus groups, participatory observation, eye-tracking, biosensors and wearable cameras, may produce new or even breakthrough results. Such an extended approach would also improve the understanding of how IC visuals are taken in and utilised by users, as well as helping assess the influence of visuals on their emotions, learning and decision-making.

It is also advisable that IC research is extended, in particular, to include stakeholders that participate in the creation and dissemination of IC visuals, such as top managers, IC managers, human resources managers and other people with a role in IC communication, such as public relations agency employees and graphic designers developing materials containing IC visuals, who have so far been outside the research scope. Extending the focus of IC research to these professionals, and the audience, would allow us to understand the intentions of the authors of IC visuals and the messages contained therein, as well as testing whether they are correctly decoded by the users of IC visuals and researchers.

The second suggestion is to expand the range of IC visuals that are analysed beyond the readily available sources (annual reports, IC reports and supplements, integrated reports) and static images (photos, graphs, diagrams, value creation maps) that most studies have focused on so far. We need to accept that the way IC visuals are communicated is evolving, and highlight the growing importance of dynamic IC visuals such as videos, animated diagrams, graphs and drill-down dashboards. In addition, IC communication channels are also undergoing transformation: the significance of visual social media and only partly controlled means of expression, such as memes and other types of viral communication, is increasing. Considering the changing nature of information exchange is a prerequisite for producing relevant research outcomes; it is also important to note that investigations examining up-to-date IC visuals offer more possibilities, such as recording changes in the viewer's level of attention, and their impact on emotions and learning and decision-making processes.

The third suggestion concerns using a more holistic approach to analysing IC information. Studying IC visuals, descriptive and numerical information at the same time is closer to the natural way of processing data by the human mind than dealing with the three dimensions separately. A holistic approach, a broader range of stakeholders involved in the evaluation and enhancement of organisational IC, and the participation of researchers from various fields, would certainly advance the attainment of the fifth stage of IC studies proposed by Dumay et al. (2018): IC research with no boundaries and as a worthwhile endeavour.

REFERENCES

Anderson, J. (1980), *Cognitive Psychology and its Implications*, Freeman, New York.

Banks, M. (2007), *Using Visual Data in Qualitative Research*, SAGE, London.

Barnabè, F., Giorgino, M.C. and M. Kunc (2019), 'Visualizing and managing value creation through integrated reporting practices: a dynamic resource-based perspective', *Journal of Management and Governance*, 23 (2), 537–575.

Barthes, R. (1964), 'Rhétorique de l'image', *Communications*, 4 (1), 40–51.

Beattie, V. and M.J. Jones (1992), 'The use and abuse of graphs in annual reports: theoretical framework and empirical study', *Accounting and Business Research*, 22 (88), 291–303.

Beattie, V. and M.J. Jones (2000a), 'Changing graph use in corporate annual reports: a time-series analysis', *Contemporary Accounting Research*, 17 (2), 213–226.

Beattie, V. and M.J. Jones (2000b), 'Impression management: the case of inter-country financial graphs', *Journal of International Accounting, Auditing and Taxation*, 9 (2), 159–183.

Bell, E. and J. Davison (2013), 'Visual management studies: empirical and theoretical approaches', *International Journal of Management Reviews*, 15 (2), 167–184.

Benschop, Y. and H.E. Meihuizen (2002), 'Keeping up gendered appearances: representations of gender in financial annual reports', *Accounting, Organizations and Society*, 27 (7), 611–636.

Bernardi, R.A., Bean, D.F. and K.M. Weippert (2002), 'Signaling gender diversity through annual report pictures: a research note on image management', *Accounting, Auditing and Accountability Journal*, 15 (4), 609–616.

Blair, M.M. and S.M.H. Wallman (2001), *Unseen Wealth: The Value of Corporate Intangible Assets*, Brookings Institution Press, Washington.

Borgatti, S.P., Mehra, A., Brass, D.J. and G. Labianca (2009), 'Network analysis in the social sciences', *Science*, 323 (5916), 892–895.

Brilliant, R. (1991), *Portraiture*, Reaktion, London.

Bujaki, M.L. and B.J. McConomy (2010), 'The portrayal of women in Canadian corporate annual reports', *Canadian Journal of Administrative Sciences*, 27, 210–223.

Burton, K., O'Connor, A. and G. Roos (2013), 'An empirical analysis of the IC Navigator approach in practice – a case study of five manufacturing firms', *Knowledge Management Research and Practice*, 11 (2), 162–174.

Campbell, R. and M.R.A. Rahman (2010), 'A longitudinal examination of intellectual capital reporting in Marks & Spencer annual reports 1978–2008', *British Accounting Review*, 42, 56–70.

Clarke, J. (2011), 'Revitalizing entrepreneurship: how visual symbols are used in entrepreneurial performances', *Journal of Management Studies*, 48 (6), 1365–1391.

Clatworthy, M.A. and M.J. Jones (2006), 'Differential patterns of textual characteristics and company performance in the chairman's statement', *Accounting, Auditing and Accountability Journal*, 19 (4), 493–511.

Cuganesan, S. and J.C. Dumay (2009), 'Reflecting on the production of intellectual capital visualisations', *Accounting, Auditing and Accountability Journal*, 22 (8), 1161–1186.

Danesi, M. (2017), 'Visual rhetoric and semiotic', accessed 28 June 2019 at http://oxfordre.com/communication/view/10.1093/acrefore/9780190228613.001.0001/acrefore-9780190228613-e-43?rskey=wUMNHw&result=2.

Davison, J. (2008), 'Rhetoric, repetition, reporting and the "dot.com" era: words, pictures, intangibles', *Accounting, Auditing and Accountability Journal*, 21 (6), 791–826.

Davison, J. (2010), '[In] visible [in] tangibles: visual portraits of the business élite', *Accounting, Organizations and Society*, 35 (2), 165–183.

Davison, J. (2014), 'Visual rhetoric and the case of intellectual capital', *Accounting, Organizations and Society*, 39 (1), 20–37.

Davison, J. and L. Skerratt (2007), 'Words, pictures and intangibles in the corporate report', Institute of Chartered Accountants of Scotland.

De Groot, E., Korzilius, H., Gerritsen, M. and C. Nickerson (2011), 'There's no place like home: UK-based financial analysts' response to Dutch-English and British-English annual report texts', *IEEE Transactions on Professional Communication*, 54 (1), 1–17.

De Groot, E., Nickerson, C., Korzilius, H. and M. Gerritsen (2016), 'Picture this: developing a model for the analysis of visual metadiscourse', *Journal of Business and Technical Communication*, 30 (2), 165–201.

Dumay, J., Guthrie, J., Ricceri, F. and C. Nielsen (2018), 'The past, present, and future for intellectual capital research: an overview', in J. Dumay, J. Guthrie, F. Ricceri and C. Nielsen (eds), *The Routledge Companion to Intellectual Capital*, Routledge, Abingdon, UK and New York, USA, pp. 1–17.

Durand, J. (1987), 'Rhetorical figures in the advertising image', in J. Umiker-Sebeok (ed.), *Marketing and Semiotics: New Directions in the Study of Signs for Sale*, Mouton, Berlin, pp. 295–318.

Edvinsson, L. and M.S. Malone (1997), *Intellectual Capital: Realizing Your Company's True Value by Finding its Hidden Brainpower* (1st edn), Harper Business, New York.

Fernstrom, L., Pike, S. and G. Roos (2004), 'Understanding the truly value creating resources – the case of a pharmaceutical company', *International Journal of Learning and Intellectual Capital*, 1 (1), 105–120.

Fu, G. (2015), 'Visual communication of aspects of human intellectual capital: a comparative study between UK and Chinese firms', Doctoral thesis, unpublished, accessed 30 July 2019 at https://core.ac.uk/download/pdf/77297287.pdf.

Goffman, E. (1959), *The Presentation of Self in Everyday Life*, Doubleday, Garden City, NY.

Guillamon-Saorin, E., Osma, B.G. and M.J. Jones (2012), 'Opportunistic disclosure in press release headlines', *Accounting and Business Research*, 42 (2), 143–168.

Guthrie, J. and R. Petty (2000), 'Intellectual capital: Australian annual reporting practices', *Journal of Intellectual Capital*, 1 (3), 241–251.

Guthrie, J., Ricceri, F. and J. Dumay (2012), 'Reflections and projections: a decade of intellectual capital accounting research', *British Accounting Review*, 44, 68–82.

Hatzivassiloglou, V., McKeown, K.R., Pang, B., Lee, L., Vaithyanathan, S., et al. (2009), 'Predicting the semantic orientation of adjectives', *ACM Transactions on Information Systems (TOIS)*, 21 (4), 315–346.

Henry, L. (2013), 'Intellectual capital in a recession: evidence from UK SMEs', *Journal of Intellectual Capital*, 14 (1), 84–101.

IIRC (2013), *The International <IR> Framework*, International Integrated Reporting Council.

Jones, M.J., Melis, A., Gaia, S. and S. Aresu (2020), 'Impression management and retrospective sense-making in corporate annual reports: banks' graphical reporting during the global financial crisis', *International Journal of Business Communication*, 57 (4), 474–496.

Kaplan, R.S. and D.P. Norton (2000), 'Having trouble with your strategy? Then map it', *Harvard Business Review*, 78, 167–176.

Kaplan, R.S. and D.P. Norton (2004), *Strategy Maps: Converting Intangible Assets into Tangible Outcomes*, Harvard Business School Press, Boston, MA.

Kok, A. (2007), 'Intellectual capital management as part of knowledge management initiatives at institutions of higher learning', *Electronic Journal of Knowledge Management*, 5 (2), 181–192.

Leach, R. (1988), 'Let the message dictate the medium', *Accountancy*, January, 93–94.

Leary, M.R. and R.M. Kowalski (1990), 'Impression management: a literature review and two-component model', *Psychological Bulletin*, 107 (1), 34–47.

Leung, S., Parker, L. and J. Courtis (2015), 'Impression management through minimal narrative disclosure in annual reports', *British Accounting Review*, 47 (3), 275–289.

Lev, B. (2004), 'Sharpening the intangibles edge', *Harvard Business Review*, 82 (6), 109–116.

Liebowitz, J. (2005), 'Linking social network analysis with the analytic hierarchy process for knowledge mapping in organizations', *Journal of Knowledge Management*, 9 (1), 76–86.

Loughran, T. and B. McDonald (2015), 'The use of word lists in textual analysis', *Journal of Behavioral Finance*, 16 (1), 1–11.

Margolis, E. and L. Pauwels (eds) (2011), *The SAGE Handbook of Visual Research Methods*, SAGE, London.

Marr, B., Schiuma, G. and A. Neely (2004), 'Intellectual capital–defining key performance indicators for organizational knowledge assets', *Business Process Management Journal*, 10 (5), 551–569.

Melloni, G. (2015), 'Intellectual capital disclosure in integrated reporting: an impression management analysis', *Journal of Intellectual Capital*, 16 (3), 661–680.

Mention, A.L. and N. Bontis (2013), 'Intellectual capital and performance within the banking sector of Luxembourg and Belgium', *Journal of Intellectual Capital*, 14 (2), 286–309.
Merkl-Davies, D.M. and N.M. Brennan (2007), 'Discretionary disclosure strategies in corporate narratives: incremental information or impression management?', *Journal of Accounting Literature*, 27, 116–196.
Michalak, J., Rimmel, G., Beusch, P. and K. Jonäll (2017), 'Business model disclosures in corporate reports', *Journal of Business Models*, 5 (1), 51–73.
Mitchell, W.J.T. (1994), *Picture Theory*, University of Chicago Press, Chicago, IL.
Mouritsen, J. (2006), 'Problematising intellectual capital research: ostensive versus performative IC', *Accounting, Auditing and Accountability Journal*, 19 (6), 820–841.
Mouritsen, J., Larsen, H.T. and P.N.D. Bukh (2001), 'Intellectual capital and the "capable firm": Narrating, visualising and numbering for managing knowledge', *Accounting, Organizations and Society*, 26, 735–762.
Norreklit, H. (2000), 'The balance on the balanced scorecard: a critical analysis of some of its assumptions', *Management Accounting Research*, 11 (1), 65–88.
Orquin, J.L. and S.M. Loose (2013), 'Attention and choice: a review on eye movements in decision making', *Acta Psychologica*, 144 (1), 190–206.
Powell, W.W., Koput, K.W. and L. Smith-Doerr (1996), 'Interorganizational collaboration and the locus of innovation: networks of learning in biotechnology', *Administrative Science Quarterly*, March, 116–145.
Rindova, V.P., Pollock, T.G. and M.L. Hayward (2006), 'Celebrity firms: the social construction of market popularity', *Academy of Management Review*, 31 (1), 50–71.
Roque, G. (2005), 'Boundaries of visual images', *Presentation, Word and Image*, 21, 111–119.
Shipilov, A.V. and S.X. Li (2008), 'Can you have your cake and eat it too? Structural holes' influence on status accumulation and market performance in collaborative networks', *Administrative Science Quarterly*, 53 (1), 73–108.
Siibak, A. (2009), 'Constructing the self through the photo selection: visual impression management on social networking websites', *Cyberpsychology: Journal of Psychosocial Research on Cyberspace*, 3 (1). https://cyberpsychology.eu/article/view/4218/3260 (accessed 19 March 2019).
Skandia (1988), *Human Capital in Transformation*, Intellectual Capital Supplement, Skandia, Stockholm.
Skandia (1995), 'Visualizing intellectual capital in Skandia. Supplement to Skandia's 1994 Annual report', Skandia, Stockholm.
Spoehr, K.T. and S.W. Lehmkuhle (1982), *Visual Information Processing*, Freeman, San Francisco, CA.
Sukhari, A. and C. De Villiers (2019), 'The influence of integrated reporting on business model and strategy disclosures', *Australian Accounting Review*, 29 (4), 708–725.
Taylor, B.G. and L.K. Anderson (1986), 'Misleading graphs: guidelines for the accountant', *Journal of Accountancy*, 162 (4), 126–135.
Teece, D.J. (1998), 'Capturing value from knowledge assets: the new economy, markets for know-how, and intangible assets', *California Management Review*, 40 (3), 55–79.
Tufte, E.R. (1983), *The Visual Display of Quantitative Information*, Graphics Press, Cheshire, CT.
Tufte, E.R. (1990), *Envisioning Information*, Graphics Press, Cheshire, CT.
Tversky, B. (1974), 'Eye fixations in prediction of recognition and recall', *Memory and Cognition*, 2 (2), 275–278.
Tweedie, D., Nielsen, C. and N. Martinov-Bennie (2018), 'The business model in integrated reporting: evaluating concept and application', *Australian Accounting Review*, 28 (3), 405–420.
Valitutti, A., Strapparava, C. and O. Stock (2004), 'Developing affective lexical resources', *PsychNology Journal*, 2 (1), 61–83.
Warren, S. (2009), 'Visual methods in organizational research', in D. Buchanan and A. Bryman (eds), *The SAGE Handbook of Organizational Research Methods*, SAGE, London, pp. 567–582.

9. Building causal maps in the intellectual capital domain: a methodological perspective

Marco Giuliani

INTRODUCTION

The academic and professional interest in intellectual capital (IC) is underpinned by the idea that it can be considered one of the main levers to create value (Edvinsson and Malone, 1997; Stewart, 1997; Sveiby, 1997). IC is typically understood to consist of three main elements, namely human capital (HC), structural capital (SC) and relational capital (RC), and it is typically approached from two different perspectives classified as 'static' and 'dynamic'. The static perspective focuses on the properties of the three IC components, identifying their size through financial and non-financial indicators in company reports. The dynamic approach, instead, assumes that none of the IC components alone is sufficient for successful performance, but rather they need to be combined to generate value. Therefore, IC becomes a phenomenon of interactions, transformations and complementarities that can be understood by focusing not only on resources but also on processes, rules, activities and connections. This dynamic perspective seeks to investigate the interactions among IC components and the linkages between IC and financial performance (Cuganesan, 2005, p. 360; Cuganesan and Dumay, 2009, p. 1163; Marr et al., 2004).

Understanding IC from a dynamic perspective requires focusing on the connections between IC components to visualize and acquire knowledge about how they contribute to the value creation process. A useful tool for this purpose is represented by causal maps. A causal map is a type of cognitive map that can be considered as a means for converting individuals' tacit knowledge about a phenomenon into an explicit model in which the different constructs are presented together with their inter-relations. In causal maps, the nodes are the constructs perceived as important and the arrows show the relations among them, that is, the links among inputs, processes and valued outcomes (Abernethy et al., 2005; Ambrosini and Bowman, 2001). This chapter aims to examine the role that causal maps can play in the development of research in the IC domain and the methodologies that can be used to build these maps for representing IC dynamics.

The chapter is structured as follows. First, some preliminary and conceptual elements are introduced. Afterwards, the different approaches for building causal maps are explained. Then some suggestions for incorporating the time dimension in causal maps are offered, together with insight about how to use causal maps in the IC domain. Finally, the above-mentioned considerations are summarized to draw some conclusions and projections.

DEFINING CAUSAL MAPS

A causal map is generally considered to be a particular type of cognitive map, which is an individual's mental model of the relationships (causal or otherwise) among the elements of a system. In other words, causal maps can be considered as representations of subjective knowledge about a phenomenon, that is, a discourse about perceived causes and effects and the perceived links between those causes and effects (Eden, 1992; Eden et al., 1992; Montibeller and Belton, 2006).

Causal maps are known by many names, including Ishikawa (fishbone) diagrams, cause-and-effect diagrams, impact wheels, issue trees, strategy maps, current reality trees, risk assessment mapping tools, and so on (Scavarda et al., 2006). This plethora of labels can be considered as an indicator of the wide range of uses these maps can have.

This form of cognitive and cause mapping aims to produce manual or electronic representations of how people perceive a situation in the form of a means–ends diagram (a directed graph). As such, the map may reveal issues of concern, how these issues relate to one another, and how changes in the character of one issue may have repercussions for another.

Topologically, a causal map is a network, where each node represents a concept, an idea or a construct, while the arcs between the nodes represent the perceived causal relationships among them (Bryson et al., 2004; Eden, 2004; Marchant, 1999; Montibeller and Belton, 2006; Wellman, 1994). The arcs may indicate only the presence or absence of a relationship, or may indicate the strength of the relationship between two nodes (Scavarda et al., 2006). In defining nodes and arrows, it is recommended that nodes are described in a clear and meaningful way to suggest possible action. This implies the need to 'dramatize' the different statements/nodes (Catasús and Gröjer, 2006).

In some approaches, the links are arrows with a positive or negative sign. A positive sign indicates a perceived positive causal connection, whereby an increase in a cause generates an increase in the linked effect (for example, 'more sales lead to more profit'). A negative sign denotes a negative connection: an increase in the cause leads to an increase in the opposite pole of the linked effect (for example, 'more sales lead to less spare production capacity') (Eden, 2004; Scavarda et al., 2006). In the case of IC, the identification of positive and negative linkages can help to understand the value creation and value destruction dimensions of IC and to avoid overly optimistic views of IC (see Figure 9.1) (Giuliani, 2013).

Information about the strength of each link may also be displayed in the map using, for example, numbers or the thickness of the arc or arrow. The indication of the strength is useful to have an idea about the probability that an activity will have an impact on a specific item (for example, if there is a strong linkage between IC and financial performance, I can expect that if I carry out activities for developing IC, my financial performance will increase) and sometimes also about the time lags between cause and effect (strong linkages tend to react quicker than weak linkages) (Kosko, 1986; Nadkarni and Shenoy, 2001).

Finally, in order to offer a more realistic interpretation of the investigated phenomenon, some suggest abandoning the traditional approach based on cause-and-effect relationships, in the form of unidirectional

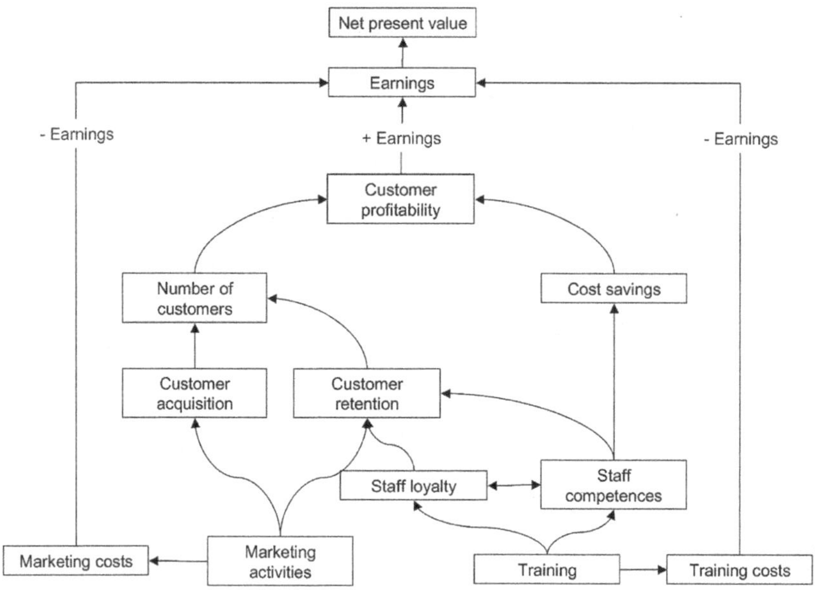

Figure 9.1 A map of positive and negative linkages for understanding value creation and value destruction

arrows, and instead consider co-influence linkages, in the form of bi-directional arrows (Montibeller and Belton, 2006).

In the case of IC, the use of bi-directional arrows may offer a more realistic representation of its complex and enigmatic nature. For example, Figure 9.2, proposed by Giuliani and Marasca (2011), shows that human capital can have a positive influence on relational capital (competent employees tend to be better able to develop and maintain relationships and satisfy customers needs) and also that relational capital can influence human capital (due to collaborations with customers, employees can acquire new competencies and develop know-how). Despite this, maps with bi-directional arrows have a higher level of complexity than those based on simple linkages and, consequently, there is a risk that they may not be used if it is difficult to understand relationships and to identify 'what causes what'. For these reasons, maps may be based only on unidirectional arrows. In all, there is a need to manage the trade-off between 'realistic representation' and understandability/usability of the map.

Some think that the main limitation of this kind of tool is the risk of offering an oversimplified view of reality (Nørreklit, 2000) and describing relationships that 'are abstracted and removed from their conditions' (Cuganesan, 2005, p. 361). Nevertheless, causal maps are still considered useful tools to understand phenomena, especially complex and/or dynamic interactions, and their reliability can be improved by adopting specific mapping processes (Abernethy et al., 2005; Cuganesan and Dumay, 2009).

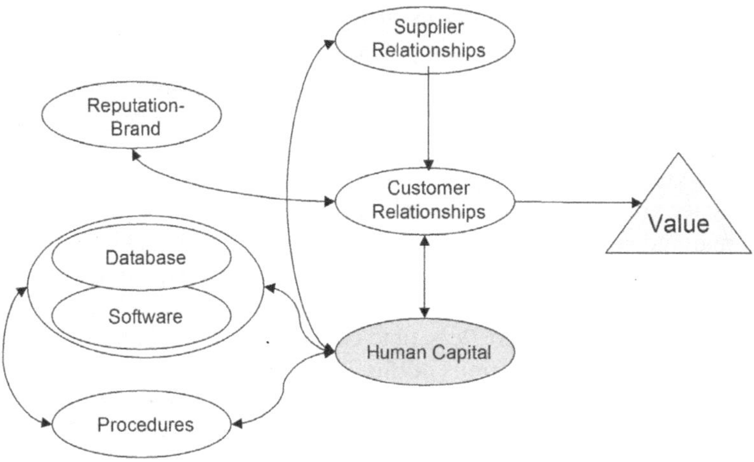

Figure 9.2 Another example of causal map regarding IC value creation process

BUILDING CAUSAL MAPS

From the analysis of the extant theory and practice, it is evident that there is not one single method but, rather, a range of different forms and methods for building a causal map (Bryson et al., 2004; Eden, 2004; Marchant, 1999; Scavarda et al., 2006; Wellman, 1994). Each of these techniques aims to provide the user with the means of capturing not only the nodes (concepts or items) but also the connections (relationships) to have both an analytical perspective (the focus on single items or single connections) but also a holistic one (patterns emerging from the overall representation). Among the different methods, I outline the following: (1) qualitative versus quantitative approaches; and (2) individual versus group versus documental methods.

Qualitative and Quantitative Approaches

Qualitative approaches design maps on the base of individual perceptions that can be collected during one-to-one interviews or focus groups. This is perhaps the most frequently used method for building causal maps, especially in the IC field where the availability of data tends to be limited.

In this case, the researcher has two main options for designing the map. The first requires that the researcher initially interviews the informed members of the organization or facilitates a focus group to gather information on the aspect they want to investigate. Afterwards, they have to transcribe the evidence collected from the qualitative research interview (Qu and Dumay, 2011) or focus group (Krueger and Casey, 2014). In this process, it is particularly important to analyse the entire transcript, as this provides a means of understanding the linkages and their properties. After analysing the data, the researcher can draw the map that will represent a rational and balanced synthesis of the ideas emerging from the interviewees. The analysis may end with a discussion between the researcher and the interviewees to gain consensus on the designed map. The main advantages of this method are the following: (1) it emphasizes the mapping competences of the researcher; (2) the map summarizes the different perceptions of the different interviewees; and (3) this method tends to be more efficient (less time-consuming) than other qualitative methods. The main limitations of this approach are the tendency to focus on confirming evidence, and the risk of incomplete analysis because of the cognitive complexity of the task (Abernethy et al., 2005; Eden, 2004; Nadkarni and Nah, 2003).

The second approach, which can be called the 'interactive approach', actively engages the expert participants in the map-building task by asking them to map causal relations among discrete themes or constructs extracted from their prior interviews. Even though this method can also be used with a single-participant interview in a one-to-one relationship, it is used more effectively and efficiently in focus groups. In comparison to the previous method, here the map is not drawn by the researcher but by the participants, typically in a focus group. Therefore, the researcher acts as a facilitator and offers methodological support. In this light, they can be asked to define the agenda of the meetings, to support the arrangement and classification of the elements provided by the focus group, to lead the discussions, to examine the issues, to design and update the map, and to obtain consensus from the participants. In this case, the researcher is not the author of the map, but leads and supports the members of the focus group in drawing their map. This method allows the experts to arrange construct cards according to their experiences of causality. This method is particularly effective for creating causal maps in the early stages of investigating complex processes when more objective data are either unavailable or pose an undue risk of dominating map-building. Care must be taken in determining the number of construct cards given to participants to successfully recall coded information. As much assistance as possible should be given to participants without leading them to predetermined results. The main limitations of this method are: (1) it is time-consuming; (2) it requires not only mapping competencies but also the ability to manage focus groups; and (3) it can be difficult to identify the 'right' focus group, that is, a group of experts able to work together and achieve results that reflect the perceptions of everyone and not just the dominant perspectives (Abernethy et al., 2005; Eden, 2004; Nadkarni and Nah, 2003).

Quantitative approaches are based on statistical or computerized analysis of data (Abernethy et al., 2005; Cuganesan and Dumay, 2009). Data regarding each construct can be quantitative from the beginning (for example, sales, investments in training, number of employees) or transformed into quantitative data through a coding process. Here, linkages are defined using different types of correlation analyses between the different constructs. The main advantages of this method are that it tries to achieve validity by establishing how reliable the discovered relations are and is not purely subjective; and the achieved results can be verified or reproduced by another researcher. The main disadvantages of this method are that it is influenced by the coding/accounting processes and by the query rules used for establishing the links; it may not be recognized as valid by the organization; and the map might be difficult to interpret as it does not necessarily reflect all of the relevant underlying theory and field experience. In addition, in some cases, it can be difficult to collect the data needed to perform robust correlation analyses.

Individual, Group and Documental Approaches

Individual maps are typically made by an 'interviewer', using the technique of interview to elicit information from another individual (that is, two parties are involved) (Bryson et al., 2004). Interviews carried out to design maps are usually structured or semi-structured and based on a deductive or inductive approach (Ackermann and Eden, 2004). This method enables interviewees to share their perceptions without peer pressure and other conformity constraints, encouraging them to open up and discuss issues as they see them rather than follow a party line (Eden and Spender, 1998). Consequently, it is possible to bring to the surface 'theories in use' rather than 'espoused theories' (Shrivastava, 1983), and therefore begin to model the situation 'as is' rather than 'as it should be'. More in-depth interviews carried out using the mapping technique also provide interviewees with the ability to say what concerns them in a manner that allows the interviewer to develop an appreciation of the situation before making judgements. While there may not be a prescribed set of questions, the agenda emerges through developing the map and visual analysis. Nodes can be further explored by asking questions to tease out details regarding options, consequences and constraints. Interviewees are therefore provided with added value both through an enhanced understanding of their own view of the world, as illustrated through the map, and through the analysis of the structure of the map, yielding some insight into emergent properties. As a result, a more thorough understanding of the interviewee's world is created as a model in the form of the map. Thus, the map becomes a vehicle for purposeful dialogue about the problem situation. In all, causal maps can become, on the one hand, a learning tool useful for the interviewees, as they enable them to have a clearer (and more organized) view of the issue and to make sense of the problem; and on the other hand, a way for the interviewers to collect rich information.

Collective or group model-building generally refers to a model-building process in which a group is deeply involved in the process of causal map construction (Morecroft and Sterman, 1994). This group-based model construction relies on facilitation processes and the design of sessions to formulate complex problems with a group of people. Group mapping can take many sub-modes (Ackermann and Eden, 2004). It can be manual or computerized. The simplest mode is manual, and this is recommended when the group is unfamiliar with technology or there is a lack of equipment and where other less overt objectives exist (for instance, a deliberate effort at team building). Manual mapping usually requires pens, chart paper and sticky-notes or stickers. A well-known interactive modelling approach is the oval mapping technique (OMT) (Ackermann and Eden,

2001, 2004; Bryson, 1995; Eden and Ackermann, 1998). This mode aims to gradually negotiate a group view of the problem and consequently develop a map that can achieve a large consensus (see: interactive approach). The computerized mode is based on specific software designed for facilitating the identification of statements and relationships. The software supports the phases of capturing, structuring and exploring the material, and it helps in the development of the map. The map is produced by the software, as a synthesis of the different contributions, in real time during the discussions or at a later point. The use of an ad hoc software allows a relevant degree of flexibility, as nodes and linkages can be easily added, removed or revised. On the contrary, usually the software does not provide the 'big picture' as the manual modes do, and it may not benefit from the richness of the interactive discussions (Ackermann and Eden, 2001; Eden et al., 1992). Both in the manual modes and in the computerized ones the intention is to enable participants to share all of their contributions, ensuring that it is clear what these statements mean and how they relate to other statements captured. This ability to capture, structure and analyse contributions from participants assists not only in ensuring an adequate level of rationality of the process, but also in encouraging participants to feel more ownership for the outcomes and therefore increase the likelihood of implementation.

Documental mapping or text mapping is probably the least-used mode of mapping. Mapping text can help to understand how the managerial and/or disclosure documents are structured, what the main topics are and how they are related to one another. Besides, text mapping can help to identify inconsistencies or contradictions and, consequently, to shed light on overlooked problems. In these cases, mapping text and then analysing the map can be seen as a useful preface to more in-depth analyses. However, working with text is perhaps the most challenging application of mapping. This can happen because there is little if any ability to ask for clarification from the sources, and consequently some items or linkages can be ambiguous or unclear. In addition, the temptation to personalize the map, through adding links that are 'obvious', is also a trap. When working in this mode, care has to be taken.

TIME AND CAUSAL MAPS

Time is a relevant variable for understanding phenomena. Examining the processes and practices at play from a temporal perspective allows a deeper exploration, beyond simple mechanics, to the pace and trajectory with which they move over time, how they align and the context of a phenomenon. Even though time appears to be very relevant to accounting, it tends to be approached as a mere variable or an element that does not deserve particular attention. In all, to understand and represent phenomena and processes correctly and completely, the time dimension has to be considered (Ancona et al., 2001; Anderson-Gough et al., 2001; Ezzamel and Robson, 1995; Huy, 2001; Mitchell and James, 2001; Mouritsen and Bekke, 1999; Nandhakumar and Jones, 2001; Nørreklit, 2000; Quattrone and Hopper, 2005).

Retrospective or Prospective Maps

Regarding the time dimensions, maps can be retrospective or prospective (Ackermann and Eden, 2004). In general, interviewees tend to take a retrospective viewpoint, and therefore implicitly if not explicitly succumb to post hoc rationalization. Thus, the resultant map usually does not reveal what took place, the perception in real time, but rather a 'sanitized' version. There are at least two reasons why this might occur: the natural sensemaking process that tends to simplify and 'reorganize' reality, and the tendency to represent problems or failures in a way that is not 'self-accusing' and consequently to provide a neat and tidy explanation and omit certain details. In all, retrospective mapping is the most common form of mapping, but there is a risk that it is not a representation of the reality 'as is' but of the reality 'as remembered' or 'as it makes sense'. In order to reduce these risks, it is possible to combine qualitative approaches with quantitative ones (based on historical data) or to triangulate different interviews or documents.

Prospective mapping inevitably reflects expectations and perceptions; therefore it tends to be more subjective than the retrospective approach. Designing prospective maps using quantitative methods can be particularly difficult due to the lack of data. Thus, a relevant aspect of this form of modelling is the increased level of importance placed on ensuring that the maps are rigorous, comprehensive and, most of all, accurate. Prospective maps, to be reliable and usable, should not incorporate unreasonable personal desires but rational expectations on which the organization converges. Consequently, it is important to balance the need for strong validation with the need for participants to have a sense of ownership over the map itself that leads to its use.

It has to be noted that according to the extant studies, the 'quality' of a map, from a temporal perspective, is related to the sensemaking process developed; that is, the quality and quantity of discussions regarding the issues represented in the map and the regularity of the mapping process influence the consistency and constancy of this practice (Anderson-Gough et al., 2001). The sensemaking and regularity of retrospective mapping enable managers and researchers to design more accurate prospective maps.

Successions and Time Lags

Most theories and representations involve fairly simple relationships of the X-causes-Y variety, with X and Y representing substantive variables other than time. Within this set of relationships, there are five major ways in which theory informs the method with respect to time. First, we need to know the time lag between X and Y. How long after X occurs does Y occur? Second, X and Y have durations. Not all variables occur instantaneously. Third, X and Y may change over time. We need to know the rate of change. Fourth, in some cases, there are dynamic relationships in which X and Y both change. The rate of change for both variables should be known, as well as how the X–Y relationship changes. Finally, in some cases we have reciprocal causation: X causes Y, and Y causes X. In all, to understand and represent a phenomenon with a correct time dimension, it is essential to understand successions, time lags, durations and possibly rates (Ancona et al., 2001; Mitchell and James, 2001).

Succession places events in their temporal order (Wittmann, 1999). Succession can be relevant because time tends to be used for ordering events over time and for identifying cause-and-effect relationships. There is often a tendency to identify an event as the cause of the following event from a temporal perspective (Lagnado and Sloman, 2006; Nørreklit, 2000). For example, if A happens before B, there can be the tendency to identify A as a cause of B. From this perspective, time can be informative as it can support the identifications of the linkages (cause-and-effect relationships) between the nodes. This idea of using the time dimension to identify causes and effects, even if it may be true in some cases, can be misleading in other circumstances, as it can mean that two unrelated events are perceived as linked (Lagnado and Sloman, 2006). In the case of IC, due to its complexity and to the interactions among IC resources, it can be difficult to identify successions. Nevertheless, even if it is not possible to identify objectively all the existing IC connections, it is useful to focus on the most relevant ones and the related successions to support IC mobilization.

A time lag can be defined as the period within which action in the context of one dimension will have an affect on another. Knowledge of time lag effects is essential because it supports the interpretation of data and phenomena, and it enables future events to be forecast. Even if time lags are relevant, they tend not to be analysed in depth, and consequently causal models and maps are often temporally biased (Gollob and Reichardt, 1987; Mitchell and James, 2001; Nørreklit, 2000). Time lags can be analysed using either quantitative approaches (statistical analysis of data) or qualitative ones (time perceptions) (Bukh and Malmi, 2005; Gollob and Reichardt, 1987; Mitchell and James, 2001; Skoog, 2003). In existing IC studies, time lags tend to be analysed through qualitative approaches based on the perceptions of different interviewees or focus groups. It has to be noted that some argue that the reliability of these perceptions tend to increase when time is discussed regularly (Giuliani, 2009, 2015b; Giuliani and Skoog, 2020; Skoog, 2003).

When the analysed phenomenon is dynamic and the map changes over time in terms of nodes and/or relationships and/or attributes of the relationships, there is a need to adopt a longitudinal perspective and consider the time lags not only between X and Y but also between X–Y and X'–Y'. In other words, in the case of dynamic phenomena, two types of time lags have to be examined. This recalls the idea of time validity, duration and rate of change. As a map is a representation of reality and reality changes over time, as well as how it is perceived, it is important to understand how often the map has to be revised to be aligned with the 'new' reality or the 'new' perception of the reality. This time validity depends on objective elements, such as changes of the context (for example, the dynamicity/competitiveness/rhythm of innovation of a market) and on subjective aspects, such as changes in the perceptions of the interviewees or changes of the interviewees. Concerning the IC field, some scholars have underlined the need to regularly update IC visualizations and maps according to the organizational strategy; otherwise, there is a risk that the organization may manage resources and connections that have become irrelevant and overlook the ones that have become important (Giuliani and Skoog, 2020; Skoog, 2003).

USING CAUSAL MAPS IN THE INTELLECTUAL CAPITAL DOMAIN

The interpretation of a map can be holistic or atomistic. The holistic approach takes place when the focus is on the big picture, on the nodes and arrows considered as a unique system. This approach is useful to understand the boundaries of the phenomenon and its overall complexity. From a holistic perspective, understanding is gained through the additional meaning given to a node not only from its content but also from the causes, consequences and explanations that are linked to that node (Ackermann and Eden, 2004).

The atomistic approach requires focusing on single aspects of the map. In this case, several aspects can be considered. For example, a first aspect to focus on is 'potency', which is represented by the number of connections an item has: the more connections, the more influential the item is (Eden, 1992, 2004). Another aspect to notice is the 'shortest path': in some cases it is important to focus on the items that have a direct connection with the target rather than on the ones that have mediated influence; here, the assumption is that direct connections are easier to manage, more predictable, more intense and faster than indirect ones (O'Donnell et al., 2002).

The proposed analysis shows that causal maps can be a useful tool for understanding and intervening in complex systems. Accordingly, causal maps have been used for developing research in the IC domain for different reasons. First, they have been successfully applied in theory and practice as they are considered to be a useful cognitive aid for managers to understand IC 'in action' (Abernethy et al., 2005; Cuganesan and Dumay, 2009; Giuliani and Marasca, 2011; Marr et al., 2004). Second, causal maps reveal and then reduce the complexity of IC, and make it possible to understand IC as a bundle of knowledge resources that produce network effects (Cuganesan and Dumay, 2009, p. 1162).

Causal Maps for Visualizing, Understanding and Mobilizing IC Value Creation Processes

From the analysis of previous studies, in the IC field, causal maps can be used for different purposes, such as:

- investigating and visualizing the interactions between different IC components (such as human capital, relational capital and structural capital), between IC and the other organizational resources and between IC and financial performance (Cuganesan, 2005; Cuganesan and Dumay, 2009; Giuliani, 2013; Giuliani and Marasca, 2011; Kaplan and Norton, 2003; Marr et al., 2004; Tayles et al., 2002);
- supporting IC mobilization (Carlucci et al., 2004; Cuganesan, 2005; Cuganesan and Dumay, 2009; Giuliani and Marasca, 2011; Kaplan and Norton, 2003; Tayles et al., 2002);
- developing and understanding IC performance measurement and evaluation models (Bontis and Fitz-Enz, 2002; Marr et al., 2004; Montemari and Nielsen, 2013);
- understanding the temporal dimension of IC (Giuliani, 2009, 2015a, 2015b; Giuliani and Skoog, 2020; Quevedo and Roberts, 2005; Skoog, 2003).

In other words, causal maps are a useful tool for understanding 'what IC does' and 'when IC should do/does what', approaching IC from a performative perspective (Mouritsen, 2006), and consequently capturing the dynamic dimension of IC to understand what flows connect the IC elements to adequately represent them.

IC maps can be focused on IC as whole or single specific resources or value creation processes (Fernstrom et al., 2004). It is important to note that while there is widespread recognition of the inter-relationships between IC elements and the consequences for value creation, in practice little empirical work on IC has been done to build on these insights (Cuganesan and Dumay, 2009; Guthrie et al., 2012). The handful of empirical analyses make several contributions that need to be considered regarding IC causal maps.

First, these analyses critique traditional, sequential cross-sectional models where, for example, human capital (HC) influences structural capital (SC) and then relational capital (RC), and finally financial capital (FC). Furthermore, they show a more complex and dynamic picture where the connections are not linear cause-and-effect linkages, but where there is co-dependence between IC resources (Cuganesan, 2005; Cuganesan and Dumay, 2009; Fernstrom et al., 2004; Kaplan and Norton, 2003; Marr et al., 2004). Consequently, there is a need to abandon the traditional logic based on input and outcome and to adopt a more complex systemic approach that emphasizes the co-influence between different IC and organizational resources.

Second, these studies further demonstrate that IC also interacts with other assets to create value. In particular, a recent study has highlighted that FC is not only an output of IC performance but can also be an input (Murthy and Mouritsen, 2011). Consequently, to some extent, an IC map will not be linear but rather circular. This implies that the 'correct' interpretation of the map will require time and regularity as people need to make sense of it to understand which action leads to the desired outcomes.

Third, the research on IC 'in action' shows that, in terms of methodology, connections can be investigated quantitatively and qualitatively adopting the methods discussed above (Abernethy et al., 2005; Cuganesan and Dumay, 2009; Murthy and Mouritsen, 2011).

Fourth, IC scholars have highlighted the problematic nature of IC, that is, that inter-relationships and their consequences for value creation are unstable and precarious, contingent upon the manner of their deployment and use within organizational processes (Cuganesan, 2005, p. 358). This implies that the identified linkages and their properties change over time and, consequently, IC maps need frequent revision.

IC mapping can also be seen as a means of facilitating conversation, sharing experiences and aiding decision-making or as a means of surfacing knowledge and structuring it as a part of knowledge management projects. This use of mapping has the potential to inform the knowledge management community both in terms of how contributions are raised and in the valuable material that is captured in the model as organizational memory.

A similar approach can be used to investigate intellectual liabilities (ILs), that is, the potential of IC to destroy value (De Santis and Giuliani, 2013). Mapping ILs can produce a systematic view of the risks related to IC. In addition, when adding to the map, possible actions for mitigating these risks and risk consequences as well as the ramifications stemming from these actions can be understood, leading to a more accurate assessment of IC. Furthermore, the comparison between the IC value creation process and the ILs' value destruction process informs understandings of the differences between the two processes and can prompt discussion on aspects – namely, the risks related to IC and the impact on organizational performance – that tend to be overlooked. In all, mapping IC and ILs produce a more complete and balanced picture of the IC phenomenon as a whole, which can then be mobilized more effectively (De Santis and Giuliani, 2013; Giuliani, 2013, 2015b).

Causal Maps for IC Performance Measurement and Evaluation

A mantra in accounting is that you need measuring for managing. According to this view, a plethora of IC measurement models has been proposed by scholars and practitioners. These models tend to measure the stock of resources and/or the IC performance using both financial and non-financial indicators. In other words, indicators can reflect both the stock of IC value and the IC value creation.

As IC measurements should support IC management, indicators should make sense for the managers and, consequently, be consistent with the strategy to mobilize IC resources to achieve the defined financial and non-financial organizational goals. Unfortunately, the choice of the 'right' indicators to be associated with specific elements is not easy, and therefore, according to some scholars, there is the risk of designing indicators that offer only a limited view of IC or that do not make sense for the users. The consequence of this is that these indicators tend to not be used or may even be abandoned (Chiucchi et al., 2018; Giuliani et al., 2016).

The starting point of a measurement process has to do with the process of deciding what to measure (Neely and Bourne, 2000). As mentioned, an IC map can be useful to identify the boundaries of IC; that is, the measurement object. IC is a 'conventional' object and it reflects the management's vision of what IC is and what forms it (Giuliani and Marasca, 2011).

With reference to the definition and implementation of the panel of indicators, causal maps can be useful to support these phases of the measurement process as well as the phase related to the use of IC indicators. As casual maps make explicit individuals' knowledge of how the company generates value, this should contribute to close the relationships between the measurement process and the management process (Chiucchi et al., 2016; Dumay and Rooney, 2011; Kaplan and Norton, 1992; Montemari and Nielsen, 2013). According to this perspective, indicators should be coupled with the IC resources (the node of the map) and with the connections related to the value creation process (the arrows between the different nodes) to potentially allow for the measurement of both the static and the dynamic aspects of IC.

Using mapping as a means of monitoring performance can overcome the problems related to working with 'too-complex models'. Working with even a 'reduced model' containing the relevant goals, strategies and actions might make it possible to use the indicators properly, rather than abandoning them if they are perceived as 'too complicated'. In this case, it is important to be selective in the identification of the nodes and linkages and of the related indicators, and to keep the map and the related indicators up to date. In all, the integration of indicators and maps increases the information content of the map and makes indicators more understandable and useful.

Causal Maps and the Understanding of the Temporal Dimension of IC

As mentioned, causal maps can be useful to understand time. As time can be a useful lens for understanding IC, causal maps can become a tool for analysing the time dimension of IC (Giuliani, 2009).

Relationships among IC resources are not stable and they change over time. The regular revision of the map will help to test the existence of the previously identified relations as well as to understand if the identified qualities have changed. This updating process could provide useful information on possible changes to the value creation process, and consequently on the need to revise the IC strategy or the IC measurements (Giuliani, 2009; Giuliani and Skoog, 2020).

Besides, matching performance indicators with the IC map can potentially provide useful information on the persistence of the effects of a particular action. This effect can be temporary or permanent and the regular use of a map can support the understanding of this aspect (Montemari and Nielsen, 2013; Nørreklit, 2000; Skoog, 2003).

Causal maps can also be useful for grasping the temporal aspects of the value creation process; that is, the time lags between actions and outcomes. Some studies have shown that causal maps stimulate discussions about time and inform the sensemaking processes about IC and time (Giuliani, 2015b; Giuliani and Skoog, 2020; Skoog, 2003).

In addition, causal maps can also be useful to compare the IC value creation process with the IC value destruction process in terms of 'pace'. Some argue that the value creation process takes more time than the value destruction process, and consequently the two processes need to be managed in different ways (Giuliani, 2015b).

CONCLUSIONS

This chapter aimed to examine the role that causal maps can play in the development of research in the IC domain and to identify the methodologies that can be used to build maps for representing IC dynamics. It has been shown that in the IC discourse, causal maps are useful for visualizing, understanding and managing IC from both a static and a dynamic perspective. Besides, they help in making sense of and using IC performance indicators according to the organizational strategy of IC creation and development. Finally, maps are also useful for grasping the temporal dimensions of IC: for instance, dynamics, pace, succession and time lags. IC casual maps can be designed according to quantitative or qualitative approaches and may adopt a retrospective or prospective approach, according to the purpose of the map and the available data.

Future research avenues may examine the roles and effects of causal maps in the IC domain, the development and comparison of different types of IC maps (qualitative, quantitative, prospective, retrospective) as well as the empirical investigation of the time dimension of IC.

REFERENCES

Abernethy, M.A., Horne, M., Lillis, A.M., Malina, M.A. and F.H. Selto (2005), 'A multi-method approach to building causal performance maps from expert knowledge', *Management Accounting Research*, 16 (2), 135–155.

Ackermann, F. and C. Eden (2001), 'Contrasting single user and networked group decision support systems for strategy making', *Group Decision and Negotiation*, 10 (1), 47–66.

Ackermann, F. and C. Eden (2004), 'Using causal mapping: individual and group; traditional and new', in Michael Pidd (ed.), *Systems Modelling: Theory and Practice*, Chichester: Wiley, pp. 127–145.

Ambrosini, V. and C. Bowman (2001), 'Tacit knowledge: some suggestions for operationalization', *Journal of Management Studies*, 38 (6), 811–829.

Ancona, D.G., Okhuysen, G.A. and L.A. Perlow (2001), 'Taking time to integrate temporal research', *Academy of Management Review*, 26 (4), 512–529.

Anderson-Gough, F., Grey, C. and K. Robson (2001), 'Tests of time: organizational time-reckoning and the making of accountants in two multi-national accounting firms', *Accounting, Organization and Society*, 26 (2), 99–122.

Bontis, N. and J. Fitz-Enz (2002), 'Intellectual capital ROI: a causal map of human capital antecedents and consequents', *Journal of Intellectual Capital*, 3 (3), 223–247.

Bryson, J.M., Ackermann, F., Eden, C. and C.B. Finn (2004), *Visible Thinking: Unlocking Causal Mapping for Practical Business Results*, Chichester: John Wiley & Sons.

Bryson, N. (1995), 'A goal programming method for generating priority vectors', *Journal of the Operational Research Society*, 46 (5), 641–648.

Bukh, P.N. and T. Malmi (2005), 'Re-examining the cause-and-effect principle of the balanced scorecard', in S. Jonsson and J. Mouritsen (eds), *Accounting in Scandinavia – The Northern Lights*, Copenhagen: Copenhagen Business School Press, pp. 87–113.

Carlucci, D., Marr, B. and G. Schiuma (2004), 'The knowledge value chain: how intellectual capital impacts on business performance', *International Journal of Technology Management*, 27 (6–7), 575–590.

Catasús, B. and J.-E. Gröjer (2006), 'Indicators: on visualizing, classifying and dramatizing', *Journal of Intellectual Capital*, 7 (2), 187–203.

Chiucchi, M.S., Giuliani, M. and S. Marasca (2016), 'The use of intellectual capital reports: the case of Italy', *Electronic Journal of Knowledge Management*, 14 (4), 245–255.

Chiucchi, M.S., Giuliani, M. and S. Marasca (2018), 'Levers and barriers to the implementation of intellectual capital reports: a field study', in J. Guthrie, J. Dumay, F. Ricceri and C. Nielsen (eds), *The Routledge Companion to Intellectual Capital*, New York: Routledge, pp. 332–346.

Cuganesan, S. (2005), 'Intellectual capital-in-action and value creation. A case study of knowledge transformation in an innovation process', *Journal of Intellectual Capital*, 6 (3), 357–373.

Cuganesan, S. and J. Dumay (2009), 'Reflecting on the production of intellectual capital visualisations', *Accounting, Auditing and Accountability Journal*, 22 (8), 1161–1186.

De Santis, F. and M. Giuliani (2013), 'A look on the other side: investigating intellectual liabilities', *Journal of Intellectual Capital*, 14 (2), 212–226.

Dumay, J. and J. Rooney (2011), '"Measuring for managing?" An IC practice case study', *Journal of Intellectual Capital*, 12 (3), 344–355.

Eden, C. (1992), 'On the nature of cognitive maps', *Journal of Management Studies*, 29 (3), 261–265.

Eden, C. (2004), 'Analyzing cognitive maps to help structure issues or problems', *European Journal of Operational Research*, 159 (3), 673–686.

Eden, C. and F. Ackermann (1998), 'Analysing and comparing idiographic causal maps', in C. Eden and J.C. Spender (eds), *Managerial and Organizational Cognition: Theory, Methods and Research*, London: SAGE, pp. 192–209.

Eden, C., Ackermann, F. and S. Cropper (1992), 'The analysis of cause maps', *Journal of Management Studies*, 29 (3), 309–324.

Eden, C. and J.C. Spender (1998), *Managerial and Organizational Cognition: Theory, Methods and Research*, London: SAGE.

Edvinsson, L. and M.S. Malone (1997), *Intellectual Capital*, New York: Harper Business.

Ezzamel, M. and K. Robson (1995), 'Accounting in time: organizational time-reckoning and accounting practice', *Critical Perspectives on Accounting*, 6 (2), 149–170.

Fernstrom, L., Pike, S. and G. Roos (2004), 'Understanding the truly value creating resources. The case of a pharmaceutical company', *International Journal of Learning and Intellectual Capital*, 1 (1), 105–120.

Giuliani, M. (2009), 'Intellectual capital under the temporal lens', *Journal of Intellectual Capital*, 10 (2), 246–259.

Giuliani, M. (2013), 'Not all sunshine and roses: investigating intellectual liabilities "in action"', *Journal of Intellectual Capital*, 14 (1), 127–144.

Giuliani, M. (2015a), 'Intellectual capital dynamics: seeing them "in practice" through a temporal lens', *Vine*, 45 (1), 46–66.

Giuliani, M. (2015b), 'Rome wasn't built in a day … Reflecting on time, intellectual capital and intellectual liabilities', *Journal of Intellectual Capital*, 16 (1), 2–19.
Giuliani, M., Chiucchi, M.S. and S. Marasca (2016), 'A history of intellectual capital measurements: from production to consumption', *Journal of Intellectual Capital*, 17 (3), 590–606.
Giuliani, M. and S. Marasca (2011), 'Construction and valuation of intellectual capital: a case study', *Journal of Intellectual Capital*, 12 (3), 377–391.
Giuliani, M. and M. Skoog (2020), 'Making sense of the temporal dimension of intellectual capital: a critical case study', *Critical Perspectives on Accounting*, 70, 101993.
Gollob, H.F. and C.S. Reichardt (1987), 'Taking account of time lags in causal models', *Child Development*, 58, 80–92.
Guthrie, J., Ricceri, F. and J. Dumay (2012), 'Reflections and projections: a decade of intellectual capital accounting research', *British Accounting Review*, 44 (2), 68–82.
Huy, Q.N. (2001), 'Time, temporal capitability and planned change', *Academy of Management Review*, 26 (4), 601–623.
Kaplan, R.S. and D.P. Norton (1992), 'The Balanced Scorecard – measures that drive performance', *Harvard Business Review*, 70 (1), 71–79.
Kaplan, R.S. and D.P. Norton (2003), *Strategic Maps: Converting Intangible Assets into Tangible Outcomes*, Boston, MA: Harvard Business School Press.
Kosko, B. (1986), 'Fuzzy cognitive maps', *International Journal of Man–Machine Studies*, 24 (1), 65–75.
Krueger, R.A. and M.A. Casey (2014), *Focus Groups: A Practical Guide for Applied Research*, Thousand Oaks, CA: SAGE Publications.
Lagnado, D.A. and S.A. Sloman (2006), 'Time as a guide to cause', *Journal of Experimental Psychology: Learning, Memory and Cognition*, 32 (3), 451–460.
Marchant, T. (1999), 'Cognitive maps and fuzzy implications', *European Journal of Operational Research*, 114 (3), 626–637.
Marr, B., Schiuma, G. and A. Neely (2004), 'The dynamics of value creation: mapping your intellectual performance drivers', *Journal of Intellectual Capital*, 5 (2), 224–229.
Mitchell, T.R. and L.R. James (2001), 'Building better theory: time and the specification of when things happen', *Academy of Management Review*, 26 (4), 530–547.
Montemari, M. and C. Nielsen (2013), 'The role of causal maps in intellectual capital measurement and management', *Journal of Intellectual Capital*, 14 (4), 522–546.
Montibeller, G. and V. Belton (2006), 'Causal maps and the evaluation of decision options – a review', *Journal of the Operational Research Society*, 57 (7), 779–791.
Morecroft, J.D. and J.D. Sterman (1994), *Modeling for Learning Organizations*, Portland, OR: Productivity Press.
Mouritsen, J. (2006), 'Problematising intellectual capital research: ostensive versus performative IC', *Accounting, Auditing and Accountability Journal*, 19 (6), 820–841.
Mouritsen, J. and A. Bekke (1999), 'A space for time: accounting and time based management in a high technology company', *Management Accounting Research*, 10 (2), 159–180.
Murthy, V. and J. Mouritsen (2011), 'The performance of intellectual capital: mobilising relationships between intellectual and financial capital in a bank', *Accounting, Auditing and Accountability Journal*, 24 (5), 622–646.
Nadkarni, S. and F.F.-H. Nah (2003), 'Aggregated causal maps: an approach to elicit and aggregate the knowledge of multiple experts', *Communications of the Association for Information Systems*, 12 (1), 25.
Nadkarni, S. and P.P. Shenoy (2001), 'A Bayesian network approach to making inferences in causal maps', *European Journal of Operational Research*, 128 (3), 479–498.
Nandhakumar, J. and M. Jones (2001), 'Accounting for time: managing time in project-based teamworking', *Accounting, Organization and Society*, 26 (3), 193–214.
Neely, A. and M. Bourne (2000), 'Why measurement initiatives fail', *Measuring Business Excellence*, 4 (4), 3–7.
Nørreklit, H. (2000), 'The balance on the balanced scorecard – a critical analysis of some of its assumptions', *Management Accounting Research*, 11 (1), 65–88.

O'Donnell, A.M., Dansereau, D.F. and R.H. Hall (2002), 'Knowledge maps as scaffolds for cognitive processing', *Educational Psychology Review*, 14 (1), 71–86.
Qu, S.Q. and J. Dumay (2011), 'The qualitative research interview', *Qualitative Research in Accounting and Management*, 8 (3), 238–264.
Quattrone, P. and T. Hopper (2005), 'A "time–space odyssey": management control systems in two multinational organisations', *Accounting, Organization and Society*, 30 (7–8), 735–764.
Quevedo, M.I. and H. Roberts (2005), 'Taking your own medicine: the relationship between Intellectual Capital and Innovativeness in the pharmaceutical sector of Peru', Paper presented at the 2nd Workshop on Visualising, Measuring, and Managing Intellectual Capital, Universiteit Maastricht, the Netherlands, 25–27 October.
Scavarda, A.J., Bouzdine-Chameeva, T., Goldstein, S.M., Hays, J.M. and A.V. Hill (2006), 'A methodology for constructing collective causal maps', *Decision Sciences*, 37 (2), 263–283.
Shrivastava, P. (1983), 'A typology of organizational learning systems', *Journal of Management Studies*, 20 (1), 7–28.
Skoog, M. (2003), 'Visualizing value creation through the management control of intangibles', *Journal of Intellectual Capital*, 4 (4), 487–504.
Stewart, T.A. (1997), *Intellectual Capital*, New York: Bantam Doubleday Dell Publishing Group.
Sveiby, K.E. (1997), 'The Intangible Assets Monitor', *Journal of Human Resource Costing and Accounting*, 2 (1), 73–97.
Tayles, M., Bramley, A., Adsead, N. and J. Farr (2002), 'Dealing with the management of intellectual capital', *Accounting, Auditing and Accountability Journal*, 15 (2), 251–267.
Wellman, M.P. (1994), 'Inference in cognitive maps', *Mathematics and Computers in Simulation*, 36 (2), 137–148.
Wittmann, M. (1999), 'Time perception and temporal processing levels of the brain', *Chronobiology International*, 16 (1), 17–32.

10. Intellectual capital and pictorial disclosures analysis: an MIA (missing in action) interpretative paradigm

Paul Davis, Mary Low, Jackie Allen and Umesh Sharma

INTRODUCTION

Intellectual capital (IC) disclosure is a voluntary reporting concept that has captured research attention in the last 20 years (Chiucchi, 2013). IC disclosure is a managerial practice that seeks to capture the intangible value of an organization by disclosing intangible items not recognized in traditional financial accounts (van der Meer-Kooistra and Zijlstra, 2001). While IC can be disclosed in written narratives, it is the direct communication of pictorial images that annual report readers and researchers are paying increased attention to (Davison, 2008).

While many studies undertake an analysis of the narrative disclosures of IC in annual reports, far fewer studies have been conducted on pictorial disclosures. Cuozzo et al. (2017) encourage finding new avenues for understanding where IC disclosures can be found. Both Steenkamp and Hooks (2011) and Yusof et al. (2015) have already asserted the significance that pictures play in disclosing IC. For instance, Steenkamp and Hooks (2011) undertook a study on the largest 28 New Zealand companies based on market capitalization in 2007, and found that when considering all forms of IC disclosure (texts, charts and pictures), 42 per cent of IC items were portrayed through pictorial disclosures. Their study also found that of all the pictures disclosed within the annual reports, 66 per cent of these pictures disclosed IC items. In a different geographical location, a similar study of 50 Malaysian companies by Yusof et al. (2015) found that 80 per cent of pictures disclosed in company annual reports were found to disclose IC items.

The importance of our study is emphasized by the viewpoints of IC researchers. For instance, Steenkamp and Hooks (2011) assert that IC disclosure is incomplete without reference to pictorial disclosures. Yusof et al. (2015) observed that insufficient research attention has been placed on visual images in annual reports. Their study also emphasized the need to analyse images and the impact that images have on annual reports. Furthermore, Dumay and Roslender (2013, p. 266) acknowledge the 'need to develop more IC research' that grapples 'with the complexities of organisational and institutional worlds ... especially research that extends beyond just "accounting" for IC'. This chapter investigates pictorial disclosures of IC of eight New Zealand universities to ascertain what aspects of IC each university is reporting pictorially in their annual reports over a period of three years.

INTELLECTUAL CAPITAL DISCLOSURE WITH THE USE OF PICTORIAL IMAGES

With annual reports of organizations now spanning over 70 pages in length, they are increasingly being used not only to showcase a set of financial statements but also to disclose narrative information about an organization's activities, with the use of images (Hooper et al., 2001). It is the use of images alongside the narratives that has become a vital part of an annual report, and these two elements combined have become a strategic marketing tool to tell a story about an organization for a given reporting period (Hooper et al., 2001). Studies have recognized that images provoke ideas and impressions which impress new memorable knowledge upon a reader, especially if images contain similar or familiar themes (Pesci et al., 2015; Davison, 2008).

Davison (2008) recognizes that pictures in an annual report are both comprised and positioned in such a way that they are like a work of fine art, in that they can carry simultaneous messages and are analysable from different image device perspectives. For instance, images are recognized to contain linguistic and iconic meanings (Barthes, 1977), make use of image rhetorical devices such as repetition (Davison, 2014; Pesci et al., 2015), and involve anadiplosis and anaphora. Davison (2008) explains visual anadiplosis 'as the repetition and variation of the subject-matter or style of image' (p. 799), and visual anaphora 'as the attachment of a business theme to a particular image, which is later repeated in the document in various forms to accompany the theme' (ibid.). Images can also be used to illustrate an organization as a global entity (Preston and Young, 2000), create impressions or, as Baudrillard (1983) and Preston et al. (1996) assert, images can present or mask a certain reality. With the common catchphrase, 'a picture is worth a thousand words', it is important to recognize the psychological influence images have to create memorable knowledge. Given the use of images in an annual report, this study sets out to focus on the impact that they may have when they disclose IC items.

It is already recognized that pictures carry out an effective role in disclosing IC items of an organization in an annual report (Steenkamp and

Hooks, 2011). However, prior studies have not considered an extended observable period within a university context to ascertain whether there is an increasing trend in IC pictorial disclosures. It is also observable that the study of interpreting pictures used in annual reports from a report reader's perspective is scarce. The importance of this type of research is twofold. First, prior studies have revealed that stakeholders reading an annual report are directing more of their attention to the non-financial components.This has significance from a marketing perspective for a university regarding what it should be disclosing, given that an annual report is one very visible communication device accessible to a stakeholder. Steenkamp and Hooks (2011) assert that visual images have become an integral part of corporate annual reports and are the favoured transparent medium to send messages to investors and the public. Second, given the increased competition amongst universities and their competition for student numbers and research grants, it has become increasingly important for universities to sell their number one intangible resource of knowledge, and this is vital for their depiction of research and human capital (Ramirez and Gordillo, 2014; Sánchez and Elena, 2006). This research undertakes an analysis of the use of IC pictorial disclosures of eight New Zealand universities to ascertain the portrayal of these items. This study uses an interpretative paradigm and applies image analysis devices.

INTELLECTUAL CAPITAL DISCLOSURES

Stakeholders require accountability from an organization (Sánchez and Elena, 2006; Wang et al., 2016), and one way in which organizations can account for their activities in a given annual period is to engage in voluntary IC disclosure reporting. While scholars do not have a consensus on the definition of IC, each study undertaken has derived a definition for its study context (Low et al., 2015). Steenkamp and Hooks (2011) note that despite the lack of consensus on an overall definition of IC, scholars recognize that it consists of the three components of external capital, internal capital and human capital. They insist that intangible value exists in: other parties outside the organization who have involvement with an organization; the knowledge and experience within the organization; and within the organization's staff. Report preparers disclose intangible IC value of an organization when they disclose information surrounding brands, patents, an entity's reputation and supply chain networks, all of which relate to the knowledge embedded in an organization (van der Meer-Kooistra and Zijlstra, 2001; Lu, 2012). In this way, IC has a recognizable economic value in a public company context.

The practice of IC disclosure has long been recognized in literature on for-profit organizations, and universities and research centres have since followed suit to engage in the practice (Sánchez and Elena, 2006). For instance, the practice of IC disclosure is mandatory for universities in Austria as of 2002 (National Council of the Republic of Austria, 2002). However, while not mandatory, other universities globally are voluntarily writing narratives and presenting pictures of items that consist of IC items. Sangiorgi and Siboni (2017) investigate the amount and nature of IC disclosure in Italian universities and find a significant amount of IC disclosures in voluntary social reports issued by these universities. They subsequently argue that IC plays a crucial role in universities given that they should represent knowledge-based institutions.

Di Berardino and Corsi (2018) analyse how IC can promote the development of a 'third mission' within the university. They present this mission as a new mandate that expands the boundaries within which institutions create value. The 'third mission' concept involves an array of activities aimed at transferring knowledge useful to society and organizations to develop entrepreneurial skills, innovation, social welfare and solid human capital, and promotes the development of science and society through various forms of communication and engagement. Di Berardino and Corsi (2018) also find that there is a positive impact of 'third mission' activities in the Italian university ecosystem, and the relevant role of structural and relational capital in the development of the third mission.

Since the beginning of the IC movement, universities have also been the subject of research on issues such as intellectual property, research and development, and reporting (Mariani et al., 2018; Secundo et al., 2018; Passaro et al., 2018; Sultanova et al., 2018). Austrian universities have made an outstanding contribution to IC research over the years, and implemented the first mandatory IC statement (Habersam et al., 2018). Martin-Sardesai and Guthrie (2018) and Di Berardino and Corsi (2018), however, argue that universities appear 'obsessed' with ranking people and publicizing research outcomes where such IC disclosures may become detrimental to staff morale.

Cricelli et al. (2018) explore the relationship between IC and performance of public universities in emerging countries. These authors found that universities need to achieve a critical mass to obtain outstanding research and innovation results. Bisogno et al. (2018) note that IC in education research is concentrated in Europe and mainly addresses IC in universities. Habersam et al. (2018) present the findings of a longitudinal study on the use of mandatory knowledge balance sheets in Austrian public universities. Habersam et al. (2018) focus on the communicative culture of the reports and the value of strategy for orientation, sense making and an effective allocation of resources. While attention has focused on the study of narrative IC disclosure in the university context (Low et al., 2015), the visual form, comprised of pictorial images, has been understudied (Yusof et al., 2015). As such, we present this issue as a 'missing in action' (MIA) interpretative paradigm.

BENEFITS OF INTELLECTUAL CAPITAL DISCLOSURE

Images in a reporting context are recognized as an effective communication device, with the ability to influence impressions and to be readily interpreted for meaning (Preston et al., 1996; Davison and Warren, 2009). Davison et al. (2012) emphasize the effectiveness of an image, stating that images can draw a reader in and create immediate interpretation. In particular, images can draw a reader into identifying intangibles such as brands, business partnerships and entrepreneurial audacity, all of which position a reporting organization towards a successful future (Davison, 2010). In addition, Yusof et al. (2015) claim that the impressions organizations may be willing to portray in images are their successes regarding rewards they have received from other organizations, successful media campaigns and sponsorships with major events.

Several scholarly opinions are given for the origin and rationale for the use of images in annual reports. Graves et al. (1996) suggest that the use of imagery is a tribute to the television epistemology that occurred in the United States in the 1960s, which emphasized the use of visual design, gloss and novelty to persuade the public of the authenticity of annual reports. Alternatively, both McKinstry (1996) and Lee (1994) observed increases in the number of pictorial images being used in annual reports in their studies, which they attributed to 'consumer engineering', where management is specifically constructing a particular image of the corporation. This idea of 'consumer engineering' is supported by Yusof et al. (2015), who claim that the non-financial information presented to annual report readers is a well-reflected description of the concerns, interests, attitudes and policies of an organization's management.

Given the additional managerial information contained in an annual report, Davison (2008) asserts that annual report readers, such as analysts who are not accountants, do read and look at the persuasive devices that extra discretionary information contains, in the form of both narratives and accompanying images. Hooper et al. (2001), in support of other scholars, acknowledge the potential that images have in an annual report context, with the observation that an increasing number of companies are using images prominently as a strategic marketing tool to convey aspects of an organization in a storytelling manner.

McKinstry (1996) analysed a series of annual reports produced by Burton Plc, a British fashion retailer, and found that its annual report became a public relations document after 1984. Similarly, Graves et al. (1996) claim that pictures in annual reports are used to refer to public relations and to assist in validating the truth claims portrayed through the financial statements.

As is known from advertising, images are used and set up in an intentional way. Barthes (1977) demonstrates the marketing power of an image by suggesting that, in an advertising context, a literal linguistic message is acquirable, and even iconic or cultural messages can be obtained by considering how the objects involved in a photograph are laid out. Yusof et al. (2015) assert that humans are quick to respond to visual images, and that appeal, comprehension and retention are common if the image is well designed. For instance, visual portraits of directing and managing the staff of an organization frequently appear in annual reports. Davison (2010) argues that intangible qualities associated with people shown in dress codes, interpersonal codes and spatial codes are used to show important intangible components of an organization, including its staff's ability to network with others, demonstrate interpersonal skills, their familiarity with the organization and a key business quality: trust.

REVIEW OF IMAGE ANALYSIS DEVICES

This section of the chapter will bring together a range of image devices in communication that are emphasized in research. Davison (2014) asserts that it is becoming more important for accountants to be aware of the communication media of pictorial disclosures in annual reports, because of the pressing visualizing and rhetorical attributes that images present.

Literal and Iconic Meanings

Scholars recognize that images have intentional meanings to be interpreted by a reader. Barthes (1977) argues that any advertising image contains at least a literal linguistic message. Usually, the caption presented with the image will help decode the literal message, but if there is none, the reader will commonly ask 'What is it?' This question anticipates its meaning from the objects that are presented. Preston et al. (1996) explain that obtaining a literal message from an image in an annual report begins and often ends in an attempt to discern the message intended from that of the designers and their corporate client. However, Davison and

Warren (2009) claim that interpreting and ascertaining meanings derived in images can be difficult, given that they can be ambiguous and even subjective if the message is interpretable. Similarly, Davison (2008) also argues that pictures can be perceived to portray unconscious messages.

One rationale behind the difficulty of interpreting images is given by Gamson et al. (1992), who reveal that image interpretation is subject to layers of meanings, with some that are naturalized, which means they are assumed to be taken for granted. For instance, Preston et al. (1996) examined the cover page of PepsiCo's 1990 annual report containing a Sumo wrestler in a ceremonial stance. As it was obvious that the image was not signifying Pepsi's diversification into Sumo wrestling, the image should, instead, be interpreted in a metaphorical sense, where the aspect of power presented in wrestling is linked to the established brand of Pepsi. This link is made explicit through the caption 'The Power of Big Brands' (Preston et al., 1996, p. 116).

Repetition

Pictures are often used to convey themed messages and have rhetorical properties associated with them, one of which is repetition, a property that is agreed upon by multiple researchers. Both Pesci et al. (2015) and Davison (2008) assert that repetition is a rhetorical device that is used with pictures to convey particular messages to an intended audience, to enhance reader memorability and to provide further emphasis. However, the authors emphasize different aspects of repetition surrounding pictorial disclosures. On one hand, Pesci et al. (2015) assert that there are different degrees of device repetition that can be used, based on the number of visual devices used to reinforce a theme. Hume (1739, as cited in Pesci et al., 2015) classifies different degrees of device repetition as none, identical, similar or accumulated.

The repetition device recognized for a given image is determined by the number of visual devices deployed. Different visual devices include narrative disclosure (for example, a caption), image disclosure and the use of a table, chart or drawing. On the other hand, Davison (2014) looks at repetition from the perspective of elements repeated within a pictorial image. Within an image, two denoted elements of a picture's properties are observed, the content (for example, people, places or things) and the form (for example, shape, colour and style). A degree of element repetition (that is, 'none', 'identity', 'similarity', 'accumulation' or 'series') is then derived based on whether objects are repeated, and if so, whether or not the form of the objects is structured and organized in a logical order within the image (Davison, 2014).

Represent or Pervert a Certain Reality

Pictorial disclosures in an annual report are often used to reflect reality or to construct reality. Baudrillard (1987) offers four phases in which an image can be used to mask reality: an image can reflect basic reality; mask and pervert a basic reality; mask the absence of a basic reality; or constitute rather than merely represent reality. Hooper et al. (2001) analysed several New Zealand companies' annual reports between 1998 and 2000 to ascertain whether there was a trend between the share price of a company and the way pictorial disclosures were used to create or mask reality. They found that companies which had been successful used pictures overtly to laud gains, and used large colourful pictures. Conversely, when a company was unsuccessful, it constructed a reality using iconic pictures that would depict a company's values (for example, endurance, progress or steadfastness), using little colour, small pictures and a small number of images.

Cultural Flow

Images can also be used to represent movements in the global cultural flow. With the movement of people globally, integrated with capital movement and the rapid pace of technological advancement, Preston and Young (2000) present a case that images have a constructive element to portray organizations as a global entity, with the influence of 'global cultural flow'. Appadurai (1990, as cited in Preston and Young, 2000) notes that 'global cultural flow' can be represented in five dimensions: ethnoscapes (people movement and the ongoing corresponding relationship people have with cultures), technoscapes (changes in technology) and financescapes (how financial capital flows around the world at a rapid pace). These three dimensions can then be represented in images presented in mediascapes (a presentation media) and ideoscapes (ideological overlays that can be contained in an image).

With all five dimensions combined, Appadurai (1990, as cited in Preston and Young, 2000) asserts that these five dimensions can be used to represent the world an organization exists in, or construct an imagined world in which the corporation supposedly operates. Similarly, Davison (2004) also recognizes the movement of the global organization in that the religious and cultural association of ascension may be prevalent in a financial statement. Often associated with staircases and multitudes of people, the organization may print the iconic notion of advancing from one area of space into another (Davison, 2004).

METHOD

This study uses a qualitative approach. Silverman (2010) states that the qualitative approach allows the researcher to ask the question 'How?' as opposed to 'How many?' and, thus, is descriptive in nature. A qualitative approach involves the collection of soft data and is appropriate for researching complex situations that may not produce precise solutions (Silverman, 2010). Ghosh and Chopra (2003, p. 75, as cited in Crowther and Lancaster, 2009) state that 'qualitative data is data in the form of descriptive accounts of observations or data which is classified by type'. This research involves the derivation of meanings. Therefore, the interpretative paradigm underpins the qualitative research approach. The interpretive paradigm allows a researcher to observe social reality from the perspective of one person and thus makes data collected very subjective (Collis and Hussey, 2014). Given that this research involves the perception of the researchers determining what IC item is disclosed in a pictorial image, and any literal messages, the interpretative paradigm was the most appropriate approach.

For any analysis to be reliable and effective, Steenkamp and Hooks (2011) highlight the importance of operating definitions for each IC category to enhance both the reader's understanding of the coding process and the degree of replicability of this study. Table 10.1 outlines the IC upper-level and lower-level categories to be used for this study. The three upper-level IC categories are: internal capital, external capital

Table 10.1 Intellectual capital categories

Internal capital	External Capital	Human Capital
Intellectual property	Brands/university image	Work-related knowledge/know-how
University culture	Students/student satisfaction	Employee
Management philosophy	Business/university partnerships	Employee's experiences in profession
Management process	Students database	Employee qualifications
Networking system/ information system	Quality standards	Employee compensation/ benefits
Research projects		Culture diversity
Financial relations		Training programmes

Source: Adapted from Low et al. (2015, p. 787).

and human capital. There are then 19 lower-level IC categories, seven each under internal and human capital, and five under external capital. Table 10.2 outlines operating definitions for each of the lower-level IC categories.

Sample

All eight New Zealand universities are considered in this study. Each university has published annual reports for the academic years of 2012, 2013 and 2014, which are analysed in this study. The annual reporting period for these universities goes from 1 January through to 31 December. The eight New Zealand universities are:

1. University of Auckland.
2. Auckland University of Technology.
3. University of Waikato.
4. Massey University.
5. Victoria University of Wellington.
6. University of Canterbury.
7. Lincoln University.
8. University of Otago.

Coding Process for this Study

To avoid common methodological problems associated with content analysis, this study establishes a coding framework. In particular, Boyatzis (1998, as cited in Beattie and Thomson, 2007) acknowledges that content analysis requires a specific description of how and when categories of IC occur, outlining explicit coding rules about specific inclusions or exclusions, and providing examples of categorized IC information.

The coding approach for interpreting IC disclosure within themed pictorial images for this study will be similar to the approach used by Steenkamp and Northcott (2007), who coded one IC item per picture and recorded one count per picture. In addition to coding one IC item per picture, the authors also used the following coding rules:

- Code the dominant IC item identified in the context unit that addresses the issue presented by the boundary issue, which adapts the approach of Husin et al. (2012) to consider the existence of each IC item presented. If one IC item causes the other IC item to co-exist, the first IC item is considered the dominant IC item.

Table 10.2 Intellectual capital components operating definitions

Category	IC Components	Description
Internal capital	Intellectual property	Includes all copyright (in relation to phonograms and broadcasts), patent rights, plant varieties, registered and unregistered trademarks, and publications (journal, books, e-journals, chapters, etc.) held by sample university
	University culture	Comprising the vision, attitudes, experiences, beliefs and values of a university
	Management philosophy	Information referred to in mission statement
	Management process	Information related to the process in the university
	Information system/networking system	Information on the development, use, application and influence of systems
	Research projects	Research projects conducted by a university
	Financial relations	Information referring to the relationships between the university and its financial relations
External capital	Brands/university image	Information of brands associated with the University
	Students/student satisfaction	Information relating to students and their satisfaction about learning
	Business/university partnership	All the activities and collaboration between universities and other organizations (firms, non-profit organizations, public authorities, local government and society as a whole)
	Student database	Database of all students
	Quality standards	Information referring to teaching quality or learning quality

Table 10.2 (continued)

Category	IC Components	Description
Human capital	Work-related knowledge/ know-how	Individual competencies of researchers, knowledge or skill obtained from the job or training
	Employees	Information regarding staff, researchers, lecturers, PhD students and administrative personnel
	Employee's experience in profession	Information referring to employees' international or national experiences in their profession
	Employee qualifications	Information relating to employees' qualifications
	Employee compensation/ benefits	Information referring to welfare or other benefits for employees and PhD students provided by a university
	Cultural diversity	Demographic information of employees
	Training programs	Education or training programmes for employees provided by a university

Source: Adapted from Low et al. (2015, p. 787).

- Record repetitive messages in different pictures as separate counts. This rule applies as more emphasis is generated when multiple images are used to convey a single message.
- Record one count per picture even if there are multiple appearances of the dominant IC item within a picture (for example, a picture representing five employees would be recorded as one count only). However, for this study, such an image is also analysed in terms of the degree of element repetition used.
- Record one count per picture regardless of the size of the picture (Steenkamp and Northcott, 2007).

To carry out the coding process, Hackston and Milne (1996, as cited in Beattie and Thomson, 2007) suggest the use of a four-digit coding approach, an approach that was used in a corporate social responsibility (CSR) disclosure study but could be adapted for IC disclosure (see Table 10.3).

By utilizing the four-digit coding approach, recording decisions and reliability calculations were performed (Beattie and Thomson, 2007). Every picture disclosed in three annual reports of each New Zealand university was tracked with a unique code to calculate the total number of pictures disclosed and the quantity of disclosures of both upper-level and lower-level classifications of IC. The quality of disclosure digit will be used to indicate the degree of surrounding text that envelops an

Table 10.3 Four-digit code approach to disclosures

Digit	IC disclosure	Adapted for this study
First Digit	The existence of IC disclosure	Does the picture contain an IC item? Yes (1) or No (0)
Second Digit	Category of IC disclosure	If the picture contains an IC themed item, what category of IC does this fit under (i.e., human, external or internal)
Third Digit	Type of disclosure	If the picture contains an IC themed item, what subcategory of IC does this best fit under (e.g., employee)
Fourth Digit	Quality of disclosure	If an IC item, what is the extent of disclosure (i.e., is there surrounding text, a caption, etc.)

Source: Adapted from Hackston and Milne (1996, as cited in Beattie and Thomson, 2007).

image, identifying textual information about the message contained in the disclosed photograph(s), and thus indicating the existence of a textual communicative device. The richness of the information is thus measured by the amount of information that is presented by the different forms of disclosure (Husin et al., 2012). Figure 10.1 illustrates the process that is used to facilitate the collection of data to analyse the trends in IC pictorial disclosures.

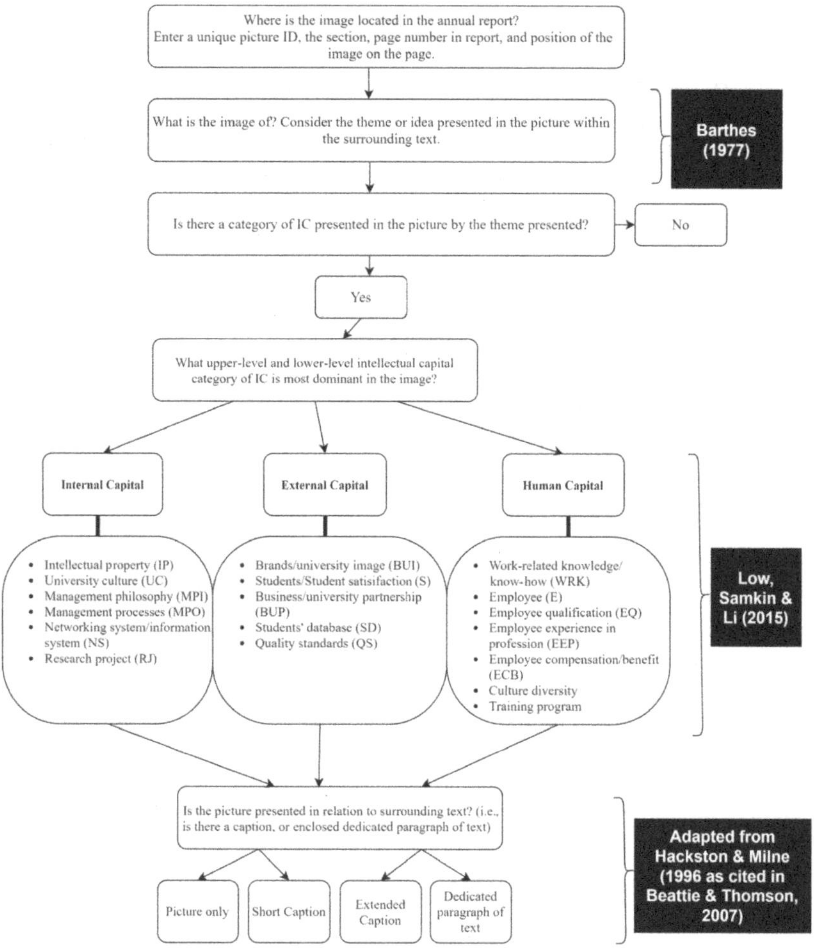

Figure 10.1 The process for collecting data and analysing trends in IC pictorial disclosures

ANALYSIS OF INTELLECTUAL CAPITAL IN PICTORIAL DISCLOSURES

This section identifies and analyses trends in the perceived pictorial disclosures over a period of three years. All eight New Zealand universities release their annual reports online, with both current and historical annual reports available. The analysis considers data from all universities to find the most frequently disclosed item, from the 19 individual subcategories of IC. This section also examines trends in both the number of disclosures each IC item has, and considers their ranking among the other categories for the three years.

To capture information for this study, each photographic image presented in the three annual reports of each university for the period 2012–2014 was coded with image placement details. The image placement details included: a unique picture identification number, the section of the annual report in which the disclosure was made, the page number of the photograph and the position of the image on the page. Collecting image placement details allowed for the easy identification and tracking of each photograph. To determine the existence of an item of IC in a photograph, a brief description of what the photograph was about was generated. Furthermore, the use of a four-digit code (see Table 10.3) was then used to capture data about the classification of the IC item depicted. The first digit (either 1 or 0) described whether the photographic image disclosed any items of IC. The second digit captured what upper-level category of IC was being depicted (external capital, internal capital or human capital; this was only used if the first digit was a 1. The third digit disclosed the classified item of the most dominant element or object of IC presented in the picture from the list of IC items (see Table 10.2). The fourth digit captured the extent of caption disclosure, based on any immediate surrounding text presented with the photographic image (with a grade range of 0–3, with 0 representing no immediate caption and 3 representing a dedicated paragraph caption). Some pictures depicted multiple IC items, and in such cases the most dominant IC item presented was counted, after taking into account all the elements and objects depicted in each picture. If an image was judged not to have an IC item, no further analysis of the image occurred on the second, third and fourth digits.

To demonstrate an example of the coding process, we explain how we analysed an image from the University of Waikato's 2014 Annual Report (for fuller details of image, see https://www.waikato.ac.nz/annualreport/2014/files/annual-report.pdf, p. 28), depicting the Deputy Vice-Chancellor with three Super XV Chiefs players. The image was surrounded by an immediate two-sentence caption that explained the importance of the image and related it to a Memorandum of Understanding (MoU) between the university and the Chiefs Rugby Club. Applying the 'four-digit code approach to disclosure' (see Table 10.3), we assigned '1' to the first digit, 'EC' (external capital) to the second digit, 'BUP' (business/university partnership) to the third digit and '2' to the fourth digit for quality disclosure ranking. The image was judged to be reinforcing a theme of 'university partnerships', and thus the image most closely aligned with the 'business and university partnerships' IC category, which is an external capital, upper-level IC category item.

The rankings of universities are based on the proportion of images perceived to portray intellectual capital, not on the total number of images. Of all the photographic images presented in annual reports of the eight New Zealand universities for the three academic years (2012, 2013, 2014), 79 per cent were perceived to contain an item of IC. Victoria University of Wellington disclosed the highest proportion of IC items, with 97.6 per cent of pictorial images perceived to disclose at least one element of IC. Massey University was a close second (96.9 per cent), with all but one image perceived to contain IC pictorial disclosure. The University of Canterbury disclosed the lowest proportion of IC items from the images used, with just 68.2 per cent of images perceived to portray IC item(s). Table 10.4 presents a summarized rank of each university with the total number of photographic images used, the number of photographic images perceived to portray IC, and the percentage of images disclosing an IC item, across all three years under consideration (2012–2014).

The University of Waikato used the highest number of pictorial images from the three annual reports, with 274 images used, but as the only university to use page header photographic images, this increased their total photographic image count by 117. The header photographic images portrayed a combination of a staircase and ceiling lighting, which were taken in the university's student centre building. If page header photographic images are not counted, Victoria University of Wellington would have disclosed the highest proportion of IC items from all the images used, and the highest number of photographic images in total. The University of Canterbury disclosed the lowest number of photographic images and the lowest number of images perceived to show IC items. A total of 885 images were counted in the annual reports of all New Zealand universities over the three-year period.

Figure 10.2 shows the trend in the number of images perceived to portray IC items for each of the three years (2012–2014) for each university. During these years, the average number of perceived IC image disclosures increased from 22 to 35, indicating that there is an increase in the quantity

Table 10.4 Overall ranking of New Zealand universities based on the proportion of images perceived to portray intellectual capital

Ranking	University	Number of images across all three reporting period annual reporting periods (2012–2014)	Number of images perceived to disclose IC items	Percentage (%) of images disclosing intellectual capital items[a]
1st	Victoria University of Wellington	168	164	97.62
2nd	Massey University	32	31	96.88
3rd	Lincoln University	118	113	95.76
4th	Auckland University of Technology (AUT)	27	25	92.59
5th	University of Waikato – no page headers[b]	157	145	92.36
	University of Waikato – page headers included[b]	(274)	(145)	(52.92)
6th	University of Otago	90	77	85.56
7th	University of Auckland	154	131	85.06
8th	University of Canterbury	22	15	68.18
Total without page headers (all universities)		768	701	91.27%
Total with page headers included (all universities)		(885)	(701)	(79.12%)

Notes:

a. Percentage (%) of images disclosing IC items is based on the total number of images disclosing IC items divided by the total number of images disclosed.

b. In the 2014 University of Waikato annual report, the preparers used a series of repeated images disclosing part of a student common area (i.e., lights and a stairwell) as part of page headers (being the only university to do so). These images were perceived not to show an IC item but were nevertheless images to be counted given the coding instructions set out in the study. The analysis in this table, however, has made an exception to this, by excluding the images perceived to be header photographs, given that their main purpose is for presentation purposes. If these page header images were accounted for in this study, the University of Waikato in the combined three years would have disclosed a total number of 274 images, with 145 being the number of images disclosing an IC item, decreasing the percentage of images disclosing IC to 52.92%. For the purposes of this study, when the University of Waikato's results are presented, both cases (with and without page headers) will be presented. As a result, the overall total and average of images disclosing IC is also affected, and both cases will be presented where relevant.

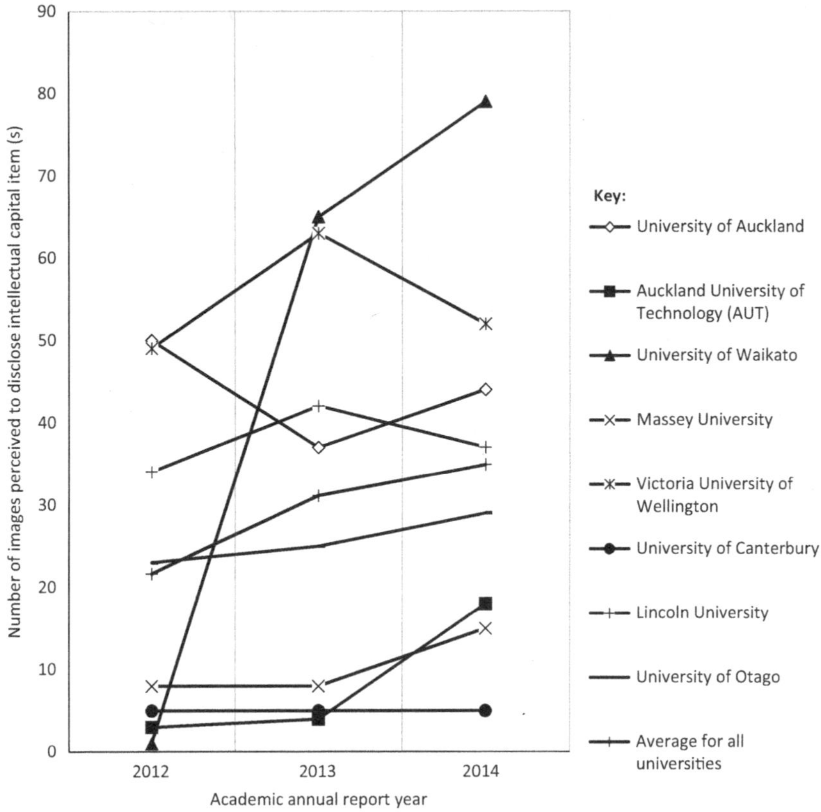

Figure 10.2 Trend in the number of images perceived to disclose intellectual capital item(s) between 2012 and 2014 for each university

of IC disclosures being made amongst New Zealand universities. Six of the eight New Zealand universities had an increase in the number of IC disclosures. The two exceptions were the University of Auckland (drop from 50 to 44), and the University of Canterbury (maintained five IC disclosures throughout). The University of Waikato had the most significant increase in image quantity used to show IC over the three-year period, going from one disclosure in 2012 to 79 disclosures in 2014. The University of Auckland had the highest number of perceived IC disclosures in 2012 with 50 counted disclosures, while University of Waikato had the highest disclosure quantities for both 2013 and 2014 with 65 and 79, respectively. The University of Auckland reduced the number of perceived IC image disclosures between 2012 and 2013, as did Lincoln University and Victoria University of Wellington between 2013 and 2014.

PORTRAYAL OF INTELLECTUAL CAPITAL VIA REPETITION ANALYSIS DEVICES

This section considers how New Zealand universities pictorially portrayed images perceived to disclose IC in their 2014 annual reports, using repetition analysis devices that were emphasized in the literature. The first repetition image analysis device considered in this study includes an analysis of the use of communication devices to reinforce themes perceived in images. The second repetition analysis device considered is element repetition, which examines whether objects are repeated within an image, and if so, whether there were variations and/or similarities in the objects' form of repetition used to invoke contrast. An analysis for each university was presented in light of evidence of perceived device and element repetition. Within each university's profile, an exemplary image was identified and analysed in light of the frameworks established earlier.

To capture information for this part of the study, each photographic image perceived to disclose IC in the 2014 annual report of each New Zealand university was coded with further details. The further details included an extended literal message analysis write-up where up to a few sentences were used to describe any key themed messages portrayed in the image. The area surrounding the image was then scanned for any further communication devices that reinforced the theme in the photographic image (for example, tabular information, photo captions, infographics, electronic drawings such as logos and other theme-related photographs). The number of communication devices identified determined the type of device repetition, which was used to emphasize the IC themed item. Each photographic image was then examined to identify key objects presented in the image, and an assessment was then made as to whether these objects were repeated in the image. Images that had repeated objects were then assessed as to whether the form of the repeated objects had variations and/or similarities in style, shape or colour appearance. Images disclosing IC that had repeated objects are said in the literature to have a higher emphasis placed on them as readers consider the differences between the objects portrayed. The degree of element repetition depended on whether the objects had evidence of both variation and similarity in form.

Extent and form of device repetition was consistent and common across all related earlier studies. While Pesci et al. (2015) considered the forms of device repetition in social and environmental reports of cooperative banks from both text and visual components, similar findings from both that study and this current study suggest that the majority of device repetition is 'similar', containing a moderate level of impact of impressions leading to memorable knowledge. Evidence of some higher level of memorable impact (for example, accumulated device repetition), where there were more than three types of stimuli acting to direct the reader to a familiar theme, was also present, although scarce given that only two New Zealand universities registered at least one image with this type of device repetition.

Furthermore, there was some evidence of the use of the rhetorical property of element repetition, which has the potential to act as a powerful tool to contribute towards communicating IC (Davison, 2008). Images presented in this study with element repetition included disclosures of multiple students, members of staff or objects that demonstrated intellectual knowledge from students or staff of the universities. Disclosing multiple people types/groups emphasized several IC disclosure categories, including student satisfaction at the university, successful group projects or achievements, and partnerships universities made with the wider community.

DISCUSSION AND CONCLUSION

The findings revealed 79 per cent of all images identified in the study disclosed some element of IC across the 24 annual reports examined. This finding was similar to the study by Yusof et al. (2015), which found that 80 per cent of the images contained in their sample of 50 Malaysian companies' annual reports alluded to IC disclosure. In their study, Yusof et al. (2015) classified most of the IC images as portraying relational capital, otherwise known as external capital. However, in this study only one of the three years (2012) had external capital as the dominantly reported category. Instead, human capital was the dominant upper-level category of IC reported on, across two of the three years (2013 and 2014).

In terms of lower-level categories of IC, both 'students/student satisfaction' and 'employee' categories were evident and had the highest quantity of images disclosed. This differs from the findings reported in Low et al. (2015), which found that research projects were the most disclosed IC item when considering narrative disclosures. With IC recognized in a range of communication devices, this study supports Steenkamp and Hooks's (2011) observation of the need to consider IC disclosure in the different forms of communication devices. With staff and students emphasized so heavily, including in terms of their successes in the form of either scholarships or projects, in annual reports of New Zealand universities, images have been strategically used to portray a university's key function as being the dissemination of knowledge to society. This finding reinforces those of Sánchez and Elena (2006), who indicated that it is a 'fact that universities' main goals are the production and diffusion of knowledge' (p. 529); and Ramirez and Gordillo (2014), who concluded that key intangible IC elements will 'produce a progressive improvement in university teaching, research and knowledge transfer' (p. 185).

This research has contributed towards the ongoing development of understandings of IC portrayed in annual reports and has generated understandings of what IC items are depicted most in a New Zealand university context. While numerous studies have considered IC in the form of text in annual reports, fewer studies had considered IC in pictorial form. Of those that considered IC in pictorial form, only a company context had been considered.

The study also considered the existence and extent of the image rhetorical device of repetition, in the form of both device repetition and element repetition, that pictures perceived to disclose IC were used to reinforce the theme presented in the image. By considering repetition, this study has examined what disclosures may be considered more important than others by annual report preparers.

Despite the contribution of this study to understandings of IC portrayed in New Zealand universities' annual reports and their depiction through the image rhetorical device of repetition, this study was subject to some limitations. First, this interpretative study on IC disclosure themes was based on the authors' understanding and judgement of the images presented. It is quite possible that different interpretations of themes and messages portrayed could lead to a different set of coded classifications of IC items by different researchers. Second, the study only considered three annual report years (2012, 2013 and 2014), and thus has some longitudinal limitations. Third, the study considered only universities in New Zealand and therefore inferences may not be extended to universities globally. Fourth, the literature identified a range of image rhetorical devices, but this study only considered the rhetorical device of repetition. Fifth, this study only considered the visual device of pictorial images and did not consider other devices that could be considered visual and could have IC disclosed, such as tables and diagrams.

There are several avenues for further research from this study. One avenue would be to consider a representational sample of annual report readers, to identify similarities and differences in the depiction of IC in a university reporting context, to ascertain a representational interpretation. Second, an extended number of years could be considered for a given university to ascertain the development of pictorial IC disclosure in a university's annual reporting. Third, another country context could be examined, and a comparison made between the findings of that study and this. Fourth, images depicting IC could be analysed not only to ascertain literal messages but also to explore instances of symbolic messages.

This research study found that the majority (79 per cent) of photographic images included in annual reports of New Zealand universities disclosed perceived IC, portraying value that cannot be seen in the accompanying set of financial statements disclosed in the same annual reports. The average number of perceived IC pictorial disclosures increased over the time frame, which suggests that preparers of these annual reports are placing an increasing emphasis on presenting a university's intangible IC value in the form of pictorial images. Given that the literature identifies images as a key communication device that stakeholders pay dedicated attention to, it could be argued that images in annual reports are becoming the most favoured communication device to find and recognize intangible value in universities.

REFERENCES

Appadurai, A. (1990), 'Disjuncture and difference in the global cultural economy', in M. Featherstone (ed.), *Global Culture*, London: SAGE Publications, pp. 295–310.

Barthes, R. (1977), 'Rhetoric of the Image', accessed 20 November 2018 at http://faculty.georgetown.edu/irvinem/theory/Barthes-Rhetoric-of-the-image-ex.pdf.

Baudrillard, J. (1983), *Simulations*, New York: Semiotext(e).

Baudrillard, J. (1987), 'Modernity', *Canadian Journal of Political and Social Theory*, 11 (3), 63–72.

Beattie, V. and S.J. Thomson (2007), 'Lifting the lid on the use of content analysis to investigate intellectual capital disclosure', *Accounting Forum*, 31 (2), 129–163.

Bisogno, M., Dumay, J., Rossi, F.M. and P.T. Polcini (2018), 'Identifying future directions for IC research education: A literature review', *Journal of Intellectual Capital*, 19 (1),10–33.

Boyatzis, R.E. (1998), *Transforming Qualitative Information: Thematic Analysis and Code Development*, Thousand Oaks, CA: SAGE Publications.

Chiucchi, M.S. (2013), 'Measuring and reporting intellectual capital', *Journal of Intellectual Capital*, 14 (3), 395–413.

Collis, J. and R. Hussey (2014), *Business Research: A Practical Guide for Undergraduate and Postgraduate Students* (4th edn), Basingstoke: Palgrave Macmillan.

Cricelli, L., Greco, M., Grimaldi, M. and L.P.L. Duenas (2018), 'Intellectual capital and university performance in emerging countries: Evidence from Colombian universities', *Journal of Intellectual Capital*, 19 (1), 71–95.

Crowther, D. and G. Lancaster (2009). *Research Methods* (2nd edn), Oxford: Butterworth-Heinemann.

Cuozzo, B., Dumay, J., Palmaccio, M. and R. Lombardi (2017), 'Intellectual capital disclosure: A structured literature review', *Journal of Intellectual Capital*, 18 (1), 9–28.

Davison, J. (2004), 'Sacred vestiges in financial reporting: Mythical readings guided by Mircea Eliade', *Accounting, Auditing and Accountability Journal*, 17 (3), 476–497.

Davison, J. (2008), 'Rhetoric, repetition, reporting and the "dot.com" era: Words, pictures, intangibles', *Accounting, Auditing and Accountability Journal*, 21 (6), 791–826.
Davison, J. (2010), '[In]visible [in]tangibles: Visual portraits of the business elite', *Accounting, Organizations and Society*, 35 (2), 165–183.
Davison, J. (2014), 'Visual rhetoric and the case of intellectual capital', *Accounting, Organizations and Society*, 39 (1), 20–37.
Davison, J., McLean, C. and S. Warren (2012), 'Exploring the visual in organizations and management', *Qualitative Research in Organizations and Management*, 7 (1), 5–15.
Davison, J. and S. Warren (2009), 'Imag[in]ing accounting and accountability', *Accounting, Auditing and Accountability*, 22 (6), 845–857.
Di Berardino, D. and C. Corsi (2018), 'A quality evaluation approach to disclosing third mission activities and intellectual capital in Italian universities', *Journal of Intellectual Capital*, 19 (1), 178–201.
Dumay, J. and R. Roslender (2013), 'Utilising narrative to improve the relevance of intellectual capital', *Journal of Accounting and Organizational Change*, 9 (3), 248–279.
Gamson, W.A., Croteau, D., Hoynes, W. and T. Sasson (1992), 'Media images and the social construction of reality', *Annual Review of Sociology*, 18, 373–393.
Ghosh, N. and P.K. Chopra (2003), *A Dictionary of Research Methods*, Leeds: Wisdom House UK.
Graves, O.F., Flesher, D.L. and R.E. Jordan (1996), 'Pictures and the bottom line: The television epistemology of US annual reports', *Accounting, Organizations and Society*, 21 (1), 57–88.
Habersam, M., Piber, M. and M. Skoog (2018), 'Ten years of using knowledge balance sheets in Austrian public universities: A retrospective and prospective view', *Journal of Intellectual Capital*, 19 (1), 34–52.
Hackston, D. and M.J. Milne (1996), 'Some determinants of social and environmental disclosures in New Zealand companies', *Accounting, Auditing and Accountability Journal*, 9 (1), 77–108.
Hooper, K., Low, M. and H. Kearins (2001), 'Pictures in New Zealand annual reports: Winners and losers', *Asian Pacific Public Relations Journal*, 3 (2), 83–107.
Hume, D. (1739), *A Treatise of Human Nature*, accessed 20 November 2018 at http://www.gutenberg.org/files/4705/4705-h/4705-h.htm#link2H_4_0006.
Husin, N.M., Hooper, K. and K. Olesen (2012), 'Analysis of intellectual capital disclosure – An illustrative example', *Journal of Intellectual Capital*, 13 (2), 196–220.
Lee, T. (1994), 'The changing form of the corporate annual report', *Accounting Historians Journal*, 21 (1), 215–232.
Low, M., Samkin, G. and Y. Li (2015), 'Voluntary reporting of intellectual capital: Comparing the quality of disclosures from New Zealand, Australian and United Kingdom universities', *Journal of Intellectual Capital*, 16 (4), 779–808.
Lu, W. (2012), 'Intellectual capital and university performance in Taiwan', *Economic Modelling*, 29 (4), 1081–1089.
Mariani, G., Carlesi, A. and A.A. Scarfo (2018), 'Academic spin offs as a value driver for the intellectual capital: The case of the University of Pisa', *Journal of Intellectual Capital*, 19 (1), 202–226.
Martin-Sardesai, A. and J. Guthrie (2018), 'Human capital loss in an academic performance measurement system', *Journal of Intellectual Capital*, 19 (1), 53–70.
McKinstry, S. (1996), 'Designing the annual reports of Burton plc from 1930 to 1994', *Accounting, Organizations and Society*, 21 (1), 89–111.
National Council of the Republic of Austria (2002), *University Organisation and Studies Act (Universities Act 2002), University Organisation Amendment Act and Universities of the Arts Organisation Amendment Act*, accessed 20 November 2018 at http://www.uibk.ac.at/index/finanzabteilung/ug2002_englisch.pdf.
Passaro, R., Quinto, I. and A. Thomas (2018), 'The impact of higher education on entrepreneurial intention and human capital', *Journal of Intellectual Capital*, 19 (1), 135–156.

Pesci, C., Costa, E. and T. Soobaroyen (2015), 'The forms of repetition in social and environmental reports: Insights from Hume's notion of "impressions"', *Accounting and Business Research*, 45 (6), 765–800.
Preston, A.M., Wright, C. and J.J. Young (1996), 'Imag[in]ing annual reports', *Accounting, Organizations and Society*, 21 (1), 113–137.
Preston, A.M. and J.J. Young (2000), 'Constructing the global corporation and corporate constructions of the global: A picture essay', *Accounting, Organizations and Society*, 25 (4), 427–449.
Ramirez, Y. and S. Gordillo (2014), 'Recognition and measurement of intellectual capital in Spanish universities', *Journal of Intellectual Capital*, 15 (1), 173–188.
Sánchez, M.P. and S. Elena (2006), 'Intellectual capital in universities: Improving transparency and internal management', *Journal of Intellectual Capital*, 7 (4), 529–548.
Sangiorgi, D. and B. Siboni (2017), 'The disclosure of intellectual capital in Italian universities: What has been done and what should be done', *Journal of Intellectual Capital*, 18 (2), 354–372.
Secundo, G., Lombardi, R. and J. Dumay (2018), 'Intellectual capital in education', *Journal of Intellectual Capital*, 19 (1), 2–9.
Silverman, D. (2010), *Doing Qualitative Research: A Practical Handbook* (3rd edn), London, UK and Los Angeles, CA, USA: SAGE.
Steenkamp, N. and J. Hooks (2011), 'Does including pictorial disclosure of intellectual capital resources make a difference?', *Pacific Accounting Review*, 23 (1), 52–68.
Steenkamp, N. and D. Northcott (2007), 'Content analysis in accounting research: The practical challenges', *Australian Accounting Review*, 17 (43), 12–25.
Sultanova, G., Svyatov, S. and N. Ussenbayer (2018), 'Transmitting competencies at universities in Kazakhstan: Intellectual capital of teachers', *Journal of Intellectual Capital*, 19 (1), 112–134.
University of Waikato (2014), *Annual Report*, accessed 15 October 2017 at https://www.waikato.ac.nz/annualreport/2014/files/annual-report.pdf.
van der Meer-Kooistra, J. and S.M. Zijlstra (2001), 'Reporting on intellectual capital', *Accounting, Auditing and Accountability Journal*, 14 (4), 456–476.
Wang, Q., Sharma, U. and H. Davey (2016), 'Intellectual capital disclosure by Chinese and Indian information technology companies: A comparative analysis', *Journal of Intellectual Capital*, 17 (3), 507–529.
Yusof, A., Rahman, M. and M. Hassan (2015), 'Firms characteristics and photography images of intellectual capital in corporate annual reports', *Prosiding Perkem*, 10 (2015), 188–195.

PART III

VALUE ADDED INTELLECTUAL COEFFICIENT (VAIC)

11. Knowledge-based organizations: an accounting point of view

Gianpaolo Iazzolino and Domenico Laise

INTRODUCTION

It is undisputed that a strategy based on investment in knowledge workers is the greatest competitive weapon for today's organizations. Furthermore, it is a kind of strategy that can lead to a sustainable advantage (Grant, 2010, pp. 150–173). By sustainable growth strategies, we generally mean the firm behaviours that in the long run tend to legitimize the social, environmental and economic expectations of all stakeholders, both internal and external (Donaldson and Preston, 1995; Drucker, 1999b). The necessary condition to create wealth for all stakeholders is, according to Drucker (1999b), the growth in productivity of knowledge workers. In fact, Drucker believes that 'knowledge worker productivity is the biggest of the 21st-century management challenges. In the developed countries, it is their first survival requirement'. He argues that 'the ability of organizations ... to survive will come to depend on their "comparative advantage" in making the knowledge worker more productive' (Drucker, 1999b). But, how can we increase the productivity of knowledge workers? Drucker sets the agenda of things to do and lists the major factors affecting the increase in the productivity of knowledge workers (Drucker, 1968, 1999a, 1999b):

1. knowledge workers themselves must plan what the task is or should be. In fact, in knowledge work, unlike manual work, the task does not programme the worker;
2. knowledge workers must manage themselves (autonomy);
3. knowledge work requires continuous innovation and learning;
4. knowledge workers must plan the quality of their output;
5. knowledge worker productivity requires that the knowledge worker is seen and treated as an asset rather than a cost.

Developed countries may have an advantage in the supply and the productivity of people educated and trained for knowledge work. But can this productivity advantage be measured, or is it purely an 'intangible thing'? Drucker does not offer an answer to this question.

Pulic (2000, 2004, 2008) accepts the challenge of measuring the productivity of knowledge workers. Pulic's main objective is to find a productivity 'measuring model' for the knowledge economy that will serve employees, management, investors and business partners (Pulic, 2008, p. 6). He believes that the method for measuring the productivity of knowledge workers is the same as the one used to measure the productivity of manual workers. The productivity of knowledge workers is equal to the ratio between the value added and the wages of workers. Other authoritative scholars share the same opinion (Kaplan and Norton, 1996). From a methodological point of view, therefore, everything we need is in the value added income statement (VAIS). However, Pulic and Drucker think that the VAIS must be reinterpreted, and this requires a 'change of mentality', namely a new 'semantic' of the value creation.

We have to start from the premise that 'people are investment and not cost any more' and that the cost of labour (intellectual), in the income statement, measures the investment in human capital rather than a cost. If this change of mentality is accepted, then the value added measures the value created by knowledge workers for the whole economy; namely, the value added measures the value creation from the stakeholders' point of view. Then, in order to increase the productivity of knowledge workers we have to increase their value added. This is Pulic's answer to the problem left open by Drucker's seminal effort. We have already published a deep methodological and critical review of Pulic's value added intellectual coefficient (VAIC) (Iazzolino and Laise, 2013). The aim was to investigate the strengths and weaknesses of the VAIC, primarily from the accounting theory perspective.

This chapter proposes two main directions of research. First, through the concept and the calculation of knowledge worker productivity, we argue that it is possible to measure the productivity of knowledge workers and use this to answer the question posed by Drucker (1968, 1993, 1999a, 1999b) at the end of the last millennium. An inter-theory relationship between Drucker's approach concerning sustainable strategies based on knowledge and Pulic's (2000, 2004, 2008) theory on human capital efficiency (HCE) can be constructed. This is useful to define a methodology for calculating knowledge worker productivity, a very practical problem for a knowledge-based organization.

Second, in the concept of the measurement of value creation for stakeholders (versus value creation for shareholders), based on the value added in the traditional way of measuring the performance of an organization, the focus is mainly on value creation for the shareholder (shareholder point of view) (Jensen, 2002). But a strategy that is socially sustainable has to create value not only for the shareholder, but also for the other stakeholders, and in particular for the employees. It is immediately evident that the economic facts of the last 20 years, dominated by the shareholder value analysis, have not brought social benefits for everyone, as promised. Mass unemployment, a characteristic of the current world economy, does not confirm that the 'philosophy' of shareholder value analysis has brought socially sustainable benefits. Some important limitations are discussed, namely the inability to measure sustainability, in the final section.

FIRST DIRECTION: THE LINK BETWEEN DRUCKER'S AND PULIC'S THEORIES AND KNOWLEDGE WORKER PRODUCTIVITY

This chapter starts with a comparative analysis of the theories of Drucker and Pulic, related to some important characteristics of the 'knowledge economy'. We identify the links between the two theories and examine the strong and weak points of the two theories.

Literature Background

This research can be mainly framed in the intellectual capital accounting (ICA) literature stream (Petty and Guthrie, 2000; Guthrie et al., 2012; Dumay, 2013; Dumay et al., 2015). Knowledge can be understood as the ability to act for survival implemented by organizations (Maturana and Varela, 1992). The firms' investments in knowledge are the greatest competitive weapon of today's organizations. A high investment in knowledge can be a very powerful tool to actuate differentiation strategies: knowledge (especially tacit knowledge) cannot be easily coded and imitated by competitors. It is a powerful barrier to the entry of competitors and a source of lasting competitive advantage (Grant, 2010).

Shakina and Barajas (2015) have proposed three strategic profiles of firms regarding intangibles. They demonstrated that investments in intangibles allow a company to be better off, even in a period of crisis. Martínez-Torres (2014) has proposed a procedure for identifying the intangible assets that generate value to knowledge-intensive organizations. Olander et al. (2015) have studied how human resources create the basis for continuing innovation and subsequent firm performance in knowledge-intensive industries. Other papers have investigated the relation between intellectual capital and firm value from the strategic point of view (Baiburina and Golovko, 2008; Huang and Wang, 2008).

The link between the topics of knowledge and accounting has been explored in other studies: Holden et al. (1995), for example, defined and applied the knowledge value added (KNOVA) approach. In relation to the productivity of knowledge workers, Phusavat et al. (2013) have used the ratio between value added and number of employees. The ratio between value created and investment in human capital was used by Duarte (2017), named VAHC. Some scholars have elaborated different models based on the measurement of the change of productivity (Hall and Mairesse, 1995). Musolesi and Huiban (2010) have proposed total factor productivity (TFP) as a measure. In addition, Pereme et al. (2016) have proposed an adaptive model to measure the productivity of the research and development (R&D) division. Davies (2004) proposed the concept of 'system integration' as a novel combination of service capabilities required to provide solutions to customers' needs.

The Main Thesis of Drucker and its Limits

Drucker states that the 21st century is characterized by the following transformation:

$$\textit{Capitalism} \rightarrow \textit{Post-capitalism}$$

This transformation is due to the following metamorphosis:

$$\textit{Manual work} \rightarrow \textit{Knowledge work}$$

In brief, for Drucker, post-capitalism is the 'knowledge economy' (Drucker, 1993). In fact, according to Drucker, knowledge work is no longer capitalistic work. It is not labour (workforce) dependent on a capitalistic firm, but autonomous and independent work. The knowledge worker is a capitalist who sells his 'human intellectual capital' to other capitalists; there are no longer conflicting social classes as in the capitalistic era.

The thesis of Drucker has stimulated debate and confusion. In fact, in the current economic system there are millions of workers who make up a non-knowledge-intensive workforce, that is, a traditional capitalistic-type workforce. It does not seem that all workers are knowledge workers, as Drucker suggests. But a knowledge-intensive workforce, employed by a multinational company, is a capitalistic type of workforce. An engineer employed by a for-profit multinational company producing software is a capitalistic employee; that is, they are not an autonomous or independent worker. These considerations are enough to state that the transition glimpsed by Drucker has not yet come about. For-profit companies and their workers still have a capitalistic nature.

This weakness in the analysis of Drucker derives from his failure to produce a clear criterion allowing one to distinguish a knowledge worker from a non-knowledge worker (manual worker). In fact, how do we know that we are in post-capitalism if we do not know who a knowledge worker is? How do we know that we are in post-capitalism if we cannot measure the quantity of knowledge incorporated in a worker? This criterion may not exist, since each job is at the same time both manual and intellectual. Certainly some jobs are more knowledge-intensive than others, but from an overall point of view it is not possible to separate brain activity from that of the human body, and as such, it is not possible to separate manual from intellectual work in a dichotomy.

The lack of a criterion to measure the quantity of incorporated knowledge in a worker creates another problem in Drucker's analysis. As already stated, he asks the following question: how can the productivity of a knowledge worker be increased? However, he does not offer any precise indication to solve this problem. The reason for the difficulties encountered by Drucker can be illustrated in the following way.

The production process is, in general, an activity that can be represented as in Figure 11.1.

The productivity (technical efficiency in the sense of Drucker) is given by the ratio:

$$Technical\ productivity = \frac{Quantity\ of\ the\ product\ of\ knowledge\ (output)}{Quantity\ of\ the\ knowledge\ (input)} \tag{11.1}$$

Now, if the quantity of knowledge (denominator of 11.1) is not measurable (because it is intangible or tacit), then productivity is not measurable. But if knowledge (especially tacit knowledge) is intangible, then we cannot know whether there is a lot or a little, and therefore we cannot know the amount of productivity of the knowledge worker (technical efficiency).

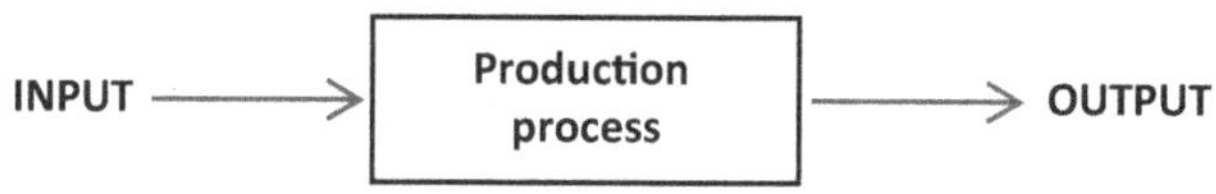

Figure 11.1 Input and output in production process

The Main Thesis of Pulic, in the Wake of the Proposal of Kaplan and Norton

Pulic follows a different direction from Drucker's standpoint. Pulic's idea is substantially simple. If knowledge productivity cannot be measured in a technical sense, Pulic employs the notion of productivity in an economic sense; work is productive if the investment in work creates a profit (income), or rather if it creates value added. For Pulic, the quantities that appear in Figure 11.1 have the following significance:

Input = investment in human capital (HC)
Output = value added obtained by HC

He suggests measuring the productivity of the knowledge worker by means of the notion of economic productivity defined as:

$$Economic\ productivity = \frac{Value\ added\ from\ investment\ in\ human\ capital}{Investment\ in\ human\ capital}$$

That is, more concisely:

$$HCE = \frac{VA}{HC} \qquad (11.2)$$

where:
HCE = human capital efficiency
VA = value added = sales – external costs
HC = human capital, that is, cost of employees (salaries and wages).

As shown, the measure of productivity of knowledge workers proposed by Pulic (human capital efficiency) does not require the measurement of the quantity of knowledge and, therefore, is free from the problems raised by the formula (11.1) of Drucker.

Investment in knowledge work (human capital, HC) is generally high, since knowledge requires a high level of training (not only scholastic) and developed skills. As a result, value added (VA) deriving from a strategy of investment in knowledge-based human resources must be high to make investment economically sustainable. Therefore, in normal conditions, investment in knowledge work is a strategy that allows the creation of value for all the stakeholders, that is, it is economically and socially sustainable. A knowledge-based strategy (in Drucker's sense) is implemented when it creates value for all stakeholders, or when it creates value added (VA) in Pulic's sense, or when it is economically and socially sustainable.

However, the use of formula (11.2) (ratio between VA and cost of employees) for measuring the productivity of work pre-dates Pulic. For example, Kaplan and Norton (1996) proposed this formula. It is included within the key performance indicators (KPIs) of the learning and growth perspective of the balanced scorecard (BSC) (Kaplan and Norton, 1996, pp. 131–132). The logic that drove them to propose the measure of productivity intended as the ratio between VA and HC is summarized in Figure 11.2.

The firm economic process is seen as a macro-process made up of four micro-processes (perspectives). Investment in human capital (HC) is the input and the main KPI of the learning and growth process. Such an investment is necessary to improve the knowledge and expertise of human resources and therefore to improve the quality of internal processes of the firm. More efficient processes are needed to improve the quality of products and customer satisfaction and, furthermore, the financial performance of stakeholders, whose primary KPI is the value added (VA).

Ultimately the efficiency of the overall process is given by the human capital efficiency (HCE), understood as the ratio between the output of the process (value added, VA) and the input of the process, measured by human capital (HC). This result evidently connects Pulic's analysis to Kaplan and Norton's work.

Analysis of Drucker and Pulic's Theories

The contribution made by Pulic can be, in another way, summarized as follows. In the social sciences, when a quantity is not easily measurable, then one resorts to a proxy, which is a quantity positively correlated to the non-measurable entity. For example, the gross domestic product (GDP) is used as proxy of the quality of life. The greater the GDP, the better, it is believed, is the quality of life, a quantity that is not easily measurable. The birthplace of a person is used as proxy of race, which is

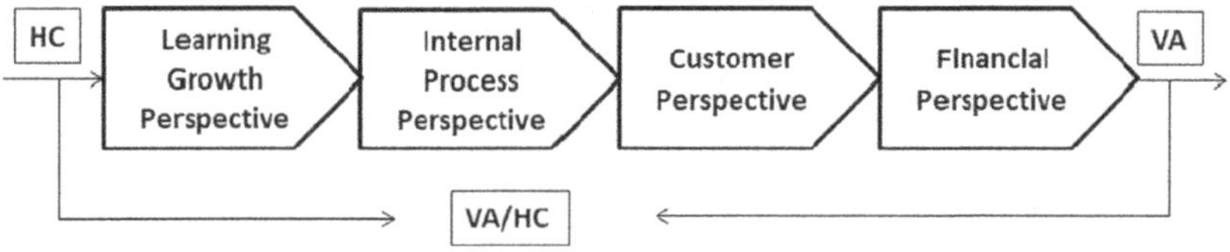

Figure 11.2 Value added (VA) and human capital (HC) as input and output of the balanced scorecard: four perspectives

a notion not easily measured or quantified. Pulic, in essence, suggests the use of the following proxies:

HC = human capital = proxy of the quantity of knowledge (input)
VA = value added = proxy of the quantity of the product of knowledge (output).

The use of HC instead of the quantity of knowledge is justified by the fact that the expense in knowledge-based human resources (HC) is positively correlated to the quantity of knowledge incorporated in the human resources.

The use of VA instead of the product created by knowledge is justified by the fact that the greater the quantity and the quality of product, the greater the value added created. In short, the value added is a quantity that reflects the knowledge content of the knowledge workers.

Let us consider the following example: a great chef has a high culinary knowledge (skill) that is incorporated in his work. This knowledge (tacit), as it can be imagined, is positively correlated to the salary of the chef (HC). It can also be imagined that the product of this knowledge is positively correlated to the value added that the chef creates for the restaurant where they work.

In general, it can be stated that the greater the knowledge incorporated in the work (skill, ability, and so on), the greater the value of the investment in human resources (HC). Moreover, the higher the quantity and the quality of the product of knowledge, the higher the value added (VA). It can be said that, according to Pulic, the VA is a kind of explicit measure (tangible) of the use of a resource that, by its nature, is intangible (tacit knowledge). According to Porter (1985), a high VA created by investment in knowledge (tacit) is a very powerful tool to actuate differentiation strategies. In fact, tacit knowledge cannot easily be coded and imitated by competitors. Therefore, it is a powerful entry barrier for competitors and a source of lasting competitive advantage (Grant, 2010).

To summarize, we agree with Pulic in the definition of the notion of 'human capital efficiency' (HCE). We do not agree, however, with other points of Pulic's analysis, particularly with the notions of 'structural capital efficiency' and 'capital employed efficiency'. These notions have no theoretical importance. In fact, the notion of 'efficiency' (productivity) is not attributable to a form of capital that is not human.

SECOND DIRECTION: VALUE CREATION FOR STAKEHOLDERS AND INVESTMENT IN HUMAN CAPITAL

In this section, we analyse: (1) value creation from the stakeholder point of view; and (2) the investment in human capital.

Literature Background

This research is focused on a particular aspect of the importance of knowledge-based drivers for value creation and sustainable competitive advantage (Grimaldi et al., 2013; Lerro et al., 2014). Demartini et al. (2015) have investigated the relationships between intellectual capital (IC), business performance and sustainability management, to propose a model for measuring and managing intangible assets. A methodology for auditing strategic resources and dynamics of value creation has been proposed by Battagello et al. (2016). The role of creativity and innovation for competitiveness in knowledge-intensive business services has been analysed by Dell'Era et al. (2015). Kianto et al. (2014) have studied the impact of both static (IC assets) and dynamic (knowledge management practices) aspects of organizational knowledge in the value creation process in organizations.

A methodology to assess the capacity of communities of innovation to improve the value creation process was proposed in Grimaldi et al. (2012). A tool based on system dynamics has been used by Zakery et al. (2017) for monitoring and improving the alignment of a firm's key resources with the market growth strategy.

Starting also from events that occurred related to human resources (Kennedy, 2013), some papers have tried to assess employee well-being in large companies (Kobayashi et al., 2018), the impact of firm decisions on human health (Pfeffer, 2010; Neate, 2015) and the relation between career paths and innovation capacity (Smets, 2016).

Stakeholder Point of View and Value Added

In the traditional way of measuring the performance of an organization, the focus is mainly on value creation for the shareholder (shareholder point of view) (Jensen, 2002). But, as already outlined, a strategy that is socially sustainable has to create value not only for the shareholder, but also for the other stakeholders and, in particular, for the employees.

A strategy that only considers the shareholder's interests is a strategy that can be satisfactory for only a part of society. The idea underlying performance measurement in terms of satisfaction only from the point of view of the shareholder is based on the idea that by maximizing profit – net operating profit after taxes (NOPAT), economic value added (EVA), dividends, and so on – social well-being is also maximized. But it is immediately evident that the economic facts of the last 20 years, dominated by the shareholder value analysis, have not brought social benefits for everyone, as promised. Mass unemployment, a characteristic of the current world economy, does not confirm that the 'philosophy' of shareholder value analysis has brought socially sustainable benefits.

The reason is that value creation has not been correctly measured. Value from the social sustainability point of view cannot be measured only by earnings before interest, taxes, depreciation and amortization (EBITDA) or by other measures, such as EVA, which are based on NOPAT which is a variant of EBITDA. The EBITDA measures the value created for all capital investors (within which there is also the shareholder), whereas value created also for the stakeholder 'employees' is measured by the value added.

In addition to value created for capital investors and for the shareholder, it is necessary to consider value created for employees, which is measured by wages and salaries, that is, by the capital invested in acquiring human resources. Value added is, therefore, the adequate measure of value creation from a stakeholder point of view.

From the point of view of society as a whole, value created is equal to (Iazzolino and Laise, 2013; Iazzolino et al., 2017; Pulic, 2000, 2008):

$$VA = HC + EBITDA \tag{11.3}$$

where:
VA = value added
HC = human capital (= cost of employees = wages and salaries)
$EBITDA$ = earnings before interest, taxes, depreciation and amortization (in Pulic's terminology it is SC = structural capital).

Expressing EBITDA in terms of its components, it holds that:

$$EBITDA = Depreciation/Amortization + Interest\ expenses + Taxes + Net\ Income.$$

The latter definition stresses the fact that in EBITDA, less taxes, there are the remunerations of various capital investors, understood in both physical and financial sense (and therefore also shareholders).

Some elucidation is needed to link the equation (11.3) with the themes of knowledge management. Knowledge that creates value is incorporated in human capital (people). If this observation is correct, then expenditure on human resources has to be seen as an investment and not as a cost: 'it is only reasonable to give this resource the status it deserves of investment and not cost anymore'. But, 'employees, who are treated as investment, are the beginning and the end of the new, knowledge-based, economy'. The reason for investing in human resources is that they are 'the main value creators of the contemporary economy' (Pulic, 2008).

Now, considering human resources as an investment and not just as a cost requires a change in managerial mentality. In fact costs, owing to their nature, have to be cut, and the traditional performance measurements are based on a logic of cost-cutting. To increase the EBITDA, the cost of human resources is also cut. But if human resources are the source of value creation then cutting them is a short-sighted strategy in the long term. Maybe the phrase 'the lower the cost, the higher the profit' captures the cost of raw materials and energy costs, but it does not accurately reflect human resources.

Building on the concept of the VAIC, the work made by the team of knowledge workers within the firm produces the value added, which is distributed on one side to the workers (cost of employees: wages and salaries) and on the other side to the capital (EBITDA).

Knowledge workers produce all the value added. A part returns to the same workers in the form of wages. The residual part is distributed to capital investors and then also to shareholders. So the value added is produced by the knowledge and the competences of human resources.

The necessary condition for reaching excellent business processes (Six Sigma) and products and a high level of value added is the availability of skilled and motivated human resources. Knowledge and competence of workers is the basis for the production of a high value added. It is for this reason that firms invest in excellent human resources ('invest in people') and that the cost of employees is not a cost but an investment. Ultimately, the value added (VA) is the labour added by knowledge workers. In the following sub-section, the special characteristics of investment in human capital are described.

Investment in Human Capital: A Type of Investment in Living Knowledge

Knowledge can be understood as an organization's ability to act for survival (Maturana and Varela, 1992). The actions for survival are solutions to problems that require creative thinking and ability for innovation. Knowledge is therefore a typical human characteristic, that should not be confused with the knowledge embedded in machines. For this reason, we distinguish between the knowledge incorporated in the human mind (living knowledge) as distinct from the knowledge embedded in technology investments (dead knowledge).

The strategy based on investment in knowledge, suggested by Drucker and Pulic, can be better described by using the distinction cited above. When investing in human resources, trust is placed in 'living knowledge', which is incorporated in the employees, that is, in people. It is believed that only human beings are able to create new knowledge and, therefore, produce value added in such a way as to justify investment. Only qualified and educated human resources are, in fact, able to create patents, copyrights, know-how, and so on. Moreover, only highly trained human resources are able to increase the quality and quantity of intangible assets (organizational relations and relations with customers). Therefore, value creation for all stakeholders necessitates heavy investments in highly trained and skilled human resources. From this type of resource, value added (VA) is produced that is suitable to make investment in human capital (HC).

The other more traditional strategy places its trust in 'dead knowledge' incorporated in ever more perfected machinery whose use is 'labour-saving'. The machine, as far as it is technologically advanced and innovative, is considered as an archive, a 'record' of human work previously provided. It is 'stored', crystallized knowledge that is no longer vital. Furthermore, dead knowledge cannot self-activate but requires other living knowledge to be used. The problem with this value creation model is that it can determine problems at the overall level in terms of social sustainability.

The model based on dead knowledge results in a low use of a workforce and, in particular, of a skilled workforce. It can be good for the firm itself, but not for the overall economic system. The more firms use the dead knowledge model, the less the social sustainability at an overall level. Therefore, there has to be a high number of industries using the living knowledge model to assure overall sustainability. The living knowledge (human resources) model determines sustainability in social terms of the global system.

At a global and social level, it is necessary to understand the fundamental driver of value creation. That is, it is necessary to place human resources at the centre of management and to understand that the following factors are crucial:

1. First and foremost, it is necessary to aim for innovation, which can continuously increase the knowledge content of products and services.

Continuous innovation is the production of new knowledge for the growth of value added (VA).
2. Second, it is necessary to develop and increase employees' skills with the aim to develop VA products and services.

It is necessary to abandon the idea that profits are low because the costs are high, and instead accept that profits are low because the VA is low.

LIMITATIONS AND IMPLICATIONS FOR FURTHER RESEARCH

This chapter aimed to propose an accounting-based point of view for studying knowledge-based organizations and strategies and their value creation process, and to indicate the main areas of research that can be investigated from this analysis.

An Important Limitation: No Possibility to Measure Sustainability

There are some aspects of the VAIC, which this chapter started from, that are linked to the concept of sustainability. Within the VAIC, there is some consideration of the social dimension of sustainability (Gladwin et al., 1995; Steurer et al., 2005; Marrewijk, 2003).

But, in general, sustainability is a multidimensional concept. For example, one of the most important dimensions is environmental, related to respect for the environment in terms of greenhouse gases and pollution, for example. Some studies have proposed new methodologies for measuring business performance related to sustainability (Bardy and Massaro, 2013). In this sense, a strategy could have a positive impact on social sustainability and also on value creation, but a negative impact in terms of pollution and on the external environment.

When studying sustainability as a multidimensional concept, it is necessary to emphasize the methodological challenges of measuring sustainability. The adoption of multiple criteria is certainly an advantage that avoids a mono-criterion myopic evaluation. However, by considering more than one dimension, it is not possible, for example, to rank different units unless the problem is reduced to a single objective function.

When performance is evaluated using only one criterion, each researcher achieves the same 'objective' and 'absolute' result using the same method (the optimization algorithm). On the other hand, when more than one criterion are considered, there are different multi-criteria algorithms that can be used, but the 'right' algorithm cannot be selected by using a multi-criteria algorithm; the choice of an algorithm ultimately depends on the subjective preference of the policy-maker. Therefore, the final ranking of the considered units ultimately depends on a policy-maker's preferences (Laise et al., 2015).

In conclusion, methodologies such as the VAIC are not able to measure sustainability in a correct and complete way because they are 'mono-dimensional' by their nature. The mono-criterial vision of business performance measurement is a weak point of VAIC.

Implications for Further Research

The chapter proposes the following directions for research: (1) the concept and the calculation of knowledge worker productivity; and (2) the concept of the measurement of value creation for stakeholders (versus value creation for shareholders). Knowledge is certainly a notably competitive weapon since it is the most important driver for value creation for all stakeholders, measured by value added. Pulic's idea is, therefore, sharable.

The first specific purpose of the chapter is the construction of an inter-theory relationship (not existing in the literature) between Drucker's approach of economically and socially sustainable strategies based on knowledge, and Pulic's theory of human capital efficiency (HCE). The existence of such a relation is necessary to provide a theoretical foundation of an accounting framework useful for evaluating knowledge-based strategies. A knowledge-based strategy (in Drucker's sense) is adopted when it creates value for all the stakeholders and, furthermore, when it provides a high VA (in Pulic's sense).

This chapter has several practical implications, as it makes it possible to reduce the risk of myopic valuation of economic performance. Managers generally underestimate the importance of performance measurement that takes into account the advantages of intangibles. The proposed approach can be very useful for top managers and accountants as it underlines the importance of the value added income statement (VAIS) and constructs a strong link to the themes of knowledge.

REFERENCES

Baiburina, E.R. and T.V. Golovko (2008), 'Empirical investigation of intellectual enterprise value and its factors for big Russian companies', *Corporate Finance*, 2 (6), 5–23.

Bardy, R. and M. Massaro (2013), 'Shifting the paradigm of return on investment: A composite index to measure overall corporate performance', *Corporate Governance*, 13 (5), 498–510.

Battagello, F.M., Cricelli, L. and M. Grimaldi (2016), 'Benchmarking strategic resources and business performance via an open framework', *International Journal of Productivity and Performance Management*, 65 (3), 324–350.
Davies, A. (2004), 'Moving base into high-value integrated solutions: A value stream approach', *Industrial and Corporate Change*, 13, 727–756.
Dell'Era, C., Landoni, P. and R. Verganti (2015), 'From creative individuals to creative capital: Value creation and appropriation strategies of creative knowledge-intensive business services', *International Journal of Innovation Management*, 19 (2), 1–32.
Demartini, P., Paoloni, M. and P. Paoloni (2015), 'Sustainability and intangibles: Evidence of integrated thinking', *Journal of International Business and Economics*, 15 (2), 107–122.
Donaldson, T. and L. Preston (1995), 'The stakeholder theory of corporation: Concepts, evidence and implications', *Academy of Management Review*, 20 (1), 65–91.
Drucker, P.F. (1968), *The Age of Discontinuity: Guidelines to our Changing Society*, London: Transaction Publishers.
Drucker, P.F. (1993), *Post-Capitalist Society*, New York: Harper Collins.
Drucker, P.F. (1999a), *Management Challenges for the 21st Century*, New York: Harper Collins.
Drucker, P.F. (1999b), 'Knowledge-worker productivity: The biggest challenge', *California Management Review*, 41 (2), 79–92.
Duarte, C.H.C. (2017), 'Productivity paradoxes revisited: Assessing the relationship between quality maturity levels and labor productivity in Brazilian software companies', *Empirical Software Engineering*, 22 (2), 818–847.
Dumay, J. (2013), 'The third stage of IC: Towards a new IC future and beyond', *Journal of Intellectual Capital*, 14 (1), 5–9.
Dumay, J., Guthrie, J. and P. Puntillo (2015), 'IC and public sector: A structured literature review', *Journal of Intellectual Capital*, 16 (2), 267–284.
Gladwin, T.N., Kennelly, J.J. and T. Krause (1995), 'Shifting paradigms for sustainable development: Implications for management theory and research', *Academy of Management Review*, 20 (4), 874–907.
Grant, R.M. (2010), *Contemporary Strategy Analysis*, 8th edition, Chichester: Wiley.
Grimaldi, M., Cricelli, L. and F. Rogo (2012), 'A methodology to assess value creation in communities of innovation', *Journal of Intellectual Capital*, 13 (3), 305–330.
Grimaldi, M., Cricelli, L. and F. Rogo (2013), 'A theoretical framework for assessing managing and indexing the intellectual capital', *Journal of Intellectual Capital*, 14 (4), 501–521.
Guthrie, J., Ricceri, F. and J. Dumay (2012), 'Reflections and projections: A decade of intellectual capital accounting research', *British Accounting Review*, 14 (2), 68–82.
Hall, B.H. and J. Mairesse (1995), 'Exploring the relationship between R&D and productivity in French manufacturing firms', *Journal of Econometrics*, 65 (1), 263–293.
Holden, T., Wilhelmij, P., Chow, W-Y., Cross, J. and R. Schade (1995), 'KNOVA: Modelling the knowledge value-added factors that influence business process performance in organisations', *Proceedings of the 28th Hawaii International Conference on System Sciences (HICSS '95)*, pp. 891–900.
Huang, C. and M. Wang (2008), 'The effects of economic value added and intellectual capital on the market value of firms: An empirical study', *International Journal of Management*, 25 (4), 722–731.
Iazzolino, G. and D. Laise (2013), 'Value added intellectual coefficient (VAIC): A methodological and critical review', *Journal of Intellectual Capital*, 14 (4), 547–563.
Iazzolino, G., Laise, D. and R. Gabriele (2017), 'Knowledge-based strategies and sustainability: A framework and a case study application', *Measuring Business Excellence*, 21 (2), 152–174.
Jensen, M.C. (2002), 'Value maximization, stakeholder theory, and the corporate objective function', *Business Ethics Quarterly*, 12 (2), 235–256.
Kaplan, R.S. and D.P. Norton (1996), *The Balanced Scorecard: Translating Strategy into Action*, Boston, MA: Harvard Business Press.

Kennedy, M. (2013), 'Bank intern Moritz Erhardt died from epileptic seizure, inquest told', *Guardian*, 22 November, pp. 14–16.
Kianto, A., Ritala, P., Spender, J.-C. and M. Vanhala (2014), 'The interaction of intellectual capital assets and knowledge management practices in organizational value creation', *Journal of Intellectual Capital*, 15 (3), 362–375.
Kobayashi, K., Eweje, G. and D. Tappin (2018), 'Employee wellbeing and human sustainability: Perspectives of managers in large Japanese corporations', *Business Strategy and the Environment*, 27 (7), 801–810.
Laise, D., Marraro, L. and Iazzolino, G. (2015), 'Metachoice for benchmarking: A case study', *Benchmarking: An International Journal*, 22 (3), 338–353.
Lerro, A., Linzalone, R. and G. Schiuma (2014), 'Managing intellectual capital dimensions for organizational value creation', *Journal of Intellectual Capital*, 15 (3), 350–361.
Marrewijk, M. van. (2003), 'Concepts and definitions of CSR and corporate sustainability: Between agency and communion', *Journal of Business Ethics*, 44, 95–105.
Martínez-Torres, M.d.R. (2014), 'Identification of intangible assets in knowledge-based organizations using concept mapping techniques', *R&D Management*, 44 (1), 42–52.
Maturana, H. and F. Varela (1992), *The Tree of Knowledge*, Boston, MA: Sambala.
Musolesi, A. and J.P. Huiban (2010), 'Innovation and productivity in knowledge intensive business services', *Journal of Productivity Analysis*, 34 (1), 63–81.
Neate, R. (2015), 'Goldman Sachs restricts intern workday to 17 hours in wake of burnout death', *Guardian*, 17 June, pp. 2–4.
Olander, H., Hurmelinna-Laukkanen, P. and P. Heilmann (2015), 'Human resources – Strength and weakness in protection of intellectual capital', *Journal of Intellectual Capital*, 16 (4), 742–762.
Pereme, F., Rose, B., Goepp, V., Radoux, J.P. and A. Belhaoua (2016), 'Toward an integrative CSDS based model of industrial R&D division efficiency', *IFAC-PapersOnLine*, 49 (12), 1785–1790.
Petty, R. and J. Guthrie (2000), 'Intellectual capital literature review: Measurement, reporting and management', *Journal of Intellectual Capital*, 1 (2), 155–176.
Pfeffer, J. (2010), 'Building sustainable organizations: The human factor', *Academy of Management Perspectives*, 24 (1), 34–45.
Phusavat, K., Comepa, N., Sitko-Lutek, A. and K.B. Ooi (2013), 'Productivity management: Integrating the intellectual capital', *Industrial Management and Data Systems*, 113 (6), 840–855.
Porter, M.E. (1985), *Competitive Advantage*, New York: Free Press.
Pulic, A. (2000), 'VAIC™ – An accounting tool for IC management', *International Journal of Technology Management*, 2 (5–8), 702–714.
Pulic, A. (2004), 'Intellectual capital – Does it create or destroy value?', *Measuring Business Excellence*, 8 (1), 62–68.
Pulic, A. (2008), *The Principles of Intellectual Capital Efficiency: A Brief Description*, Zagreb: Croatian Intellectual Capital Center.
Shakina, E. and A. Barajas (2015), 'Intangible-intensive profile of a company: The key to outperforming', *Journal of Intellectual Capital*, 16 (4), 721–741.
Smets, M. (2016), 'Career pathing and innovation in professional', *Academy of Management Perspectives*, 30 (4), 369–383.
Steurer, R., Langer, M., Konrad, A. and A. Martinuzzi (2005), 'Corporations, stakeholders and sustainable development I: A theoretical exploration of business–society relations', *Journal of Business Ethics*, 61 (3), 263–281.
Zakery, A., Afrazeh, A. and J. Dumay (2017), 'Analysing and improving the strategic alignment of firms' resource dynamics', *Journal of Intellectual Capital*, 18 (1), 217–240.

12. Re-examination of the value added intellectual coefficient (VAIC™): a test of value relevance

Oren Mooneeapen, Subhash Abhayawansa and Dinesh Ramdhony

INTRODUCTION

Intellectual capital (IC) is increasingly recognised as an important strategic asset for creating sustainable competitive advantage and value (Chen et al., 2005). However, reporting of IC in corporate reports and measuring IC remain problematic. Pulic's (2000) value added intellectual coefficient (VAIC), which measures the intellectual capital efficiency, has been used by researchers and practitioners in the past two decades as a proxy for the value creation potential of firms' IC due to the challenges associated with measuring IC in monetary terms (Fijałkowska, 2014). The purpose of this chapter is to question whether VAIC can be treated as a reliable proxy for the value creation potential of IC that the capital market uses to assess firms' future cash flows. It does not, however, question the appropriateness of using VAIC as a measure of firms' past IC efficiency or performance where it is likely that the capital market has already factored in.

Companies voluntarily disclose IC information to the public assuming that it is incremental to what can be inferred about firms' IC from their financial statements, including VAIC, which is calculable from publicly accessible accounting data. If companies voluntarily disclose information about IC that is not accounted for by the VAIC, then the validity of the findings of research and the effects of decisions that use VAIC to proxy for the value creation potential of IC is questionable. In contrast, if VAIC is a reliable and valid proxy for firms' IC potential and conveys the majority of information contained in voluntary IC disclosure, then voluntary disclosure of IC information by companies – for instance, through integrated reports and strategic reports – would be a non-value adding endeavour. This study investigates whether VAIC is a valid proxy for the value creation potential of IC communicated through IC disclosure (ICD) insofar as the capital market is concerned.

The study uses longitudinal data from 34 out of 40 companies listed on the Stock Exchange of Mauritius for the four years from 2014 to 2017. Content analysis of voluntarily disclosed IC information in the annual reports of the sample companies provides the data to measure the extent of ICD. The findings of the study do not support the contention that VAIC communicates information relevant to the capital market. It does, however, show that ICD, while controlling for VAIC, is value relevant. Only capital employed efficiency (CEE), which is a subcomponent of VAIC, is found to be value relevant, but this indicator communicates the value creation potential of physical and financial capitals rather than IC.

Although the plethora of studies that use VAIC as a proxy for the value creation potential of IC and promote VAIC for use by practitioners, the findings of this study suggest that, at best, VAIC is a partial proxy of IC performance.[1] This finding has important implications for IC research and practice.

The present chapter makes several contributions to the literature; its main contributions are methodological. First, it adds to the IC literature by explaining the incremental informativeness of ICD when the possible influence of VAIC is taken into consideration. Prior research has only explained the value relevance of ICD or VAIC separately. Second, our chapter provides a nuanced understanding of VAIC as a proxy for the value creation potential of IC by examining the value relevance of the subcomponents that it comprises. As VAIC also incorporates CEE, which measures value creation performance and potential of financial and physical capital, its validity as a measure of IC performance is dependent on the extent to which VAIC is explained by its IC components of human capital and structural capital. Thus, separately examining human capital efficiency (HCE) and structural capital efficiency (SCE) not only enables a more detailed understanding of IC value relevance but also overcomes any biases associated with an analysis based on VAIC alone. Our finding that CEE is the only subcomponent of VAIC that is value relevant downplays the importance of VAIC as a proxy for IC potential.

These contributions to the IC literature are important from a methodological point of view as our findings directly question the appropriateness of using VAIC as a convenient proxy for the value creation potential of IC, and support the use of ICD scores for this purpose. In this regard, we add to the growing debate about the reliability and validity of VAIC as a measure of firms' IC (for a critique of VAIC, see Ståhle et al., 2011) and encourage disclosure of IC by companies.

The chapter first reviews the literature related to this study and highlights how this research stands out from previous studies. Next, it describes the research design, where the sample, variables and analytical models are detailed. The results are then presented and discussed. The final section discusses the findings and concludes the chapter, outlining the implications of this study and recommendations for further studies.

RELATED LITERATURE

The literature relevant to the present investigation can be categorised into three strands: (1) studies examining the relationship between VAIC (including its separate components) as a measure of IC efficiency and company performance and/or market value; (2) studies investigating the value relevance of ICD; and (3) studies exploring the relationship between ICD and VAIC.

The VAIC method was created by Pulic (2000) to measure and monitor, using accounting figures, the efficiency of companies' IC in creating value. It is argued that VAIC is a determinant of companies' market value as it provides information about IC performance. Several studies have tested this proposition. The majority of the studies find that VAIC is positively correlated with market-to-book value (for example, Chen et al., 2005). Other studies find no support for the relationship between VAIC and market-to-book value (see Chu et al., 2011; Ståhle et al., 2011) or find a negative relationship between VAIC and market-to-book value (see Celenza and Rossi, 2014).

It is argued that these results can be explained by the fact that different investors and capital markets place different emphasis or value on the value creation capabilities of the two IC components (that is, HCE and SCE) and CEE comprising VAIC (Chen et al., 2005; Chu et al., 2011) and the efficiency of the capital markets in incorporating IC information in stock prices. For instance, Gigante's (2013) study of European banks reveals a positive relationship between HCE and market-to-book value and a negative relationship between SCE and market-to-book value. In contrast, Chu et al.'s (2011) analysis of data from constituent companies of the Hang Seng Index of the Hong Kong Stock Exchange for the period 2001 to 2009 reveals a positive correlation between SCE and market value and a negative correlation for HCE and market value.

The negative relationships for HCE and SCE are attributed to investors not considering expenditures on human capital or structural capital as investments but rather as costs, owing to the way these measures are constructed. It is also possible that the inability of the VAIC methodology to capture synergies and interactions between IC components and financial and physical capitals (Murthy and Mouritsen, 2011) may be contributing to the counterintuitive results.

Another reason for the inconsistency in the findings of the studies using VAIC might be that investors use information on firms' IC garnered through other sources (for example, voluntarily provided by the firms and/or accessed through third parties) to interpret VAIC and its constituents. Such information is also capable of enlightening investors of the interactions and synergies between IC components and enabling them to determine whether expenditure on various IC components are value creating or not. These arguments support our contention that the value relevance of VAIC and its subcomponents should be examined in tandem with the informational role of ICDs.

The reduction of information asymmetry between a company and external users of information is one major reason for voluntary ICD. Research confirms the value relevance of IC information (Abdolmohammadi, 2005; Abhayawansa and Guthrie, 2010; Gamerschlag, 2013; Uyar and Kılıç, 2012) and demonstrates how such information is used by capital market participants (Abhayawansa et al., 2015). Further support for the value relevance of ICD is provided by the evidence that firms provide more ICDs when the information asymmetry is high, for instance companies in the pharmaceutical industry.

Research on the relationship between firms' VAIC and the extent of ICD is scarce. One notable exception is Williams (2001), who examined the relationship between ICD and VAIC using data from a sample of Financial Times Stock Exchange (FTSE) 100 companies for the period 1996–2000. Contrary to the author's predictions, the study reveals that in a given year when a firm's level of VAIC increases, the extent of IC information the entity discloses decreases. Williams (2001) invokes proprietary cost theory to explain the finding, arguing that the fear of losing competitive advantage makes companies reluctant to disclose information about their IC when IC performance reaches a threshold level. If proprietary costs prevent companies from disclosing IC information, then one would expect to see the explanatory power of ICD being subsumed substantially by the explanatory power of VAIC in a model that examines value relevance. Williams's (2001) findings and explanations inform the formulation of research questions in the present study, as shown in the next section.

DEVELOPMENT OF RESEARCH QUESTION

According to the resource-based view of the firm, sustainable competitive advantage of the modern firm lies in its use of tangible as well as intangible assets that are inimitable, heterogeneous (that is, differing across firms), immobile, irreplaceable (not replaceable by another resource) and add value to the firm (Wright and McMahan, 1992; Wright et al., 1994). These internal resources or strategic assets include brand names, patents, in-house knowledge of technology, employee skills, trade contact and efficient procedures (Grant, 1991). As IC, by definition, encompasses such intangible assets, the resource-based view would also imply that efficient use of IC results in greater financial performance (Bounfour, 2003; Youndt et al., 2004). According to the efficient market hypothesis, information about IC that determines future financial performance has information content, and thus should be associated with the firm's market value. Supporting this argument, prior studies provide ample evidence of the value relevance of IC (see, Abhayawansa and Guthrie, 2010).

The proprietary cost theory explains the economic consequences of full disclosure, whereby the threat of competitors motivates firms to limit the disclosure of information insofar as benefits offered by disclosure are less than perceived costs of disclosure (Healy and Palepu, 2001). Accordingly, the greater the IC of a company and more efficiently it is used, the less likely it is to disclose IC in fear that the company's competitors may derive an advantage, at the expense of the company, from the information.

Firms having a substandard level of IC will also have disincentives to disclose IC information. The ICDs of such firms will demonstrate the firms' lack of IC potential and value creation capabilities, triggering adverse action by investors and other stakeholders such as lenders, suppliers and labour unions (Williams, 2001). These actions may include investors diverting their investments from or stopping further investment in the firm; lenders renegotiating credit terms; and labour unions demanding more resources to be allocated to employee development and well-being. A firm performing poorly in terms of IC would struggle to deal with such reprisals. If predictions based on proprietary cost theory and the arguments above hold, then ICDs will not provide more information to the market than what is discernible about the firm's IC from publicly accessible accounting information. Hence, if VAIC calculated based on publicly accessible accounting information is a proxy for IC potential, then ICDs will not be value relevant.

An alternative to the above hypothesis is predicted by theories that support greater disclosure of IC information by firms. Impression management theory views corporations as social actors who engage in managing impressions to enhance their respectability and impressiveness (Highhouse et al., 2009). This theory predicts that the management of companies with lower IC performance will attempt to influence the perceptions of stakeholders by providing more ICDs to portray the companies in a more favourable light. Discretionary disclosure theory, which explains disclosures as a tool to lower the perceived risks of investors, predicts that firms provide IC information for investors to assess firms' future cash flows, leading to lower cost of capital and better valuation by the market. The managerial branch of stakeholder theory explains that firms respond to the information needs of dominant stakeholders, which might include investors wanting more information about firms' IC or trade unions, and others interested in firms' investments in human capital. Also, signalling theory predicts firms will disclose more information, including information on IC performance and potential, to signal their future performance to the capital market.

If firms are motivated to enhance ICDs, then firms with greater IC are likely to have greater ICDs. Thus, ICDs in such a scenario would convey information incremental to what is conveyed about firms' IC through publicly accessible accounting information, such as VAIC. Accordingly, ICD would be value relevant after controlling for the informational value of VAIC as a proxy for IC performance.

The above discussion shows that there are theoretically informed arguments supporting as well as rejecting the contention that informativeness of voluntary ICDs would be incremental to the informativeness of IC performance discernible through publicly available financial statements. As a result, this chapter avoids making predictions, and poses the following research question: Is voluntary ICD value relevant when the information content of VAIC as a proxy for IC potential is controlled?

RESEARCH METHOD

Sampling and Data Collection

An examination of the value relevance of IC should be done in a setting where business and investors place high importance on IC. We selected Mauritius as the context for this study because it provides an IC-intensive setting. Mauritius belongs to the category of small island developing states (SIDS) that share social, economic and environmental vulnerabilities, such as small but growing populations, narrow resource base, remoteness, susceptibility to natural disasters and excessive dependence on international trade (United Nations, 2015). These characteristics, coupled with the fact that Mauritius has few natural resources to exploit for economic advantage, means the country relies heavily on its IC.

Conscious of this fact, successive governments have come up with the motto of 'putting people first'. Mauritius is one of the rare countries where education from pre-primary to tertiary level and health care services are free for its citizens. Public transport is provided to students free of charge as well. These policies have arguably helped Mauritius to achieve the highest literacy rate among African countries (UNICEF, 2019). Moreover, businesses are encouraged to invest in human capital, with the government reimbursing 80 per cent of the cost incurred on staff training and development. It can thus be inferred that the selected context provides an IC-intensive setting for our investigation.

We intended to include the entire population of companies listed on the Stock Exchange of Mauritius to maximise representativeness. There were 40 companies listed on the Stock Exchange of Mauritius in 2014. However, due to a lack of available information required to calculate the IC variables, six companies were excluded, limiting the sample to 34 companies. As the study covers the four years from 2014 to 2017, the 34 companies should yield 136 company-year observations. However, one company-year observation was excluded as a company in the sample did not publish an annual report for the year 2014. Hence, the analyses conducted in this study are based on 135 company-year observations. Twenty firm-year observations were removed as they corresponded to firm-years with losses, reducing the number of observations included in our analyses to 115.

The main source of data to measure the extent of ICD is the annual reports of the companies. As the companies studied are listed companies, they are required to publish audited financial reports. We obtained data about the historical market values and financial information necessary to calculate VAIC values and other variables required for the analyses from Datastream.

Measuring ICD

The extent of ICD is determined by coding references to IC in the annual reports based on an ICD index. The ICD index includes 21 IC items developed by Guthrie and Petty (2000). These items are classified into structural, relational and human capital categories. The ICD index is shown in Table 12.1. If an ICD index item is disclosed by a firm in its annual report, then it is assigned a score of one for that item, or zero otherwise. The ICD score for each company is calculated as the total number of IC items disclosed in the company's annual report divided by the maximum number of ICD index items (21). Hence, a company disclosing all 21 IC items included in the ICD index would be assigned an ICD score of one (21 divided by 21).

Table 12.1 Intellectual capital disclosure index

Structural capital index	Relational capital index	Human capital index
1. Research and Development	8. Brands/Reputation	16. Employees
2. Intellectual Property	9. Suppliers	17. Education & Qualifications
3. Management Philosophy	10. Customers	18. Training
4. Corporate Culture	11. Customer Satisfaction/Loyalty	19. Work-Related Knowledge/ Competencies
5. Management Processes	12. Marketing	20. Teams of Employees
6. Information Systems	13. Distribution Channels	21. Entrepreneurial Spirit
7. Infrastructure Assets	14. Business Collaborations	
	15. Research Collaborations	

Value Added Intellectual Coefficient (VAIC)

The VAIC model was created as a response to the argument that the past accounting systems could not meet the requirements of modern companies because they did not explain the future value creation capabilities of modern businesses (Pulic, 2000). VAIC purportedly indicates total efficiency of value creation from human, structural and physical capital. The three components that comprise VAIC can be separated in analyses to provide greater explanatory power (Chen et al., 2005).

VAIC is calculated by adding up CEE, HCE and SCE. CEE is the amount of value created from a unit of capital employed and it is calculated as valued added (sales – cost of sales – depreciation) divided by capital employed (total assets – intangible assets). CEE is included in the calculation of VAIC because a company's efficiency in managing its financial and physical capital affects its IC performance due to interrelationships between IC and financial and physical capitals (Jhunjhunwala, 2009). HCE measures the amount of value created for each Mauritian rupee spent on human resources, and it is calculated as value added divided by total expenditure on employees. SCE measures how successful a firm's structural capital is in creating value. It is measured as the amount of structural capital (value added – total expenditure on employees) divided by the amount of value added.

VAIC is a model that has attracted significant criticism in the IC literature although it continues to be widely used. A main criticism relates to the calculation of HCE. Andriessen (2004) argues that considering all expenses relating to employees as assets (human capital) is incorrect, as most costs associated with employees cannot be a source of future benefit and thus do not fit within the definition of an item of IC. Chu et al. (2011) highlight that there is an inverse relationship between HCE and SCE in the VAIC model, incorrectly implying that one capital cannot be increased without decreasing the other.

Furthermore, it is possible for a company that is using its IC less efficiently, but other capitals (for example, financial, physical and natural) more efficiently, to have a higher VAIC, leading to a false conclusion about that company's IC. A more fundamental criticism of VAIC relates to its reliance on operating profit as the basis for calculating value added, because operating profit can fluctuate over time due to factors not associated with IC (Ståhle et al., 2011). Also, HCE can be sensitive to industry or sector, with biases towards capital-intensive companies and away from labour-intensive companies (Ståhle et al., 2011).

Analytical Model

Barth et al. (2001) explain that an information item is value relevant if it has a predicted association with equity market values. In line with prior studies on value relevance (see Aboody and Lev, 1998; Baboukardos and Rimmel, 2016), and based on Ohlson (1995) who shows how firm value relates to accounting data and other information, the following linear price-level model is employed. Kothari and Zimmerman (1995) show that price-level models, compared to return-models, produce unbiased estimates due to better specification. In this model, an association between ICD or VAIC and equity values indicates the extent to which information contained in ICD or VAIC is consistent with that used by investors:[2]

$$SP_{i,t} = \beta_0 + \beta_1 BVS_{i,t} + \beta_2 EPS_{i,t} + \beta_3 ICD_{i,t} + \beta_4 VAIC_{i,t} + \beta_5 ROA_{i,t} + \beta_6 LEV_{i,t} + \beta_7 TA_{i,t} + \varepsilon_{i,t} \quad (12.1)$$

where SP_{it} is the natural logarithm of firm i's stock price (of common shares) three months after the fiscal year end in year t;[3] BVS_{it} is the book value of equity per share for firm i at the end of fiscal year t; EPS_{it} is reported annual earnings per share for firm i in fiscal year t; ICD_{it} is ICD index score for firm i in fiscal year t; $VAIC_{it}$ is value added intellectual coefficient for firm i at the end of fiscal year t; ROA_{it} is return on assets for firm i in fiscal year t; LEV_{it} is total debt as a percentage of total equity for firm i at the end of fiscal year t; and TA_{it} is the logarithm of total assets for firm i at the end of fiscal year t.

Model 1 is a modified version of the model developed by Ohlson (1995) and assumes that firm value is a function of three variables: the book value of equity, current period earnings and future benefits that are modified based on other information. In the above model ICD, VAIC, ROA and LEV are considered other information that can modify future benefits accruing to the company. Barth and Kallapur (1996) argue that regression variables in price-level models are likely affected by cross-sectional scale differences among sample firms. As a remedy, they demonstrate that, 'including a scale proxy as an independent variable is more effective than deflation at mitigating coefficient bias, even if the proxy is 95 percent correlated with the true scale factor' (Barth and Kallapur, 1996, p. 527). Thus, rather than deflating VAIC and ICD by a size measure, we use TA to control for scale in Model 1. Moreover, LEV and ROA are included to control for leverage and profitability as they are related to investments in and future performance of IC (Jhunjhunwala, 2009; Murthy and Mouritsen, 2011). If VAIC is informative and encompasses the information content in ICDs, then we expect β_4 to be, and β_3 not to be, statistically significantly different from zero.

Model 2 shown below is commonly adopted in value relevance studies (Chen et al., 2005; Johnston et al., 2008). This model assumes that investors will factor in the cash flow consequences of IC estimated from all publicly available information, increasing the difference between book value and market value of the firm as the value of IC is not reflected in the financial statements. Hence, firms with greater IC performance will have a higher market-to-book value. Thus, Model 2 is estimated to determine whether the ICDs provide information about future cash flows that is not ascertainable from VAIC:

$$MBV_{i,t} = \beta_0 + \beta_1 ICD_{i,t} + \beta_2 VAIC_{i,t} + \beta_3 ROA_{i,t} + \beta_4 LEV_{i,t} + \beta_5 TA_{i,t} + \varepsilon_{i,t} \qquad (12.2)$$

where $MBV_{i,t}$ is market-to-book value and the definition of other variables are the same as in Model 1.

Since the sample includes data on several firms over four years, this study uses panel data analysis. The Hausman test is commonly used to choose between fixed-effects and random-effects models when analysing panel data. The results of the Hausman test affirmed the appropriateness of a fixed-effects over a random-effects model for both regressions. A fixed-effects model controls for unobservable factors that are likely to be constant over time for each firm (for example, firm's culture), yet may affect the relationship between the independent and dependent variables. Our panel data models are estimated using ordinary least squares with firm and year fixed-effects and White's (1980) heteroscedasticity-consistent standard errors. We adopt robust (heteroscedasticity-consistent) standard errors because price-models often suffer from heteroscedasticity. Using the augmented Dickey–Fuller test, we determined that the VAIC and ICD variables met the stationarity assumption. The Durbin–Watson test was carried out to test for autocorrelation in the residuals from the regression in Model 1 and Model 2. The values obtained from the Durbin–Watson test are around two, which indicates the absence of autocorrelation in the residuals in both models.

SUMMARY STATISTICS AND EMPIRICAL RESULTS

Table 12.2 presents the summary statistics for all variables used in the two models we estimated. Given that the potential maximum ICD score is one, a mean of 0.78 indicates that, on average, the level of voluntary ICDs of companies listed on the Stock Exchange of Mauritius (SEM) is relatively high. This justifies our selection of Mauritius as the context for

Table 12.2 Summary statistics

	N	Mean	Standard deviation	Minimum	Maximum
SP	135	1.46	0.58	−0.06	2.69
MBV	135	1.47	2.53	0.33	23.28
BVS	135	65.09	75.52	0.36	365.56
EPS	120	5.10	8.19	0.00	39.83
ICD	135	0.78	0.16	0.24	1.00
VAIC	129	3.94	3.62	0.18	21.60
ROA	119	0.05	0.06	0.00	0.37
LEV	135	3.11	2.97	1.00	18.12
TA	135	15.72	1.79	10.71	19.66

Notes: SP is the natural logarithm of stock price three months after the fiscal year end; MBV is market-to-book value; BVS is the book value of equity per share; EPS is reported annual earnings per share; ICD is ICD index score; VAIC is value added intellectual coefficient; ROA is return on assets; LEV is total debt as a percentage of total equity; TA is the logarithm of total assets.

our investigation. The mean debt to total equity (LEV) ratio is considered high at 3.11 with a maximum of 18.12. Companies listed on the SEM have low profitability on average with a mean ROA of 0.05 and a maximum of only 0.37. High variation is found in MBV, BVS, EPS, VAIC, LEV and TA while variables SP, ICD and ROA have lower standard deviations.

We conducted pairwise correlations between the variables. The Pearson correlation coefficients and variance inflation factors for each independent variable suggest minimal collinearity and multicollinearity is not a cause of concern.

Empirical results of the model estimations are shown in Table 12.3. Model 1 is statistically significant at 1 per cent and Model 2 at 10 per cent. ICD is positively related to both SP (p = 0.063) and MBV (p = 0.09). The coefficient for VAIC is not statistically significant even at the 10 per cent level in any of the models, but in Model 1 it has a negative sign, contrary to a priori expectations. Contrary to the theoretical

Table 12.3 Main empirical results

Dependent variable	Model (1)		Model (2)	
	SP		MBV	
	Standardised coefficients	Probability	Standardised coefficients	Probability
EPS	−0.002	0.793		
BVS	0.003	0.027		
ICD	0.234	0.063	4.032	0.090
VAIC	−0.004	0.388	0.055	0.705
ROA	0.368	0.070	24.082	0.193
LEV	0.000	0.976	0.289	0.046
TA	0.028	0.225	0.662	0.071
Constant	0.744	0.071	−13.110	0.084
F-statistic	4.98	0.0003	2.18	0.0571
R^2 (within)	0.2533		0.2525	
R^2 (between)	0.5080		0.1336	
Firms	31		32	
Observations	112		115	

Notes: SP is the natural logarithm of stock price three months after the fiscal year end; MBV is market-to-book value; BVS is the book value of equity per share; EPS is reported annual earnings per share; ICD is intellectual capital disclosure index score; VAIC is value added intellectual coefficient; ROA is return on assets; LEV is total debt as a percentage of total equity; TA is the logarithm of total assets. All regressions include time fixed-effects.

expectations raised by Ohlson's (1995) model, the coefficient for EPS is not statistically significant at 10 per cent in Model 1. Among the control variables, the coefficient for ROA is positively and statistically significantly related to SP at the 10 per cent significance level in Model 1; and in Model 2, coefficients on LEV and TA are positively related to MBV and statistically significant at 5 per cent and 10 per cent levels, respectively.

The positive relationship between MBV and ICD explains that companies that disclose more information about their IC see a greater gap between their market values and book values. The gap between the market and book values increases because the market adjusts upwards the cash flow estimates of companies that disclose IC information, given that IC information provides information relevant to the market in determining the future value creation potential of companies. The results from Model 1, which shows that ICD score is associated with stock price, further support our contention that the capital market factors in the information contained in ICDs. On the other hand, the fact that the coefficient for VAIC is not statistically significant, while the coefficient for ICD is significant in both models, highlights that VAIC does not provide information about firms' IC that is of relevance to assessing future cash flow consequences of firms' IC over and above what is already known by the market.

We conducted further analysis to examine whether any of the subcomponents of VAIC (specifically, HCE, SCE or CEE) were value relevant despite the finding that VAIC as a whole is not. We used Model 2 for this purpose and analysed the three subcomponents of VAIC separately; the regression results are presented in Table 12.4. Untabulated results of the estimated Model 1 are qualitatively like that of Model 2.

As per the results shown in Table 12.4, the estimated coefficients on HCE and SCE are not statistically significant, while CEE is. This is an interesting finding as it indicates that only the efficiency of employing financial and physical capitals ascertained from VAIC is considered relevant by the capital market. Thus, our findings support the contention that VAIC does not convey new information about intangible drivers of firm value that has not already been incorporated in the stock price.

If VAIC does not convey information about future value creation potential of IC and thus future cash flows, then a question arises as to what information is conveyed by VAIC. To answer this question, we examine whether VAIC measures IC efficiency that is reflected in firm performance. Table 12.5 provides the results of this analysis which treats ROA as a measure of firm performance.

Table 12.4 Empirical results on value relevance of VAIC subcomponents

Dependent variable	Model (2) – MBV		
	Model HCE	Model SCE	Model CEE
ICD	3.742*	3.760	3.892*
HCE	−0.039		
SCE		0.327	
CEE			0.962***
ROA	25.987	24.757**	26.88
LEV	0.288*	0.305*	0.290**
TA	0.638*	0.654*	0.733**
Constant	−12.34*	−12.87*	−14.51*
F-statistic	2.59**	2.65**	19.92***
R^2 (within)	0.2483	0.2482	0.3041
R^2 (between)	0.1444	0.1323	0.1997
Firms	33	33	33
Observations	119	119	119

Notes: The table provides coefficient estimates and the statistical significance level. MBV is market-to-book value; ICD is intellectual capital disclosure index score; HCE is human capital efficiency; SCE is structural capital efficiency and CEE is capital employed efficiency; ROA is return on assets; LEV is total debt as a percentage of total equity; TA is the logarithm of total assets. All regressions include time fixed-effects.
*, **, and *** indicate significance at the 10 per cent, 5 per cent, and 1 per cent levels, respectively.

The results show that the estimated coefficient for VAIC is positively and statistically significantly associated with ROA. Given that IC drives firm performance, as advocated by the resource-based view of the firm, this result suggests that VAIC is a measure of past value creation efficiency, which according to our previous analysis is already known by the market. It is also found that among the IC subcomponents of VAIC, HCE is positively associated and SCE is not associated with ROA, suggesting that firm financial performance is a function of human capital and less so structural capital. Prior studies (for example, Gigante, 2013) also find that HCE seems to be the IC subcomponent of VAIC that has the most statistically significant association with firm financial performance. Although the estimated coefficients of VAIC and HCE are statistically significant, they are not economically significant. Hence, we avoid making any inferences based on these results.

Table 12.5 Empirical results on the relationship between VAIC and financial performance

Dependent variable	ROA		
	Model VAIC	Model HCE	Model SCE
HCE	0.006**	0.007***	
SCE			0.026
CEE			
LEV	−0.003	−0.003	−0.003
TA	0.0004	0.0001	−0.002
Constant	0.029	0.035	0.0809
F-statistic	20.01***	20.01***	2.80**
R^2 (within)	0.1910	0.2322	0.0867
R^2 (between)	0.2335	0.1639	0.1578
Firms	32	33	33
Observations	115	119	119

Notes: The table provides coefficient estimates and the statistical significance level. HCE is human capital efficiency; SCE is structural capital efficiency and CEE is capital employed efficiency; LEV is total debt as a percentage of total equity; TA is the logarithm of total assets. All regressions include time fixed-effects.
*, **, and *** indicate significance at the 10 per cent, 5 per cent, and 1 per cent levels, respectively.

DISCUSSION AND CONCLUSION

Our findings show a significant positive association of ICD with both SP and MBV, thus rejecting the proprietary cost theory-based explanation of companies' willingness to provide IC information, and upholding theory and arguments supporting greater voluntary disclosure of IC information. The results should, however, be cautiously interpreted, as ICD, similarly to other disclosures, can be subject to impression management. As ICD, which includes information not accessible from financial statements, is found to be value relevant and VAIC not to be so, the reliability of VAIC as a proxy for IC value creation potential is questionable. While VAIC might convey information about IC efficiency or performance, which is backward-looking information, as it is meant to be, it does not seem to provide forward-looking value relevant information. Thus, our findings highlight that the information about IC in ICD and VAIC, should it measure what it purports to, would be different and one is not a substitute for the other.

The only significant relationship we found between the subcomponents of VAIC and market valuation is with CEE; meanwhile, the IC components of VAIC, HCE and SCE, along with VAIC as a whole, showed no significant association with MBV. This finding indicates that information content in VAIC in relation to IC, if there is any, is not taken into consideration in assessing firms' future cash flows. Two explanations could be put forth to answer why the capital market does not react to VAIC, which purportedly conveys IC value creation efficiency. Either the market participants do not consider VAIC to be a reliable measure of value creation efficiency, or VAIC does not represent what it claims to represent. Regardless of which of these two explanations is most salient, the implication is crucial for IC research and practice. Evidently, there is a need for a measure of IC that can be derived relatively easily for decision-making purposes by both companies and investors, as in the knowledge-based business world of today, value creation from IC cannot simply be ignored.

It comes as no surprise that our findings evidence a positive association of VAIC with company performance, through ROA, as VAIC includes a CEE component that is merely a return on assets ratio that does not take into account intangible assets included in the balance sheet. The results relating to the individual IC components of VAIC can thus be considered to be of greater interest, since VAIC also includes CEE. HCE is seen to be positively associated with ROA and this emphasises how crucial human resources are for the performance of companies.

As for structural capital, we can say that companies with highly efficient structural capital perform better. As such, the lack of any significant association between SCE and MBV can be explained by the shortcomings of the SCE measurement. As Ståhle et al. (2011) argue, there is no reason to class the SCE variable as structural capital, since it is calculated as the difference between a company's value added and its human capital. Again, we see a methodological implication as, even though VAIC is among the rare measures that can place a monetary value on IC value creation efficiency, its improvement is of utmost importance. This would require more robust and critical research into it.

Our findings have implications for companies and policy-makers. Companies can benefit by voluntarily disclosing more information on IC as a way to improve their market valuation, and putting a greater emphasis on their IC value creation potential. Our results may inform policy-makers on the importance of formulating and implementing policy regarding ICDs to ensure that these disclosures show a true and fair view, particularly as the impact of ICDs on the market valuation of shares may motivate management to manipulate such disclosures.

This study highlights several future research opportunities. First, our findings help rejuvenate research using content analysis to measure ICD, which has been subject to recent criticism (see Dumay and Cai, 2014; Dumay et al., 2015). Second, the evidence we provide of the value relevance of ICDs (that is, not moderated by VAIC) highlights the importance of future research on the presence of impression management with regard to ICDs. Third, future research should investigate the value relevance of separate components of ICDs. Our study is unable to provide the level of analysis necessary to make inferences on the three types of ICDs as variations in these capitals need to be captured using a more detail disclosure index. Fourth, further studies conducted on different time periods and countries may be required in order to understand what VAIC truly measures, and how it can be improved to overcome its current shortcomings. Finally, including ICD as a variable in future VAIC research will also allow the parallel determination of trends in ICD practices to demonstrate whether the findings of this study are consistent with other time periods and countries, thus supporting their generalisability.

NOTES

1. As CEE can interact with IC in driving future firm performance, and as this indicator is value relevant, we can argue that VAIC provides at least some information related to value creation potential associated with firms' IC.
2. However, as highlighted by Aboody and Lev (1998), such an association does not indicate that investors in fact used ICD in assessing security values.
3. We use stock prices three months after the fiscal year end to allow time for the IC information in annual corporate reports to be assimilated by the market. Selection of this time period is consistent with prior studies.

REFERENCES

Abdolmohammadi, M. (2005), 'Intellectual capital disclosure and market capitalization', *Journal of Intellectual Capital*, 6 (3), 397–416.

Abhayawansa, S., Aleksanyan, M. and J. Bahtsevanoglou (2015), 'The use of intellectual capital information by sell-side analysts in company valuation', *Accounting and Business Research*, 51 (5), 279–306.

Abhayawansa, S. and J. Guthrie (2010), 'Intellectual capital and the capital market: a review and synthesis', *Journal of Human Resource Costing and Accounting*, 14 (3), 196–226.

Aboody, D. and B. Lev (1998), 'The value relevance of intangibles: the case of software capitalization', *Journal of Accounting Research*, 36 (3), 161–191.

Andriessen, D. (2004), *Making Sense of Intellectual Capital: Designing a Method for the Valuation of Intangibles*, Oxford: Elsevier Butterworth-Heinemann.

Baboukardos, D. and G. Rimmel (2016), 'Value relevance of accounting information under an integrated reporting approach: a research note', *Journal of Accounting and Public Policy*, 36 (4), 437–452.

Barth, M.E., Beaver, W.H. and W.R. Landsman (2001), 'The relevance of the value relevance literature for financial accounting standard setting: another view', *Journal of Accounting and Economics*, 31 (1–3), 77–104.

Barth, M.E. and S. Kallapur (1996), 'The effects of cross-sectional scale differences on regression results in empirical accounting research', *Contemporary Accounting Research*, 13 (2), 527–567.

Bounfour, A. (2003), 'The IC-dVAL approach', *Journal of Intellectual Capital*, 4 (3), 396–413.

Celenza, D. and F. Rossi (2014), 'Intellectual capital and performance of listed companies: empirical evidence from Italy', *Measuring Business Excellence*, 18 (1), 22–35.

Chen, M.C., Cheng, S.J. and Y. Hwang (2005), 'An empirical investigation of the relationship between intellectual capital and firms' market value and financial performance', *Journal of Intellectual Capital*, 6 (2), 159–176.

Chu, S.K.W., Chan, K.H. and W.W. Wu (2011), 'Charting intellectual capital performance of the gateway to China', *Journal of Intellectual Capital*, 12 (2), 249–276.

Dumay, J. and L. Cai (2014), 'A review and critique of content analysis as a methodology for inquiring into IC disclosure', *Journal of Intellectual Capital*, 15 (2), 264–290.

Dumay, J., Cai, L. and R. Chase (2015), 'Using content analysis as a research methodology for investigating intellectual capital disclosure: a critique', *Journal of Intellectual Capital*, 16 (1), 121–155.

Fijałkowska, J. (2014), 'Value Added Intellectual Coefficient (VAIC™) as a tool of performance measurement', *Przedsiebiorczosc I Zarzadzanie*, 15 (1), 129–140.

Gamerschlag, R. (2013), 'Value relevance of human capital information', *Journal of Intellectual Capital*, 14 (2), 325–345.

Gigante, G. (2013), 'Intellectual capital and bank performance in Europe', *Accounting and Finance Research*, 2 (4), 120–129.

Grant, R.M. (1991), 'The resource-based theory of competitive advantage: implications for strategy formulation', *California Management Review*, 33 (3), 114–135.

Guthrie, J. and R. Petty (2000), 'Intellectual capital: Australian annual reporting practices', *Journal of Intellectual Capital*, 1 (3), 241–251.

Healy, P.M. and K.G. Palepu (2001), 'Information asymmetry, corporate disclosure, and the capital markets: a review of the empirical disclosure literature', *Journal of Accounting and Economics*, 31 (1–3), 405–440.

Highhouse, S., Brooks, M.E. and G. Gregarus (2009), 'An organizational impression management perspective on the formation of corporate reputations', *Journal of Management*, 35 (6), 1481–1493.

Jhunjhunwala, S. (2009), 'Monitoring and measuring intangibles using value maps: some examples', *Journal of Intellectual Capital*, 10 (2), 211–223.

Johnston, D.M., Sefcik, S.E. and N.S. Soderstrom (2008), 'The value relevance of greenhouse gas emissions allowances: an exploratory study in the related United States SO_2 market', *European Accounting Review*, 17 (4), 747–764.

Kothari, S.P. and J.L. Zimmerman (1995), 'Price and return models', *Journal of Accounting and Economics*, 20 (2), 155–192.

Murthy, V. and J. Mouritsen (2011), 'The performance of intellectual capital: mobilising relationships between intellectual and financial capital in a bank', *Accounting, Auditing and Accountability Journal*, 24 (5), 622–646.

Ohlson, J.A. (1995), 'Earnings, book values, and dividends in equity valuation', *Contemporary Accounting Research*, 11 (2), 661–687.

Pulic, A. (2000), 'VAIC™ – an accounting tool for IC management', *International Journal of Technology Management*, 20 (5–8), 702–714.

Ståhle, P., Ståhle, S. and S. Aho (2011), 'Value Added Intellectual Coefficient (VAIC): a critical analysis', *Journal of Intellectual Capital*, 12 (4), 247–268.

UNICEF (2019), *Key Demographic Indicators*, accessed 15 July 2019 at data.unicef.org/country/mus/.

United Nations (2015), *Small Island Developing States in Numbers: Climate Change Edition 2015* (Vol. 2019), New York: Office of the High Representative for the Least Developed Countries, Landlocked Developing Countries and Small Island Developing States (UN-OHRLLS).
Uyar, A. and M. Kılıç (2012), 'Value relevance of voluntary disclosure: evidence from Turkish firms', *Journal of Intellectual Capital*, 13 (3), 363–376.
White, H. (1980), 'A heteroskedasticity-consistent covariance matrix estimator and a direct test for heteroskedasticity', *Econometrica*, 48, 817–838.
Williams, S.M. (2001), 'Is intellectual capital performance and disclosure practices related?', *Journal of Intellectual Capital*, 2 (3), 192–203.
Wright, P.M. and G.C. McMahan (1992), 'Theoretical perspectives for strategic human resource management', *Journal of Management*, 18 (2), 295–320.
Wright, P.M., McMahan, G.C. and A. McWilliams (1994), 'Human resources and sustained competitive advantage: a resource-based perspective', *International Journal of Human Resource Management*, 5 (2), 301–326.
Youndt, M.A., Subramaniam, M. and S.A. Snell (2004), 'Intellectual capital profiles: an examination of investments and returns', *Journal of Management Studies*, 41 (2), 335–361.

13. Measuring intellectual capital efficiency: going beyond the VAIC model

Muhammad Nadeem and Rashid Zaman

INTRODUCTION

The world's economy has significantly transitioned from the industrial era to the knowledge era over the last three decades. In a knowledge-driven economy, the traditional factors of production, such as land, buildings and machinery, are being replaced with knowledge-based resources, such as employees' knowledge and skills (Stewart and Ruckdeschel, 1998; Nadeem et al., 2019b). The resource-based view (RBV) of the firm also focuses on the long-term competitive advantage of the firm by maintaining its strategic resources, such as knowledge and skills, which in turn can yield above-average profits for the firm (Peteraf, 1993). These knowledge-based resources, which create value for the firm, are commonly termed 'intellectual capital' (Stewart and Ruckdeschel, 1998). According to Barney (1991), a firm should develop inimitable, valuable and rare resources to build a sustainable competitive advantage, which defines a firm's profitability (Amit and Schoemaker, 1993). Knowledge is a vital resource of a firm that can be developed, transferred and used for competitive advantage within and across industries (Nonaka, 1991; Grant, 1996).

With this shift from a physical assets-based economy to a knowledge-based intellectual capital economy, intellectual capital (commonly known as the difference between market value and book value of the firm) has become the key to the value creation process of a firm (Petty and Guthrie, 2000). This new trend makes the measurement and management of intellectual capital (IC) an important topic in today's knowledge-based economies (Roos et al., 1997; Bontis, 1999). Knight (1999) argues that a business must invest in its personnel for the better management of IC, which will in turn build competitive organizational and relational capital. Thus, spending on intellectual capital is no longer being treated as cost, rather it is recorded as an investment (Guthrie, 2001).

The above discussion highlights the importance of effective measurement and management of intellectual capital resources within a firm. As argued by Kannan and Aulbur (2004), the major aim in measuring intellectual capital is to explore the value of hidden assets and develop those assets to help to achieve a firm's goals. The importance of intellectual capital measurement can be seen in the statement, 'what you can measure, you can manage, and what you want to manage, you need to measure' (Roos et al., 1997). The following advantages of intellectual capital measurement have been explored in the literature (Čater and Čater, 2009; Zangoueinezhad and Moshabaki, 2009; Nadeem et al., 2017b):

1. IC measurement helps to identify the real value of intangible assets.
2. Evaluation of intellectual capital helps to identify the true pattern of knowledge flow within firms.
3. Learning patterns of firms will accelerate through effective intellectual capital measurement.
4. IC measurement, from time to time, will help monitor the intangible assets and explore new methods to increase the value of these intangibles.
5. IC measurement helps in understanding and enhancing a firm's relationships with different stakeholders, such as customers.
6. IC measurement can help increase investment in research and development (R&D), which will enhance innovation in products and services.
7. IC can increase knowledge-sharing activities among the employees and firms once the benefits of knowledge management are realized.
8. Measurement and effective management of human capital, one component of IC, will increase the motivation of employees.

IC MEASUREMENT MODELS

The RBV of a firm holds that a firm's intangible assets contribute equally towards the financial performance as its tangible assets, and value added should be recognized as a measure of performance rather than the return to owners. The value added augments the true measure when it comes to an economy's production in today's knowledge-based era (Sveiby, 1997). Firer and Williams (2003) argue that different perceptions of accounting income have led to different performance measurements based on different theories. For example, under the enterprise resource perspective, an organization acts as a decision-making unit on behalf of its stakeholders including employees, shareholders and creditors; and the profit, the reward for these stakeholders, is termed 'value added'.

In accordance with the different theories on a firm's income, different models have been introduced in the literature to measure intellectual

Table 13.1 Monetary and non-monetary models for intellectual capital measurement

Monetary models	Non-monetary models
Market capitalization models	Scorecard models
M/B value model	Balance scorecard by Kaplan and Norton (1995)
Tobin's Q by Luthy (1998)	Technology broker model by Brooking (1996)
ROA models	Skandia Navigator by Edvinsson and Malone (1997)
EVA[a] & MVA[b] models by Bontis (1999)	IC-Index model by Roos et al. (1997)
Calculated intangible value by Dzinkowski (2000)	Intangible assets monitoring model by Sveiby (1997)
VAIC[c] by Pulic (1998)	Heuristic frame by Joia (2000)
Intangible-driven value model by Lev (2000)	
Residual income model by Ohlson (1995)	

Notes:
a. Economic value added.
b. Market value added.
c. Value added intellectual coefficient.

capital efficiency. These models can be classified into two broad groups: monetary and non-monetary. Table 13.1 summarizes these models.

The Skandia Navigator model is among the pioneers in acknowledging the importance of intellectual capital and its disclosure on the balance sheet. The model classifies intellectual capital into four elements, namely, human, process, renewal and customer capital.

Kaplan and Norton (1995) propose an intellectual capital measurement model known as the balanced scorecard. The idea was to measure the efficiency of intangible assets, which were previously ignored. This model produces results in the form of scores for different elements of IC, such as human, structural and innovation capital. Using Skandia Navigator as a base, Bontis (2004) constructed a new measure called the national intellectual capital index (NICI) aimed at measuring and managing intellectual capital at the national level. The model includes market capital, process capital, renewal capital and human capital as different indicators of the intellectual capital of a nation. The author applied the NICI model to several Arab countries to measure national intellectual capital, and concluded that national intellectual capital represents almost 20 per cent of the total financial wealth of each country in the study's sample.

Based partially on the Skandia Navigator framework, Pulic (1998) developed a new but more comprehensive, easy to calculate measure called value added intellectual coefficient (VAIC). The VAIC model is unique since it measures the intellectual capital size and efficiency, thereby giving a base for comparison between firms, industries and economies (Pulic, 1998). Unlike previous models, which are either customized or fit for some specific profile of firms, the VAIC model uses data from audited reports of firms, which increase its authenticity (Pek, 2005).

THE VAIC MODEL

Several models in the literature can be used to measure intellectual capital efficiency. These models, as shown in Table 13.1, are classified into monetary and non-monetary measures (Edvinsson and Malone, 1997). According to Sydler et al. (2014), non-monetary models (qualitative) limit benchmarking and provide limited information because of a company's specific characteristics. It is more challenging when there are no set guidelines regarding the disclosure of intellectual capital by companies. Cheng et al. (2008) classify intellectual capital research into survey questionnaire and financial data methods. The former approach uses a survey questionnaire to ask respondents to rate their agreement on a five-point Likert scale. This indirect method contains several questions depending upon the purpose of the study, and measures the relationships between the respondent's behaviour and the results (Bontis, 2001; Cabrita and Vaz, 2005; Martínez-Torres, 2006). The latter approach, however, uses financial data obtained from the financial reports of firms. Monetary-based models allow users to compare firms or industries and sometimes countries. Another benefit from using quantitative models is that these models use publicly available information that has usually been audited, which increases the reliability of the results.

One of the most widely used monetary models to measure intellectual capital efficiency is the value added intellectual coefficient (VAIC) model, developed at the Austrian Intellectual Capital Centre (Pulic, 1998, 2004). The VAIC model measures the value added by the business along with individual contributions of each asset category towards the firm's value. These asset categories include tangible and intangible assets, such as intellectual resources. Unlike other assessment-based measures that are unable to measure the asset value of intellectual capital of a firm, VAIC is an indicator-based measure that uses financial report data and calculates the asset value and intellectual capital efficiency of a firm, which is useful for decision-making by management.

The literature (Firer and Williams, 2003; Pek, 2005; Chan, 2009; Joshi et al., 2013) identifies the following benefits from using the VAIC model to measure intellectual capital efficiency:

1. The VAIC model results in numerical indicators that are equally important for all stakeholders, such as creditors, investors, customers, shareholders, providing them with the basis for comparing the components of intellectual capital.
2. Unlike other measures, which demand scores or grading award criteria, VAIC is a quantitative measure that uses statistical analysis and computations for many companies covering millions of data items collected over time.
3. Because of the quantitative measurement, VAIC results can be compared with traditional financial measures such as turnover ratios and profitability ratios that are found in firms' financial reports.
4. VAIC is a simple measure in terms of computational procedures and is easy to understand by management and other stakeholders who are familiar with corporate financial information.
5. According to Chan (2009), the VAIC model can be consistently applied and its results can be compared at departmental, firm, industry and country level, thereby providing a benchmark for effective intellectual capital management.
6. Using publicly available information from audited financial reports increases the reliability of the results.
7. The VAIC model is based on a value-added approach that is consistent with the RBV of the firm, which highlights the importance of intellectual capital for the firm.
8. The VAIC model has been used rigorously to measure the efficiency and effectiveness of intellectual capital of publicly listed companies in several countries, such as Australia, Taiwan, Malaysia, India, Austria, Pakistan and the United Kingdom (Chan, 2009).

Calculations of VAIC

This section discusses in detail how the VAIC model works and what steps are involved in the calculations of VAIC. The VAIC calculations involve a two-step process (Pulic, 1998), where value added is calculated in the first step and VAIC is calculated in the second step.

Step 1

In the VAIC model, total value added (VA) by the business can be calculated as:

$$VA = OUT - IN \quad (13.1)$$

where VA is value added, OUT is output, which represents the total revenue of a firm earned by selling its products or services. IN is input, which includes all expenses a firm makes in raw materials, operational overheads. Pulic (1998) did not include staff costs as expenses in the VAIC model. The author argues that since this money is spent on employees who play a major role in the value creation process, these expenses should be treated as an investment. By replacing output and input with their individual variables in equation (13.1), we can write equation (13.2) as follows:

$$VA = R - C \quad (13.2)$$

where R is total revenues, C is total material cost incurred during the year. Equation (13.2) can also be written as:

$$VA = NI + LC + I + T + DP \quad (13.3)$$

where NI is net income for the year, DP is depreciation and amortization, LC is labour cost, I is interest cost and T is taxes.

Net income can be calculated as:

$$NI = R - C - DP - LC - I - T \quad (13.4)$$

The VA equation (13.3) can also be written as:

$$R - C = NI + LC + I + T + DP \quad (13.5)$$

The left hand side of equation (13.5) represents the total value added by the firm and the right hand side explains its distribution to different stakeholders, such as wages for employees, interest for creditors, taxes to government and net income for the shareholders and retained earnings.

Step 2

In step two, the VAIC is calculated by measuring the human capital (HCE), structural capital (SCE) and capital employed (CEE) efficiencies:

$$VAIC = ICE + CEE \quad (13.6)$$

where ICE is the intellectual capital efficiency and is expressed as:

$$ICE = HCE + SCE \quad (13.7)$$

Human capital efficiency (HCE) measures the ability of the firm to create value through making a \$1 investment in employees and is calculated as:

$$HCE = VA / HC \tag{13.8}$$

Structural capital efficiency (SCE) measures how much capital has been created by structural capital and is calculated as:

$$SCE = SC / VA \tag{13.9}$$

Capital employed efficiency (CEE) measures how much value has been created from each dollar of shareholders' capital and can be calculated as:

$$CEE = VA / CE \tag{13.10}$$

Hence, VAIC can also be written as:

$$VAIC = VA / HC + SC / VA + VA / CE \tag{13.11}$$

where HC is human capital and is measured as the total cost of employees in wages and salaries; CE is capital employed is the book value of total capital employed in the business; and SC is structural capital, which is calculated as:

$$SC = VA - HC \tag{13.12}$$

The VAIC model has been extensively used in the literature to measure intellectual capital efficiency. For example, Chen et al. (2005) used the VAIC model to study the relationship between intellectual capital and a firm's financial performance in Taiwan, and reports a significant positive relationship. Firer and Williams (2003), studying the relationship between intellectual capital and a firm's financial performance, found the relationship to be limited and mixed. The VAIC model has been extensively used in previous studies (Tan et al., 2007; Ting and Lean, 2009; Pal and Soriya, 2012; Joshi et al., 2013; Nadeem et al., 2017b) because of its usefulness and ease of understanding. Table 13.2 provides a summary of selected studies that have applied the VAIC model to measure intellectual capital efficiency.

Table 13.2 Selected studies on the VAIC model

Aim	Sector	Country	Authors
Intellectual capital and performance	Banks and insurance	Turkey	Yalama and Coskun (2007)
		Malaysia	Ting and Lean (2009)
		Australia	Joshi et al. (2013)
		Multiple countries	Al-Musali and Ismail (2016)
		Egypt	Sherif and Elsayed (2016)
		Ghana	Alhassan and Asare (2016)
		Malaysia	Chen et al. (2014)
	Pharmaceutical industry	India	Bharathi Kamath (2008)
			Ghosh and Mondal (2009)
	Technology-intensive firm	Serbia	Janošević et al. (2013)
		Spain	María Díez et al. (2010)
		China	Kai Wah Chu et al. (2011)
		Australia	Clarke et al. (2011)
			Nadeem et al. (2018)
	Multiple firms	India	Pal and Soriya (2012)
		Serbia	Komnenic and Pokrajčić (2012)
		Multiple countries	Nadeem et al. (2017b)
			Janošević et al. (2013)
	Manufacturing firms	Italy	Guerrini et al. (2014)
	Service-related companies	Malaysia	Kamardin et al. (2015)
	Agricultural firms	European companies	Mrazkova et al. (2016)
	Real estate	Bosnia and Herzegovina	Pucar (2012)
	Football clubs	Italy	Pietrantonio and Iazzolino (2014)
		Malaysia	Lee and Mohammed (2014)
		Brazil	Pitelli Britto et al. (2014)

Interaction between VAIC and Corporate governance	Manufacturing firms	Turkey	Aras et al. (2011)
	Multiple industries	China	Nadeem et al. (2017a)
	Service firms	Australia	Appuhami and Bhuyan (2015)
Comparing different evaluation models	Multiple sectors	Northern Italy	Iazzolino and Laise (2013)
IC and risk management	Insurance	Malaysia	Chen et al. (2014)

Source: Adapted from Nadeem et al. (2019a).

THE VAIC CRITIQUE

Despite its popularity, the VAIC model has been critiqued for its construction and ability to capture the full information of intellectual capital resources. The VAIC model is based on the VA concept and VA is calculated as the sum of a firm's operating profit (OP), its personnel costs (LC) and depreciation and amortization (D&A) expenses. The basic argument of Pulic (1998) is that since money spent on human resources creates value for the firm, these expenses should be treated as investments; this is consistent with Frederickson et al. (2010). Ståhle et al. (2011) argue that OP and D&A expenses are generally affected by the decisions of firms, meaning that OP is the outcome of current investment whereas D&A are the outcomes of previous investment. Furthermore, structural capital (SC) is calculated by subtracting personnel costs from value added ($SC = VA - LC$); in other words $SC = OP + D\&A$. Ståhle et al. (2011) therefore state that $OP + D\&A$ is comparable to the operating margin of the firm; thus, there is no reason to call it structural capital. Matching the concept of the VAIC model with different definitions of intellectual capital in the literature, Ståhle et al. (2011) argue that VAIC does not meet the full criteria to examine IC. However, the VAIC model has been used extensively in spite of major criticisms. Vishnu and Kumar Gupta (2014) believe that the VAIC model fairly represents important components of IC. However, there is one serious problem in the VAIC model: that is, the SCE measure of the VAIC model is not justifiable (Ståhle et al., 2011; Vishnu and Kumar Gupta, 2014; Nimtrakoon and Chase, 2015).

In addition to the structural capital measure, the VAIC model exhibits another serious problem in terms of structural capital efficiency (SCE). SEC is measured by dividing structural capital by value added ($SCE = SC/VA$). There are two basic problems in this calculation. First, since SC is the difference between VA and LC or human capital, there is perfect dependency upon each other. This means that the value of SC depends on the value of HC as shown in the equation below:

$$SC = VA - HC \tag{13.13}$$

Moreover:

$$HCE = VA / HC \tag{13.14}$$
$$SCE = SC / VA \tag{13.15}$$

Hence, SCE can also be written as:

$$SCE = 1 - 1 / HCE \tag{13.16}$$

Similarly, HCE can also be written as:

$$HCE = 1 / (1\text{–}SCE) \tag{13.17}$$

This scenario leads to two problematic situations. First, because of the dependency between HCE and SCE, which stems from equation (13.13), one can say that an increase in human capital will lead to a decrease in structural capital, VA being constant. Second, based on equation (13.15), one can interpret that an increase in VA will lead to a decrease in structural capital efficiency, which is against the basic principles of accounting and finance. Because of the severity of the problems with SCE in the VAIC model, many researchers have tried to overcome the problem by using alternative measures of structural capital.

ADJUSTMENTS TO VAIC: THE A-VAIC MODEL

This section discusses in detail the proposed adjustment that Nadeem et al. (2019a) have made to the original VAIC model and introduces the adjusted VAIC model, which they call the 'Adjusted-VAIC' (A-VAIC).

As indicated by Ståhle et al. (2011), calculation of SC in the VAIC model is problematic. Pulic (1998) subtracts human capital from VA to obtain SC, which is equal to OP but has nothing to do with SC (Ståhle et al., 2011). Definitions of intellectual capital vary. For example, according to Bassi (1997), intellectual capital consists of knowledge and its components, including HC, SC and customer capital. Choong (2008) defines intellectual capital as the sum of investments such as R&D, human costs, copyrights and brand names. These definitions agree that there are at least three components of IC: human, structural and relational capital. The structural capital component of intellectual capital has been referred to as unique production processes, copyrights, R&D, and sometimes those infrastructural facilities that help employees make use of their knowledge (Mehralian et al., 2013).

Structural capital refers to investment in R&D, which is the main source of unique processes, and copyrights. Furthermore, R&D investment is the main source of innovation; the literature sometimes refers to SC as innovation capital (INVC) (Choong, 2008). Nadeem et al. (2019a) therefore replace the structural capital measure of the VAIC model with R&D and copyrights investment. Previous studies (Nimtrakoon and Chase, 2015; Vishnu and Kumar Gupta, 2014) that extended the original VAIC model also replaced SC with R&D costs. The use of R&D costs as an SC measure has at least two advantages. First, the R&D investments directly represent

SC; therefore, the Adjusted-VAIC (A-VAIC) introduced by Nadeem et al. (2019a) uses R&D as a measure of SC, unlike the original VAIC model where SC is the difference between VA and HC. Second, the use of R&D investments overcome the superimposition of VA and HC because R&D is an independent variable in their A-VAIC model.

Pulic (1998) also measured structural capital efficiency (SCE) as SC divided by VA, which was criticized by Ståhle et al. (2011). It is worth noting here that the previous studies (Nimtrakoon and Chase, 2015; Vishnu and Kumar Gupta, 2014) that modified the original VAIC model calculated SCE similarly to the original VAIC model and thus produced inclusive results. HCE or CEE, which are calculated as VA divided by HC or CE, measure how much value has been added per dollar of investment in HC or CE. However, SCE is calculated as SC divided by VA, which resembles VA efficiency rather than SCE. Since, in the A-VAIC model, INVC (R&D) is an independent variable, the structural capital efficiency (referred to as INVCE) is calculated by Nadeem et al. (2019a) as follows:

$$INVCE = VA \,/\, INVC \tag{13.18}$$

where INVC is equal to R&D investments. Equation (13.18) measures how much value has been added as a result of each dollar of investment in INVC. Thus, equation (13.18) is the true representation of INVC as per general accounting and finance principles.

Finally, Pulic (1998) calculates VA by adding labour costs and depreciation and amortization to operating profit. Pulic (1998) argues that since money spent on employees generates long-term benefits for the firm, these expenses should be treated as investments. By the same token, several authors (Bontis, 1999; Mouritsen et al., 2005; Stewart and Ruckdeschel, 1998) also argue that investment in R&D creates wealth for firms in the long run, hence these expenses should be treated as investments rather than expenditure. Further, if employees use their knowledge and skills to create value for the firm then it is structural capital (INVC) which enables employees to make use of their skills (Choong, 2008). Therefore, if employee cost is added back to VA, R&D investment should also be added back since this investment also creates value for firms. Moreover, R&D investment converts knowledge and skill into unique processes that then form the basis of competitive advantage according to resource-based view (RBV) theory. Therefore, Nadeem et al. (2019a) modify the VA equation to add R&D and copyrights investment to obtain net VA:

$$VA = NI + LC + I + T + DP + R\&D \tag{13.19}$$

Following the above discussed changes, Nadeem et al. (2019a) propose their A-VAIC model as:

$$A - VAIC = \frac{VA}{HC} + \frac{VA}{INVC} + \frac{VA}{CE} \tag{13.20}$$

where VA/HC is human capital efficiency (HCE), $VA/INVC$ is innovation capital efficiency (INVCE) and VA/CE is capital employed efficiency (CEE).

Nadeem et al. (2019a) then test their A-VAIC model to measure intellectual capital efficiency using data from ten developed and emerging markets worldwide. Their results suggest a significant positive relationship between A-VAIC and its components (HC, INVC and CE) and firm performance, across almost all ten countries in their study. More importantly, their proposed A-VAIC model produced more consistent results than the original VAIC model, showing how effective the changes they made are. Nadeem et al. (2019a) claim that the contributions of their study are twofold. First, it highlights the importance of intellectual capital for firm performance, especially in terms of building sustainable competitive advantage. Second, and most importantly, the A-VAIC model introduced and tested in their study can confidently be used by researchers and industry to measure and manage the efficiency of IC. However, they also note that the biggest limitation of their study is that their findings are limited to selected developed and emerging markets; therefore, more studies are required to implement the A-VAIC model, especially in emerging markets, to test the reliability of their model.

VALUE CREATION: GOING BEYOND FINANCIAL RETURNS

Nadeem et al. (2019a) argue that prior literature on firms' value creation for stakeholders has oversimplified and narrowed the concept of value down to 'economic returns'. While economic returns are fundamental to a firm's core stakeholders (that is, shareholders), other legitimate stakeholders want 'value' beyond economic returns. The closer investigation of the original VAIC as well as the A-VAIC models show that these models still rely on financial numbers and, hence, sidestep value creation for the environment and the society. Stakeholder theory suggests that organizations have multiple stakeholders (including governments, shareholders, suppliers, employees, customers and the environment) whose activities impact on the firm and vice versa (Freeman, 1984). These stakeholders contribute inputs to the organization to obtain benefits from the firm (Donaldson and Preston, 1995). This is also the reason for firms to maximize value from more than one direction.

It is also argued that, rather than focusing on economic returns, firms may concentrate on a value measure that incorporates the value required by all legitimate stakeholders. This view is also rooted in stakeholder theory and emphasizes the 'joint-ness' of stakeholder interests, so that all legitimate stakeholders benefit over time (Freeman, 1984; Freeman et al., 2007). In this regard, Nadeem et al. (2019a) define stakeholder value as firms' aggregate performance on environmental, social and economic metrics. They argue that this definition of stakeholder value serves the interests of most legitimate stakeholders. For example, firms' environmental performance is based on value created for stakeholders, such as communities, suppliers and customers. Similarly, the social performance incorporates value for employees, customers and communities. Finally, the economic metric measures firms' performance on value created for shareholders and economic utility for overall stakeholders.

Based on this literature review, it is evident that neither the original VAIC model nor its modified versions incorporate value creation from environmental and social perspectives. Due to increasing stakeholder pressure on firms to promote environmentalism, socialism and sustainability, it is vital for firms to monitor their performance on multiple indicators. Therefore, there is a strong need for future research to develop a measure that not only measures firm value creation for shareholders but also satisfies the demands of different stakeholders.

CONCLUSION

Intellectual capital has been among the most investigated strands of accounting and corporate finance fields over the last couple of decades. The emergence of a specific journal, namely the *Journal of Intellectual Capital*, and enormous numbers of theoretical and empirical studies published in various other journals, such as *Measuring Business Excellence*, are evidence of the growth of this research field. The importance of intellectual capital increased especially after the 1997 Asian financial crisis and the great financial crisis of 2008. IC's pivotal role during financial turmoil can be explained due to the fact that when firms are financially hampered during a crisis, they look for other means of survival, such as the use of intellectual resources. Consequently, the measurement of intellectual capital becomes vital for firms as they can then make efficient use of available intellectual capital resources.

The accounting literature has, to date, produced several measures of calculating the intellectual capital efficiency. One of the most widely used numerical measures of intellectual capital is the VAIC model. These models use accounting numbers from audited financial reports, which increases the models' usefulness and allows comparisons across firms, industries and even economies. However, the VAIC has received criticism recently, and as a result, several authors have attempted to make changes to this model to overcome the criticism. For example, Nadeem et al. (2019a) review some of the earlier changes to this model and they then propose some changes and introduce the A-VAIC model. They test their A-VAIC model using data from firms in ten countries and report more consistent results. Therefore, they conclude that adjustments to the original VAIC model are possible to increase its ability to effectively measure the intellectual capital efficiency.

However, recent research and practice suggests that firms should measure and manage their performance on environmental and social indicators as well. This seems to be the biggest critique of both the original VAIC model and the A-VAIC model. Therefore, scholars should develop a multidimensional measure that can serve the interests of broader stakeholders, such as customers, suppliers, employees, community and shareholders.

REFERENCES

Alhassan, A.L. and N. Asare (2016), 'Intellectual capital and bank productivity in emerging markets: evidence from Ghana', *Management Decision*, 54 (3), 589–609.

Al-Musali, M.A. and K.N.I. Ku Ismail (2016), 'Cross-country comparison of intellectual capital performance and its impact on financial performance of commercial banks in GCC countries', *International Journal of Islamic and Middle Eastern Finance and Management*, 9 (4), 512–531.

Amit, R. and P.J. Schoemaker (1993), 'Strategic assets and organizational rent', *Strategic Management Journal*, 14 (1), 33–46.

Appuhami, R. and M. Bhuyan (2015), 'Examining the influence of corporate governance on intellectual capital efficiency: evidence from top service firms in Australia', *Managerial Auditing Journal*, 30 (4/5), 347–372.

Aras, G., Aybars, A. and O. Kutlu (2011), 'The interaction between corporate social responsibility and value added intellectual capital: empirical evidence from Turkey', *Social Responsibility Journal*, 7 (4), 622–637.

Barney, J. (1991), 'Firm resources and sustained competitive advantage', *Journal of Management*, 17 (1), 99–120.

Bassi, L.J. (1997), 'Harnessing the power of intellectual capital', *Training and Development*, 51, 25–30.

Bharathi Kamath, G. (2008), 'Intellectual capital and corporate performance in Indian pharmaceutical industry', *Journal of Intellectual Capital*, 9 (4), 684–704.

Bontis, N. (1999), 'Managing organisational knowledge by diagnosing intellectual capital: framing and advancing the state of the field', *International Journal of Technology Management*, 18 (5), 433–462.

Bontis, N. (2001), 'Assessing knowledge assets: a review of the models used to measure intellectual capital', *International Journal of Management Reviews*, 3 (1), 41–60.
Bontis, N. (2004), 'National intellectual capital index: a United Nations initiative for the Arab region', *Journal of Intellectual Capital*, 5 (1), 13–39.
Brooking, A. (1996), *Intellectual Capital – Core Asset for the Third Millennium Enterprise*, London: International Thomson Business Press.
Cabrita, R.M. and J. Vaz (2005), 'Intellectual capital and value creation: evidence from the Portuguese banking industry', *Electronic Journal of Knowledge Management*, 4 (1), 11–20.
Chan, K.H. (2009), 'Impact of intellectual capital on organisational performance: an empirical study of companies in the Hang Seng Index (Part 1)', *Learning Organization*, 16 (1), 4–21.
Chen, F.C., Liu, Z.J. and Q.L. Kweh (2014), 'Intellectual capital and productivity of Malaysian general insurers', *Economic Modelling*, 36, 413–420.
Chen, M.C., Cheng, S.J. and Y. Hwang (2005), 'An empirical investigation of the relationship between intellectual capital and firms' market value and financial performance', *Journal of Intellectual Capital*, 6 (2), 159–176.
Cheng, M.-Y., Lin, J.-Y., Hsiao, T.-Y. and T.W. Lin (2008), 'Censoring model for evaluating intellectual capital value drivers', *Journal of Intellectual Capital*, 9 (4), 639–654.
Choong, K.K. (2008), 'Intellectual capital: definitions, categorization and reporting models', *Journal of Intellectual Capital*, 9 (4), 609–638.
Clarke, M., Seng, D. and R.H. Whiting (2011), 'Intellectual capital and firm performance in Australia', *Journal of Intellectual Capital*, 12 (4), 505–530.
Čater, T. and B. Čater (2009), '(In) tangible resources as antecedents of a company's competitive advantage and performance', *Journal for East European Management Studies*, 14 (2), 186–209.
Donaldson, T. and L.E. Preston (1995), 'The stakeholder theory of the corporation: concepts, evidence, and implications', *Academy of Management Review*, 20 (1), 65–91.
Dzinkowski, R. (2000), 'The value of intellectual capital', *Journal of Business Strategy*, 21 (4), 33.
Edvinsson, L. and M. Malone (1997), *Realizing your Company's True Value by Finding its Hidden Brain Power*, New York: Harper Collins.
Firer, S. and S.M. Williams (2003), 'Intellectual capital and traditional measures of corporate performance', *Journal of Intellectual Capital*, 4 (3), 348–360.
Frederickson, J.R., Webster, E. and I.O. Williamson (2010), 'Is the current accounting treatment of education and training costs appropriate?', *Australian Accounting Review*, 20 (3), 265–273.
Freeman, R.E. (1984), *Strategic Management: A Stakeholder Perspective*, Boston, MA: Pitman.
Freeman, R.E., Harrison, J.S. and A.C. Wicks (2007), *Managing For Stakeholders: Survival, Reputation, and Success*, New Haven, CT: Yale University Press.
Ghosh, S. and A. Mondal (2009), 'Indian software and pharmaceutical sector IC and financial performance', *Journal of Intellectual Capital*, 10 (3), 369–388.
Grant, R.M. (1996), 'Toward a knowledge-based theory of the firm', *Strategic Management Journal*, 17 (S2), 109–122.
Guerrini, A., Romano, G. and C. Leardini (2014), 'Does intellectual capital efficiency affect financial performance? The case of Italian listed firms', *International Journal of Learning and Intellectual Capital*, 11 (2), 127–148.
Guthrie, J. (2001), 'The management, measurement and the reporting of intellectual capital', *Journal of Intellectual Capital*, 2 (1), 27–41.
Iazzolino, G. and D. Laise (2013), 'Value added intellectual coefficient (VAIC): a methodological and critical review', *Journal of Intellectual Capital*, 14 (4), 547–563.
Janošević, S., Dženopoljac, V. and N. Bontis (2013), 'Intellectual capital and financial performance in Serbia', *Knowledge and Process Management*, 20 (1), 1–11.
Joia, L.A. (2000), 'Measuring intangible corporate assets: linking business strategy with intellectual capital', *Journal of Intellectual Capital*, 1 (1), 68–84.

Joshi, M., Cahill, D., Sidhu, J. and M. Kansal (2013), 'Intellectual capital and financial performance: an evaluation of the Australian financial sector', *Journal of Intellectual Capital*, 14 (2), 264–285.

Kai Wah Chu, S., Hang Chan, K. and W.W. Wu (2011), 'Charting intellectual capital performance of the gateway to China', *Journal of Intellectual Capital*, 12 (2), 249–276.

Kamardin, H., Abu Bakar, R. and R. Ishak (2015), 'Proprietary costs of intellectual capital reporting: Malaysian evidence', *Asian Review of Accounting*, 23 (3), 275–292.

Kannan, G. and W.G. Aulbur (2004), 'Intellectual capital: measurement effectiveness', *Journal of Intellectual Capital*, 5 (3), 389–413.

Kaplan, R.S. and D.P. Norton (1995), 'Putting the balanced scorecard to work. Performance measurement, management, and appraisal sourcebook', *Harvard Business Review*, 66–74.

Knight, D.J. (1999), 'Performance measures for increasing intellectual capital', *Strategy and Leadership*, 27 (2), 22–27.

Komnenic, B. and D. Pokrajčić (2012), 'Intellectual capital and corporate performance of MNCs in Serbia', *Journal of Intellectual Capital*, 13 (1), 106–119.

Lee, S.P. and S. Mohammed (2014), 'Intellectual capital on listed agricultural firms' performance in Malaysia', *International Journal of Learning and Intellectual Capital*, 11 (3), 202–221.

Lev, B. (2000), 'Intangibles: management, measurement and reporting', available at www.baruch-lev.com.

Luthy, D.H. (1998), 'Intellectual capital and its measurement', *Proceedings of the Asian Pacific Interdisciplinary Research in Accounting Conference (APIRA), Osaka, Japan*, August, pp. 16–17.

María Díez, J., Lizet Ochoa, M., Begona Prieto, M. and A. Santidrián (2010), 'Intellectual capital and value creation in Spanish firms', *Journal of Intellectual Capital*, 11 (3), 348–367.

Martínez-Torres, M.R. (2006), 'A procedure to design a structural and measurement model of intellectual capital: an exploratory study', *Information and Management*, 43 (5), 617–626.

Mehralian, G., Rasekh, H.R., Akhavan, P. and A.R. Ghatari (2013), 'Prioritization of intellectual capital indicators in knowledge-based industries: evidence from pharmaceutical industry', *International Journal of Information Management*, 33 (1), 209–216.

Mouritsen, J., Bukh, P.N. and H.K. Bang (2005), 'Understanding intellectual capital in an innovative medium-sized firm: the case of Maxon Telecom', *Australian Accounting Review*, 15 (36), 30–39.

Mrazkova, S., Perzelova, I. and J. Glova (2016), 'Impact of the value-added intellectual coefficient and its components on overall performance of selected European companies', *Polish Journal of Management Studies*, 14 (2), 161–171.

Nadeem, M., De Silva, T.A., Gan, C. and R. Zaman (2017a), 'Boardroom gender diversity and intellectual capital efficiency: evidence from China', *Pacific Accounting Review*, 29 (4), 590–615.

Nadeem, M., Dumay, J. and M. Massaro (2019a), 'If you can measure it, you can manage it: a case of intellectual capital', *Australian Accounting Review*, 29 (2), 395–407.

Nadeem, M., Farooq, M.B. and A. Ahmed (2019b), 'Does female representation on corporate boards improve intellectual capital efficiency?', *Journal of Intellectual Capital*, 20 (5), 680–700.

Nadeem, M., Gan, C. and C. Nguyen (2017b), 'Does intellectual capital efficiency improve firm performance in BRICS economies? A dynamic panel estimation', *Measuring Business Excellence*, 21 (1), 65–85.

Nadeem, M., Gan, C. and C. Nguyen (2018), 'The importance of intellectual capital for firm performance: evidence from Australia', *Australian Accounting Review*, 28 (3), 334–344.

Nimtrakoon, S. and R. Chase (2015), 'The relationship between intellectual capital, firms' market value and financial performance: empirical evidence from the ASEAN', *Journal of Intellectual Capital*, 16 (3), 587–618.

Nonaka, I. (1991), 'The knowledge-creating company', *Harvard Business Review*, 69 (6), 96–104.

Ohlson, J.A. (1995), 'Earning, book values, and dividends in equity valuation', *Contemporary Accounting Research*, 11 (2), 661–687.
Pal, K. and S. Soriya (2012), 'IC performance of Indian pharmaceutical and textile industry', *Journal of Intellectual Capital*, 13 (1), 120–137.
Pek, C.G. (2005), 'Intellectual capital performance of commercial banks in Malaysia', *Journal of Intellectual Capital*, 6 (3), 385–396.
Peteraf, M.A. (1993), 'The cornerstones of competitive advantage: a resource-based view', *Strategic Management Journal*, 14 (3), 179–191.
Petty, R. and J. Guthrie (2000), 'Intellectual capital literature review: measurement, reporting and management', *Journal of Intellectual Capital*, 1 (2), 155–176.
Pietrantonio, R. and G. Iazzolino (2014), 'Intellectual capital and business performances in Italian firms: an empirical investigation', *International Journal of Knowledge Management Studies*, 5 (3–4), 211–243.
Pitelli Britto, D., Monetti, E. and J. da Rocha Lima Jr (2014), 'Intellectual capital in tangible intensive firms: the case of Brazilian real estate companies', *Journal of Intellectual Capital*, 15 (2), 333–348.
Pucar, S. (2012), 'The influence of intellectual capital on export performance', *Journal of Intellectual Capital*, 13 (2), 248–261.
Pulic, A. (1998), 'Measuring the performance of intellectual potential in knowledge economy', Paper presented at the 2nd McMaster Word Congress on Measuring and Managing Intellectual Capital by the Austrian Team for Intellectual Potential.
Pulic, A. (2004), 'Intellectual capital–does it create or destroy value?', *Measuring Business Excellence*, 8 (1), 62–68.
Roos, J., Edvinsson, L. and G. Roos (1997), *Intellectual Capital: Navigating in the New Business Landscape*, New York: New York University Press.
Sherif, M. and M. Elsayed (2016), 'The impact of intellectual capital on corporate performance: evidence from the Egyptian insurance market', *International Journal of Innovation Management*, 20 (3), 1650034.
Ståhle, P., Ståhle, S. and S. Aho (2011), 'Value added intellectual coefficient (VAIC): a critical analysis', *Journal of Intellectual Capital*, 12 (4), 531–551.
Stewart, T. and C. Ruckdeschel (1998), 'Intellectual capital: the new wealth of organizations', *Performance Improvement*, 37 (7), 56–59.
Sveiby, K.E. (1997), *The New Organizational Wealth: Managing and Measuring Knowledge-based Assets*, San Francisco, CA: Berrett-Koehler Publishers.
Sydler, R., Haefliger, S. and R. Pruksa (2014), 'Measuring intellectual capital with financial figures: can we predict firm profitability?', *European Management Journal*, 32 (2), 244–259.
Tan, H.P., Plowman, D. and P. Hancock (2007), 'Intellectual capital and financial returns of companies', *Journal of Intellectual Capital*, 8 (1), 76–95.
Ting, I.W.K. and H.H. Lean (2009), 'Intellectual capital performance of financial institutions in Malaysia', *Journal of Intellectual Capital*, 10 (4), 588–599.
Vishnu, S. and V. Kumar Gupta (2014), 'Intellectual capital and performance of pharmaceutical firms in India', *Journal of Intellectual Capital*, 15 (1), 83–99.
Yalama, A. and M. Coskun (2007), 'Intellectual capital performance of quoted banks on the Istanbul stock exchange market', *Journal of Intellectual Capital*, 8 (2), 256–271.
Zangoueinezhad, A. and A. Moshabaki (2009), 'The role of structural capital on competitive intelligence', *Industrial Management and Data Systems*, 109 (2), 262–280.

PART IV

NOVEL APPROACHES

14. An introduction to network analysis in intellectual capital research

Rosa Lombardi and Federico Schimperna

INTRODUCTION

The purpose of this chapter is to introduce network analysis and its main principles (Wasserman and Faust, 1994; Haythornthwaite, 1996; Provan et al., 2005; Scott, 2011) to intellectual capital researchers who may not be familiar with this research method. Thus, this chapter provides an overview of network analysis and the opportunities to apply this to intellectual capital research (Trequattrini et al., 2012; Trequattrini et al., 2015b; Trequattrini et al., 2017), especially intellectual capital measurement. Results are discussed across the international context showing applications, principles and characteristics (Trequattrini et al., 2015a) that illuminate the value of network analysis in intellectual capital research.

This chapter provides an outline of network analysis, its main principles and existing literature (Granovetter, 1973; Wasserman and Faust, 1994; Borgatti et al., 2009; Scott, 2011), to understand how it is applied in accounting research, its main features and the renewed application to intellectual capital measurement. Particularly, this chapter advances the study of intellectual capital measurement (Montemari and Nielsen, 2013), proposing a different perspective, based on the analysis of the relationships of a specific phenomenon. Through the analysis of relationships, this chapter introduces a new set of network indicators composing a system useful to interpret various phenomena (Trequattrini et al., 2015a). Thus, network analysis becomes a relevant tool for academic and professional communities, offering quick indicators to understand different aspects of a phenomenon.

As established in the literature, managers need to govern the value creation process of their organisation and especially the networks in which they are involved (Montemari and Nielsen, 2013). Measuring and managing intellectual capital dynamism is essential to achieve such an objective. Over the past 20 years, academics and practitioners have developed intellectual capital measurement, such as the utilisation of cognitive maps, causal maps, strategy maps and network analysis (Montemari and Nielsen, 2013). Unlike traditional methods, network analysis focuses its analysis on relationships and not on the organisation (Provan et al., 2005). Network analysis allows researchers to investigate network phenomena (Borgatti et al., 2009; Trequattrini et al., 2015a), in which nodes are social actors (Worrell et al., 2013) and ties or links represent connections between nodes.

In this chapter we show the relevance of network analysis to intellectual capital research from the accounting perspective. However, it is possible to apply insights from this chapter to other qualitative and quantitative accounting research projects. The remainder of the chapter is organised as follows: we start by defining network analysis and then explain the software and review the literature on network analysis. The last section presents the main conclusions from the literature review and proposes directions for future research.

DEFINING NETWORK ANALYSIS

Network analysis is a research method adopted by researchers in several economic fields (Trequattrini et al., 2017), to investigate the social structure of a network. Particularly, the application of network analysis allows researchers to explore connections and relationships between actors in a network (Granovetter, 1973; Borgatti et al., 2009; Scott, 2011). Such methodologies have been used to investigate intellectual capital measurement (Montemari and Nielsen, 2013).

Over the past 20 years, academics and practitioners have developed tools for intellectual capital measurement, such as the utilisation of cognitive maps, causal maps, strategy maps or network analysis (Montemari and Nielsen, 2013). A cognitive map helps to define how causal relationships and concepts relate to each other. Concepts in cognitive maps are represented by points and causal links between them by arrows (Axelrod, 1976). Causal maps are a typology of cognitive maps and a network of inter-linked concepts (Montibeller and Belton, 2006), useful to highlight the causal structure of individuals' ideas and what influences the decision-making process (Hodgkinson et al., 2004; Montemari and Nielsen, 2013). Conversely, strategy maps are a tool aimed at measuring only the company's strategy, particularly focused on intangibles (Kaplan and Norton, 2001, 2008).

Unlike traditional methods, network analysis focuses its analysis on relationships instead of on the organisation (Provan et al., 2005). According to Provan et al. (2005), 'Network analysis is a method of collecting and analyzing data from multiple individuals or organizations that may be interacting with one another'. Network analysis is not a formal or unitary theory, nor a deductive system. It is a broad strategy useful to investigate social structure. Network analysis is regarded as a paradigm or a perspective, rather than a predictive social theory (Emirbayer and Goodwin, 1994) adopted through the utilisation of specific software to analyse phenomena.

According to Scott (2011), social network analysis (Wasserman and Faust, 1994), as applied to the investigation of social interactions among individuals (Provan et al., 2005), was developed from graph theory. A graph is a set of lines connecting points, while graph theory is a group of mathematical axioms and formulae, which describe the properties of the patterns formed by the lines (Scott, 1988). In the last few years, social network analysis has been applied as a research method to many different kinds of interactions and relationships in numerous disciplines, such as accounting, management, physics, biology, crime/war and public health (Borgatti et al., 2009; Trequattrini et al., 2012; Trequattrini et al., 2015a; Trequattrini et al., 2017). Thus, the social network analysis approach seeks to investigate various kinds of patterns and phenomena, trying to determine their characteristics and discover their potential consequences (Freeman, 2004).

In the last three decades, network analysis has received increasing attention, and its application has extended across several economic fields (Knoke and Yang, 2008). Recently, the application of network analysis in research projects has centred on connections and relationships (links or ties) between individuals, groups and organisations (nodes) (Granovetter, 1973; Borgatti et al., 2009; Scott, 2011). In these studies, network analysis has been used as an inductive approach to investigate numerous social structures and relational phenomena, enriching individual and corporate strategies (Otte and Rousseau, 2002; Emirbayer and Goodwin, 1994).

The strength of network analysis is that it allows researchers to investigate network phenomena (Borgatti et al., 2009; Trequattrini et al., 2015a). Each network is characterised by a set of nodes connected by ties or links (Haythornthwaite, 1996; Worrell et al., 2013). Nodes are social actors (Worrell et al., 2013), and ties or links represent connections between nodes, changing in content, direction and strength (Granovetter, 1973; Garton et al., 1999). Ties can carry and exchange resources, such as information or money. The directions of ties show who gives and who takes resources in the network, whereas strength provides the ties' level of intensity or activity (Worrell et al., 2013). Thus, relationships between nodes create social capital and add value to the context in which they are placed (Burt, 2000; Trequattrini et al., 2015a).

In this way, network analysis is a useful tool for understanding the significance of relationships and showing social actions in a network (Worrell et al., 2013), even if network analysis's implementation is based on specific rules. Trequattrini et al. (2015a) outlined that: 'Network analysis (Wan Hui, 1971) is a formal instrument for analysing relationships, based on a mathematical and statistical approach, where graphs and diagrams are used to express and summarise relationships based on nodes (dots) and arches (lines) or, in other words, on individuals/entities and relationships'. Thus, network analysis is based on: (1) systematic empirical data; (2) the use of graphic imageries; and (3) mathematical-statistical and computational models supporting the analysis (Freeman, 2004).

Through a literature review of the network analysis approach (Trequattrini et al., 2012), it is clear that such studies often use software, such as UCINET, to illustrate the social network and the descriptive network measures. Some specific applications of network analysis have focused on board interlocks and their ability to contribute to strategic decision-making (Blanco-Alcántara et al., 2018), the knowledge creation capacity of project teams in the building construction industry (Ginevičius et al., 2011), the firms' transactions (Solitander and Tidström, 2010) and the knowledge of workers' performance (Burton et al., 2012). Additionally, network analysis has been employed in several accounting studies and in intellectual capital research, analysing the impact of structural capital on exploitative and exploratory innovations (Yan and Guan, 2018), relational capital and the relationships phenomena (Cricelli and Greco, 2013; Barão and da Silva, 2013) and the key employees' and knowledge-management programmes (Hollenbeck and Jamieson, 2015). Thus, the network analysis research method is applied to a wide range of phenomena, explored in terms of structural patterning and social actors' interactions (Freeman, 2004).

A notable example of what a network analysis looks like is included in the study by Trequattrini et al. (2015a). These authors applied network analysis to the football industry, drafting passes (links or ties) among professional football players (nodes) to define their relationships during the match, proposing a tool to define strategy, their decision-making process and corporate tactics. Thus, investigating nodes and links by a network requires the definition of a set of measures that support the analysis and its aims (Borgatti et al., 2009).

Through a mathematical-statistical approach, network analysis allows researchers to inductively define characteristics of relational phenomena activated by two or more nodes and their links (Granovetter, 1973). Thus, network analysis is applied through the utilisation of the software that obtains graphs, images and a wide range of descriptive indexes (for example, centrality, cohesion, frequency, betweenness, ego-network), defining the relational perspective of a phenomenon.

SOFTWARE FOR NETWORK ANALYSIS

Network analysis provides an approach to structurally analyse networks, investigating the relationships linking individuals rather than investigating individuals themselves (Freeman, 2004). Carrying out a network data analysis is difficult. Huisman and van Duijn (2004) argued:

> The main reason for this is the dependence structure of the network. The ties from and to the same actor are not independent, and therefore statistical analysis cannot be based on broad independence assumptions as is usually done. Also, the ties are often dichotomous, making methods or models based on normal distributions inappropriate.

Because statistical analysis of network data is difficult, software for network analysis is crucial to develop the following five types of analysis: (1) statistical network descriptives; (2) relations within and between networks; (3) relations between networks and actor attributes; (4) comparison and categorisation of actors; and (5) network dynamics (Huisman and van Duijn, 2004).

Thus, the application of network analysis to investigate research phenomena is developed through the utilisation of specific software tools (Scott, 1996; Freeman, 2004; Knoke and Yang, 2008; Borgatti et al., 2009). Software is essential to facilitate network analysis, handle particular routines or problems, such as the identification of subgroups or statistical testing (Knoke and Yang, 2008) and provide descriptive network measures. According to Huisman and van Duijn (2004), the main network analysis software tools are: FATCAT, GRADAP, JUNG, KliqFinder, MatMan, MultiNet, NetMiner II, Pajek, PermNet, PREPSTAR, SNA, SNAP, Snowball, StOCNET, Structure and UCINET. Up to now, UCINET seems to be the most complete and updated software for processing and analysing research data and applying network analysis to accounting and intellectual capital research phenomena.

In the light of its high number of non-statistical and statistical procedures (Borgatti et al., 2009; Trequattrini et al., 2015a; Trequattrini et al., 2017), it is important to present a more detailed review of UCINET software. The interface, similar to Excel with a set of procedures by UCINET software, makes it the most complete and updated analysis tool compared to others. Thanks to its greater specificity (Cordaz, 2005), the main advantages of UCINET software are the high number of descriptive network measures (for example, centrality, cohesive subgroups and structural holes, cohesion) and procedure-based methods (for example, cluster analysis, two-mode scaling and structural equivalence). Additionally, UCINET has a built-in spreadsheet editor (Huisman and van Duijn, 2004). Thus, it is probably the most well-known and used software for processing and analysing relational data.

Using UCINET software, network analysis requires the construction of a data and entering matrix (DEM), in which data are registered, organised and prepared for the analysis and research aims. The following phases involve data recoding (DR) through the dichotomisation of data, transforming the numerical values in binary values (BVs) and building a binary matrix (BM). Particularly, the BM allows for the creation of the social network graphically displayed in the graph-net. Additionally, the UCINET software's application allows descriptive network measures (DNMs) to be built, among which the most relevant is the cohesion degree (CD) of the network, the subgroups of the network (SN) and actors' position (AP) in the network. The indexes grouped by the degree of network cohesion (CD) are included in Table 14.1, and network centrality is in Table 14.2.

Table 14.1 The descriptive network measures

Network measures	Description
Density	It represents one of the main indicators of the degree of network cohesion, allowing a network with many links to be considered cohesive
Distance	It analyses the network cohesion based on actors' distance estimating the average distance, the distance-based cohesion and the distance-weighted fragmentation
Connectivity	It is the number of nodes that need to be removed to disconnect the network

Table 14.2 Network centrality indexes

Indexes	Description
Degree centrality	The centrality of each node depends on the number of relationships concerning it
Closeness centrality	It is a centrality measure expressed analysing distance between points; if a node is close to many of the other nodes, it is more central in the network
Betweenness centrality	It indicates how much a node is in an intermediate position between two other nodes, showing if a node is in the shortest path connecting every other pair of nodes

Table 14.3 Clusters

AC MILAN	
Clique	Players
1	23, 17, 5
2	23, 17, 32
3	4, 23, 5
4	10, 18, 20
5	18, 17, 20
6	4, 21, 5
7	17, 5, 20
FC BARCELONA	
Clique	Players
1	8, 10, 4, 16, 6, 18, 3
2	8, 10, 4, 16, 6, 3, 2
3	8, 4, 16, 6, 18, 5, 3
4	17, 4, 16, 6, 3, 2

Source: Trequattrini et al. (2015a, pp. 100–101).

Additionally, the decomposition of the network into cliques is posited as a relevant strategy definition tool (Trequattrini et al., 2015a). The clique creation consists of cohesive subsets of actors (nodes) who share strong ties (links) to each other, as reported in Table 14.3 (for example, the number of football team players in common for each clique). Lastly, another strategy is grouping the actors based on the frequency associated with each pair of actors belonging to the same clique, building a co-membership matrix, as reported in Figure 14.1. For example, the number of overlaps where the players are classified according to the frequency with which they belong to the same clique. The highest values define the closest or strongest nodes. The values contained in this matrix indicate how many times each pair of actors is in the same clique, showing a strong link between these actors if they are together in a high number of cliques.

NETWORK ANALYSIS AND INTELLECTUAL CAPITAL LITERATURE

In the last few years, network analysis has been applied to many different kinds of interaction and relationship analysis in numerous disciplines

	92	11	10	4	18	23	21	17	5	20	32
92	**0**	0	0	0	0	0	0	0	0	0	0
11	0	**0**	0	0	0	0	0	0	0	0	0
10	0	0	**1**	0	1	0	0	0	0	1	0
4	0	0	0	**2**	0	1	1	0	2	0	0
18	0	0	1	0	**2**	0	0	1	0	2	0
23	0	0	0	1	0	**3**	0	2	2	0	1
21	0	0	0	1	0	0	**1**	0	1	0	0
17	0	0	0	0	1	2	0	**4**	2	2	1
5	0	0	0	2	0	2	1	2	**4**	1	0
20	0	0	1	0	2	0	0	2	1	**3**	0
32	0	0	0	0	0	1	0	1	0	0	**1**

	8	10	17	4	16	6	18	5	3	2	1
8	**3**	2	0	3	3	3	2	1	3	1	0
10	2	**2**	0	2	2	2	1	0	2	1	0
17	0	0	**1**	1	1	1	0	0	1	1	0
4	3	2	1	**4**	4	4	2	1	4	2	0
16	3	2	1	4	**4**	4	2	1	4	2	0
6	3	2	1	4	4	**4**	2	1	4	2	0
18	2	1	0	2	2	2	**2**	1	2	0	0
5	1	0	0	1	1	1	1	**1**	1	0	0
3	3	2	1	4	4	4	2	1	**4**	2	0
2	1	1	1	2	2	2	0	0	2	**2**	0
1	0	0	0	0	0	0	0	0	0	0	**0**

Source: Trequattrini et al. (2015a, p. 101).

Figure 14.1 Matrix of co-belonging

(Borgatti et al., 2009), including in intellectual capital measurement (Montemari and Nielsen, 2013). Intellectual capital has an impact on recent economic, managerial, sociological and technological developments (Petty and Guthrie, 2000) that should be analysed separately from other specific topics. Assuming the growing importance of intellectual capital, this section examines the literature that applies network analysis to intellectual capital research.

Starting from the 1980s, intangibles rapidly became one of the main sources of competitive advantage for companies, changing the world's economy and leading to a knowledge-based economy (Ricceri and Guthrie, 2009). Knowledge resources involved in the value creation process were commonly embedded in the field of intellectual capital research (Stewart, 1997; Sveiby, 1997; Brooking, 1998; Chaminade and Roberts, 2003; Guthrie et al., 2011). Thus, intellectual capital became a strategic asset composed of human capital, relational capital and structural capital (Stewart, 1997; Guthrie et al., 2011). Intellectual capital has been contextualised in relation to: the information technology and information society; the knowledge and knowledge-based economy; the network society;

and innovation as the main source of competitive advantage (Petty and Guthrie, 2000).

In the last few years, several scholars have investigated intellectual capital from a network analysis perspective (Trequattrini et al., 2015a). Intellectual capital research (Stewart, 1997; Petty and Guthrie, 2000; Mouritsen et al., 2001; Dumay and Garanina, 2013; Dumay, 2016) and its stages (Petty and Guthrie, 2000; Dumay, 2009; Dumay and Roslender, 2012; Chiucchi and Dumay, 2015) have been developed through the application of several research methods, including network analysis and its software tools (Solitander and Tidström, 2010; Schmutte, 2014; O'Hagan, 2017).

It is now recognised that intellectual capital research has undergone several phases of development (Edvinsson and Malone, 1997; Petty and Guthrie, 2000; Dumay and Garanina, 2013). During the first stage of intellectual capital research (Sveiby, 1988, 1997; Edvinsson and Malone, 1997; Celemi, 1998), the awareness of intellectual capital and related intangibles was translated into its centrality in creating and managing competitive advantage by organisations. The principle 'to render the invisible visible by creating a discourse that all could engage in' (Petty and Guthrie, 2000) fostered several frameworks (Kaplan and Norton, 1992; Edvinsson, 1997; Sveiby, 1997) and became the proposition for the second stage of intellectual capital research. By investigating intellectual capital as a value driver source (Dumay, 2009) for organisations, the theoretical background of intellectual capital was born (Dumay and Garanina, 2013).

In the first stages of intellectual capital research (Petty and Guthrie, 2000; Dumay, 2009), network analysis and its software tools were used in several studies as a research method supporting the intellectual capital investigation. Network analysis was applied to describe the value creation dynamics of working groups, organisations, business webs and purposeful networks engaging in intangible value (Allee, 2009), the knowledge creation process as a source of competitive advantage (Kase and Zupan, 2009) and understanding intellectual capital individual components and performance (Pedro et al., 2018). As the intellectual capital classification was an interesting issue (Pedro et al., 2018), network analysis approaches allowed individual intellectual capital components to be determined by drafting the network's structure, features and interconnections. Thus, network analysis identified the type of networks embracing groups, individual intellectual capital components and performance (Pedro et al., 2018).

Interestingly, the utilisation of network analysis in several studies has led to the explanation of how intellectual capital flows contribute to improving organisations' competitive position (Solitander and Tidström, 2010). Solitander and Tidström (2010) analysed relational capital in terms of transactions between companies using network analysis to draft competitive business relationships. Notably, these authors assumed the identification of internal and external groups, playing key roles in the company's network and recognising tangible and intangible transactions occurring between companies. Thus, the business environment surrounding a company becomes more complex, assuming the presence of cooperative and competitive flows (Solitander and Tidström, 2010).

The study by Solitander and Tidström (2010) provides one example of the application of network analysis in the field of intellectual capital research. Additionally, the research by Barão and da Silva (2013) based on social network analysis and re-engineering environment (SNARE) is an interesting study. These authors used the network analysis approach to assess the relational capital of a knowledge-intensive organisation. Specifically, they evaluated partner–developer relationships in an international software company, demonstrating the existence of relevant intangible aspects involved in the product innovation process.

Furthermore, network analysis was applied as a research method to study intellectual capital implications in corporate management and performance measurement (Capece and Costa, 2009; Trequattrini et al., 2012; O'Hagan, 2017). The third stage of intellectual capital research (Cuozzo et al., 2017; Dumay and Garanina, 2013; Chiucchi and Dumay, 2015; Lombardi and Dumay, 2017) is the most relevant in terms of network analysis application. Trequattrini et al. (2012) explained how network analysis can be applied to prevent company turnaround and crisis. Network analysis is a tool for investigating relationships between the company and its stakeholders as a way to understand a company's well-being.

Capece and Costa (2009) have examined the relationship between the structural non-hierarchical configuration of virtual teams and the performance resulting from their knowledge creation process, using network analysis and a set of indexes (for example, network degree centralisation, network flow betweenness centralisation, information and communication technologies usage variety, information and communication technologies usage variability, leadership style, average frequency of communication). O'Hagan (2017) has investigated relationship measurement in network connections of gender diversity and boards of directors applying betweenness index to measure centrality, determining which directors in the analysis are the most relevant. Thus, network analysis is applied as a validation research method to previous applications of statistical tools (for example, regression analysis) (O'Hagan, 2017).

It is worth emphasising that network analysis is also used to understand managerial implications from intellectual capital research. Sarker et al. (2011) identified individuals who emerge as 'stars' in globally distributed teams involved in knowledge labour. Kasztler and Leitner (2009) analysed dynamic relationships through network analysis, allowing managers to visualise and understand details of the relationship that can either facilitate or obstruct knowledge creation and transfer. Blanco-Alcántara et al. (2018) investigated whether the influence of the board interlocks depended on their ability to contribute to strategic decision-making. Thus, the application of network analysis is related to the calculation of the centrality measures to verify the research hypothesis (Blanco-Alcántara et al., 2018).

Network analysis is also relevant in the field of human capital to identify and select key employees and improve knowledge-management programmes (Hollenbeck and Jamieson, 2015). Ginevičius et al. (2011) pointed out, from a theoretical standpoint, the relevance of social network analysis as a powerful technique to reveal specific expertise or influence, how people cooperate, and with whom, who is overburdened with requests for assistance and who fails to collaborate at all. Aliev and Sigov (2017) applied network analysis to assess the ability and willingness of employees to work in groups and identify active or passive employees in terms of the communication and transfer of organisational knowledge. Ujwary-Gil (2019) highlighted relevant managerial implications in terms of knowledge, skills, tasks and resources within a library context through a network analysis of network efficiency. In these examples, network analysis is a useful method for identifying and evaluating human resources in a firm.

The fourth stage of intellectual capital research builds on the third stage and incorporates network analysis methods, extending intellectual capital's analysis from specific organisations to a wider ecosystem composed of countries, cities or communities (Dumay and Garanina, 2013) and relationships with stakeholders (Secundo et al., 2018). For example, Cricelli and Greco (2013) analysed the relational capital in an inter-university consortia using network analysis. Díez-Vial and Montoro-Sánchez (2014) studied knowledge flows and local networks in the Madrid Science Park in Spain using network analysis to test relationships between firms in the park. Di Vincenzo et al. (2012) described the structural characteristics of individuals' social capital through a sample of 22 Swedish pharmacies. Thus, network analysis is an essential tool for understanding relationships in a broader context in which the company survives.

Applying network analysis to investigate an ecosystem represents a new stream of research. For example, Schmutte (2014) investigated job transitions using network analysis (for example, adjacency matrix) to find the boundaries of labour market mobility. A mobility network is an undirected graph where nodes represent workers only connected to nodes representing employers. The graph of indirect connections between workers and employers reports the degree distribution and the clustering nodes. Including statistics on network density, Schmutte (2014) showed that network analysis provides simple descriptive statistics characterising market complexity and is useful in several research applications. Thus, network statistics produced through network analysis are a useful source of information for a cross-sectional and dynamic analysis of ecosystems.

Additionally, network analysis has been used to analyse relationships between actors in a wide field, such as an economic sector (Viren et al., 2015). For example, political connections have been investigated through network analysis to point out the impact of political dealings on innovation, affirming a connection between firms and their surrounding environment due to political relationships (Tsai et al., 2019). Lastly, Trequattrini et al. (2017) applied network analysis to understand the network of Italian economic sectors involved in the copyright industry. Thus, they evaluated the economic contribution of the copyright industry to an individual nation.

CONCLUSIONS AND FUTURE APPLICATIONS

In this chapter, we analysed network analysis and its application in intellectual capital research, generating insights for academic and practice-based communities. Through an analysis of existing literature (Trequattrini et al., 2012; Lombardi, 2015; Trequattrini et al., 2015a; Trequattrini et al., 2015b), we found that the application of network analysis is useful for identifying key people or emerging groups within organisations, focusing on their links, measuring the value of trust in relationships or knowledge and analysing formal and informal relationships (Allee, 2009; Sarker et al., 2011; Massingham, 2016; Blanco-Alcántara et al., 2018), which are all important elements of intellectual capital.

The application of network analysis mainly derives from quantitative indicators and graphs to identify the quality of relationships and connected issues (Granovetter, 1973; Wasserman and Faust, 1994; Scott, 2011). As a strategic tool, network analysis is a useful instrument for managers to evaluate the performance of organisations and assume decision-making processes in the ecosystem approach (Dumay and Garanina, 2013; Secundo et al., 2018). Additionally, network analysis is used to identify and select key employees, improve knowledge-management programmes (Hollenbeck and Jamieson, 2015), measure social capital, find internal and external relations and distinguish trust.

Considering that our results can be extended to all economic sectors, we provided a useful network analysis for investigating intellectual capital measurement, contributing to the literature on this theme (Montemari and Nielsen, 2013). Even though this contribution has several limitations (for example, the absence of empirical research), this literature review aimed to identify future research agendas for intellectual capital research, and in the process highlighted the value of the network analysis method across several economic fields. Future investigations should be focused on applying network analysis to several phenomena.

The future application of network analysis to intellectual capital research should aim to study the organisational and strategic aspects of dynamic company systems. Network analysis is able to provide a set of measures interpreting strategic and tactical decision-making processes, roles and functions at the organisational level, as well as corporate governance and management issues related to intellectual capital. Thus, future directions for the use of this research method in intellectual capital studies should recognise the validity of graphs and indicators (for example, centrality, density, distance, and betweenness centrality) for explaining and measuring intangibles in the company system, such as competence and skills by human resources, brands and stakeholder relationships, patents and client databases.

Additionally, it seems from the previous analysis that network analysis has not been applied to investigate border-crossing intangibles assets such as artificial intelligence, big data, Internet of Things (IoT) and blockchains (Lombardi, 2019), nor to interpret related phenomena and changing corporate processes influenced by smart technologies. Thus, several applications of intellectual capital phenomena are required to establish core indicators by network analysis, directly explaining intellectual capital measurement in traditional and border-crossing intangibles assets. This chapter calls for more contributions to network analysis and its application in the intellectual capital research agenda.

REFERENCES

Aliev, I.M. and V.I. Sigov (2017), 'Creating a learning organization as an increase in the adaptability of a company's human capital to the volatility of the external environment', *European Research Studies Journal*, 20 (4), 57–69.

Allee, V. (2009), 'Value-creating networks: organizational issues and challenges', *Learning Organization*, 16 (6), 427–442.

Axelrod, R. (1976), *Structure of Decision: The Cognitive Maps of Political Elites*, Princeton, NJ: Princeton University Press.

Barão, A. and A.R. da Silva (2013), 'Applying SNARE-RCO to evaluate the relational capital of an organization: the SH case study', in M.M. Cruz-Cunha, J.E. Varajão and

A. Trigo, *Sociotechnical Enterprise Information Systems Design and Integration*, Idea Group Inc, pp. 136–153.
Blanco-Alcántara, D., Díez-Esteban, J.M. and M.E. Romero-Merino (2018), 'Board networks as a source of intellectual capital for companies: empirical evidence from a panel of Spanish firm', *Management Decision*, 57 (10), 2653–2671.
Borgatti, S.P., Mehra, A., Brass, D.J. and G. Labianca (2009), 'Network analysis in the social sciences', *Science*, 323 (5916), 892–895.
Brooking, A. (1998), *Intellectual Capital*, Andover: Cengage Learning EMEA.
Burt, R. (2000), 'The network structure of social capital', *Research in Organizational Behavior*, 22 (1), 345–423.
Burton, P., Wu, Y., Prybutok, R. and G. Harden (2012), 'Differential effects of the volume and diversity of communication network ties on knowledge workers' performance', *IEEE Transactions on Professional Communication*, 55 (3), 239–253.
Capece, G. and R. Costa (2009), 'Measuring knowledge creation in virtual teams through the social network analysis', *Knowledge Management Research and Practice*, 7 (4), 329–338.
Celemi (1998), 'Growing a knowledge company', www.celemi.com.
Chaminade, C. and H. Roberts (2003), 'What it means is what it does: a comparative analysis of implementing intellectual capital in Norway and Spain', *European Accounting Review*, 12 (4), 733–751.
Chiucchi, M.S. and J. Dumay (2015), 'Unlocking intellectual capital', *Journal of Intellectual Capital*, 16 (2), 305–330.
Cordaz, D. (2005), *Le misure dell'analisi di rete e le procedure per la loro elaborazione mediante UCINET V*, Appendice al volume Salvini, A., L'analisi delle reti sociali. Risorse e meccanismi, Ed Plus, Pisa: Pisa University Press.
Cricelli, L. and M. Greco (2013), 'Relational capital and performances in interuniversity research consortia', *International Journal of Engineering Business Management*, 5 (1), 830–841.
Cuozzo, B., Dumay, J., Palmaccio, M. and R. Lombardi (2017), 'Intellectual capital disclosure: a structured literature review', *Journal of Intellectual Capital*, 18 (1), 9–28.
Di Vincenzo, F., Hemphälä, J., Magnusson, M. and D. Mascia (2012), 'Exploring the role of structural holes in learning: an empirical study of Swedish pharmacies', *Journal of Knowledge Management*, 16 (4), 576–591.
Díez-Vial, I. and Á. Montoro-Sánchez (2014), 'Social capital as a driver of local knowledge exchange: a social network analysis', *Knowledge Management Research and Practice*, 12 (3), 276–288.
Dumay, J.C. (2009), 'Intellectual capital measurement: a critical approach', *Journal of Intellectual Capital*, 10 (2), 190–210.
Dumay, J. (2016), 'A critical reflection on the future of intellectual capital: from reporting to disclosure', *Journal of Intellectual Capital*, 17 (1), 168–184.
Dumay, J. and T. Garanina (2013), 'Intellectual capital research: a critical examination of the third stage', *Journal of Intellectual Capital*, 14 (1), 10–25.
Dumay, J. and R. Roslender (2012), 'Utilising narrative to improve the relevance of intellectual capital', *Journal of Accounting and Organizational Change*, 9 (3), 248–279.
Edvinsson, L. (1997), 'Developing intellectual capital at Skandia', *Long-range Planning*, 30 (3), 366–373.
Edvinsson, L. and M. Malone (1997), *Intellectual Capital: Realising Your Company's True Value by Finding its Hidden Brainpower*, New York: Harper Collins.
Emirbayer, M. and J. Goodwin (1994), 'Network analysis, culture, and the problem of agency', *American Journal of Sociology*, 99 (6), 1411–1454.
Freeman, L. (2004), *The Development of Social Network Analysis: A Study in the Sociology of Science*, Vancouver: Empirical Press.
Garton, L., Haythornthwaite, C. and B. Wellman (1999), 'Studying online social networks', in S. Jones (ed.), *Doing Internet Research: Critical Issues and Methods for Examining the Net*, Thousand Oaks, CA: SAGE, pp. 75–105.

Ginevičius, T., Kaklauskas, A. and P. Kazokaitis (2011), 'Knowledge model for integrated construction project management', *Business: Theory and Practice*, 12 (2), 162–174.

Granovetter, M.S. (1973), 'The strength of weak ties', *American Journal of Sociology*, 78 (6), 1360–1380.

Guthrie, J., Ricceri, F. and J. Dumay (2011), 'Reflections and projections: a decade of intellectual capital accounting research', *British Accounting Review*, 44 (2), 68–82.

Haythornthwaite, C. (1996), 'Social network analysis: an approach and technique for the study of information exchange', *Library and Information Science Research*, 18 (4), 323–342.

Hodgkinson, G.P., Maule, A.J. and N.J. Bown (2004), 'Causal cognitive mapping in the organizational strategy field: a comparison of alternative elicitation procedures', *Organizational Research Methods*, 7 (1), 3–26.

Hollenbeck, J.R. and B.B. Jamieson (2015), 'Human capital, social capital, and social network analysis: implications for strategic human resource management', *Academy of Management Perspectives*, 29 (3), 239–253.

Huisman, M. and M.A.J. van Duijn (2004), 'Software for statistical analysis of social networks', Sixth International Conference on Logic and Methodology, Amsterdam.

Kaplan, R.S. and D.P. Norton (1992), 'The balanced scorecard: measures that drive performance', *Harvard Business Review*, 70 (1), 71–79.

Kaplan, R.S. and D.P. Norton (2001), 'Transforming the balanced scorecard from performance measurement to strategic management: part I', *Accounting Horizons*, 15 (1), 87–106.

Kaplan, R.S. and D.P. Norton (2008), *The Execution Premium – Linking Strategy to Operations for Competitive Advantage*, Boston, MA: Harvard Business Press.

Kase, R. and N. Zupan (2009), 'Human capital and structural position in knowledge networks as determinants when classifying employee groups for strategic human resource management purposes', *European Journal of International Management*, 3 (4), 478–494.

Kasztler, A. and K.H. Leitner (2009), 'An SNA/based approach for management control of intellectual capital', *Journal of Intellectual Capital*, 10 (3), 329–340.

Knoke, D. and S. Yang (2008), *Social Network Analysis*, Quantitative Applications in the Social Sciences, 154, Thousand Oaks, CA: SAGE Publications.

Lombardi, R. (2015), *Le reti d'impresa in economia aziendale. Profili critici e interpretativi*, Collana Studi di Ragioneria e di Economia Aziendale, Vol. 67, Torino: Giappichelli Editore.

Lombardi, R. (2019), 'Knowledge transfer and organizational performance and business process: past, present and future researches', *Business Process Management Journal*, 25 (1), 2–9.

Lombardi R. and J. Dumay (2017), 'Guest editorial. Exploring corporate disclosure and reporting of intellectual capital: revealing emerging innovations', *Journal of Intellectual Capital*, 18 (1), 2–8.

Massingham, P. (2016), 'Knowledge accounts', *Long Range Planning*, 49 (3), 409–425.

Montemari, M. and C. Nielsen (2013), 'The role of causal maps in intellectual capital measurement and management', *Journal of Intellectual Capital*, 14 (4), 522–546.

Montibeller, G. and V. Belton (2006), 'Causal maps and the evaluation of decision options: a review', *Journal of the Operational Research Society*, 57 (7), 779–791.

Mouritsen, J., Larsen, H.T. and P. Bukh (2001), 'Intellectual capital and the "capable firm": narrating, visualising and numbering for managing knowledge', *Accounting, Organizations and Society*, 26 (7), 735–762.

O'Hagan, S.B. (2017), 'An exploration of gender, interlocking directorates, and corporate performance', *International Journal of Gender and Entrepreneurship*, 9 (3), 269–282.

Otte, E. and R. Rousseau (2002), 'Social network analysis: a powerful strategy, also for the information sciences', *Journal of Information Science*, 28 (6), 441–453.

Pedro, E., Leitão, J. and H. Alves (2018), 'Intellectual capital and performance: taxonomy of components and multi-dimensional analysis axes', *Journal of Intellectual Capital*, 19 (2), 407–452.

Petty, R. and J. Guthrie (2000), 'Intellectual capital literature review: measurement, reporting and management', *Journal of Intellectual Capital*, 1 (2), 155–176.

Provan, K.G., Veazie, M.A., Staten, L.K. and N.I. Teufel-Shone (2005), 'The use of network analysis to strengthen community partnerships', *Public Administration Review*, 65 (5), 603–613.

Ricceri, F. and J. Guthrie (2009), 'Critical analysis of international guidelines for the management of knowledge resources', in D. Jemielniak and J. Kociatkiewicz (eds), *Handbook of Research on Knowledge-intensive Organisations*, New York, NY and Hershey, PA: Information Science Press, pp. 375–392.

Sarker, S., Kirkeby, S. and S. Chakraborty (2011), 'Path to "stardom" in globally distributed hybrid teams: an examination of a knowledge-centered perspective using social network analysis', *Decision Sciences*, 42 (2), 339–370.

Schmutte, I.M. (2014), 'Free to move? A network analytic approach for learning the limits to job mobility', *Labour Economics*, 29, 49–61.

Scott, J. (1988), 'Social network analysis', *Sociology*, 22 (1), 109–127.

Scott, J. (1996), 'Software review: a toolkit for social network analysis', *Acta Sociologica*, 39 (2), 211–216.

Scott, J. (2011), 'Social network analysis: developments, advances, and prospects', *Social Network Analysis and Mining*, 1 (1), 21–26.

Secundo, G., Massaro, M., Dumay, J. and C. Bagnoli (2018), 'Intellectual capital management in the fourth stage of IC research: a critical case study in university settings', *Journal of Intellectual Capital*, 19 (1), 157–177.

Solitander, M. and A. Tidström (2010), 'Competitive flows of intellectual capital in value-creating networks', *Journal of Intellectual Capital*, 11 (1), 23–28.

Stewart, T.A. (1997), *Intellectual Capital: The New Wealth of Organisations*, London: Doubleday Currency.

Sveiby, K.E. (1988), 'Den Nya Årsredovisningen' (The New Annual Report) Workgroup 'Konrad', Ledarskap Förlag, Stockholm.

Sveiby, K.E. (1997), *The New Organizational Wealth: Managing and Measuring Knowledge, Based Assets*, San Francisco, CA: Berrett-Koehler.

Trequattrini, R., Lombardi, R. and M. Battista (2015a), 'Network analysis and football team performance: a first application', *Team Performance Management*, 21 (1/2), 85–110.

Trequattrini, R., Lombardi, R., Lardo, A., Della Rosa, S. and F. Bolici (2015b), 'A review of virtual health networks: online communities that manage health information reducing environmental uncertainty', in J.C. Spender, G. Schiuma and V. Albino (eds), *10th International Forum on Knowledge Assets Dynamics, IFKAD 'Culture, Innovation and Entrepreneurship: connecting the knowledge'*, Bari, 10–12 June, pp. 1504–1514.

Trequattrini, R., Manfredi, S., Lombardi, R. and L.D. Scordino (2017), 'Copyright-based industry and network theory: exploring new horizons', *International Journal of Digital Culture and Electronic Tourism*, 2 (2), 83–102.

Trequattrini, R., Russo, G. and R. Lombardi (2012), 'The crisis of company networks and tools for its prediction', *International Business Research*, 5 (10), 46–55.

Tsai, L.C., Zhang, R. and C. Zhao (2019), 'Political connections, network centrality and firm innovation', *Finance Research Letters*, 28, 180–184.

Ujwary-Gil, A. (2019), 'Organizational network analysis: a study of a university library from a network efficiency perspective', *Library and Information Science Research*, 41 (1), 48–57.

Viren, P.P., Vogt, C.A., Kline, C., Rummel, A.M. and J. Tsao (2015), 'Social network participation and coverage by tourism industry sector', *Journal of Destination Marketing and Management*, 4 (2), 110–119.

Wasserman, S. and K. Faust (1994), *Social Network Analysis: Methods and Applications*, Cambridge: Cambridge University Press.

Worrell, J., Wasko, M. and A. Johnston (2013), 'Social network analysis in accounting information systems research', *International Journal of Accounting Information Systems*, 14 (2), 127–137.

Yan, Y. and J. Guan (2018), 'Social capital, exploitative and exploratory innovations: the mediating roles of ego-network dynamics', *Technological Forecasting and Social Change*, 126, 244–258.

15. The usefulness of exercises for identifying critical IC in organizations

Susanne Durst

INTRODUCTION

In organizations, a large amount of intellectual capital (IC) or knowledge is personalized; that is, it exists in an individual's mind (Wong and Aspinwall, 2004). If this knowledge is critical, especially in terms of organizational performance, the possessor of this essential knowledge takes on a central position within the organization (Bridge et al., 2003). These people have competencies, professional experience or access to business networks that are viewed as fundamental for running the organization. Given that people retire or may leave an organization, this IC knowledge can be at risk (Durst and Wilhelm, 2012).

Consequently, all organizations need to identify and implement systematic approaches to cope with present and future IC-related challenges and their possible internal and external consequences with respect to the organizations' capability to take actions and survive. As not all IC is critical to organizations, initial activities should strive to identify critical knowledge that is most at risk of being lost.

Even though the relevance of knowledge is normally emphasized in organizations, members of organizations often have difficulties in specifying which specific knowledge and skills different individuals possess (Van Zolingen et al., 2001). Thus, in order to study critical IC in organizations, I argue that we as researchers should go beyond the application of traditional research methods, such as interviews and questionnaires, and turn to research methods that allow us to capture deeper insights into people's perceptions of IC in general, and critical IC in particular. Thus, methods need to be applied that make it possible to look beyond the surface. I believe that more indirect approaches may help to achieve this goal.

Against this background, this chapter's intention is to illustrate how to identify critical IC knowledge in organizations by means of exercises. These exercises involve a small number of people representing different functions and roles and are supported by the application of a software that is intended to provide insights into the concentration of relevant knowledge with certain individuals, respectively, in certain departments.

The tool calculates an overall 'knowledge at risk' scale representing the total of the four dimensions: human capital, structural capital, relational capital and social capital (Durst and Wilhelm, 2013). The task of the group is to jointly discuss the 'knowledge at risk' as found (perceived) in their departments or with certain individuals while going step by step through the software tool. In light of my experience, the outcome of this activity not only assists the individuals to view IC knowledge from a risk point of view, but in addition helps them to understand which members of the organization are key actors, and to evaluate what makes those people so essential. From a research perspective, I believe that running such exercises provides valuable insights into how different individuals view and perceive (critical) IC knowledge.

The examples used in this chapter are based on previous research activities undertaken by myself and some of my colleagues in the context of studying risks related to IC, intangibles and knowledge in both private and public organizations. The chapter is structured as follows. In the following section, the relevant IC literature is briefly outlined to frame the chapter. This is followed by sections that describe the method and its execution. The chapter ends with a discussion and conclusion.

INTELLECTUAL CAPITAL

IC is 'the sum of everything everybody in a company knows that gives it a competitive edge ... Intellectual Capital is intellectual material, knowledge, experience, intellectual property, information ... that can be put to use to create [value]' (Dumay, 2016, p. 169). IC is vital to innovation and competitive differentiation in many sectors; it stimulates organizational learning, enhances individual and organizational performance and innovative behaviour (Lerro et al., 2014). Consequently, IC management needs to be a core strategic effort. Unfortunately, many companies fail to understand the requirements for managing IC, and the complexity involved (Sullivan, 1999). This may be why many corporate initiatives focusing on the management of IC knowledge have only moderate success (Hislop, 2005). IC management is difficult because it does not only involve decisions from managers and allocation of resources. It is also a dimension in many other management issues. IC is created or exploited by humans and their mindsets, organizational values and beliefs, as well as the full commitment of all organization members. Companies that fail to properly manage their IC to secure its value creation potential run significant risks (Jääskeläinen, 2007, quoted in Kupi et al., 2008), for example loss of expertise or reinvention of know-how. Therefore, it is important to carefully manage the risky side of IC, as managers and entrepreneurs cannot afford to neglect IC risks even though they might be more familiar with financial capital and the risks related to this asset category (Brunold and Durst, 2012).

IC can be addressed through two approaches: a static and a dynamic approach (Kianto, 2007). The static approach emphasizes the development of IC classification schemes: human capital, structural capital and relational capital. This is now a standard perspective (Edvinsson and Kivikas, 2007). Human capital comprises the knowledge, competences, abilities and skills of employees (Schultz, 1961). Thus, a central feature of human capital is that it belongs to the organization members themselves (Hussi, 2004). According to Bontis (1998, p. 65), the 'essence' of human capital is the pure intelligence of the company's members. Structural capital covers everything that supports employees' productivity, such as organizational structure and processes, software and corporate culture (Marr, 2005). Finally, relational capital embodies all the relationships with customers, suppliers and other critical partners (Roos et al., 2001). This classification may seem convenient, but often IC is created through a combination of different resources. This suggests that the actual value of IC lies in the combined power of the IC elements, not in their individual existence (Lev, 2001; Andriessen, 2004). This brings us to the dynamic approach to IC, which underlines the relationship between the IC elements/intangibles with an emphasis on the 'organizational capabilities to leverage, develop and change intangible assets for value creation' (Kianto, 2007, p. 344).

CRITICAL IC

It is generally agreed that not all IC knowledge is critical – in this chapter, understood as 'essential' – for organizations to master present and future opportunities and challenges. In fact, IC that has been relevant in the past may have become obsolete or forgotten over time (Tan et al., 2006). Also, simply holding specific knowledge does not make an individual a critical person (Van Zolingen et al., 2001). Instead, the specific ties an individual has that are critical to executing knowledge transfer could point to critical knowledge, as the dissolution of these ties could result in a loss of this specific knowledge (Cattani et al., 2013). Thus, IC knowledge is in a constant state of change and should be continuously monitored and updated as required. One may also argue that critical IC is 'the' resource that is most at risk of being lost (Frigo, 2006). Moreover, the risk of losing critical IC is high, it can occur at different levels, have either anticipated or unanticipated effects, and create immediate or delayed costs (DeLong, 2004).

Critical IC can reside in many repositories; the focus of this chapter is on the knowledge that resides in individual members of an organization (Argote and Ingram, 2000). Even though the relevance of IC knowledge is usually emphasized in organizations, they have difficulties in specifying which specific knowledge and skills different individuals actually possess (Van Zolingen et al., 2001), which may reflect the division of labour (Brown and Duguid, 1998) or a lack of interest in getting to the bottom of this issue. Finally, critical IC is context-dependent and complex; thus, a type of IC relevant to one firm is irrelevant to other firms (Spender, 1996). Given the relevance of IC knowledge to both private and public organizations, these organizations need to be in a position to identify their critical IC.

Identification of Critical IC

Extant literature has discussed a number of different methods to identify critical IC. The identification of critical IC can be considered as the critical basis for subsequent IC management activities such as retention. Thus, as Liebowitz and Beckman (1998) put it, the identification stage determines the core competencies that are critical to business success. In the literature, the development of knowledge maps has been highlighted as a means of supporting the identification of IC knowledge. These maps locate important knowledge in organizations and provide information on where to find it (Davenport and Prusak, 1998). Also, the use of social network analysis (SNA) has been recommended to better understand who the key players are in an organization and their critical relationships (Parise, 2007).

To raise awareness about the different qualities IC knowledge may assume in different situations – for example, being an asset or a liability – Durst and Wilhelm (2013) developed a tool intended to provide a better understanding of the likely dependency on certain organization members. To do so, the tool calculates a so-called 'knowledge at risk' scale. This scale represents the sum of values across four dimensions: human capital, structural capital, relational capital and social capital. The tool consists of different levels, which need to be filled and can be adjusted to the requirements of the organization in question. In the end, the instrument provides a report displaying the overall result (the 'knowledge at risk' score) and the results for each of the four dimensions.

The measures and approaches available intend to contribute to an improved understanding of the IC knowledge situation in organizations, and based on this, facilitate the development and execution of subsequent measures needed to cope with the given situation. Thus, it can be concluded that these methods could form the basis for studying and identifying relevant IC in organizations.

From a research point of view, and in order to better understand individuals' opinions and views regarding IC knowledge in general, and the perceived difference between ordinary knowledge and critical knowledge in particular, I argue that researchers need to apply additional approaches. Based on my experience I believe that the application of one of these methods/approaches could be integrated within a measure that is designed to develop our understanding of IC practices in organizations, of which the identification of critical IC should be central. Thus, in order to come closer to this aim, the focus should be less on the outcome of the application of these methods – which could be a knowledge map of the organization, for example – but more on an in-depth investigation of the processes that will ultimately lead to this outcome.

I have been studying IC knowledge in general, and the risky side of IC knowledge in particular, for several years; I have learned over this time that to better understand how organizations approach and view IC knowledge, a researcher needs to be innovative. The strengths of traditional research methods such as surveys and different types of interviews are generally known, but they fall short when the primary research interest is to understand how people think about IC knowledge: their own IC and that of others, what makes this IC critical, as well as the link between this IC and the organization's value creation. As people tend to overestimate their own competencies (Dunning et al., 2003) and underestimate those of others (Song et al., 2004), the validity of data obtained is significantly affected.

THE EXERCISE

Before I can enter into an in-depth discussion about the exercise and its potential usefulness, I need to define the term 'exercise'. In line with Lexico (n.d.), I view an exercise as an activity that is carried out for a specific purpose. In the present case, this is a specific research purpose. The exercise is conducted with the aim to identify critical IC in an organization. Moreover, the exercise is to be run in a planned, structured and repetitive manner for the purpose of reliability (Diekmann, 2005).

The Tool

As mentioned before, the exercise is shaped and executed around the tool developed by Durst and Wilhelm (2013). The tool's origin goes back to a research project that investigated a mid-sized company's handling of the constant threat of knowledge attrition due to staff turnover or long-term absence. In this study, it was argued that an understanding of the potential danger of knowledge attrition is important due to the immense direct and indirect costs it can cause. Thereby, the smaller the organization, the greater the danger.

The tool in question was specifically developed for smaller organizations (that is, small and medium-sized organizations) facing the danger of knowledge attrition due to different circumstances. The primary aim of the tool is to raise awareness about the concentration of relevant IC knowledge with certain individuals, respectively, in certain departments (Starke et al., 2003). To reach this aim, a composite measure was created to calculate an overall 'knowledge at risk' scale.

The scale represents the sum of four dimensions, namely, human capital, structural capital, relational capital and social capital. The default setting (the weighting) for the four dimensions is set at 30 per cent for human capital, 10 per cent for structural capital, 30 per cent for relational capital and 30 per cent for social capital. The organization in question can change these weightings according to its requirements. Thus, the persons involved can specify the emphasis of the organization depending on the firm size and structure. The tool consists of various levels, which need to be filled by the people using the tool. For instance, the age and length of service of the individuals are needed. To calculate the scores of the individual dimensions, different information is needed. For example, in the case of the human capital dimension, the tool questions whether the organization member under investigation possesses expert knowledge. Regarding the dimension of social capital, the tool asks about the type of knowledge flow (one-dimensional versus bilateral). In the context of the relational capital and structural capital, the issues of quality of business relations and an individual's contribution to the development of structural capital are covered.

The calculation for each individual dimension is executed once the data are collected. In the end, the tool issues a report displaying the overall result (the 'knowledge at risk' score) and the results for each of the four dimensions. The total score may be characterized by the use of various colours to highlight the quality of risk (Table 15.1).

The outcome of this tool identifies organization members who are considered key players in the organization. In addition, the tool generates

Table 15.1 'Knowledge at risk' scoring

Surname	First name	Initial	Age	Length of service	Total score	Human capital	Social capital	Structural capital	Relational capital
Schulz	Katrin	KS	25	4	0.55	0.82	0.70	0.25	0.25
Rose	Walter	WR	59	15	0.41	0.76	0.60	0	0.10
Lundvall	David	DL	41	8	0.63	0.76	0.10	1	1
Trudeau	Emilie	ET	36	12	0.66	0.58	0.80	1	0.5
Chang	Lynn	LC	55	25	0.75	0.78	0.40	1	1

information about what makes those organization members critical. Durst and Wilhelm (2013) assume that the latter information is valuable as it provides the necessary in-depth information about the types of knowledge that are available in the organization and about the people who possess this knowledge. Thus, with the help of the tool, relevant knowledge becomes visible. Based on these insights, more concrete measures and actions will be possible with regard to the management of IC in general, and specific IC measures in particular.

According to Durst and Wilhelm (2013), the tool's main strength is its simplicity, as it is easy to use and not based on complex technology that may cause any barriers or resistance, and participants do not need training to use the tool. Thus, the exercise may be undertaken within the time and resource constraints of contemporary organizations.

Conditions for Running the Exercise

From experience, it is advisable to run the exercise in the facilities of the respective organization. A familiar setting increases the chances of the participants focusing on the exercise and its relevance to the environment they are operating in. Moreover, establishing an open environment will enhance the execution of the exercise, which means that the participating individuals should feel free to talk about their own IC and that of others in a rather neutral and open way to identify critical knowledge. It is the role of the organization's leadership to establish such an environment; this may be easier in organizations that are less competitive and do not have 'closed doors'.

For example, the important role of the leadership was highlighted in a recent exercise that I conducted in a Swedish public organization. One of the executives was particularly interested in obtaining information about the issue of knowledge concentration in the respective departments involved. Thus, he did internal marketing communications to involve the staff, and during the actual execution of the exercise I did not get the feeling that the participants feared sanctions or criticism and therefore could speak openly.

In regard to the composition of the groups, it is appropriate to form groups that consist of individuals representing different functions, roles and units. This ensures a balanced discussion about knowledge in general, and critical knowledge in particular. Involving individuals representing one role or function increases the likelihood that discussions will focus on specific knowledge domains, and thus risks overlooking other important knowledge domains. For example, a few years ago the exercise was run with the leadership of a medium-sized enterprise, and the discussion was dominated by a rather narrow focus on the leadership's own relevant human capital and relational capital. Running the exercise with other organization members of this company, however, revealed the role of an external partner's capacities and skills for the company's overall business model.

With the above in mind, I turned to mixed groups when running the exercises. Thus, this insight also means that a researcher needs to be prepared to work at persuading an organization's leadership, which might not immediately be convinced of the benefits of having mixed groups involved in the exercise. In a recent execution of the exercise, the groups involved managers, administrators, women and men, but also younger and older workers to account for any generation gaps regarding the perception of knowledge and its relevance. The inclusion of different generations proved to be quite useful, as the link between function and relevance was questioned by the younger generation; older workers tended to attribute critical knowledge to people higher in the organization's hierarchy, while younger workers did this less.

In terms of the duration of the exercise, it seems that one hour is an appropriate time. This gives the participants enough time not only to discuss IC and the different IC dimensions but also for filling out the necessary fields of the tool. Practical experience also shows that one hour is a time that is considered appropriate by the managers, as they must release the individuals from work during the execution of the exercise. This seems to hold for smaller companies too. Finally, in terms of the size of the group, experience shows that groups ranging from four to six people are most suitable for discussions about IC knowledge.

The Execution of the Exercise

As mentioned, the primary task of the exercise (or different rounds, depending on the size of organization involved) is to get a picture of how the participants perceive critical knowledge and people through the software tool. At the beginning of the exercise, the participating researcher gives a brief introduction to the exercise and its execution. This researcher will also enter the information the group provides into the software program; thus, the group can focus on their discussions rather than entering the data. In addition, experience has shown that involving a second researcher is advisable, as this person could concentrate on capturing the views and opinions shared by the participants while doing the exercise. These views and opinions are captured through taking notes. This means that the exercise rounds are not recorded. Consequently, a second researcher not only adds to the data collection but also reduces the risk of misunderstandings or misinterpretations. During the execution of the exercise, the participating researcher acts as a moderator, who initiates discussions and makes sure that the group continues the discussion productively. However, the researcher takes a passive role, as the discussion should be run by the group.

To initiate the discussion about IC knowledge in general, and critical IC knowledge in particular, the group is invited to think of key people in their departments or their organization. The aim is for the group to identify these people and determine what makes them key to the organization; what would be the consequence for the organization/department if this person left? Based on past exercises, every organization has these 'critical' people. When it comes to the discussion of the special characteristics of these people, differences between group participants and how they perceive crucial individuals become clear. Observations have shown that while ordinary employees tend to have difficulty specifying what makes these individuals critical, participants in leadership roles have fewer problems. For example, an older person who participated in the execution of the exercise conducted in a public organization, and who formerly held a leading position, explained that for him a person in a leading position is automatically linked to being a key person; while a young person working in the same organization, who was part of another round, stressed that the role of managers should not be overestimated. This underlines again the importance of diversity and carefully selecting the group members. In terms of keeping the exercise going, so far I have not experienced a faltering of discussions; on the contrary, the participants seem interested in discussing knowledge in more depth.

Suitability of the Exercise for Identifying IC

Based on the number of exercise rounds conducted in different organizations, including public and private organizations, large and small companies, I have come to the conclusion that the approach presented is a useful addition to the study of IC, and critical IC in particular, as it gives individuals the opportunity to discuss knowledge in depth. Thus, it enables discussions that could help fill in gaps. While the notion of knowledge loss is often abstract, through these exercises it becomes more tangible for a group of people and not just for a few individuals. By involving different organization members, it also increases the chances of establishing a common understanding of what critical IC means for the organization. Based on this understanding, it may be easier to communicate and execute

IC-related practices in favour of the organization as a whole, as well as the individual organization member.

From a research point of view, one can say that these insights are significant, as they increase our understanding of IC in general, and in turn enable more concrete research activities. As the researchers develop a more concrete understanding of the differences between ordinary IC and critical IC, they can develop and propose more concrete IC tools and measures. Therefore, researchers can not only highlight the importance of IC, but also develop more specific examples of this in practice when working with practitioners.

CONCLUSIONS

To address present and future business and organizational challenges, organizations of all kinds need to have an in-depth overview of their critical IC knowledge at any time. This overview allows the organizations to apply their IC knowledge in the best possible way. Thus, from a research point of view, it is vital to understand what specific IC knowledge is considered as relevant in organizations, among different departments and individuals, and why. Traditional research methods such as interviews or questionnaires often reach their limits, as they may only capture the perception of critical IC knowledge from the viewpoint of certain groups (for example, managers), or the findings may be vague (for example, the relevance of critical IC knowledge is generally highlighted for the future well-being of the organization). Regarding the latter, such an insight is of little importance, as IC knowledge differs in degree and quality, which needs to be understood to actually manage it.

On the other hand, people may find it difficult to determine critical knowledge; this may have something to do with the tendency to overestimate one's own knowledge and underestimate another person's knowledge. In order to overcome this dilemma, IC research should focus more on groups, rather than individuals, and should also take advantage of more indirect methods when trying to research and understand the sensitive issues of IC knowledge.

As such, this chapter has proposed specific exercises to further develop research on IC. More precisely, in this chapter, the proposed exercise is supported by software that helps determine knowledge concentration in organizations. By engaging smaller groups in this exercise, the main intention is to give the participating individuals a platform to discuss IC and critical IC in depth. Such an exchange is viewed as crucial to improve the success of any IC management activities in the organization. Thus, the content presented in this chapter fits nicely with the third stage of IC research: the praxes of IC as found in organizations, as proposed by Dumay (2013). Moreover, by focusing on the possible downsides of IC knowledge, the chapter contributes to recent research efforts to develop a more balanced discussion about IC knowledge and its management (Brunold and Durst, 2012; Durst and Zieba, 2018).

The insights provided in the present chapter appear to be valuable for researchers, as the proposed approach offers an alternative research method to study critical IC in organizations, which could bring researchers closer to understanding the thinking of practitioners regarding IC knowledge and its perceived relevance. Consequently, a more advanced and balanced understanding of critical IC knowledge will be possible, which in turn can help in further developing the research field as a whole.

Lastly, but not least, the participating organizations also benefit from the process. By including mixed groups in the exercise, the discussion of IC knowledge and its relevance has a broader basis, which not only raises awareness of the topic among a greater number of organization members, but also increases the opportunity of developing more (and even better) solutions to address any form of knowledge concentration in the organization. My experience also indicates that the results of the process could lead to improved coordination between the managers and the personnel department, as a concerted approach to managing critical knowledge IC is required.

REFERENCES

Andriessen, D. (2004), *Making Sense of Intellectual Capital. Designing a Method for the Valuation of Intangibles*, Burlington, MA: Butterworth-Heinemann.

Argote, L. and P. Ingram (2000), 'Knowledge transfer: a basis for competitive advantage in firms', *Organizational Behavior and Human Decision Processes*, 82 (1), 150–169.

Bontis, N. (1998), 'Intellectual capital: an exploratory study that develops measures and models', *Management Decision*, 36 (2), 63–76.

Bridge, S., O'Neill, K. and S. Cromie (2003), *Understanding Enterprise, Entrepreneurship, and Small Business*, 2nd edn, New York: Palgrave Macmillan.

Brown, J.S. and P. Duguid (1998), 'Organizing knowledge', *California Management Review*, 40 (3), 90–111.

Brunold, J. and S. Durst (2012), 'Intellectual capital risks and job rotation', *Journal of Intellectual Capital*, 13 (2), 178–195.

Cattani, G., Dunbar, R.L.M. and Z. Shapira (2013), 'Value creation and knowledge loss: the case of Cremonese stringed instruments', *Organization Science*, 24 (3), 813–830.

Davenport, T.H. and L. Prusak (1998), *Working Knowledge*, Cambridge, MA: Harvard Business School Press.

DeLong, D.W. (2004), *Lost Knowledge. Confronting the Threat of an Aging Workforce*, Oxford: Oxford University Press.

Diekmann, A. (2005), *Empirische Sozialforschung. Grundlagen, Methoden, Anwendungen*, Hamburg: Rowohlt.
Dumay, J. (2013), 'The third stage of IC: towards a new IC future and beyond', *Journal of Intellectual Capital*, 14 (1), 5–9.
Dumay, J. (2016), 'A critical reflection on the future of intellectual capital: from reporting to disclosure', *Journal of Intellectual Capital*, 17 (1), 168–184.
Dunning, D., Johnson, K., Ehrlinger, J. and J. Kruger (2003), 'Why people fail to recognize their own incompetence', *Current Directions in Psychological Science*, 12 (3), 83–87.
Durst, S. and S. Wilhelm (2012), 'Knowledge management and succession planning in SMEs', *Journal of Knowledge Management*, 16 (4), 637–649.
Durst, S. and S. Wilhelm (2013), 'Do you know your knowledge at risk?', *Measuring Business Excellence*, 17 (3), 28–39.
Durst, S. and M. Zieba (2018), 'Mapping knowledge risks: towards a better understanding of knowledge management', *Knowledge Management Research and Practice*. DOI: 10.1080/14778238.2018.1538603.
Edvinsson, L. and M. Kivikas (2007), 'Intellectual capital (IC) or Wissensbilanz process: some German experiences', *Journal of Intellectual Capital*, 8 (3), 376–385.
Frigo, M. (2006), 'Knowledge retention: a guide for utilities', *Journal American Water Works Association*, 98 (9), 81–84.
Hislop, D. (2005), *Knowledge Management in Organizations*, Oxford: Oxford University Press.
Hussi, T. (2004), 'Reconfiguring knowledge management – combining intellectual capital, intangible assets and knowledge creation', *Journal of Knowledge Management*, 8 (2), 36–52.
Kianto, A. (2007), 'What do we really mean by the dynamic dimension of intellectual capital?', *International Journal of Learning and Intellectual Capital*, 4 (4), 342–356.
Kupi, E., Sillanpää, V. and K. Ilomäki (2008), 'Risk management of intangible assets', paper presented at the International Forum on Knowledge Asset Dynamics (IFKAD), Matera, 26–27 June.
Lerro, A., Linzalone, R. and G. Schiuma (2014), 'Managing intellectual capital dimensions for organizational value creation', *Journal of Intellectual Capital*, 15 (3), 350–361.
Lev, B. (2001), *Intangibles. Management, Measurement, and Reporting*, Washington, DC: Brookings Institution Press.
Lexico (n.d.), 'Exercise', https://www.lexico.com/definition/exercise.
Liebowitz, J. and T. Beckman (1998), *Knowledge Organizations. What Every Manager Should Know*, Boca Raton, FL: St Lucie Press.
Marr, B. (2005), 'Strategic management of intangible value drivers', *Handbook of Business Strategy*, 6 (1), 147–154.
Parise, S. (2007), 'Knowledge management and human resource development: an application in social network analysis methods', *Advances in Developing Human Resources*, 9 (3), 359–383.
Roos, G., Bainbridge, A. and K. Jacobsen (2001), 'Intellectual capital analysis as a strategic tool', *Strategy and Leadership Journal*, May, 21–26.
Schultz, T.W. (1961), 'Investment in human capital', *American Economic Review*, 2 (1), 1–17.
Song, F., Cadsby, C.B. and T. Morris (2004), 'Other-regarding behavior and behavioral forecasts: females versus males as individuals and as group representative', *International Journal of Conflict Management*, 15 (4), 340–363.
Spender, J.C. (1996), 'Making knowledge the basis of a dynamic theory of the firm', *Strategic Management Journal*, 17 (Winter), 45–62.
Starke, F.A., Dyck, B. and M.K. Mauws (2003), 'Coping with the sudden loss of an indispensable employee', *Journal of Applied Behavioral Science*, 39 (2), 208–228.
Sullivan, P.H. (1999), 'Profiting from intellectual capital', *Journal of Knowledge Management*, 3 (2), 132–142.
Tan, H.C., Carrillo, P., Anumba, C., Kamara, J.M., Bouchlaghem, D. and C. Udeaja (2006), 'Live capture and reuse of project knowledge in construction organizations', *Knowledge Management Research and Practice*, 4, 149–161.

Van Zolingen, S.J., Streumer, J.N. and M. Stooker (2001), 'Problems in knowledge management: a case study of a knowledge-intensive company', *International Journal of Training and Development*, 5 (3), 168–184.

Wong, K.Y. and E. Aspinwall (2004), 'Characterizing knowledge management in the small business environment', *Journal of Knowledge Management*, 8 (3), 44–61.

16. Interventionist research into value creation mechanisms

Christian Nielsen and Morten Lund

INTRODUCTION TO QUALITATIVE RESEARCH

Without moving into the wider discussion about the purpose of science and discussing differing world-views, it is the purpose of this chapter to provide insights into the conduct of interventionist type studies and how to ensure plausible research results in this process. However, it must be recognized that from a paradigmatic stance, interventionist research is positioned in an understanding of the importance of subjective natures regarding the distinction between objective and subjective (Burrell and Morgan, 1979). As a researcher, it is important to understand one's own perspective and comprehension of the world, the truth and how the truth is derived. This is the essence of the theory of science (Arbnor and Bjerke, 2008). Here, qualitative research differs from quantitative research methods.

The key issues in the quantitative–qualitative debate are generally of an ontological and epistemological nature. In the words of Phillips (1988), quantitative researchers perceive truth as something which describes an objective reality, separate from the observer and waiting to be discovered. This definition is gravely in opposition to qualitative researchers, who are concerned with the changing nature of reality created through people's experiences; an evolving reality in which the researcher and researched are mutually interactive and inseparable. Sale et al. (2002) argue that the paradigms upon which quantitative and qualitative methods respectively are based, incorporate different perspectives of reality (Burrell and Morgan, 1979) and therefore, at least from a paradigmatic perspective of the world (Guba, 1987), constitute different and incommensurable views (Kuhn, 1962) of the phenomenon under study.

According to Morgan and Smircich (1980), the prevailing dichotomy between quantitative and qualitative methods is a rough and oversimplified one. Rather, they argue for a more nuanced perspective towards this discussion and conclude that aspects such as the underlying perception of the nature of knowledge, ontological assumptions and assumptions about human nature must be taken into consideration. As humans, we are rationally bounded and are affected by our identities, experiences and acquired rules-of-thumb. According to March and Olson (1989, p. 160), 'rather than calculating outcomes, a person is motivated by appropriate behaviour, considering which rules apply to a specific situation'. Therefore, in qualitative research, not only is knowledge created in conjunction with the object under scrutiny, but the understanding and reflection created is also influenced by our prior knowledge, experience and the context in which the research is conducted.

Qualitative research is concerned with understanding, exploring and explaining phenomena. It is not the purpose here to define qualitative research, except that it is concerned with answering questions of the type: 'How?', 'Why?' and 'In which way?' For a more thorough review on qualitative research in social sciences, we refer to Lune and Berg (2016).

Often, case studies are mistaken for qualitative research. Such studies, however, are a frequently applied approach to qualitative research and comprise a methodology that encompasses several potential research methods. Many researchers in social sciences adopt qualitative approaches using case studies. Eisenhardt and Graebner (2007) argue that case studies are particularly suitable when investigating theories in new contexts to provide insights to and potentially enrich theory with new cases, making comparisons across cases, and to evaluate relationships among constructs and hence provide new insights (Yin, 2018; Eisenhardt and Graebner, 2007).

Qualitative research can mobilize methods that help to answer the research question(s). Such methods may include interviews, observation, workshops, focus groups, as well as background and secondary information regarding the phenomena being studied, and these methods may in fact also include quantitative data about customers, markets, products or other forms of statistics. For a thorough review of conducting qualitative research interviews, we refer to Qu and Dumay (2011).

Interventionist research may take the form of a case study, and may apply multiple methods of intervening and non-intervening. The choices and applications would be made in order to ensure the best possible results. This chapter is particularly concerned with interventionist research of organizations, and organizational networks and the business ecosystem around them, including strategic partners, suppliers, customers, competitors and other relevant public institutions (Laughlin and Puxty, 1983). The imperative of this level of analysis is an inductive and interpretive perspective, taking its point of departure in the appeal of the company's top management team and their decisions. In this sense, the remaining functions in the company (for example, accounting, business development, logistics, sales, production, marketing) all become a part of developing the company and its strategic imperatives. From such a meta-theoretical perspective, contributions to research are based upon empirical arguments (Mouritsen, 1990, p. 162).

In general, investigating a problem or a phenomenon can be achieved at the level of individual agents or on a collective social action level (see also Peters, 2001). Choosing which level to take as the point of departure for a study relates to whether the study can be perceived as individualistic or holistic (Rosenberg, 2000). This so-called structure–agency problem is a dichotomy where on one side we view the patterns of social behaviour as instigators of individual behaviour, and on the other side observe individuals in their social action.

In methodological individualism, the aim is to explain social phenomena as caused by individuals and the mechanism influencing the behaviour of individual agents. Social action thus becomes a result of the decisions and actions performed by individual agents, while explanation of a social phenomenon is achieved by analysing the behaviour of individuals.

In methodological holism, social phenomena are explained as whole systems rather than only by the actions of individual agents. There is a qualitative difference between the social phenomenon within the social system and the sum of actions performed by the agents constituting the whole. The social phenomenon is explained as a whole. It comprises individual agents holding positions in the social system, and these agents are controlled by laws affecting the system as a whole. From a holistic perspective, such laws cannot be explained only by observing individual behaviour, and individuals are perceived as being created by social systems.

An applicable model of social reality for the purpose of analysis is to distinguish between macro, meso and micro levels in relation to relevance of the analysis (Ritzer, 1996, p. 647; see also Stones, 1998, p. 293). Table 16.1 depicts three different levels with which the analysis of our object of study could take its point of departure, namely macro, meso and micro. It is evident that this dissertation is concerned with investigating a phenomenon that relates to the meso level, namely the production and consumption of business reporting metrics in the market for information. However, the specific point of departure for the analyses conducted is on both meso and micro levels.

Economics-based theories would argue that the emergent properties of individuals' patterns of behaviour and action cannot influence the behaviour of organizations on another level, including that of markets. However, in relation to understanding how large systems function, it may be argued that it is naïve to believe that rationality is a primary form of social interaction. The point of view crafted by these authors is that large systems do not work rationally because rationality is overridden

Table 16.1 Different levels of analysis in social science

	Level of analysis	Specific object of analysis
Macro level	Society	The world around us, markets
Meso level	Institutions and organizations	The companies Related organizations Public institutions
Micro level	Individuals and groups	Individuals inside the organization, for example, managers and individuals outside the organization Groups of decision-makers

by a logic of appropriateness that destroys the rationality of systems. On the micro level, the individual interprets situations according to their identity and situation, because we as humans are not rational beings. On the meso level, the market for information can be regarded as a social system. Understanding the sociology of this financial phenomenon thus entails '[t]he recognition of the importance of human actions ... [as] ... an essential feature of such an approach' (Ryan et al., 2002, p. 146). From such a perspective, the role of theory is to understand rather than generate hypotheses.

According to Sutton and Staw (1995), theory-building is a key aspect of research. Moreover, because there seem to be inconsistent beliefs regarding what theory is, Sutton and Staw (1995) argue that there is probably increased consensus about what theory is not. In fact, theory could be anything from a guess to a general falsifiable explanation (Weick, 1995, p. 386). In criticizing the claims to theory often mobilized in academic papers, they argue that: 'listing references to existing theories and mentioning the names of such theories is not the same as explicating the causal logic they contain' (Sutton and Staw, 1995, p. 372). Thus, Sutton and Staw (1995), in arguing that theory is about causality, adopt a somewhat functionalistic standpoint.

DiMaggio (1995) provides an alternative account, stating that theory as a surprise machine is a narrative describing the world as we see it, and an account of a social process requiring that 'hypotheses detailing regularities in relations among variables be accompanied by plausible accounts of how the actions of real humans could produce the associations predicted and observed' (p. 391). Thus, theory in some manner illustrates connections among phenomena. According to Weick (1995, p. 385), theorizing is a process rather than a product, and theory work can take a variety of forms because theory itself is a continuum, and because most verbally expressed theory leaves tacit some key portions of the originating insight (Weick, 1995, p. 387). Van Maanen (1979) argues that a field of research first requires interim struggles (Runkel and Runkel, 1984) in the form of descriptive narratives before theory can be formulated.

WHAT IS INTERVENTIONIST RESEARCH?

In this chapter, we distinguish between qualitative studies that are interventionist of nature and non-interventionist of nature (see Lukka, 2005 for a further explication). In the literature, we find multiple labels for what we here choose to call interventionist research, including the likes of action research, participatory action research and engaged scholarship. Arguably, there are different typologies of performing interventionist research depending on the aim of the research, as argued by Van de Ven and Johnson (2006) and Van de Ven (2007).

In non-interventionist studies, researchers must be careful not to influence the object under scrutiny through their actions and questions, in order for the research to be as objective as possible. It is a general perception of non-interventionist qualitative studies that validity and reliability features follow those of the more quantitative sciences, best exemplified by the structures set out by Yin (2018). For interventionist research, this strategy of objectivity and non-influence disappears, because it is the purpose to study the effects of intervention, influence and opinion.

As argued above, epistemology concerns how knowledge is generated or derived. 'For action researchers, solutions to problems are negotiated among the interests of stakeholders with different power and resources', and 'current knowledge represent our best efforts but will likely be revised', as Ozanne and Saatcioglu (2008) state. In addition, it is the epistemological approach, and purpose, of interventionist research not only to derive information, produce knowledge and understand phenomena, but also to make change happen and to study the effects of calculated and uncalculated interventions. In this context, who sets the research agenda and the interventions, and who benefits from them, becomes of more importance than how the data are gathered.

In the interventionist research tradition, reality is typically considered a social construction, and the world is not independent in itself or existing externally (Koshy and Pascal, 2011). Intervention-oriented researchers assume that the social world we inhabit is co-created, context bound, relational, and situated (Susman and Evered, 1978). In other words, it is possible to change the world through interaction and influence.

Hence, researchers make subjective accounts from the participants, the context, the activities and the data collection (Koshy and Pascal, 2011). Interventionist research is an approach which is often used to improve and change practices and conditions, more than producing knowledge and research (Koshy and Pascal, 2011; Coghlan, 2004). Interventionist research typically has an ambition to improve the phenomenon being studied; for example, in the case of the project illustrated below, to improve the business model of the organization and to create a new network-based business model.

Interventionist research has risen from the idea that if you want to understand a problem properly, then you have to try to change it. Lewin (1946) presents a seminal interventionist-based research method and paradigm and argues that it changes the relationship between the researcher and the participating stakeholders from non-interventionist methods. Here, non-scientific participants are involved and seen as a key resource in the process because it is their perception that has to be changed. Reason and Bradbury (2001, p. 1) define interventionist research as 'a participatory, democratic process concerned with developing practical knowing in the pursuit of worthwhile human purposes'. Interventionist research resulted in the involvement of the participants throughout the process, from problem definition to project design, data collection and analysis; the idea of the interventionist research is that you 'have to work with local participants to improve local practices' and the ideas of the participants must be considered to transform their practices (Ozanne and Saatcioglu, 2008). To summarize, we provide some of the essential characteristics of interventionist research, using Coghlan's (2004) framework, in Table 16.2.

Understand Your Own Motivation

Why should you bother to carry out research that will be vastly criticized because you have affected the phenomenon you are studying? This is a question we have asked ourselves and our colleagues frequently. Interventionist research is important to the development of theories; however, as researchers we need to be realistic about the reach of the contributions possible. Therefore, we urge you to ask yourself the following questions:

- What is your personal motivation for being an interventionist researcher?
- What do you want to change?
- What do you what to learn from the interventions that you make?

Table 16.2 Addressing the characteristics of interventionist research

Characteristic of interventionist research	How this is addressed in the research project
Interventionist researchers act. Interventionist researchers are not merely observers, they are actively working at making something happen.	The researchers helped the companies innovate their business models through participatory innovation activities.
Interventionist research always involves two goals: solve a problem and contribute to science. There is no clear distinction between theory and empirics.	The researchers contributed to developing the business models of the case companies and contributed with narratives and storytelling to the business model theory-complex.
Interventionist research is interactive. Interventionist research requires cooperation between the researchers and the client personnel, and continuous adjustment to new information and new events.	The development of new business models has been conducted with the companies and through the processes in the project.
Interventionist research aims at developing holistic understanding during a project and recognizing complexity.	When developing new business models, the use of knowledge of the companies' market conditions was essential to ensure relevance and real problem-solving in the project.
Interventionist research is fundamentally about change. Interventionist research is applicable to the understanding, planning and implementation in groups, organizations and communities.	The purpose of the project has been to solve problems by interacting with the involved companies and changing the way they work with their business models and improve their growth through new ways of thinking, innovating also.
Interventionist research requires an understanding of the ethical framework, values and norms within which it is used in a particular context.	The researchers had background knowledge of business development, financing and market knowledge.
Interventionist research can include all types of gathering data methods.	The data were collected in different ways, through summaries, interviews, video clips, workshops, evaluations and reflections, and also informal meetings.
Interventionist research requires a pre-understanding of the corporate and organizational environment.	The researchers had background knowledge of business development, financing and market knowledge.

What you should get out of answering these questions is to reflect upon why this research is interesting for you, and why you should bother to go that 'extra mile' to produce new knowledge. Perhaps it is the case that you cannot answer the question that is in your mind without using this methodology, or it may be that you could but are curious on certain elements that cannot merely be observed. Whatever your answers here, we hope that you will be sincere and reflect upon why it is that this methodology is the best option for the question you would like to answer.

It is common knowledge that researchers, particularly professors, are the most knowledgeable people in the world; at least probably in relation to something highly specific. The positive side of this possession of knowledge is that they are motivated to stay on top of their field, and this motivation typically brings with it a lot of energy and inspiration. Without going into a personality test of academics, with this knowledge often comes a self-confidence that can pressure even stubborn practitioners into thinking outside of the box. Thereby, if this on-the-edge knowledge is brought into play, it can create innovative and creative situations and solutions that, when tested in the real world, not only lead to advantages for the participating companies but also lead to the generation of new theory.

However, there is a potential flip-side to this. Bringing such impressive resources into an interventionist process requires a certain degree of modesty on the part of the researcher. It is important that the researcher ensures they bring knowledge into play at the right time and do not take over the process unnecessarily. Finally, the good interventionist researcher explicitly links expected learning outcomes and how the contribution from the intervention leads to a value-added contribution in comparison to performing non-interventionist type research. This ability can be achieved through the creation of organizational and personal narratives.

As mentioned in Table 16.2, the interventionist researcher acts, changes things and interacts, and creates both change and knowledge. The interventionist researcher is therefore not an ordinary researcher. Ozanne and Saatcioglu (2008) note that a research partnership between researcher and participant is ideal, but in practice the researcher's position can vary from insider to outsider, as from high to low level of participation. In the cases involved in the current project, the research practice varied over time, the tendency leaning towards a higher involvement during the first steps of the collaboration and less involvement as the process developed from the initial stages.

In interventionist research, it is a prerequisite that the participants in the project are somehow affected, perhaps leading to change in behaviour or seeking help to solve problems. It is therefore also a condition that the participants have an interest in attempting to influence the research project in this case. The relationship between researchers and participants is an issue to address: on the one hand, connecting with the participants, gaining trust and getting access to all knowledge; and on the other hand, acknowledging that the close relationship that may be built could affect the documentation and data collection going forward.

'Participants are collaborators in the research project because action researchers assume that people who participate and are committed to the process will generate more-thorough social accounts and will be more invested in the successful application of the findings' (Reason and Bradbury, 2001). Ozanne and Saatcioglu (2008) note that it is this specific assumption that drives many of the methodological choices action researchers make, and this approach is unique to interventionist research. However, working closely with practitioners often results in struggles for the researchers because practitioners often have considerable expertise and insider knowledge; practitioners also may be guided by prejudice, ignorance and self-interest, not seeing their behaviour as being harmful to the process (Ozanne and Saatcioglu, 2008).

Introducing Plausibility

The normative take on establishing quality parameters for qualitative research is to assess a given study's reliability, internal validity and external validity (Yin, 2018). The goal here is to help readers assess the quality of the research processes being undertaken, and thereby to affirm that the conclusions can be generalized to other contexts in a trustworthy manner. Generalizability is a major quality criterion for all types of research because it is the notion of applying results and new theory to other places, situations, and so on, that makes research fruitful. Lukka and Kasanen (1995, p. 72) define generalization as the 'derivation of and argumentation for conclusions covering many or all cases of a certain type based on one or more observations of the real world', and argue that qualitative research such as case studies is often considered as merely being able to offer anecdotal evidence only.

Qualitative approaches to research are often criticized for a lack of generalizability (Lukka and Kasanen, 1995), but also to a significant extent for their lack of internal validity and reliability (Miles and Huberman, 1994). Parker and Northcott (2016) articulate two approaches to qualitative generalization, namely theoretical and naturalistic generalization. Qualitative researchers can use these two distinct avenues for enhancing and justifying the general applicability of findings and conclusions, either through theoretically argued explanations or through analogical reasoning.

According to Easton (1998), validity concerns the inter-subjective convincibility of a study (that is, the extent to which scholars agree that a study and its results cover the phenomena they claim to embrace). Thus, by taking the point of departure in this conception, validity as a general concept relates to securing the quality of the research being reported. As will be evident from the sections below, validity – research quality and convincibility, and so on – is in fact far from a homogenous concept, and it relates to a whole array of different research controls and strategies.

According to Modell (2009), considerations of validity require a series of trade-offs between efforts directed at external, internal and construct validation. 'Validity', to a quantitative researcher, would mean that results correspond to things in the real world; whereas to a qualitative researcher, 'valid' is a label applied to an interpretation or description with which one agrees (Smith and Heshusius, 1986). Thus, the validity controls applied across the separate articles in the study will vary. Some of the most cited authors within the fields of qualitative accounting research, such as Yin (2018) and Ryan et al. (2002), distinguish between three types of validity, namely: procedural validity, external validity and internal validity. Procedural validity, by Yin (2018) labelled construct validity, relates to whether 'the researcher has adopted appropriate and reliable research methods and procedures … addresses clearly specified research questions … and the case analysis should be fully documented' (Ryan et al., 2002, p. 155), for example by leveraging a tight chain of evidence through the case study database. Eisenhardt (1989) argues that achieving strong case studies is a question of inducing a research strategy focusing on a clear problem definition and 'construct validity' through iteration and tightly linked to data.

External validity is often mentioned as a problem for qualitative research because of the inherent difficulties that may exist in relation to generalizability. In this manner, external validity concerns the extent to which the findings of a study can be generalized to other settings (that is transferability).

Ultimately, validity concerns the organization of the research process (Turner, 1981) and reliability the ability for someone else to conduct the study again under the same conditions and to reach the same conclusions. In case studies, for example, the reliability criterion can be strengthened during the data collection phase by using a case study protocol. Another way of strengthening the reliability is to construct a case study database.

From the perspective of a philosophy of social science, hermeneutics is an example of one approach that is concerned with processes of interpretation. Hermeneutics is often interlinked with intentionality of action that can provide concepts and terminology and designate a procedure from which a field to be investigated can be described and explained (Gilje and Grimmen, 2002; Rosenberg, 2000). Hermeneutics is often applied as an investigation process for the analysis of phenomena described by meaningful expressions where the task is to explain intentions, situations, conditions, decisions and actions. These notions are similar to the meta-theoretical perspective described above.

The term 'hermeneutic circle' denotes the inter-relationship between a phenomenon that is being studied, interpreted and explained, and the context in which that phenomenon exists as an alternation between parts of a system and the whole system (Højbjerg, 2004, p. 312). The conditions and specific context under which a phenomenon exists must also be interpreted. The idea posed here is that the interpretation process proceeds in a constant circular movement between the phenomenon and the context. In our case, this is the company's business reporting and that company's surroundings. What creates meaning is the relationship between parts and the whole, and the fact that these relations make it possible to understand, describe and interpret.

Because we are interpreting our own actions as well as the actions performed by others, every interpretation of a social phenomenon by the researcher includes the interpretation of the researcher. Thus, in this 'double hermeneutics', the researcher becomes a part of the context wherein the phenomenon exists (Gilje and Grimmen, 2002). Therefore, research procedures must consider these possible influences in order to overcome critique in relation to validity and reliability.

In moving towards the application of notions of plausibility rather than reliability and validity, descriptions of the processes of interpretation become crucial to assessing the quality of research processes. We therefore pose a set of questions that must be clarified in order to enhance the plausibility of interventionist research:

- How do you record the events and interactions that you have with the organization/phenomenon you are studying?
- How do you store and access the data and different data-formats?
- How do you analyse the data?
- How do you ensure the validity of the patterns/events you are seeing in the data?

These questions are covered through the case described below. Notable examples of studies of intellectual capital where such research strategies are used actively are in, for example, Demartini and Paoloni's (2013) study of a company's transition from intellectual capital measurement to intellectual capital management, and Chiucchi and Giuliani's (2017) study of the role of the project leader in intellectual capital reporting.

Combining Intervention and Non-Intervention

Mixed-methods research is simultaneously emphasized as a fruitful strategy for developing novel insights and new knowledge. However, such research is also at risk of being attacked from both sides of the paradigm trench. This problem is not as clear in the case of mixing intervention and non-intervention methods; however, the combinatorial application of intervention and non-intervention may raise issues for the researcher and their documentation and interpretation. Our suggestion, based on the extensive application of both methods with and without combination, is to divide these roles between two researchers, as is described below.

EXPERIENCES FROM STUDYING VALUE CREATION MECHANISMS

This section reflects the empirical data gathering in a large-scale research and business development project called the International Center for Innovation (ICI) and a series of related spinoff projects. The project, how it was structured and the networks will be described in detail. The International Center for Innovation project started in 2008. It was initiated as a business development initiative under the Northern Denmark Region funded by European Structural Funds. The regional government had an ambition to provide new knowledge and tools to strengthen the growth potential of the local businesses so that they could cope better with the global competition.

Background for the Interventionist Research Project

The challenge the project was supposed to take on was that many companies in the region were experiencing that their business model could not maintain sufficient competitiveness and profitability, and global competitors were rapidly copying or developing alternative new products, despite many of these companies having spent many years perfecting their ability to innovate products and generally having a high innovation rate.

This problem formed an assumption that the many business development programmes offered by the North Denmark Region Growth Forum were focusing on product development, and product development was seen not to be able to stand alone: there needed to be a focus on the business model innovation as well. The core of the International Center for Innovation projects was the objective to establish ten sub-projects formed as business networks (ICI Networks) that each aimed to create a new network-based global business model (see Appendix). The cases all represent business model challenges that led to development and innovation of new business models, and testing thereof in the project.

The International Center for Innovation project focused on the fact that many companies were experiencing that their business model could not maintain sufficient competitiveness, and during the International Center for Innovation project came to understand that a part of the problem was that the companies were focusing on product development, and as it turned out, this was not a sufficient focus. As the project evolved, it became clear that there was a requirement for some sort of business model innovation, leading to the research question: How is it possible to capture the essence of business models through the use of narratives, and can business model narratives be structured into a framework that leads us to a new perspective in designing and testing business models?

The research project included a range of activities in the ten networks, such as workshops, interviews and board meetings, and during the research there was continuous progress in testing the use of narratives by using video clips and other tools for storytelling and innovation of new business models within the networks. The essence of using the data is the researcher making selected accounts of all the data that the researcher has been reading and analysing. Thus, the researcher brings selected accounts to the table to present the relevant data to answer the research question.

The finding in the (ongoing) case study on the narratives in business models has led to a number of new insights that have been published in internationally renowned academic journals (Lund and Nielsen, 2014; Nielsen and Lund, 2018).

Organization of the Interventionist Research Project

See Figure 16.1. It is important to be aware of the role of the researcher in a given research project.

In each of the ten International Center for Innovation networks, there were three primary functions; a project assistant and a project advisor representing the International Center for Innovation project, and a project manager that represented the companies in the business network. The project assistant worked as an active part of the project, ensuring that as much as possible of what is going on related to the International Center for Innovation project was documented and archived. The typical profile

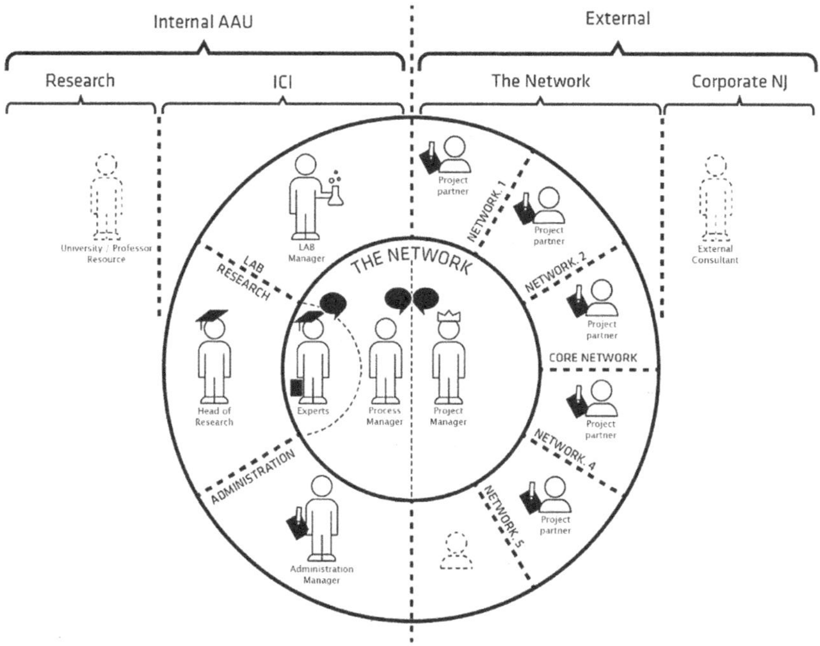

Figure 16.1 Organization of the International Center for Innovation project

for a project assistant was a young consultant, with expertise in process design and a basic understanding of the concept of business models. These assistants proved to be a valuable asset in the International Center for Innovation project because they documented the process stringently and served as a vast resource to both the project advisor and the project manager.

In most networks, the project advisor was a researcher with expertise in business model research. The researcher was asked not only to advise by providing knowledge but also to interact in the process of using this knowledge to create network-based global business models. The researchers were responsible for the business model focus in each network and the involving of experts if required in the individual networks. The project manager represented the companies in the individual business network. In most networks, the project manager was in charge of the entire project (business results) and was a key decision-maker.

To support all these actors, different functions played different roles: project management, administration, a board, a senior advising board and a lab. The project management consisted of the project manager (a professor, also managing the centre for industrial production), the administration manager and the lab manager, and had frequent meetings overseeing, planning and executing the project. Administration performed the usual tasks. The board met frequently between two and four times a year, and had different responsibilities. They approved the International Center for Innovation networks, had continuous follow-ups with the network and generally oversaw the project. The board consisted of representatives from the funding source, key figures in the public sector (one person representing the municipalities, one person representing the region of North Denmark and the managing director of Business Development Centre Northern Denmark) and three chief executive officers (CEOs) of three companies from the north region of Denmark. The senior advising board was a group formed by the chairman of the International Center for Innovation consisting of CEOs and figures among the most successful, noteworthy industries in the area. They offered the International Center for Innovation network to pitch their business model, and give feedback and potential help with specified assignments.

Last but not least, the lab was a support cornerstone in the International Center for Innovation project because it was responsible for supporting the project process, as well as having responsibility for a platform that generally would provide tools for the process of understanding, designing and prototyping business models in the International Center for Innovation networks, documentation, and so on.

The Data Collection

Data collection in interventionist research encompasses a variety of different data collection methods and types of data. The data in the project are collected in a variety of ways including summaries of official meetings, interviews, using video clips interactively, workshops, evaluations and informal meetings. Examples of activities in the data collection of the International Center for Innovation project are depicted in Table 16.3.

An interesting part of the qualitative data is the use of video as a tool in the process, providing interesting opportunities in the research, used for example for discussing the insights from the workshops. The contact and dialogues from the project include email correspondence, video and videoconferencing recordings of live workshops and conversations. Video and video clips can be used in showing the meanings that people bring to their work situations, and can provide new visualizations to the participants. Video provides context and offers pictures of the lived practice and new

Table 16.3 Data collection examples

Phase	Activity	Examples of data
Collecting data in the first part of the period		
Activities in the Networks	Board meetings Workshops on business models	Summaries from meetings Video clips from workshops Visualizations from workshops (graphics)
Interviews with participants	Interviews	Summaries from interviews
Evaluations of the International Center for Innovation Networks	Consultants evaluating the International Center for Innovation Networks	Evaluation reports from COWI
Literature study	Searching and reading the business model literature	Papers on the business model theory
Data collection in the later part of the period		
Activities in the Networks	Developing new business models within the Networks	Learning and descriptions of new business models
Using video clips for storytelling	Workshops	New insights and narratives on the business model in the Networks
Developing a new framework for business models in narratives and storytelling	Analysis of the business model framework, collected data and process	A supplement to the business model theory on narratives and storytelling

insights, more than summaries and our memories can achieve. In applying the data, we must be aware that the researcher makes selected accounts on behalf of all the data in order to present the relevant data to answer the research question.

INSIGHTS

Following our introduction to qualitative research and from that what interventionist research is, how the quality of such research can be evaluated and communicated, and finally by providing insights from a concrete interventionist research project on improving value creation mechanisms, we now intend to provide a set of insights that we have not encountered previously in the literature.

Build Relationships and Trust

As an interventionist researcher, you will be affecting your object of study. Your prior knowledge, your own goals and ambitions as well as your experiences and personality will be a part of this research. Our recommendation is to work actively on building a good relationship with the key participants in the project. Without openness and trust, your interventions risk being whisked away.

Building relationships and trust take time, and therefore, if you do not know the participants in advance, we suggest that you spend some weeks getting to know them, being in the organization, sharing lunch and having a laugh together. These recommendations can easily be accomplished while preparing tasks for other assignments.

Stages in an Interventionist Research Project

Our experiences lead us to believe that it is a good idea to consider the different stages that an interventionist research project goes through in relation to your planning and the way you interact with the organization:

1. Piloting the project and devising the initial research question.
2. Organizing the project and contacting a relevant organization.
3. Building knowledge of the organization, relationships and trust.
4. Initiating the research.
5. Iteration of interventions.
6. Evaluating the outputs and effects.
7. Repeating steps 5 and 6 until time has run out or desired results are achieved.
8. Analysing results.
9. Analysing processes.
10. Writing up the research and disseminating it to practice and to academia.

Across these stages, the design of the interventionist research project should account for whether there may be a difference between the weight of intervention versus non-intervention research methods across these steps in the given project. In some projects, it may be an advantage not to affect the object of study too much, or too early, in the process; in other projects, it will be the other way around. The most important aspect here is to be explicit about it, because the best solution will be context-dependent. In some instances, the organization being studied requires an early boost of inspiration to get going, and in others the organization is already innovating at full speed, but perhaps without clear direction. Make sure to note down your thoughts on entering the process, and provide an explanation for the strategy of engagement that you choose to go with. Remember, participating and taking over are two different ways of engaging with an organization. Make sure you act appropriately despite probably being the most knowledgeable person in the world.

There is a natural tendency for the need to build upon the relationship in the early stages of an interventionist research project and to let the relationship and trust grow during the iteration of interventions and collaborative evaluations of the results. However, in steps 9 and 10, the researcher will experience the backdrop of the closeness in the relationship in the analysis process and should make careful note of when they may not be truthful to the data, but rather are affected and subjective in the conclusions being drawn.

Four-Step Process to Making Interventions that Matter

Above, we described ten steps in an interventionist research project. In steps 5 to 7, you are 'on stage', so to speak; and therefore, how do you handle that situation and what do you do? Many novice interventionist researchers ask themselves: How do I intervene? When do I intervene? When do I know not to intervene but let things go with the flow? When do I know what to do next? And how do I keep at least one step ahead of the participants?

When planning interventionist research, it is important to leave space for the unexpected. However, not having expectations, or worse yet, not being properly prepared, is not a good option. As is the case with all other research, good planning is never a bad thing. In the worst-case scenario, your good plan needs to be adjusted after it meets reality. Remember, the devil is always in the detail, and therefore having thought through potential scenarios and having a backup plan of action is always a good idea.

Any monkey can make an intervention. However, how do you make interventions that matter and make a real difference? This is a subjective matter, and will most likely be in the eyes of the beholder. In other words, what matters for you, might not matter for us, or for the participating organization. The customer is always right, and therefore whether the intervention made a difference or not can only be judged by the entity being researched. We may have an opinion about it too, and we may have measures of resulting performance and impactful publications to back up our commitment. However, remember: customers first.

Plan to be agile. Be prepared to go with the flow. But do not turn up without options, plans, thoughts and hopes.

These remarks have similarities to the type of thinking related to rapid prototyping processes. Therefore, always keep your process in mind; and try to envision the next step. As any good chess-player, once you are trained in the skills of intervention research, you will find yourself acting on pre-established patterns that reveal themselves throughout the process. Below, we have identified a 'four-step process to making interventions that matter':

1. Depart from a contextual understanding. Make sure you understand the context and how existing practices may be rooted in institutionalized and culturally borne practices that may be difficult to alter in the short term.
2. Provide an air of change or newness. Challenge existing knowledge, existing structures and existing ways of doing things. Your intervention must introduce something to the participants that represents newness.
3. Plan your process and your communication of the intervention. Make sure to create some form of excitement among the participants to ensure that what you are discussing is viable and that it will have an effect that can be seen outside of the room.
4. Keep it simple and concrete. Make sure your intervention is concrete enough for the participants to understand how they should react to it, and make sure that if you propose a change that it is implementable.

Data Structure and Data-Discipline

Data-discipline is crucial. Leaning on the recommendations of Yin (2018), maintaining a research protocol is an important aspect of qualitative research. Hence, we also recommend using a researcher diary to enable reflection upon how your own thoughts have developed throughout a given research process. Below, we illustrate how the data were organized in the International Center for Innovation project.

From the beginning of the International Center for Innovation project, effort was made to ensure that as much as possible of the activity of the project was documented, and that this documentation was structured. Several different information technology tools that could support and document the work and processes in the International Center for

Innovation networks were tested. It remained an excessive challenge that so many different stakeholders (for example. project manager, project advisor, ICI lab, consultants) were involved. Therefore, a project assistant was assigned to each International Center for Innovation Network to assist with documentation and data collection. In the beginning of the project, a protocol was made where each role in the project was described; for example, how to handle and document data. The most important stakeholders and their responsibilities are listed in Table 16.4.

The data were structured and stored through a system based on open source and web-based services that were shared in different security levels to participants in the individual networks, project managers, assistants and advisors included in the project. The different stakeholders were motivated to use the system because it became a part of sharing and collaborating during the project. Other than documenting the process, a series of documents were a part of the formal requirements,

Table 16.4 Responsibilities of different stakeholders

Project assistant	Document all planned events and processes Coordinate and collect and store data from relevant research projects related to the International Center for Innovation Network, if any Take minutes from meetings Update calendar with activities Responsible for the Project Definition Report (PDR) document, and ensures that this is followed Participate in frequent status reports to the International Center for Innovation management and board
Project advisor	Responsible for the PDR being followed, and that any deviations are reported in frequent reports to the International Center for Innovation management and board Document processes
Project manager	Document internal activities in relation to the project Participate in frequent status reports to the International Center for Innovation management and board
International Center for Innovation administration	Time sheets, with detailed descriptions Financial documents, accounting for expenses made in relation to the project Archive contracts, letters and other formal material

Note: NJ = Northern Jutland, AAU = Aalborg University.

Figure 16.2 An example of a data structure

including for example the International Center for Innovation application, Project Definition Report (PDR), quarterly status reports on the project, internal management reports and the closing report to the regional government.

Every network had a fixed data structure, which was divided into three main categories: activities, documentation and PDR. As seen in the illustrated screen dump in Figure 16.2, the data were either structured by date or by project, depending on the nature of each category. Because there were more than 50 gigabits of pictures, videos and recordings stored from the project, it was decided that these data should be stored in a separate structure to make the documents and notes more accessible and shareable.

CONCLUDING REMARKS

In this chapter, we set out to contribute to how the quality of interventionist research may be enhanced. We discussed differences between qualitative and quantitative research as well as variations between interventionist and non-interventionist research approaches. Accordingly, we introduced the notion of plausibility as a preferred measure of research quality in opposition to quantitative research and a major fraction of qualitative research. From these outlines, and through the example of an empirical interventionist research project, four main insights were provided.

First, our empirical probing uncovered the importance of building a relationship and building trust between yourself and the responding partners in the interventionist research. This is an aspect that has not received much attention and would warrant further research for the sake of training younger scholars. From our studies, we argue that interventionist research projects should adhere to a set number of stages, and that the motivation for intervention should be linked to expected learning outcomes and how the contribution from the intervention leads to a value-added contribution in comparison to carrying out non-interventionist type research, for example through the creation of organizational and personal narratives, in which you as a researcher must partake.

Our examples led us to provide indications for what a good intervention is. We argue that as an interventionist researcher, you should always plan to be agile. To improve the quality of your interventions, you need a good understanding of the contextual setting and to provide an air of change or newness to your audience. Further, take care to plan your process and your communication of the intervention, and keep interventions simple and concrete.

Finally, we also found indications that the application of intervention and non-intervention in conjunction creates a strong format for plausible research outputs because it releases the researcher from the paradox of not affecting the object of study too early in the process but still wanting to provide intervention before participants become impatient.

REFERENCES

Arbnor, I. and B. Bjerke (2008). *Methodology for Creating Business Knowledge*. London: SAGE.

Burrell, G. and G. Morgan (1979). *Sociological Paradigms and Organizational Analysis*. New York: Heinemann Educational Books.

Chiucchi, M.S. and M. Giuliani (2017). Who's on stage? The roles of the project sponsor and of the project leader in IC reporting. *Electronic Journal of Knowledge Management*, 15(3), 183–193.

Coghlan, D. (2004). Action research in the academy: why and whither? Reflections on the changing nature of research. *Irish Journal of Management*, 25(2), 1–10.

Demartini, P. and P. Paoloni (2013). Implementing an intellectual capital framework in practice. *Journal of Intellectual Capital*, 14(1), 69–83.

DiMaggio, P.J. (1995). Comments on 'What Theory is Not'. *Administrative Science Quarterly*, 40, 391–397.
Easton, G. (1998). Case research as a methodology for industrial networks: a realist apologia. In P. Naudé and P. Turnbull (eds), *Network Dynamics in International Marketing*. London: Pergamon, pp. 73–87.
Eisenhardt, K.M. (1989). Building theories from case study research. *Academy of Management Review*, 14(4), 532–550.
Eisenhardt, K.M. and M.E. Graebner (2007). Theory building from cases; opportunities and challenges. *Academy of Management Journal*, 50(1), 25–32.
Gilje, N. and H. Grimmen (2002). *Samfundsvidenskabernes forudsætninger: Indføring I Samfundsvidenskabernes Videnskabsfilosofi*. Copenhagen: Hans Reitzels Forlag.
Guba, E. (1987). What have we learned about naturalistic evaluation? *Evaluation Practice*, 8, 23–43.
Højbjerg, H. (2004). Hermeneutik. In L. Fuglsang and P.B. Olsen (eds), *Videnskabsteori i Samfundsvidenskaberne: På Tværs af Fagkulturer og Paradigmer*. Frederiksberg: Roskilde Universitetsforlag, pp. 309–348.
Koshy, V. and C. Pascal (2011). Nurturing the young shoots of talent: using action research for exploration and theory building. *European Early Childhood Education Research Journal*, 19(4), 433–450.
Kuhn, T.S. (1962). *The Structure of Scientific Revolutions*. Chicago, IL: University of Chicago Press.
Laughlin, R. and T. Puxty (1983). A rational reconstruction of the decision-usefulness criterion. *Journal of Business Finance and Accounting*, 10(3), 451–480.
Lewin, K. (1946). Action research and minority problems. *Journal of Social Issues*, 2(4), 34–46.
Lukka, K. (2005). Approaches to case research in management accounting: the nature of empirical intervention and theory linkage. In S. Jönsson and J. Mouritsen (eds), *Accounting in Scandinavia – The Northern Lights*. Kristianstad, SW: Liber & Copenhagen Business School Press, pp. 375–399.
Lukka, K. and E. Kasanen (1995). The problem of generalizability: anecdotes and evidence in accounting research. *Accounting, Auditing and Accountability Journal*, 8(5), 71–90.
Lund, M. and C. Nielsen (2014). The evolution of network-based business models illustrated through the case study of an entrepreneurship project. *Journal of Business Models*, 2(1), 105–121.
Lune, H. and B.L. Berg (2016). *Qualitative Research Methods for the Social Sciences*. Harlow: Pearson Higher Education.
March, J.G. and J.P. Olsen (1989). *Rediscovering Institutions: The Organizational Basis of Politics*. New York: Free Press.
Miles, M.B. and A.M. Huberman (1994). *Qualitative Data Analysis: An Expanded Sourcebook*. Thousand Oaks, CA: SAGE.
Modell, S. (2009). In defence of triangulation: a critical realist approach to mixed methods research in management accounting. *Management Accounting Research*, 20(3), 208–221.
Morgan, G. and L. Smircich (1980). The case for qualitative research. *Academy of Management Review*, 5, 491–500.
Mouritsen, J. (1990). Det Eksterne Regnskabsvæsen i Videnskabsteoretisk Belysning. In H. Andersen (ed.), *Videnskabsteori og Metodelære*. Copenhagen: Samfundslitteratur, pp. 147–168.
Nielsen, C. and M. Lund (2018). Building scalable business models. *MIT Sloan Management Review*, 59(2), 65–69.
Ozanne, J.L. and B. Saatcioglu (2008). Participatory action research. *Journal of Consumer Research*, 35(3), 423–439.
Parker, L.D. and D. Northcott (2016). Qualitative generalising in accounting research: concepts and strategies. *Accounting, Auditing and Accountability Journal*, 29(6), 1100–1131.

Peters, B.G. (2001). *Institutional Theory in Political Science: The 'New Institutionalism'*. New York: Continuum.
Phillips, J.R. (1988). Research blenders. *Nursing Science Quarterly*, 1, 4–5.
Qu, S.Q. and J. Dumay (2011). The qualitative research interview. *Qualitative Research in Accounting and Management*, 8(3), 238–264.
Reason, P. and H. Bradbury (2001). *Handbook of Action Research: Participative Inquiry and Practice*. London: SAGE Publications.
Ritzer, G. (1996). *Sociological Theory*. Singapore: McGraw-Hill International Editions.
Rosenberg, A. (2000). *Philosophy of Social Science: A Contemporary Introduction*. New York: Routledge.
Runkel, P.J. and M. Runkel (1984). *A Guide to Usage for Writers and Students in the Social Sciences*. Totowa, NJ: Rowman & Allanheld.
Ryan, B., R.W. Scapens and M. Theobald (2002). *Research Method and Methodology in Finance and Accounting*. London: Academic Press.
Sale, J.E.M., L.H. Lohfeld and K. Brazil (2002). Revisiting the quantitative–qualitative debate: implications for mixed-methods research. *Quality and Quantity*, 36, 43–53.
Smith, J.K. and L. Heshusius (1986). Closing down the conversation: the end of the quantitative–qualitative debate among educational inquirers. *Educational Researcher*, 15(1), 4–12.
Stones, R. (ed.) (1998). *Key Sociological Thinkers*. London: Macmillan Press.
Susman, G. and R.D. Evered (1978). An assessment of the scientific merits of action research. *Administrative Science Quarterly*, 23(4), 582–603.
Sutton, R.I. and B.M. Staw (1995). What theory is not. *Administrative Science Quarterly*, 40, 371–384.
Turner, B.A. (1981). Some practical aspects of qualitative data analysis: one way of organising the cognitive processes associated with the generation of grounded theory. *Quality and Quantity*, 15, 225–247.
Van de Ven, A.H. (2007). *Engaged Scholarship: A Guide for Organizational and Social Research*. Oxford University Press on Demand.
Van de Ven, A.H. and P.E. Johnson (2006). Knowledge for theory and practice. *Academy of Management Review*, 31(4), 802–821.
Van Maanen, J. (1979). The fact of fiction in organizational ethnography. *Administrative Science Quarterly*, 24, 539–550.
Weick, K.E. (1995). What theory is not, theorizing is. *Administrative Science Quarterly*, 40, 385–390.
Yin, R.K. (2018). *Case Study Research and Applications: Design and Methods*. Los Angeles, CA: SAGE Publications.

APPENDIX 1: THE TEN INTERNATIONAL CENTER FOR INNOVATION NETWORKS

Provital
Eye in the sky
Seafood
Mobil tracking
HR-IT
Cspot
ViewWorld
EBB
SAFE
Space Creator

17. Combining the measurement and management approaches: the fuzzy logic methodology

Stefania Veltri

INTRODUCTION

The chapter focuses on the use of a well-known quantitative method, the fuzzy logic methodology, to measure intellectual capital (IC). The chapter describes briefly the method, its strengths and weaknesses, and some applications in published journal articles. In the chapter I refer to IC as a dynamic system of intangible, knowledge-based resources and activities capable of creating value for stakeholders (European Commission, 2006). Originally derived from for-profit strategic management techniques, IC, which encompasses three primary interrelated components – namely human capital (HC), structural capital (SC) and relational capital (RC) – also provides a conceptual framework for public and non-profit strategic management (Mouritsen et al., 2004; Kong and Prior, 2008).

In their 2003 article, Habersam and Piber identified two fundamental strategies seen as alternative ways to deal with IC: measurement and management (Habersam and Piber, 2003). Considerable attention has been paid to this issue over the years, and it remains a relevant one in the current stage of IC research (Mouritsen and Roslender, 2009; Guthrie et al., 2012). I argue that the main strong point of measuring IC through the fuzzy expert system (FES) model is its capability to combine management and measurement views, to reflect the newest concepts regarding IC, and to take into consideration the 'vague' interactions between IC categories. Thus, the aim of the chapter is to combine measurement and management views, by presenting a different way to determine a comprehensive IC index.

The chapter contributes to the broadening of the research community's understanding regarding an alternative measurement of an organisation's IC value. From a measurement perspective, the results may be regarded as valuable proof that IC performance can be measured by 'tangible values', that is, quantitatively. On the management side, the possibility of retracing the determinants of the different IC intermediate indicators composing the final IC index allows corporate managers to use this information for decision-making purposes.

The chapter presents two applications of the FES model: to a non-profit and to a for-profit context. For the non-profit sector, a FES model is applied to data derived from the Austrian universities' mandatory IC reports. For the for-profit sector, the model is applied to a firm involved in a strategic alliance.

The remainder of the chapter is organised as follows: it discusses the motivation to propose a FES model to measure IC; FES model main pros and cons; and two applications where a FES model has been used to measure IC, one dealing with the public sector, the other with the private sector.

MOTIVATION TO MEASURE IC THROUGH THE FES METHOD

The well-known Sveiby matrix (Sveiby, 2009) classified the existing IC measurement models into four main categories: (1) market capitalisation; (2) return on asset; (3) direct intellectual capital; and (4) scorecard. The first three models belong to the measurement perspective, as they focus on the financial side of measurement and the monetary value of intangible assets; while the scorecard approaches belong to the management perspective, as they look for quantitative and qualitative indicators able to measure intangible resources and activities, and aim at showing the role of IC in a firm's value creation (Serrano-Cinca et al., 2004; Coakes and Bradburn, 2005; Leitner et al., 2007).[1]

Fuzzy logic methodology does not fit any of these approaches, as it aims to combine measurement and management perspectives, by developing an IC index through a technique which is able to give a numeric measurement of an organisation's comprehensive IC (and its subcategories), at the same time allowing to retrace the determinants of IC value creation (Schiuma, 2009). A fuzzy logic approach, unlike traditional mathematics used within the financial methods for measuring IC, is able to consider the qualitative nature of most IC indicators developed within the scorecard methods, thus combining measurement and management approaches. This issue is relevant in the IC literature, as in the last decades the measurement approach has aimed at providing a number expressive of the IC value, while the management approach, aimed at using the IC indicators derived from strategy for decision-making purposes, has emerged as a different way of dealing with IC (Habersam and Piber, 2003).

I argue that the issue remains relevant even in the actual stages of IC research, characterised by critical and performative analysis of

IC in action (Mouritsen, 2006; Guthrie et al., 2012). This is because it remains questionable whether an excessive focus on the measurement perspective can lead to there being little attention paid to management processes (Chaminade and Roberts, 2003; Mouritsen and Roslender, 2009).

I argue that, to be useful, a method to measure IC should respect the inner features of IC, that is, its potential value and its dynamic and firm-specific nature. The first feature implies that, in order to create value, IC subcategories must interact with each other and with tangible resources (Helm-Stevens et al., 2011). Furthermore, the relationships which can develop among the indicators are never univocal, but rather are of 'concomitant cause and multiple effect' with obvious implications in terms of the complexity of the IC framework (Chiucchi, 2004). The dynamic nature of IC implies that it is a concept in evolution, which undergoes change over time, and which must be constantly understood and interpreted (Kianto, 2007). The implications for researchers working with IC indicators are that an exhaustive list of IC components does not exist due to these constant changes of classification (Gröjer, 2001). The firm-specific nature of IC implies that IC indicators are specific for each single organisation, sector, industry, typology, size of organisation, and so on. Even the more accredited guidelines for drawing up an IC report do not propose an exhaustive list, but include only some firm-specific examples. The implication for researchers is that they must manage different IC indicators even when they carry out research in the same sector. Moreover, researchers working with IC indicators must bear in mind that IC indicators, which are derived from the organisation's knowledge strategy and can have both a non-financial and a financial nature, have to be centred on the intangible resources, on the actions carried out to develop intangible resources and also on the effects of these actions. Indicators derived in applying an FES model can take account of these inner features of IC, and the next sections illustrate the FES model's main advantages and how it works.

FES MAIN ADVANTAGES

To date, several IC indices have been developed, mainly within the pioneering IC scorecard measurement models, which revealed from the beginning the need to develop a comprehensive IC index which is able to express the IC value of an organisation. They focused on IC category content and were geared towards both measurement and evaluation (Chiucchi, 2004).

Consistent with the pioneering IC scorecard measurement models, two synthetic IC measures, namely the intellectual capital index and the IC-index, have been proposed by Edvinsson and Malone (1997) and by Roos et al. (1997), respectively. In detail, the intellectual capital index (Edvinsson and Malone, 1997) is a synthetic monetary measure given by the product of the potential future development of IC (C) and the efficiency in using IC (i); while the IC-index (Roos et al., 1997) is a numeric ratio given by the weighted sum of selected IC indicators. Nonetheless, previous IC measurement models fail in considering the qualitative nature of intangibles and the interactions among IC variables and categories as a source of an organisation's value creation (Chiucchi, 2004).

The FES is the methodology to develop an IC index able to include the inner features of IC, that can be calculated in an easy and rational manner (that is, using a mathematical basis without being difficult to understand), and that can be adapted to the different sectors, giving an effective tangible measure of the IC at the same time. Moreover, the FES is an extremely flexible model, as it is possible to introduce several value drivers and change the rules connecting drivers and intermediate variables at any time, and it is a transparent model, as the experts involved put their experience and knowledge into the building of the FES and their choices are transparent, visible and manifest at any given step. The advantages of developing an IC index using an FES can be summarised as follows.

The FES Combines the Measurement and Management Perspectives

In IC literature, the measurement view suggests that formal models are needed for a better description and rationalisation of the IC value (Neely et al., 1995; Mettänen, 2005; Arena et al., 2009), while the managerial perspective suggests that reality cannot be described by merely relying on mathematical models which are complex in their application and simplified in their assumptions (Kujansivu, 2009; Lönnqvist et al., 2009). The FES, allowing codification of human knowledge in the form of a mathematical algorithm, takes the two different approaches into account.

The FES is Easy to Understand and Implement

Working with a multidisciplinary model like the one I present, the advantage of using an FES approach is that an advanced knowledge of mathematics is not required for all the experts involved. The solution is derived from a heuristic approach based on logical implications ('if, then' rules), so even those not expert in mathematics can easily understand the formal applications and hence can support the implementation of the FES.[2]

The FES is a Formal Model

The FES model is a formal one, which rationalises the evaluation process. The final result gives a proper numerical value for the organisation.

The FES Integrates Qualitative and Quantitative Data

A fuzzy approach, unlike standard mathematical approaches, is capable of integrating qualitative and quantitative analysis, so that the model is not forced to limit its scope to numerical variables with well-specified units of measures, but can handle any type of qualitative driver (which is an impossible task for classical mathematics).

The FES can Handle a High Number of Value Drivers

An FES model can handle a high number of value drivers, simplifying the design of the whole system, thus reducing its complexity and intelligibility; the system is modular, therefore not explosive, since it is run from branch to trunk.

The FES is Flexible

The FES model is extremely flexible; it is possible to introduce several value drivers and change the rules connecting drivers and intermediate variables at any time.

The FES is Transparent

The experts involved put their experience and knowledge into the building of the FES. Their choices are transparent, visible and manifest at any given step. In this way, their opinions are subject to debate and eventual change if not accepted by most of the assembly.

FES METHODOLOGY: HOW IT WORKS

Technically speaking, the FES is a cognitive framework that adequately replicates the natural way human beings react cognitively to the world and think about problems and situations, and it enables us to formulate qualitative concepts (Magni et al., 2006). The underlying logic of the FES is fuzzy logic, that is, an extension of Boolean logic (or two-valued logic: true and false), introduced to manage the concept of intermediate degrees of truth (Zadeh, 1965).

FESs are expert systems which rely on fuzzy logic. Fuzzy logic is a cognitive framework that adequately replicates the natural way human beings cognise the world and think about problems and situations. In other words, fuzzy logic overcomes Boolean logic (true or false) and enables researchers to formalise qualitative (linguistic) and vague concepts such as 'low', 'medium', 'high', 'good', 'excellent', and so on (Magni et al., 2006). An expert system is a tool designed to replicate the way of reasoning of one or more experts, which consists of a knowledge base and an inferential engine. An FES model is thus an information system using fuzzy data, fuzzy rules and fuzzy inference, usable to merge the capabilities of an expert system to simulate the decision-making process with the vagueness typical of human reasoning, which is present in fuzzy logic (Magni et al., 2002, 2006). Behaviours and decisions are encoded in blocks of rules and processed through a fuzzy logic inference engine.

The FES construction requires the participation of experts, whose knowledge of the problem is accumulated in the form of blocks of rules. These features meet the needs of the proposed methodology: to formalise and automate the decision-making process relating to the valuation of IC, handling qualitative and quantitative variables, exploring the cognitive mechanisms underlying this process, reducing the distortions often found in the real decision-making context.

The implementation of an FES system is generally divided into the following phases:

1. focus group with experts to define the inputs, conditions for the aggregation of intermediate variables and output;
2. layout of the model (modular decision tree);
3. definition of linguistic attribute (fuzzy value) for each variable, range of variables and blocks of fuzzy rules;
4. trial processing and optimisation; and
5. analysis of the final output.

The design of an FES is the first and most important step of the study. With the help of a panel of experts, a modular system is selected, consisting of several fuzzy modules linked together. The main structure of the model is based on the aggregation of its subcomponents. Starting from the right (going from branches to trunk), the final output is determined by its main factors, which are determined by other intermediate variables, which in turn are determined by other variables and so on until, proceeding backward, a set of initial independent variables (the inputs) is reached.

From a mathematical point of view, the connection between the set of the n input variables and the output can be represented by a function f of n independent variables x_i, $i = 1, 2,..., n$, affecting the dependent variable y (intermediate variable), so that $y = f(x_1, x_2, \dots x_n)$.

All the knowledge needed to design and build the system components (variables and elements for their evaluation, blocks of rules and weights for aggregation) is 'pulled' by the experts using various techniques of investigation. The FES model thus relies heavily on the knowledge and competence of the focus experts' group.

Summarising, an IC index calculated using the FES model is not only able to include the inner features of IC, but it could also be calculated in an easy and rational manner (that is, using a mathematical basis without being difficult to understand), and it can be adapted to the different sectors, giving an effective tangible measure of the IC at the same time. The next section provides evidence of the application of an FES model to two very different sectors.

THE USE OF FES METHODOLOGY IN IC LITERATURE

The number of scientific contributions using fuzzy logic methodology has sharply increased in the recent past in many sectors (Bagnoli and Smith, 1998; Magni et al., 2002; Malagoli et al., 2009). As regards the possibility to integrate expert systems and fuzzy logic for IC evaluation, I believe that it represents a reliable methodology that could be appealing for managers, practitioners and analysts, because of the 'fuzzy' nature of IC (O'Donnell et al., 2000). In empirical literature, the fuzzy logic methodology has been recently applied in empirical research work addressed to evaluating knowledge and IC (Bozbura et al., 2007; Zandi and Tavana, 2010; Wu et al., 2010).

This section examines two recent applications of the FES model to IC measurement: Veltri et al. (2014), which applies the FES model to Austrian data drawn from the mandatory IC statements, and Veltri et al. (2015), which applies the FES model to an Italian firm belonging to a strategic alliance.

Applying FES Methodology to the Public Sector: Measuring IC of Austrian Universities

Veltri et al.'s (2014) contribution aimed to define an FES able to return an IC index for the Austrian university sector. The experts to set up the

FES model were the authors of the article; one of them was an expert in fuzzy models, and he selected the type of fuzzy system to employ; two of them were competent in the subject of IC (one of them was a teacher in an Austrian university), and they designed the fuzzy system (that is, they chose the inputs and output variables) and defined the linguistic attributes (fuzzy values) for each variable along with the corresponding function (fuzzification of input and output). The three authors together defined the set of fuzzy rules ('if, then' rules), chose the fuzzy inference method, translated the fuzzy output in a 'crisp' value (defuzzification), then validated the fuzzy system. The results have thus been commented upon under an IC point of view. Figure 17.1 illustrates the structure of the fuzzy logic model used in Veltri et al.'s (2014) article.

The correct way to read this figure is by starting from the right and going to the left. Starting from the right, we have the final evaluation IC, which is the aggregation of the three main factors HC, RC and SC. All the variables that are not initial drivers are called 'intermediate variables' (IVs). They are not, from the beginning, directly measurable, but will be so by the modularity of the FES. The authors had several dialogues to correctly identify the subcomponents of IC (HC, RC and SC) in the university sector. They ended up with a list of HC, RC and SC indicators. In choosing these indicators, the authors refer to the IC literature, their IC competence, and the Austrian University Organization and Studies Act (UG) 2002.

In Table 17.1, HC is the aggregation of didactics (IV) and research (IV). Research is the aggregation of direct drivers but didactics is obtained by another aggregation of staff abilities (IV) and dynamic staff composition (IV).

In Table 17.2, SC is the aggregation of hardware and databases (IV), university culture (IV) and the innovation value driver.

In Table 17.3, RC is the direct aggregation of four direct drivers involving scientific relationships.

The IV as well as the final IC are obtained by several aggregations using linguistic rules and ad hoc selected inference machines (fuzzy inference method), procedure graphically represented in the layout by rule blocks (RBs). In these blocks, the lines of the variables to be evaluated go in, and a single line summarising the evaluation goes out. This procedure, which combines the contribution of experts and mathematical elaboration, is the main force of the FES; therefore, the building of the RBs is of major importance. RBs have been obtained using a standard method which speeds up the experts' answers, reducing disagreement.

Experts find, linguistically, the monotonicity of heuristic functions starting from independent variables; this produces a partial or final output.

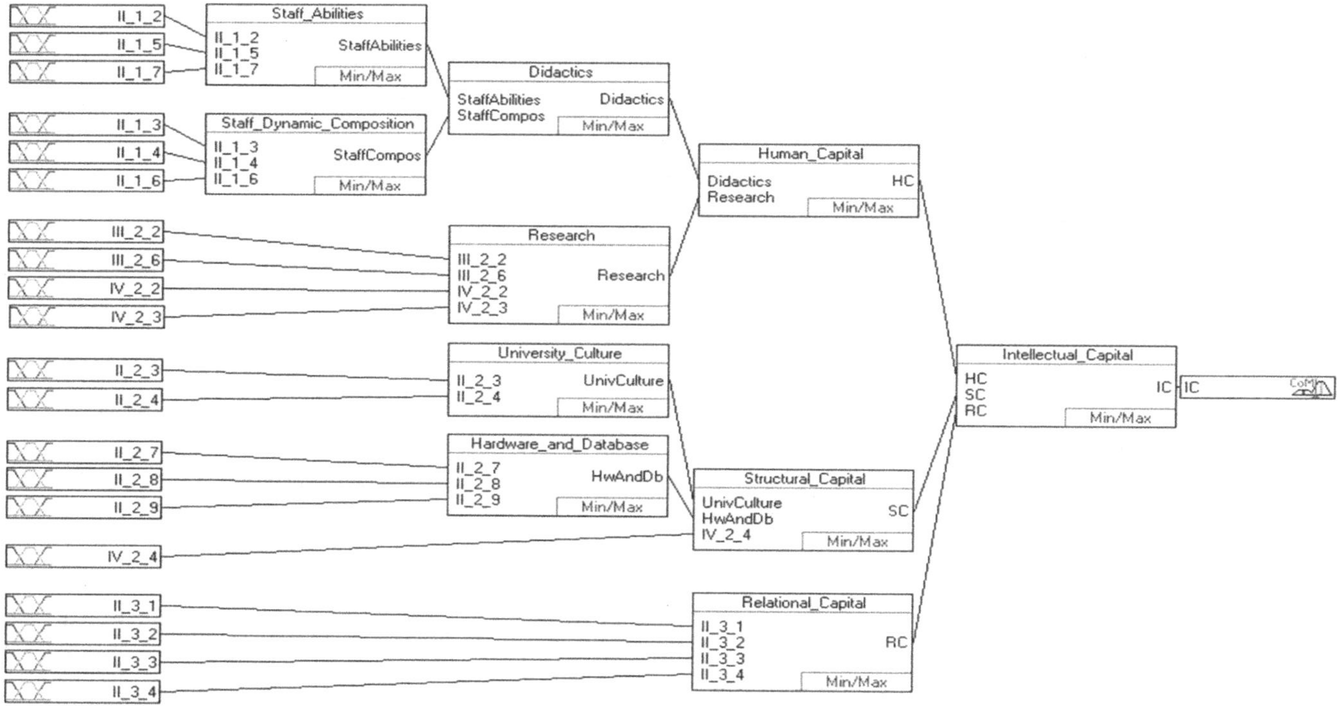

Figure 17.1 Structure of the FES model

Table 17.1 The human capital indicators selected for the model

Variables to measure	Intellectual capital report (ICR) numeration	Indicators
Didactics		
Staff's abilities		
Didactics qualifications	II 1.2/II 1.1	Number of awarded teaching qualifications (habilitations)/ staff
Training	II 1.7/II 1.1	Number of participants in programmes for continuing education and personnel development/staff
Activities that improve teaching qualifications	II 1.5/II 1.1	Number of academic staff who have completed a temporary stay abroad amounting to at least 5 days (outgoing)/staff
Staff's dynamic composition		
Professors called to work at universities	II 1.3/II 1.1	Number of appointments to the university/staff
Professors who leave university for an external professorship	II 1.4/II 1.1	Number of appointments from the university/staff
New teachers	II 1.6/II 1.1	Number of incoming academic staff/staff
Research		
Number of ongoing research and development projects supported by external funds	III 2.2	Number of ongoing projects within research and development supported by third-party funds
Acknowledgement of the research ability of researchers	IV 2.3	Number of presentations held as invited speaker or selected presenter at scientific events
Researcher's productivity	IV 2.2	Number of scientific publications of the staff
Investments in future university researchers	III 2.6	Number of doctoral programmes

Table 17.2 The structural capital indicators selected for the model

Variables to measure	Intellectual capital report (ICR) numeration	Indicators
Hardware and databases		
Databases	II 2.7	Cost for available online research databases in euros
Scientific journals	II 2.8	Cost for available scientific journals in euros
Infrastructure	II 2.9	Total funding for large equipment for research and development
Innovation		
Patents	IV 2.4	Number of patents awarded to the university
University culture		
The social culture	II 2.3	Number of staff active at special institutions
	II 2.4	Number of staff active in institutions for students with special needs or with chronic conditions or both

Table 17.3 The relational capital indicators selected for the model

Variables to measure	Section	Indicators
Scientific relationships		
External relationships	II 3.1	Number of staff in function as chairs, members or reviewers on external appointment committees and habilitation committees
Cooperation agreement	II 3.2	Number of partner institutions/enterprises incorporated in cooperation agreement
Scientific relationships	II 3.3	Number of staff with function on scientific journals
	II 3.4	Number of staff on scientific panel

The system translates these statements by means of suitable operations. The inference method is chosen according to the related problem. Finally, experts test the system using input data whose output is already known.

An example of an RB, the rule block 'Staff's abilities', is represented in Table 17.4.

The RB is self-explanatory. As an example, row 8 is to be read as follows: whatever the value of the other variables, if the 'Didactics qualifications' (input II.1.2) is low, the 'Activities that improve teaching qualifications' (input II.1.5) is high and the 'Training' (input II.1.7) is medium, then the 'Staff's abilities' is medium.

Table 17.4 Rule block 'Staff's abilities'

IF			THEN	
II1.2	II1.5	II1.7	DoS	Staff Abilities
low	low	low	1.00	very low
low	low	medium	1.00	very low
low	low	high	1.00	low
low	medium	low	1.00	very low
low	medium	medium	1.00	low
low	medium	high	1.00	medium
low	high	low	1.00	low
low	high	medium	1.00	medium
low	high	high	1.00	high
medium	low	low	1.00	very low
medium	low	medium	1.00	low
medium	low	high	1.00	medium
medium	medium	low	1.00	low
medium	medium	medium	1.00	medium
medium	medium	high	1.00	high
medium	high	low	1.00	medium
medium	high	medium	1.00	high
medium	high	high	1.00	very high
high	low	low	1.00	low
high	low	medium	1.00	medium
high	low	high	1.00	high
high	medium	low	1.00	medium
high	medium	medium	1.00	high
high	medium	high	1.00	very high
high	high	low	1.00	high
high	high	medium	1.00	very high
high	high	high	1.00	very high

The next step is the production of the numerical evaluation of IC. This step is called 'defuzzification' as the final output is, at this point, a fuzzy quantity and not a number. This step is feasible even for intermediate variables and this is one of the main reasons for using a modular system with respect to the use of a global vision.

The final step is the validation test of the FES, which in the article is obtained by looking at the three macro-indexes (HC, SC, RC) defuzzified. The final output is a ranking of the 20 Austrian universities ranked following the IC index.

Applying FES Methodology to the Private Sector: Measuring IC of a Network's Company

The second application of a FES model to measure IC is Veltri et al.'s (2015) article in which FES is used to measure the IC of a firm, 3C Catene srl, belonging to an Italian network agreement, the PIB network, localised in the province of Lecco in the northern Lombardy region of Italy. An ad hoc FES model is developed in the article.

To build it, the data needed was collected as inputs through the qualitative tool of the semi-structured interview to the general managers of the selected firm, then the data was interpreted by researchers. Based on qualitative data, the researchers acted as experts (content experts) and, together with an expert on the FES models (methodology expert), worked on developing the ad hoc FES quantitative model.

All the knowledge needed to design and build the system components (variables and elements for their evaluation, blocks of rules and weights for aggregation) was extracted by the experts using various techniques of investigation. For the purposes of this paper a focus group with partially structured discussions was used. A nominal group technique (NGT) approach was employed for the meeting procedure. NGT uses a group of experts who hold discussions chaired by a moderator (Duggan and Thachenkary, 2004; Dunham, 2006), with the aim to reduce to a minimum distortions due to personal interaction during the discussion. The NGT model in a first phase does not rely on oral communication; instead individuals communicate in a written form, to enable individuals to overcome possible obstacles to the expression of their opinions (from shyness, deference towards important experts or unwillingness to offer views conflicting with those of any superiors present). Subsequent phases involve the presentation and discussion of proposals; each idea is discussed by all the members of the group, then classified by each member using an ordinal scale. Finally, mathematical calculations – for example, the average of all the individual assessments – are made based on the scores given.

As with all methodologies, the experts' focus group has its weaknesses, including factors such as: individual stereotypes, which lead to the creation of a cognitive filter in the analysis (even by experts) of social phenomena; the relational dynamics, of a psychological and social nature, which affect communication between the different social protagonists; the selection processes and the representativeness of the group of experts referred to; and the definition of the level of reliability of the analyses carried out. To overcome any possible measurement errors, several corrective measures were applied to counterbalance the use of the experts' focus group. Top management people were interviewed twice, in order to better focus on some of the insights they offered. Interviews were recorded and typed, and in case of misunderstandings a further and shorter interview was scheduled in order to clarify or detail some of the aspects of the previous interview. Once typed, interviews were submitted to interviewees in order to check for potential inconsistencies or mistakes. Internal documents were also collected in order to support interviewees' statements and to better detail the analysis. Moreover, the inter-rater reliability was assessed, meaning that data were independently coded and the coding compared for agreement (Armstrong et al., 1997). The rule to follow in the case of disagreement was also foreseen (one main referent chosen in the group). Finally, the model was corroborated by testing its reliability against a series of simulations, varying the value of one or more value drivers simultaneously while leaving the others fixed.

As it was for the FES model used in Veltri et al. (2014), in Veltri et al. (2015) a modular system was also selected, consisting of several fuzzy modules linked together. The main structure of the model is based on the aggregation of the three main components of IC: human capital (HC), structural capital (SC) and relational capital (RC) (Figure 17.2).

Starting from the right (going from branches to trunk), the final output 'ICinNetAgr' is determined by the three main factors HC, SC and RC, which are determined by other intermediate variables, which in turn are determined by other variables and so on until, proceeding backward, a set of initial independent variables (the inputs) is reached.

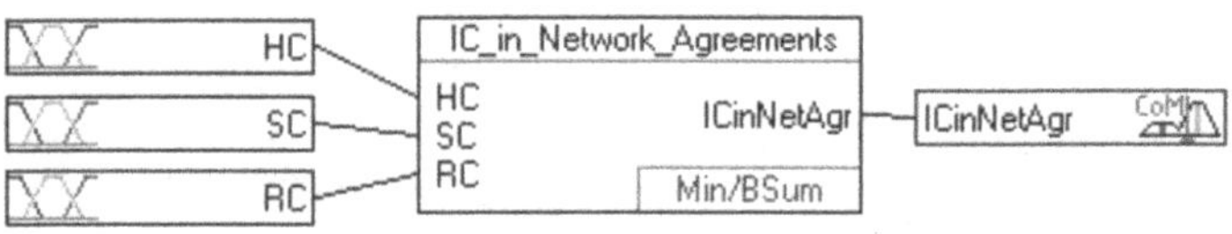

Figure 17.2 Main structure of the FES model

The HC system is based on the evaluation of two large areas: the level of knowledge, understood both as level of education and as ability to perform well on their own work, and human resources, evaluated through the profile and the staff satisfaction and through an index of the productivity of managers. The system is constructed by aggregating 23 inputs through 16 blocks of rules, to get 15 intermediate variables, and final evaluation (the HC output). Figure 17.3 illustrates the structure of the HC subcategory.

The evaluation of the RC is made by combining the assessment of Market and Network areas with the input 'SupStability' (stability of suppliers). The system is constructed by aggregating 21 inputs through 14 blocks of rules, to get 13 intermediate variables and the RC output. Figure 17.4 illustrates the structure of the RC subcategory.

The output of the SC system is obtained by comparing the result of the substructure Research, composed of 11 inputs (Table 17.5), with the input 'InvITonTI', which compares the amount of investment in information technology (IT) to the total of investments. The aggregation is done through eight blocks of rules and seven intermediate variables. Figure 17.5 illustrates the structure of the SC subcategory. The results produced by the system are displayed in Table 17.5.

CONCLUSIONS

The structure of the models employed in the Veltri et al. (2014) and Veltri et al. (2015) articles are consistent with the IC strategic management conceptual framework, allowing also to obtain a synthetic number expressive of the IC evaluation. The model produces a numerical evaluation, as do the financial and accounting models; but while the numbers derived from these models are a sort of 'black box' where the determinants of the IC index are not highlighted, the FES model employed explicitly takes account of these variables.

FES methodology relies heavily on the knowledge and competence of the experts' focus group to provide input for the model, thus one of its main limitations is the high level of subjectivity involved. This could translate into measurement errors. Nonetheless, although this methodology clearly involves a high level of subjectivity and is subject to measurement error, it is worth remembering that it addresses some of the inherent limitations of the inferential statistical methods which are based on the direct observation of phenomena (Krueger and Casey, 2009; Bertin, 2005), such as the need to produce information quickly, to create a shared set of terms and concepts for the different parties involved in a communication process, and to involve all these parties in the evaluation process.

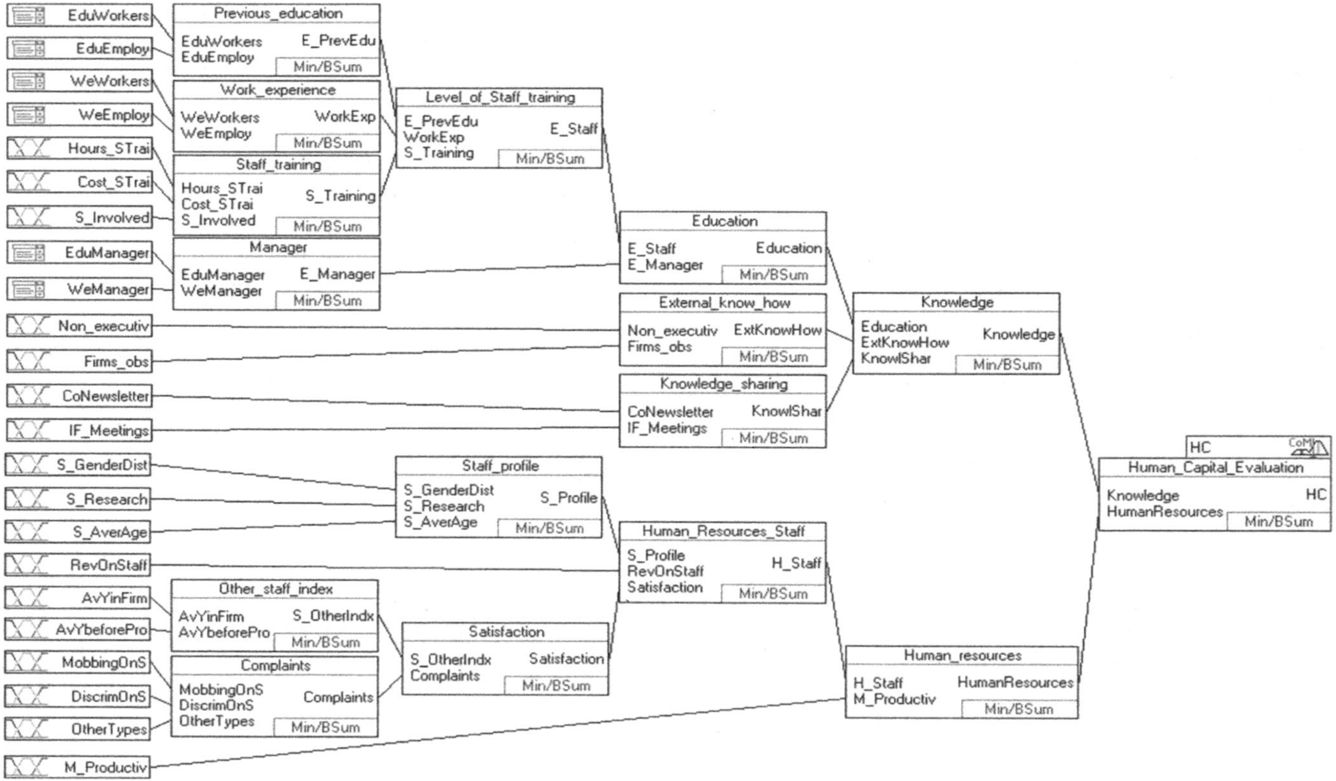

Figure 17.3 Structure of human capital subcategory

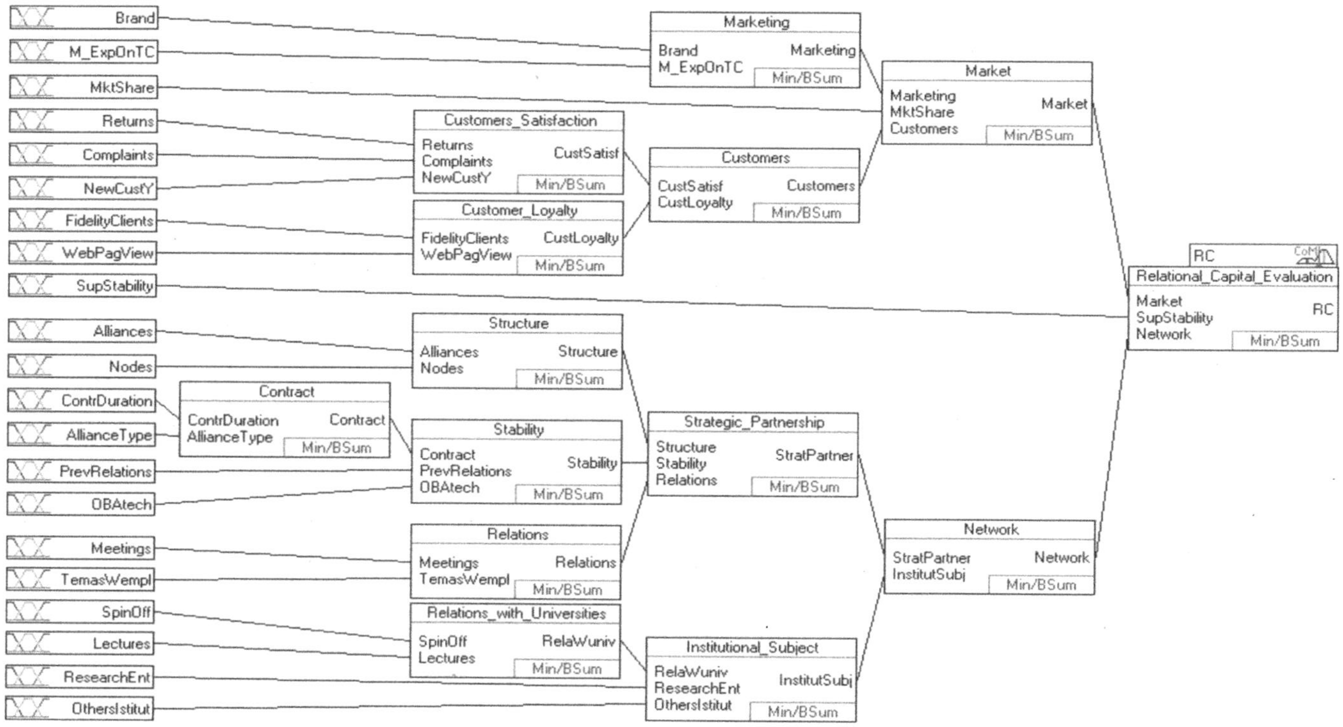

Figure 17.4 Structure of relational capital subcategory

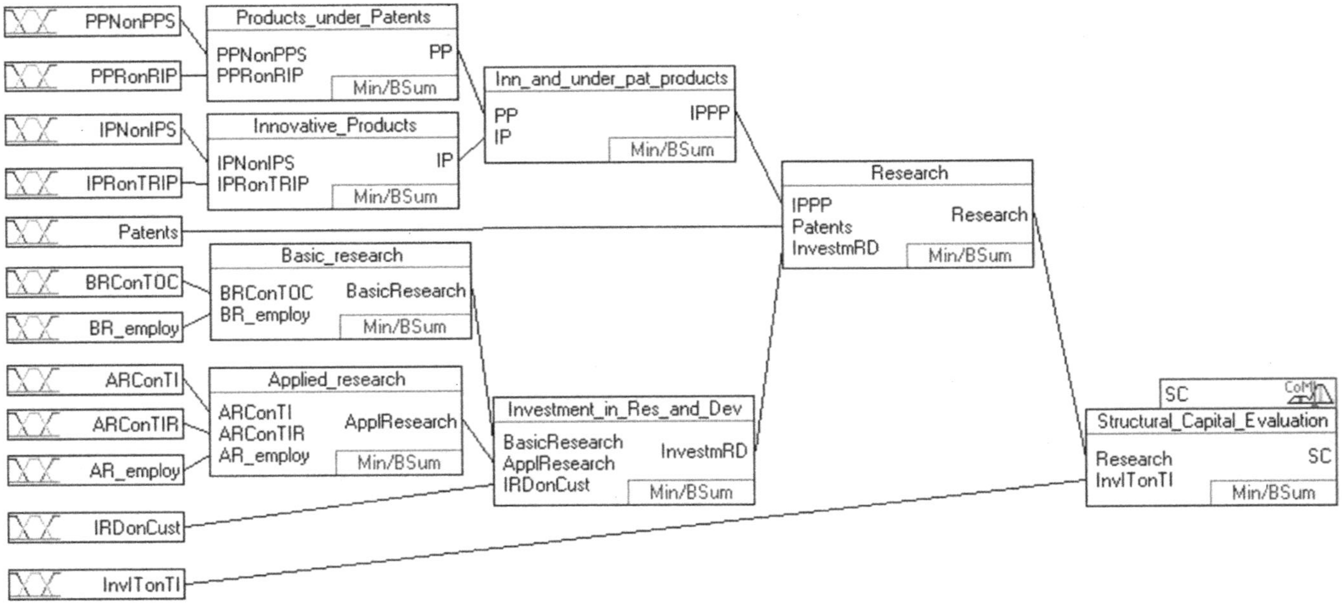

Figure 17.5 Structure of structural capital subcategory

Table 17.5 Rule block 'Staff's abilities'

1°level int. Var.	1°level int. Var.	HC System	Input	1°level int. Var.	1°level int. Var.	RC System	Input	1°level int. Var.	SC System	Output
Knowledge	Human resources	HC	SupStability	Market	Network	RC	InvITonTI	Research	SC	ICinNetAgr
27.60	100.00	70.30	very high	68.33	44.64	76.13	very low	14.29	0.11	52.68

Therefore, for FES methodology to produce reliable results it is dependent on the researchers' knowledge of the specific theme (content experts) and expertise on the FES model (methodology experts) working together to build an ad hoc FES model, as only researchers who have an in-depth knowledge of a particular phenomenon could assign reliable values and construct reliable rule blocks, and only experts of the FES model are able to build rule blocks, defuzzify input values and build intermediate variables to obtain the final output.

Of course the FES model presents implementation problems: that is, the problems typical of the experts' focus group (which could be managed) and the mathematical competence needed (even if it uses a mathematical basis without being difficult to understand), but I believe that it is worthwhile investing in, as the FES model, which combines the intuition and the experience of experts with the formal rigour of a logic system, is flexible enough to be adapted to different sectors, providing an effective tangible measure of IC while at the same time revealing its determinants, so combining effectively the measurement and management sides.

Regarding the main implications of the application of the FES model to measure IC, it can be concluded that both applications propose an alternative IC evaluation model using an FES approach, able to combine the intuition and the experience of experts, who supply the system with the knowledge base, with the formal rigour of a logic system.

Regarding the FES model as applied to the Austrian universities, it was designed ad hoc for them. It is a pilot model that has been built on the IC report model under the Austrian University Organization and Studies Act (UG) 2002 (UG 2002). It suffers from the limitations proper to all intellectual capital reports (ICRs), such as the lack of 'soft' activities-related and process IC indicators, due to the difficulty in defining them, therefore only further corroboration both within the university sector other than in the Austrian one, and also in other sectors, can lead to the improvement of the model. The FES model applied to Austrian universities represents a first step, but it is flexible enough for individual adaptations and adjustments and has potential for further improvements and elaborations.

The main limitation to the study is that it has been applied to a non-random sample, with the obligation to use for the model the IC indicators already defined in the ICR. The model would require the carrying out of further tests in different university contexts, but this will be possible only in the presence of available and comparable IC data. The main advantage of the IC score developed through an FES model is undoubtedly its return of a reliable IC index (that is, based on its inner features) to be used in comparisons and in the models that investigate a relation between IC and other firm performance measures, but also should be mentioned the possible external and internal benefits related to the ranking of the universities based on their IC ratings. Internally, university managers may have suggestions regarding which IC area needs to be improved and in which area IC should be maintained at the current levels. Externally, a list of universities based on their IC would allow for evaluation of the effectiveness of universities in maintaining and developing their IC, increasing transparency throughout the university system and the flow of information on IC issued by universities for their various stakeholders. Ranking or benchmarking universities by their IC, ministries could get information about the strengths and weaknesses of the science system and, if these rankings are used to reallocate resources to universities higher in the list, this could lead to an increase in the performance of universities, as IC could be a good indicator of a university's future performance. Moreover, if ministries ranked universities on their IC, linking some benefits to best-performing universities, the message that supranational organisations wish to send would become clear: universities are pivotal actors in the knowledge era and they must assume a key role in developing the IC of nations.

Regarding the FES model created and implemented for 3C Catene srl, a firm belonging to the Italian PIB network, the main findings of the paper could have implications for both the theoretical and empirical communities. Theoretically, the study contributes to broadening the research community's understanding regarding the alternative measurement of IC created within strategic alliances, and the results obtained for the selected firm may be regarded as valuable proof that IC performance within strategic alliances can be measured quantitatively. On the management side, the possibility of retracing the determinants of the different IC intermediate indicators composing the final IC index offered by this model allows managers to use this information for their decision-making purposes. In fact, the framework that enables the calculation of the IC index considers the manager's concept of IC, the elements that constitute and influence IC production and the IC value creation process itself. Moreover, the model proposed is intuitive and comprehensible, flexible (it can be changed by the evaluator), and usable to handle many quantitative and qualitative variables: as the system is modular, going from branches to trunk, it allows a high number of value drivers to be handled.

The main limitation of the research is related to the difficulty of quantifying the real contribution made by the selected firm to the network production of IC, this being possible only when the relevant data have been collected from the other firms in the network. Further empirical investigations are therefore planned to follow to all the other companies in the network, but the pilot model applied to the PIB Italian network is a good reference for other similar situations, as it is flexible enough for individual adaptations and adjustments. Once it is validated, it will be possible to apply the model, with a minimum of modifications, to other vertically integrated types of network.

NOTES

1. Scorecard methods evolved from pioneering IC measurement and management models (Edvinsson and Malone, 1997; Roos et al., 1997; Sveiby, 1997) to advanced ones (ARC, 2000; DATI, 2000; Meritum Report, 2002; DMSTI, 2003). The advanced models adopt the evolved notion of IC as a dynamic system of intangible resources based on knowledge. These models focus their attention on the interactions between the IC items, at the basis of the organisation's value creation, and on intangible activities which are essential in the production and development of intangible resources.
2. An example of 'if, then' implication is the following: *if* market forecasts are favourable *and* the quality of the products is very high *and* the intensity of rivalry is low, *then* prospective profits are high. In this example an FES has to specify to what degree the market forecasts are favourable, to what degree the quality of the products is very high, and to what degree the intensity of rivalry is low. If the system receives this information, the system will infer, using its inferential engine, that 'prospective profits are high' (Magni et al., 2006).

REFERENCES

Arena, M., M. Arnaboldi, G. Azzone and P. Carlucci (2009), 'Developing a performance measurement system for university central administrative services', *Higher Education Quarterly*, 63(3), 237–263.

Armstrong, D., A. Gosling, J. Weinman and T. Marteau (1997), 'The place of inter-rater reliability in qualitative research: an empirical study', *Sociology*, 31(3), 597–606.

Austrian Research Centers (ARC) (2000), *Wissensbilanz 1999 Seibersdorf*, accessed 14 May 2017 at http://www.arcs.ac.at.

Bagnoli, C. and H.C. Smith (1998), 'The theory of fuzzy logic and its application to real estate valuation', *Journal of Real Estate Research*, 12(2), 169–199.

Bertin, G. (2005), 'Tecniche basate sulle conoscenze degli esperti', in L. Bernardi (ed.), *Percorsi Di Ricerca Sociale*, Vol. 1, Rome: Carocci, pp. 216–236.

Bozbura, F.T., A. Beskese and C. Kaharaman (2007), 'Prioritization of human capital measurement indicators using fuzzy AHP', *Expert Systems with Applications*, 32(4), 1100–1112.

Chaminade, C. and H. Roberts (2003), 'What it means is what it does: a comparative analysis of implementing intellectual capital in Norway and Spain', *European Accounting Review*, 12(4), 733–751.

Chiucchi, M.S. (2004), *Sistemi di misurazione e di reporting del capitale intellettuale: criticità e prospettive*, Turin: Giappichelli.

Coakes, E. and A. Bradburn (2005), 'What is the value of intellectual capital?', *Knowledge Management Research and Practice*, 3(2), 60–68.

Danish Agency for Trade and Industry (DATI) (2000), *A Guideline For Intellectual Capital Statements – A Key To Knowledge Management*, accessed 9 December 2017 at http://efs.dk/download.pdf/viden.uk.pdf.

Danish Ministry of Technology and Innovation (DMSTI) (2003), *Intellectual Capital Statements. The New Guideline*, accessed 9 December 2017 at http://wwr.videnskapsministeriet.dk/fsk/publ/2003/guideline_uk/guideline_uk.pdf.

Duggan, E.W. and C.S. Thachenkary (2004), 'Integrating nominal group technique and joint application development for improved systems requirements determination', *Information and Management*, 41(4), 399–411.

Dunham, R. (2006), *Nominal Group Technique: A User's Guide*, Madison, WI: University of Wisconsin.

Edvinsson, L. and M.S. Malone (1997), *Intellectual Capital – Realising Your Company's True Value by Finding its Hidden Brainpower*, New York: Harper Business Publisher.

European Commission (2006), Ricardis (Reporting intellectual capital to augment research development and innovation in SMEs), *Report to the Commission from the High Level Expert Groups on Ricardis*, Directorate General of Research, Brussels: European Commission.

Gröjer, J. (2001), 'Intangibles and accounting classifications: in search of a classification strategy', *Accounting, Organizations and Society*, 26(7–8), 695–713.

Guthrie, J., F. Ricceri and J. Dumay (2012), 'Reflections and projections: a decade of intellectual capital accounting research', *British Accounting Review*, 44(2), 68–82.

Habersam, M. and M. Piber (2003), 'Exploring intellectual capital in hospitals: two qualitative case studies in Italy and Austria', *European Accounting Review*, 12(4), 753–779.

Helm-Stevens, R., K.C. Brown and J.K. Russel (2011), 'Introducing the intellectual capital interplay model: advancing knowledge frameworks in the not-for-profit environment of higher education', *International Education Studies*, 4(2), 126–140.

Kianto, A. (2007), 'What do we really mean by the dynamic dimension of intellectual capital?', *International Journal of Learning and Intellectual Capital*, 4(4), 342–356.

Kong, E. and D. Prior (2008), 'An intellectual capital perspective of competitive advantage in nonprofit organisations', *International Journal of Nonprofit Voluntary Sector Marketing*, 13(2), 119–128.

Krueger, R.A. and M.A. Casey (2009), *Focus Groups: A Practical Guide for Applied Research*, 4th edn, Thousand Oaks, CA: SAGE Publications.

Kujansivu, P. (2009), 'Is something wrong with intellectual capital management models?', *Knowledge Management Research and Practice*, 7(4), 300–307.

Leitner, K.-H., J. Prikoszovits, M. Schaffhauser-Linzatti, R. Stowasser and K. Wagner (2007), 'The impact of size and specialization on universities' department performance: a DEA analysis applied to Austrian universities', *Higher Education*, 53(4), 517–538.

Lönnqvist, A., V. Sillanpää and D. Carlucci (2009), 'Intellectual capital management in practice: assessment of implementation and outcomes', *Knowledge Management Research and Practice*, 7(4), 308–316.

Magni, C.A., S. Malagoli and G. Mastroleo (2006), 'An alternative approach to firm's evaluation: expert systems and fuzzy logic', *International Journal of Information Technology*, 5(1), 195–225.

Magni, C.A., G. Mastroleo and G. Facchinetti (2002), 'A fuzzy expert system for solving real option decision processes', *Fuzzy Economic Review*, 6(2), 51–73.

Malagoli, S., C.A. Magni, F. Buttignon and G. Mastroleo (2009), 'Rating and ranking firms with fuzzy expert systems: the case of Camuzzi', *IUP Journal of Applied Finance*, 15(10), 63–88.

Meritum Report (2002), *Guidelines for Managing and Reporting on Intangibles*, Fundación Aritel Móvil, Madrid: Meritum.

Mettänen, P. (2005), 'Design and implementation of a performance measurement system for a research organization', *Production Planning and Control*, 16(2), 178–188.

Mouritsen, J. (2006), 'Problematising intellectual capital research: ostensive versus performative IC accounting', *Auditing and Accountability Journal*, 19(6), 820–841.

Mouritsen, J. and R. Roslender (2009), 'Critical intellectual capital', *Critical Perspectives on Accounting*, 20(7), 801–803.

Mouritsen, J., S. Thorbjørnsen, P.N. Bukh and M.R. Johansen (2004), 'Intellectual capital and new public management: reintroducing enterprise', *Learning Organization*, 11(4–5), 380–392.

Neely, A.D., M.J. Gregory and K.W. Platts (1995), 'Performance measurement system design: a literature review and research agenda', *International Journal of Operations and Production Management*, 15(4), 80–116.
O'Donnell, D., P. O'Regan and B. Coates (2000), 'Intellectual capital: a Habermasian introduction', *Journal of Intellectual Capital*, 1(2), 187–200.
Roos, J., G. Roos, N.C. Dragonetti and L. Edvinsson (1997), *Intellectual Capital: Navigating in the New Business Landscape*, Basingstoke: Macmillan.
Schiuma, G. (2009), 'The managerial foundations of knowledge assets dynamics', *Knowledge Management Research and Practice*, 7(4), 290–299.
Serrano-Cinca, C., C. Marmoliero and F. Chaparro (2004), 'Spanish savings banks: a view on intangibles', *Knowledge Management Research and Practice*, 2(2), 103–117.
Sveiby, K.E. (1997), 'The Intangible Assets Monitor', *Journal of Human Resource Costing and Accounting*, 2(1), 73–97.
Sveiby, K.E. (2009), 'Methods for measuring intangible assets', accessed July 2017 at http://www.sveiby.com/articles/intangiblemethods.htm.
Universitaetsgesetz (UG) (2002), *University Organisation and Studies Act. University Organisation Amendment Act and Universities of the Arts Organisation Amendment Act*, No. 120/2002/9th August, (English Translation), Vienna: Federal Ministry of Education, Science and Culture.
Veltri, S., G. Mastroleo and M. Schaffhauser-Lizatti (2014), 'Measuring intellectual capital in the university sector using a fuzzy logic expert system', *Knowledge Management Research and Practice*, 12, 175–192.
Veltri, S., A. Venturelli and G. Mastroleo (2015), 'Measuring intellectual capital in a firm belonging to a strategic alliance', *Journal of Intellectual Capital*, 16(1), 174–198.
Wu, H., J. Chen and I. Chen (2010), 'Innovation capital indicator assessment of Taiwanese universities: a hybrid fuzzy model application', *Expert Systems with Applications*, 37(2), 1635–1642.
Zadeh, L.A. (1965), 'Fuzzy sets', *Information and Control*, 8(3), 338–353.
Zandi, F. and M. Tavana (2010), 'A hybrid fuzzy real option analysis and group ordinal approach for knowledge management strategy assessment', *Knowledge Management Research and Practice*, 8(3), 216–228.

18. Operationalising the resource-based view of the firm

Göran Roos

BACKGROUND

The resource-based view (RBV) of the firm, by putting the determinants of the firm's performance inside the firm, developed as an approach to complement the strategic views that placed the determinants of the firm's performance outside the firm, that is, the structure–conduct–performance (SCP) paradigm. This SCP paradigm originated with Mason (1939) and was exemplified by the industrial organisation view. The SCP paradigm is represented by the writings of, for example, Bain (1968) and Porter (1979, 1980, 1981, 1985, 1989, 1991, 1996, 2008).

Following a detailed analysis of the underlying philosophical and epistemological foundations of the RBV, as well as the fundamental assumptions employed by key scholars, Seoudi (2009) identified that the RBV is one of three distinct 'strategic views' of the firm; the other views being the dynamic capability view (exemplified by the writings of Nelson and Winter, 1982; Teece et al., 1997; Helfat and Peteraf, 2003) and the competence-based view (exemplified by Hamel and Heene, 1994; Sanchez and Heene, 1997). Although the focus of this chapter is on the practical aspects of using the RBV within a firm context, it has applicability to all three schools since their differences do not outweigh their similarities around the challenges of applying them in practice.

Rumelt (1984, p. 557) states that 'a firm's competitive position is defined by a bundle of unique resources and relationships and that the task of general management is to adjust and renew these resources and relationships as time, competition, and change erode their value'. The ability to execute this process of abandoning, acquiring, reallocating and integrating resources in a reactive or proactive way as the operating environment changes is implicit in Rumelt's statement, but is explicitly defined as the firm's dynamic capabilities by Eisenhardt and Martin (2000).

The RBV provided a major contribution to the strategy field by explaining persistent differences in firm profitability that could not be explained by differences in industry conditions (Peteraf, 1993). The focus of much research in the RBV field has been on identifying the attributes of heterogeneous resources. Barney (1991) stated that resources that can form the basis of a firm's competitive advantage must be strategically valuable, rare among existing or potential competitors, imperfectly imitable, and there must not exist strategically equivalent substitutes that are valuable but neither rare nor imperfectly substitutable. Peteraf (1993, p. 186) also argues that the requisite conditions for sustained rent-generation are 'heterogeneity', 'imperfect mobility', 'ex-ante limits to competition' and 'ex-post limits to competition'.[1] As several scholars have stated, heterogeneity can be derived from uncertainty and immobility (for example, Foss and Knudsen, 2003), path dependence, chance events, governmental largesse and unevenly distributed property rights (Nelson, 1991). The RBV does not aim to explain heterogeneity, but rather to proceed from the assumption of its existence to investigate the resource conditions underlying sustained competitive advantage (Peteraf and Barney, 2003). Empirical studies show that the more valuable and rarer a given firm's resource–capability combination, the more likely the firm will achieve a competitive advantage (Newbert, 2008).

Barney (1986) points out that once relevant resources have been acquired, they can be combined and recombined in a variety of ways to implement different strategies. From this, it follows that the way resources are combined will determine the success by which a strategy is implemented. In other words, a firm's competitive position fundamentally relates to both the uniqueness of a bundle of resources (Dierickx and Cool, 1989) and the value creating effectiveness of this bundle. High effectiveness in combining and deploying resources requires understanding of the cause and effect relations between deployment decisions and economic returns (Lippman and Rumelt, 1982). This view is echoed by Martín-de-Castro et al. (2006), who state that capabilities arise from the coordination of different resources, and hence are dynamic and more complex than resources. In Newbert's (2007) survey of empirical work relating to the RBV, individual resources were found to enhance firm performance in 37 per cent of the studies reviewed, whereas the ability to configure and reconfigure a resource deployment system enhanced performance in 71 per cent of the studies.

Barney (1986, p. 1238) poses the question: 'How can firms become consistently better informed about the value of strategies they are implementing than any other firms?' The answer provided by Barney is that in principle there are two different approaches. The first is to analyse the external environment in which the firm operates (the SCP paradigm). It is unlikely, however, that this will generate the insights needed for the firm to achieve supra-normal returns, since the tools and the information required, as well as the skills needed to put the tools to use for this type of analysis, are available in the public domain. Most firms pursuing this route will arrive at approximately the same conclusions. Thus Barney (1986, p. 1238) concludes: 'Analysing a firm's competitive environment cannot, on average, be expected to generate the expectational advantages that can lead to expected above normal returns in strategic factor markets'. The second approach is to analyse the resources that the firm has at its disposal. This information does not exist in the public domain. Therefore, possessing the skills or techniques to use tools for this purpose would provide the basis for supra-normal returns. At the time of Barney's (1986) writing, neither the tools nor the skills to use them existed.

To capture the practical value of the RBV, some form of tool to evaluate the ability of resources to form the basis for competitive advantage is needed, and for this purpose Barney and Griffin (1992) proposed the VRIO framework (that is, Valuable, Rare, Inimitable, Organised to capture value). This framework is qualitative in nature and encompasses the following questions: Is the firm able to exploit an opportunity or neutralise an external threat with the resource/capability? Is control of the resource/capability in the hands of a relative few? Is it difficult to imitate, and will there be significant cost disadvantages to a firm trying to obtain, develop or duplicate the resource/capability? Is the firm organised, ready and able to exploit the resource/capability? Is the firm organised to capture value? For each of the questions there is a possible yes or no answer, and only those resources for which the answer is yes can form the basis of a competitive advantage. If the answer is yes, then the competitive advantage can be sustained until the external market conditions change sufficiently.

Qualitative approaches that align with the one developed by Barney and Griffin have also been developed by Collis and Montgomery (1995) and Grant (2005). As there seem to be no further tools developed and these tools are all qualitative in nature, there is a need for a quantitative tool to analyse a larger palette of managerial action recommendations. This conclusion is supported by Warnier et al. (2013), who conclude that the tool development within the strategy field, as relates to the RBV, has not gone much further than qualitative reasoning and, even in these approaches, weaknesses are obvious. The lack of quantitative tools to support managerial use of the RBV was lamented by Dagnino (2012). Davidsson et al. (2009) also point out that the RBV lacks the ability to explicitly assess key variables, which is challenging because mere quantification of generic resource stocks does not suffice for adequate research testing of RBV-based hypotheses. A similar implied request for tools that would guide decisions is made by Bowman and Collier (2006, p. 192), who also call for such tools in their statement: 'the RBV literature currently lacks any meaningful or useful prescriptions that practitioners can use to move their firms forward'.

CRITIQUE OF THE RESOURCE-BASED VIEW

As a theory, the RBV looks at the firm through a static lens with the relevant resources being used to generate a given output rather than a dynamically unfolding complex multi-stage process (Kim and Mahoney, 2006). This means that the RBV is essentially reductionist, in contrast to holistic or emergent theories that view firms as analogous to biological organisms, which incorporate complex feedback mechanisms focused on maintaining the boundaries of the organisation (Kraaijenbrink et al., 2010).

Accepting that the focus of any strategy work using the RBV lens must also cover the dynamic aspects of firms' resource deployment, two issues arise: the first relates to the ways attributes of resources may and likely will change over time; and the second relates to the present and potentially future way in which these resources are deployed to generate the desired value. The first issue recognises that the value of a given resource has an objective component (for example, new technological developments making a given resource obsolete, thus removing it from the potential portfolio of resources that can form the basis of a competitive advantage). In addition, there is a subjective component, related to the perception of the value and value creating potential of a resource, the analysis of which requires an analysis of the resource–beholder–environment system[2] (Mahoney, 1995; Lewin and Phelan, 2002; Kor, 2003; Foss et al., 2005; Kor et al., 2007; Foss et al., 2008). Future deployment must consider an environment in constant disequilibrium, which requires continuous reconfiguration of the resource deployment system as conceived by the beholder in the resource–beholder–environment system (Mathews, 2010; Sirmon et al., 2011).

There has been much criticism of weaknesses in the RBV; some of this has been indirect or unintended, and some of it has been direct and intended (Sanchez, 2008; Lockett et al., 2009; El Shafeey and Trott, 2014). Kraaijenbrink et al. (2010, pp. 351–359) reviewed the critique of the RBV in an excellent paper. They summarised the critique under eight core themes and addressed each of them:

- (1) The RBV has no managerial implications. (2) The RBV implies infinite regress. (3) The RBV's applicability is too limited.

(4) Sustainable competitive advantage (SCA) is not achievable. (5) The RBV is not a theory of the firm. Kraaijenbrink et al. found that these first five critiques are incorrect, or irrelevant, or apply only when the RBV is taken to its logical or impractical extreme and, hence, can be ignored.

- (6) Valuable, rare, inimitable and non-substitutable resources and capabilities, plus having the organisation in place that can absorb and apply them, are neither necessary nor sufficient for SCA. Their reflection on this critique is that: the listed criteria are not always necessary and not always sufficient to explain a firm's SCA; the RBV does not sufficiently consider the synergy within resource bundles as a source of SCA; the RBV does not sufficiently recognise the role that judgement and mental models of individuals play in value assessment and creation. Hence, this is a serious critique and needs to be addressed to strengthen the RBV.
- (7) The value of a resource is too indeterminate to provide for useful theory. Regarding this critique, Kraaijenbrink et al. conclude that the current conceptualisation of value turns the RBV into a trivial heuristic, an incomplete theory or a tautology, and a more subjective and creative notion of value is needed to address this weakness of the RBV.
- (8) The definition of resource is unworkable. Kraaijenbrink et al. find that definitions of resources are all-inclusive and that the RBV does not recognise differences between resources as inputs and resources that enable the organisation of such inputs. They also find that there is no recognition of how different types of resources may contribute to SCA in different ways.

One of the key consequences of the weaknesses identified in the RBV is that management is unable to test or simulate a given resource deployment structure and get feedback on its potential effectiveness in value creation. The RBV and the associated strategy lenses need an associated toolbox that allows management to deploy tools in strategy-making processes. Hence, the existing qualitative tools need to be complemented with quantitative tools allowing, for example, for simulation of alternative resource deployment systems. Only when such tools are available will the practical use of the RBV reach that of the SCP strategy paradigm.

INTRODUCING THE TOOL FOR OPERATIONALISING THE RESOURCE-BASED VIEW OF THE FIRM

Creating the Resource Taxonomy

The development of a resource taxonomy must take its starting point in existing resource behaviours and characteristics. The intellectual capital view (ICV) of the firm, drawing on economics, accounting and strategy literature, has identified the different resource attributes in terms of: decreasing marginal return, increasing marginal return and network economic behaviour; additive and non-additive; rivalry and non-rivalry; known conversion rate to monetary value and unknown conversion rate to monetary; owned by the firm and not owned by the firm; high information asymmetry and low information asymmetry; full excludability exists, partial excludability exists and no excludability exists. Based on these attributes the smallest number of resource categories possible is five, and they are summarised in Figure 18.1.

Whether a resource is tangible or intangible reflects the debate about the accounting recognisability of the resource. Whereas the debate around whether a resource is a traditional economic resource (monetary or physical) or an intellectual capital (IC) resource (relational, organisational or human) represents a debate about the form, and ultimately the economic behaviour, of the resource. This is not a semantic distinction, since the argument that intangibles and IC resources are not the same thing is self-evident. There are plenty of IC resources that have a tangible expression. Likewise, there are plenty of traditional economic resources that have intangible expressions. Figure 18.2 separates resource type from the issue of accounting recognisability with some illustrative examples.

There are four criteria (extracted from measurement theory) for identifying a resource on each level of a hierarchy:

1. Each resource must be distinct, meaning that the definition of a resource must be clear and separate from the definitions of all other resources at that level.
2. Each resource level must be complete, meaning that there must be no relevant resources missing from a given level of the distinction tree.
3. Each resource must be independent from other resources, meaning that if one of the resources changes there must be no automatic and instantaneous change in any of the other resources on that level.

	Resource category				
	Monetary Resources	**Physical Resources**	**Relational Resources**	**Organisational Resources**	**Human Resources**
Description	Financial resources that take the form of cash assets (such as marketable securities) that can easily be converted to pure cash	Anything that can be touched, for example have a physical presence (that is what you would normally find under the heading of plant and equipment in the balance sheet)	The relationships held by individuals on behalf of the firm or that are embodied in the form of contracts with the firm as one party. The outcome of desires to hold explicit or implicit relationships with the firm by external parties	The result of human endeavours developed internally in the firm or acquired externally by the firm that is now owned by the firm and that are not physical or monetary in nature	All to the firm useful resources that are embodied in people
Owned and controlled by	Firm	Firm	No one owns, and the resource is co-controlled	Firm	Individual
Economic behaviour	Decreasing marginal return	Decreasing marginal return	Network economic behaviour	Network economic behaviour	Increasing marginal return
Known conversion rate to monetary value	Yes	No	No	No	No
Additive	Yes	Yes	No	No	No
Information asymmetry	Low	Low	High	High	High
Rivalry resource	Yes	Yes	No	No	No
Excludability	Yes	Yes	No	Partial	No
Value appropriation mechanisms	Finance structure and cost of capital	IP Firm specific assets	First mover advantage Network size Reputation Bargaining power Customer retention	Causal ambiguity Contracts Agreement stability Imperfect mobility Brand	Shared Values/ Goals Innovativeness Absorptive capacity
Drives towards a strategic logic (in the meaning of Stabell & Fjelstad, 1998) of:	Value chain	Value chain	Value network Although can drive towards a value shop logic in the very early stages of the resource lifecycle and towards value chain in the very late stages of the resource lifecycle	Value network Although can drive towards a value shop logic in the very early stages of the resource lifecycle and towards value chain in the very late stages of the resource lifecycle	Value shop

Source: After Roos et al. (2005).

Figure 18.1 Resource characteristics

		Intellectual capital resource type				
		Monetary Resources	**Physical Resources**	**Relational Resources**	**Organisational Resources**	**Human Resources**
Accounting recognisability	**Tangible**	Cash	Building	Repeat Order	Employee Contract	Physical presence
	Intangible	Borrowing capacity	Building location	Preferred supplier status	Organisational culture	Problem-solving ability

Source: After Roos et al. (2005).

Figure 18.2 Separation of resource type from accounting recognisability (with examples)

4. Finally, the resource portfolio on the detailed level to which the resource types are broken down must be agreeable, meaning that it must be broken down to a level that is suitable for the purpose for which it is intended.

If these requirements are adhered to, the resulting resource portfolio will, in a structured and easily accessible way, show all resources, broken down to a suitable level of granularity, which the organisation can access for value creating purposes.

MAPPING THE RESOURCE DEPLOYMENT SYSTEM

As discussed in the literature around the RBV, the dynamic capability view, the core competence-based view and the knowledge-based view, it is necessary to have a dynamic perspective on resources since it is the interaction of resources within the resource portfolio of the firm that creates the value that the firm can deliver, and in addition, interacting bundles of resources can form the basis for a temporary competitive advantage.[3] This means that there needs to be a clear distinction between identifying what resources are present in the resource portfolio (the static view) and the way they are 'put to use'; the latter is labelled the resource deployment system of the firm (the dynamic view).

There is no automatic correlation or causality between the amount of a given resource that the organisation has at its disposal and the value that the organisation can create, since the provision of more resources does not automatically result in the production of more value. Instead, the value that the organisation manages to produce is a function of how it puts its resources to use – the configuration of the resource deployment system – and how well it manages the transformation from one type of resources into another. Consequently, mapping this resource deployment system is critical for any analysis of the firm's value creation using the RBV (and other inside-out views of the firm) and for the ability to point out potential improvements in effectiveness.

In summary, a given organisation is made up of a unique resource portfolio deployed in a unique transformation structure; no two organisations are the same. All resources in an organisation are directly or indirectly interconnected in some way or other, and value is created through the sequential transformation of one resource into another.

There are several problems to be overcome in identifying and mapping resources and the way they are deployed to create value:

- Problem 1: Not all resources are additive (for example, customer relationships), so just because more of something real (for example, money, time, and so on) is invested into a resource that does not necessarily result in more of that resource.
- Problem 2: Transformations take different forms: some are physical flows, some are monetary flows, some are knowledge transfer, some are reputation or trust transformations. Most transformations are made up of several of these different types of sub-transformations and, for practical purposes, become difficult if not impossible to identify and map.

Hence, an analytical model that represents what actually happens will be far too difficult and complicated, not to say impractical, to reach a meaningful insight with a reasonable amount of work. To overcome this, a concept from system dynamics – influence space – can be used. To describe a system, two things need to be known: first, what happens; and, second, which of the things that happen matter for the outcome or behaviour of the system.

Making the (not unreasonable) assumption that the system can be approximated as a linear dynamic system means that a rich set of mathematical properties can be applied to produce exact solutions. This contrasts with nonlinear dynamic systems, which as a rule do not have closed-form solutions, meaning that they do not have a mathematical expression that can be evaluated in a finite number of operations.[4]

Moving to influence space means looking at to what extent a given resource and a given transformation influence the overall system. Taking this approach provides the added benefit that influences can be treated as additive. This suggests problem 1 can be overcome. If the generic term 'effort' is introduced to encompass all the different forms that influence can take, it is possible to produce a concept that will take care of problem 2.

At this point the objection that 'this discussion is about principle not reality' may be raised. This is normally not a problem since a beneficial behavioural effect comes into play: Asking someone to describe a complex system results in them not describing the actual system in some objective sense, instead they will describe the system as they perceive it.[5] If someone that controls the firm's resource deployment system (for example the chief executive officer, CEO) is asked to describe the desired future and present position of the firm, it does not matter if the resulting description of the present position of the firm is a 'true' representation of the firm in some objective sense. This person will act as if it is, and will therefore drive the firm from wherever it is to what is described as the desired position. The conclusion is that a methodologically sound approach to capturing the principle or perceived reality of something is as good as (or even better than) trying to catch the actual reality of something; and, in addition, this is a much easier task.

The tool created through this approach is named the Intellectual Capital Navigator (IC Navigator). The IC Navigator is used to identify and map, for further evaluation, the organisation's unique transformations structure, that is, its resource deployment system.

The IC Navigator generates a numeric representation of how management views the way in which resources are deployed to create value in the organisation. The process of creating the IC Navigator also captures and categorises the resources in the firm's resource portfolio, management's view of their relative importance, the way management views their existing resource deployment system, and the relative influence of the transformations in this system.

The core of the IC Navigator lies in identifying transformations from one resource to another. This requires a detailed step-by-step understanding of what is taking place in an organisation, and is different to the more overarching thinking (where steps are taken for granted, ignored or overlooked) that is normal when organisational value creation is discussed. It is important to note that from an IC Navigator viewpoint all transformations are possible; it is just that in a specific organisation they are not all relevant. Figure 18.3 provides a non-exhaustive example of transformations as an illustration of this.

By mapping how resources influence each other, the IC Navigator provides an overall map of the logic used by management when it comes to resource deployment in a specific organisation. The IC Navigator must not be confused with different types of models that try to map the real flow of things in the organisation. These 'real flow' models are insufficient to capture what goes on in organisations. They can only capture transformations of a physical, monetary or informational nature. This

		Transformation into				
		Monetary	**Physical**	**Relational**	**Organisational**	**Human**
Transformation from	**Monetary**	Investment in financial instruments	Investment in physical assets	Investment in building relationships	Investment in brands, systems, information, etc.	Investment in recruitment, training, etc.
	Physical	Sales of products	Chemical synthesis	Design and/or Chemical effect	New processes	New knowledge
	Relational	Relationship arbitrage	Use of others' assets	Word of mouth	Access to process	Co-learning
	Organisational	Sale of IP, process, software, system, information, etc.	Process-driven production	Customer relationship management system	Automated process development or data-to-information transformation	Automated training
	Human	Sale of competence or knowledge (normally in the form of man-hours)	Prototype development or output of artistic or design endeavours	Building or developing relationships	Codification of knowledge	Apprenticeship

Source: After Roos et al. (2005).

Figure 18.3 Examples of transformations from the resource category named in the row headings to the resource category named in the column headings

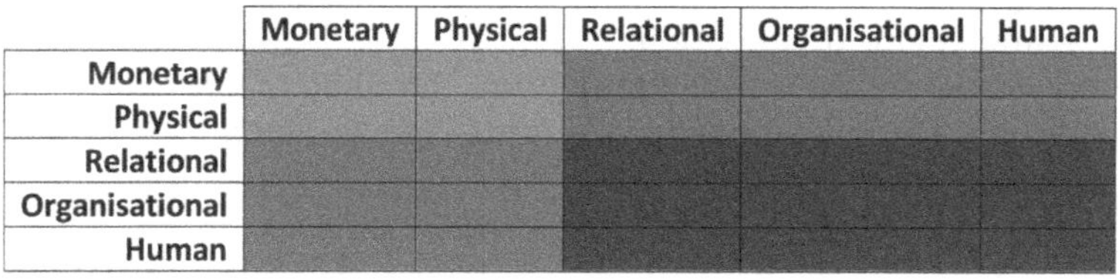

Figure 18.4 Capture possibilities for models aiming to capture real transformations

means that, due to the multidimensional nature of transformations, as well as the non-additiveness of transformations, not all transformations can be captured. Figure 18.4 shows the level of capture possible if the aim is to capture real transformations. These models can only capture the transformations in the upper left, light grey area in Figure 18.4; they are able to capture either the input or the output, but not both in the upper right and lower left medium grey area; and they are not able to capture anything in the lower right black. This is due to the multidimensional nature of the transformations as well as the non-additiveness of the transformations that include IC resources.

The IC Navigator both operates on a higher level of abstraction than these real transformation models and is more useful (see below) since it provides a total picture of all transformations and resources that contribute to the organisation's value creation.

The IC Navigator provides a useful bridge between strategy crafting and strategy implementation by assisting both strategic thinking and strategic analysis. In a recent study (Roos, 2013), it was ranked by firm managers as the third most valuable approach among 14 approaches to understand important dimensions of a firm's business model.

USING THE TOOL FOR OPERATIONALISING THE RESOURCE-BASED VIEW OF THE FIRM

The process used to create an IC Navigator is a consensus process aimed at capturing the tacit knowledge in the management team as it relates to how value is perceived to be created in the organisation. The necessary steps in this process are:

1. Identification of the firm's resources and the classification of these into the different categories.
2. Weighting of the resources according to their ability to influence value creation in the organisation.
3. Evaluation of the identified resources according to their suitability to form the basis for competitive advantage and evaluation of the quality and quantity of each resource.

The first major process step, using the distinction tree's most detailed level of classification (for example, level 3 or more detailed levels), is to create a resource matrix where the level 3 resources appear along the two axes and are grouped in the five level 2 resource categories. This step is illustrated in Figure 18.5 with an example of a resulting matrix.

This is a very structured way of looking at resources by category, and is an improvement on the more general way in which resources have been treated in the RBV (and other inside-out views of the firm).

The requirement to identify, label and categorise resources under the four constraints described above can be challenging for managers the first time, and is best done in a facilitated discussion process. The knowledge to do this does reside within the combined heads of the senior management team, but it may not previously have been expressed in this way.

The creation of the matrix is the fundamental starting point for the IC Navigator process, and this matrix is the tool for capturing the combined

Resource Weight		Resource Weight	From / To	Cash	Bonds & Stocks	Guarantees	Facilities	Equipment	Products	Customers	Suppliers	Partners	Knowledge Providers	Capital Providers	IT Systems	Brand	Organisational Culture	Accumulated Data & Information	Processes	Knowledge	Problem-Solving Ability	Interpersonal Skills	Attitude	Creativity
5%	Monetary	3%	Cash																					
		1%	Bonds & Stocks																					
		1%	Guarantees																					
15%	Physical	2%	Facilities																					
		3%	Equipment																					
		10%	Products																					
20%	Relational	10%	Customers																					
		2%	Suppliers																					
		6%	Partners																					
		1%	Knowledge Providers																					
		1%	Capital Providers																					
40%	Organisational	4%	IT Systems																					
		4%	Brand																					
		4%	Organisational Culture																					
		8%	Accumulated Data & Information																					
		20%	Processes																					
20%	Human	5%	Knowledge																					
		4%	Problem-Solving Ability																					
		4%	Interpersonal Skills																					
		4%	Attitude																					
		3%	Creativity																					

Figure 18.5 The resulting resource matrix template from the distinction tree above

management team's understanding of the resources the firm has at its disposal, the relative importance of these resources to the firm, the way these resources are put to use and the relative influence that each of the resource uses has on the firm's ability to create value. Hence, care must be taken to ensure that the resource portfolio that forms the starting point for the matrix is perceived to reflect well management's perception of reality.

The next step is to weight the resource transformations on each row by distributing 100 points across all the possible transformations in that row. This fixed-sum allocation approach is aimed at capturing latent utility (Carson et al., 1994). The alternative approaches[6] to achieve the same objective have not worked equally well when tried in executive MBA settings.

This fixed-sum allocation is done by asking the question: 'How relatively influential is this transformation when it comes to contributing to the organisation's value creation?' It is not about how large the transformation is, it is about how much it matters. This is a very important distinction, since small transformations may matter a lot (for example, the creation of a new mental concept in a development team based on a discussion with a customer), whereas large transformations may not matter a great deal (for example, paying rent for a large service organisation in a city centre location).

The result of this step is a matrix where every row adds up to 100 and where each transformation that has been assigned a weight greater than zero is defined. This answers the question: 'What do we mean by this transformation?' An example of the resulting transformation matrix is shown in Figure 18.6.

At this stage of the process, the matrix can only be read and interpreted row by row since the different rows operate on different scales (see below) and, hence, cannot be compared.

It is important to point out here, in terms of sensemaking and the subjectivity of the process, that the aim is not to identify some objective truth but instead to capture management's perception of their reality. One of the benefits at this point in the process is that it provides opportunities for reflection within the management team on the level of agreement around the firm's perceived value creating pathway.

The next step in the process is to convert the IC Navigator from a row-based description of the transformations to a total picture. This requires that all the transformations in the matrix must add up to 100. This is possible since the influence matrix is additive, whereas a matrix that tries to capture real flows would not be additive and therefore this step is impossible in such a matrix. This step is done by weighting the numbers on a given row by the weighting of the resource that is the starting point of the transformations. Figure 18.7 shows this converted (or normalised) transformation matrix based on the transformation matrix shown in Figure 18.6.

Insights that follow from a simple look at what has been provided by management (since the matrix reflects – albeit in a different way – what management have put into it) can sometimes provide surprises, as illustrated in a statement by the Apion CEO in Peppard and Rylander (2001, p. 521): 'When [we began this process] we said that people are our most important resource. But as we went through the analyses process we saw something quite different that caused us to think quite differently about what to do in order to create shareholder value'.

Given the statement above that all the numbers, given that they depict influence, are additive, it is now possible to construct the transformation matrix on any of the more aggregate levels in the resource distinction tree by summing up the transformation in the respective groups. For the matrix in Figure 18.7, this adds up to the outcome shown in the matrix in Figure 18.8.

Resource Weight		Resource Weight	From \ To	Cash	Bonds & Stocks	Guarantees	Facilities	Equipment	Products	Customers	Suppliers	Partners	Knowledge Providers	Capital Providers	IT Systems	Brand	Organisational Culture	Accumulated Data & Information	Processes	Knowledge	Problem-Solving Ability	Interpersonal Skills	Attitude	Creativity	Total
5%	Monetary	3%	Cash	0	1	0	4	8	8	9	6	6	6	2	13	11	2	6	11	3	1	1	1	1	100
		1%	Bonds & Stocks	100	0	0	0	0	0	0	0	0	0	0	0	0	0	0	0	0	0	0	0	0	100
		1%	Guarantees	50	0	0	14	14	22	0	0	0	0	0	0	0	0	0	0	0	0	0	0	0	100
15%	Physical	2%	Facilities	0	0	0	0	7	12	14	15	15	12	0	0	0	0	0	25	0	0	0	0	0	100
		3%	Equipment	3	0	0	4.8	4.8	39	0	3	0	0	0	5.2	0	0	5.2	31	4	0	0	0	0	100
		10%	Products	46	0	0	0	5	0	6	6	6	6	1	0	10	0	3	5	4	2	0	0	0	100
20%	Relational	10%	Customers	7	0	0	0	1	7	22	6	6	6	3	3	3	3	6	3	11	5	0	3	5	100
		2%	Suppliers	12	0	8	1	1	11	3	3	3	3	1	3	3	3	6	6	12	6	6	6	3	100
		6%	Partners	0	0	0	0	1	5	2	2	2	2	0	6	12	3	23	12	10	5	5	5	5	100
		1%	Knowledge Providers	3	0	0	0	1	2	2	2	2	2	0	2	2	2	27	11	24	4	4	4	6	100
		1%	Capital Providers	89	0	0	5	0	0	0	0	0	0	6	0	0	0	0	0	0	0	0	0	0	100
40%	Organisational	4%	IT Systems	4	0	0	0	0	2	1	1	1	1	1	6	0	0	50	31	2	0	0	0	0	100
		4%	Brand	48	0	0	0	0	15	25	3	3	3	3	0	0	0	0	0	0	0	0	0	0	100
		4%	Organisational Culture	19	0	0	8	8	4	7	7	7	7	7	0	12	2	0	3	0	0	0	9	0	100
		8%	Accumulated Data & Information	10	0	0	2	8	16	7	8	4	4	4	2	2	0	2	23	4	4	0	0	0	100
		20%	Processes	19	0	0	4	8	16	3	3	3	3	3	6	6	3	3	12	3	3	0	1	1	100
20%	Human	5%	Knowledge	0	0	0	1	5	10	3	3	3	3	1	6	4	3	11	11	13	13	0	5	5	100
		4%	Problem-Solving Ability	22	0	0	1	18	2	0	0	0	0	0	1	1	1	9	20	2	21	0	0	2	100
		4%	Interpersonal Skills	3	0	0	0	0	0	4	3	3	3	1	0	12	11	0	0	12	12	12	12	12	100
		4%	Attitude	0	0	0	0	0	0	4	4	4	4	0	0	17	0	0	0	14	14	13	13	13	100
		3%	Creativity	0	0	0	5	20	24	2	2	2	3	0	0	6	2	7	7	5	5	0	5	5	100
100%		100%																							

Figure 18.6 The resulting resource matrix containing the row-wise weighted transformations

Resource Weight		Resource Weight	From \ To	Cash	Bonds & Stocks	Guarantees	Facilities	Equipment	Products	Customers	Suppliers	Partners	Knowledge Providers	Capital Providers	IT Systems	Brand	Organisational Culture	Accumulated Data & Information	Processes	Knowledge	Problem-Solving Ability	Interpersonal Skills	Attitude	Creativity	Total
5%	Monetary	3%	Cash	0.0	0.0	0.0	0.1	0.2	0.2	0.3	0.2	0.2	0.2	0.1	0.4	0.3	0.1	0.2	0.3	0.1	0.0	0.0	0.0	0.0	3
		1%	Bonds & Stocks	1.0	0.0	0.0	0.0	0.0	0.0	0.0	0.0	0.0	0.0	0.0	0.0	0.0	0.0	0.0	0.0	0.0	0.0	0.0	0.0	0.0	1
		1%	Guarantees	0.5	0.0	0.0	0.1	0.1	0.2	0.0	0.0	0.0	0.0	0.0	0.0	0.0	0.0	0.0	0.0	0.0	0.0	0.0	0.0	0.0	1
15%	Physical	2%	Facilities	0.0	0.0	0.0	0.0	0.1	0.2	0.3	0.3	0.3	0.2	0.0	0.0	0.0	0.0	0.0	0.5	0.0	0.0	0.0	0.0	0.0	2
		3%	Equipment	0.1	0.0	0.0	0.1	0.1	1.2	0.0	0.1	0.0	0.0	0.0	0.2	0.0	0.0	0.2	0.9	0.1	0.0	0.0	0.0	0.0	3
		10%	Products	4.6	0.0	0.0	0.0	0.5	0.0	0.6	0.6	0.6	0.6	0.1	0.0	1.0	0.0	0.3	0.5	0.4	0.2	0.0	0.0	0.0	10
20%	Relational	10%	Customers	0.7	0.0	0.0	0.0	0.1	0.7	2.2	0.6	0.6	0.6	0.3	0.3	0.3	0.3	0.6	0.3	1.1	0.5	0.0	0.3	0.5	10
		2%	Suppliers	0.2	0.0	0.2	0.0	0.0	0.2	0.1	0.1	0.1	0.1	0.0	0.1	0.1	0.1	0.1	0.1	0.2	0.1	0.1	0.1	0.1	2
		6%	Partners	0.0	0.0	0.0	0.0	0.1	0.3	0.1	0.1	0.1	0.1	0.0	0.4	0.7	0.2	1.4	0.7	0.6	0.3	0.3	0.3	0.3	6
		1%	Knowledge Providers	0.0	0.0	0.0	0.0	0.0	0.0	0.0	0.0	0.0	0.0	0.0	0.0	0.0	0.0	0.3	0.1	0.2	0.0	0.0	0.0	0.1	1
		1%	Capital Providers	0.9	0.0	0.0	0.1	0.0	0.0	0.0	0.0	0.0	0.0	0.1	0.0	0.0	0.0	0.0	0.0	0.0	0.0	0.0	0.0	0.0	1
40%	Organisational	4%	IT Systems	0.2	0.0	0.0	0.0	0.0	0.1	0.0	0.0	0.0	0.0	0.0	0.2	0.0	0.0	2.0	1.2	0.1	0.0	0.0	0.0	0.0	4
		4%	Brand	1.9	0.0	0.0	0.0	0.0	0.6	1.0	0.1	0.1	0.1	0.1	0.0	0.0	0.0	0.0	0.0	0.0	0.0	0.0	0.0	0.0	4
		4%	Organisational Culture	0.8	0.0	0.0	0.3	0.3	0.2	0.3	0.3	0.3	0.3	0.3	0.0	0.5	0.1	0.0	0.1	0.0	0.0	0.0	0.4	0.0	4
		8%	Accumulated Data & Information	0.8	0.0	0.0	0.2	0.6	1.3	0.6	0.6	0.3	0.3	0.3	0.2	0.2	0.0	0.2	1.8	0.3	0.3	0.0	0.0	0.0	8
		20%	Processes	3.8	0.0	0.0	0.8	1.6	3.2	0.6	0.6	0.6	0.6	0.6	1.2	1.2	0.6	0.6	2.4	0.6	0.6	0.0	0.2	0.2	20
20%	Human	5%	Knowledge	0.0	0.0	0.0	0.1	0.3	0.5	0.2	0.2	0.2	0.2	0.1	0.3	0.2	0.2	0.6	0.6	0.7	0.7	0.0	0.3	0.3	5
		4%	Problem-Solving Ability	0.9	0.0	0.0	0.0	0.7	0.1	0.0	0.0	0.0	0.0	0.0	0.0	0.0	0.0	0.4	0.8	0.1	0.8	0.0	0.0	0.1	4
		4%	Interpersonal Skills	0.1	0.0	0.0	0.0	0.0	0.0	0.2	0.1	0.1	0.1	0.0	0.0	0.5	0.4	0.0	0.0	0.5	0.5	0.5	0.5	0.5	4
		4%	Attitude	0.0	0.0	0.0	0.0	0.0	0.0	0.2	0.2	0.2	0.2	0.0	0.0	0.7	0.0	0.0	0.0	0.6	0.6	0.5	0.5	0.5	4
		3%	Creativity	0.0	0.0	0.0	0.2	0.6	0.7	0.1	0.1	0.1	0.1	0.0	0.0	0.2	0.1	0.2	0.2	0.2	0.2	0.0	0.2	0.2	3
100%		100%																							100

Figure 18.7 The resulting normalised transformation matrix starting with the transformation matrix outlined in Figure 18.6

	Monetary	Physical	Relational	Organisational	Human	*Row Sum:*
Monetary	1.5	1.1	0.9	1.3	0.2	5.0
Physical	4.7	2.3	3.7	3.5	0.7	15.0
Relational	2.0	1.5	5.2	6.0	5.3	20.0
Organisational	7.4	9.2	8.2	12.5	2.7	40.0
Human	1.0	3.1	2.1	5.3	8.5	20.0
Column Sum:	16.7	17.2	20.1	28.6	17.4	

Figure 18.8 *The level 3 transformation matrix shown in Figure 18.7 consolidated to a level 2 transformation matrix*

The row sum in the rightmost column equals, by definition, the weighting of the resources, so Figure 18.8 excludes the weighting column on the left to show the result more clearly. What has been created is the numerical representation of the IC Navigator, and it is possible to use this to evaluate the effectiveness of the resource deployment structure. As an example, the matrix in Figure 18.8 fully describes the system and its response to any given set of inputs. Hence, the resources and resource transformations captured are the state variables[7] and the system matrix[8] of this system.

The behaviour of the resources that underpin the firm's value creating activities will determine the behaviour of the firm. These behaviours are generally called strategic logics and are summarised in Figure 18.9.

	Type of Strategic Logic (Value chain named by Porter (1985) and Value Shops and Value Networks named by Stabell & Fjelstad, 1998)		
Attribute	**Value Chain**	**Value Shop**	**Value Network**
Original designation by Thompson (1967)	Long-linked technology	Intensive problem-solving technology	Mediating and facilitating technology
Business problem	Transforming inputs to outputs	Mobilising resources and structure activities to solve unique customer problems	Linking willing participants across time and space to enable direct and indirect exchanges
Business Focus	Product or Service	Solutions to problems (enabling shift from one state to a more desirable state)	Connections
Competitive Focus	Scale, Capacity utilisation	Scope, Personnel utilisation	Coverage, Network utilisation
Value creation process is	Sequential	Cyclical and iterative	Simultaneous and parallel
Value creation Logic	Understood by disaggregating the value creation process of the firm into discrete activities that contribute to the firm's relative cost position and create a basis for differentiation. Disaggregation must be complete in the sense that it captures all the activities performed by the firm.	Understood by recognizing that the flow of activities is not linear but iterative between activities and cyclical across the activity set resulting in a high degree of both sequential and reciprocal interdependence between activities often involving multiple disciplines and specialties in spiralling activity sets (where each cycle implements the solution to the problem that follows from the solution implemented in the previous cycle).	Understood by recognizing that a concurrent and layered set of activities is required to service efficiently a random need for mediation services between many customers.
Inherent organisational focus	Efficiency	Effectiveness	Neither Efficiency nor Effectiveness
Underpinned by resource categories	Monetary Physical Organisational (in the last phase of the resource life cycle) Relational (in the last phase of the resource life cycle)	Human Organisational (in the first phase of the resource life cycle) Relational (in the first phase of the resource life cycle)	Organisational (in intermediate phases – almost all – of the resource life cycle) Relational (in intermediate phases – almost all – of the resource life cycle)

Source: Extracted from Roos et al. (2005, Table 1.2, pp. 23–26).

Figure 18.9 *Brief overview of the three strategic logics*

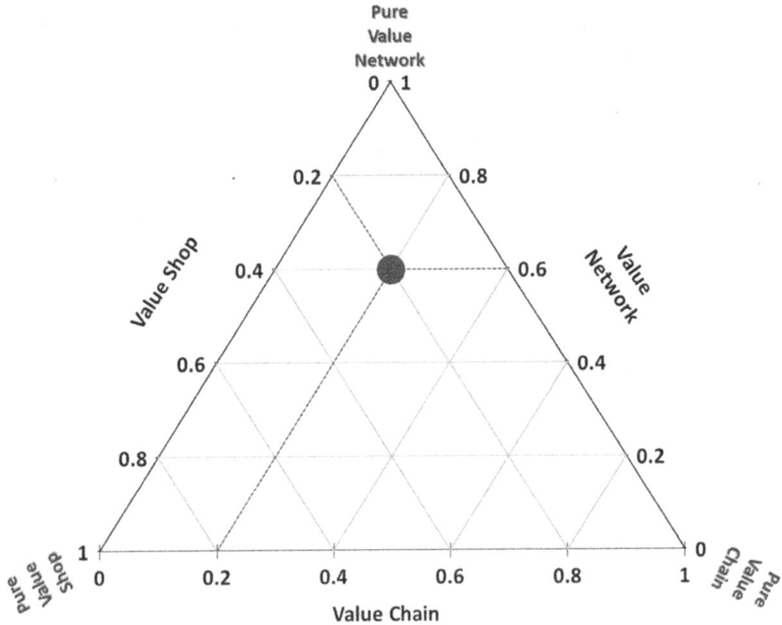

Figure 18.10 *The strategic logic centre of gravity for the transformation matrix in Figure 18.8*

Using a ternary plot (Figure 18.10) the balance between the value chain, value shop and value network logic for this organisation can be shown (drawing on the data in Figure 18.8).

Looking at Figure 18.10, it is possible to infer that this firm is predominantly operating as a value network (60 per cent weighting), but with aspects of value shop (20 per cent weighting) and value chain (20 per cent weighting). One consequence of this mix (drawing on Figure 18.9) is that unless management put a high emphasis on it, the organisation will struggle to achieve and maintain both efficiency and effectiveness.

To address this, it is necessary to capture how the value created by the organisation is embodied. For an organisation that is listed on the stock exchange, the primary stakeholders are the shareholders, albeit their relative importance has declined with the ascendants of other stakeholders. In many markets this means that the shareholder primacy paradigm is being challenged. In markets, or for contexts where the shareholder primacy paradigm is valid, these shareholders are typically looking for total shareholder returns, which are driven by both the free cash flow that the organisation is generating and the growth in this free cash flow.

In such a case, the value created by the organisation is embodied in monetary resources.

For other organisations or contexts, the answer is not so straightforward. To be able to articulate how the organisation embodies the value it delivers to different stakeholders, managers need to understand how value is perceived by stakeholders from an operational and strategic point of view.

PROCESSING AND ANALYSING THE INFORMATION COLLECTED AND PROVIDED BY THE TOOL FOR OPERATIONALISING THE RESOURCE-BASED VIEW OF THE FIRM

The first step in the analysis is to identify which resources are value sinks – those that absorb more effort[9] than they generate; and which resources are value sources – those that generate more effort than they absorb. This aids in assessing how the different resources contribute to the overall value creation path of the organisation. In a well-run organisation, all the influential intermediary resources are value sources; the firm gets more out of them than it puts into them.

This value sink and value source information, as relates to a given resource, is captured in the effector ratio and the effector plot. The effector plot captures the importance or influence of the individual resource on the axis of abscissas (x-axis) and the effector ratio on the axis of ordinates (or y-axis).

The effector ratio of a resource is the sum total of all transformation flows originating in the resource divided by the sum total of all transformation flows terminating in the resource in the normalised transformation matrix. The normalised transformation matrix must be used to benefit from the additiveness of the transformation flows on the same scale (before normalisation, each row in the transformation matrix operates on its own scale and all rows do not operate on the same scale). Following Western conventions the human mind tends to perceive right and up as good positions (directions) and down and left as bad positions (directions) and, hence, using the axis of abscissas for importance and influence would position the most important or most influential resource towards the right, which is helpful for intuitive interpretation (Tversky, 2014). As relates to the effector ratio, there is a conflict between the human mind's preference for linearity and the mathematical challenge being posed, as the effector ratio also contains the resource importance or influence as one of its constituent variables, which means that the axis of ordinates is not independent from the axis of abscissas.

If resources transform to other resources (including to themselves) in proportion to the intrinsic importance of the receiving resource, then the gradient of a line fit is zero. Similarly, if a resource transforms only to itself then the gradient of a line fit is zero. Since at any level in the resource portfolio above the finest level of distinctions possible to create (where all resources would be expressed on a level not possible to subdivide into other resources; a utopian situation not possible to achieve in practice since there will always be transformations from a resource to itself), there will always be the problem that the gradient of a line fit will be partly dependent on the self-transformation proportion. While other transformations may and usually do overwhelm this, for the less important resources it does not give clear guidance on what the appropriate gradient should be for an organisation, especially since the gradient is very sensitive to changes in the perceived influence of resources.

The convention adopted is that the base ten logarithm ($\log_{10}$) of the effector ratio is plotted on the axis of ordinates. The justification for choosing the base ten logarithm transformation is that since the resource importance apportionment uses a fixed-sum (100) approach, an increase in the importance of one resource is matched by an equal reduction in the importance of the others. Thus, the scale is $\frac{y}{(1-y)}$ in its simplest form and this is non linear as y increases. Indeed, in the useful working range wherein the most important resource could be 20 times as important as the least, the scale is nonlinear to the extent shown by the black line in Figure 18.11.

This nonlinearity can be compensated for by using the logarithm (base 10) of the ratio (grey line in Figure 18.11) as it conforms reasonably well to a perfect linear relationship (within the useful working range). Hence, the choice of the base ten logarithmic transformation of the effector ratio numbers before plotting.

As stated above, the effector ratio is calculated by taking the row sum for the resource in question divided by the column sum for the resource in question. This is shown in Figure 18.12, with the resulting effector ratios shown in Figure 18.13.

The resulting logarithmic effector plot is shown in Figure 18.14, with the values marked in the label linked to the information in Figure 18.13.

In this plot, the more influential a resource is, the further to the right it appears. Also, in this plot value sinks have a y-axis value below 0.0, and value sources have a y-axis value above 0.0, so they appear below and above the x-axis, respectively. In Figure 18.14, monetary resources are a clear value sink; which they should be, since

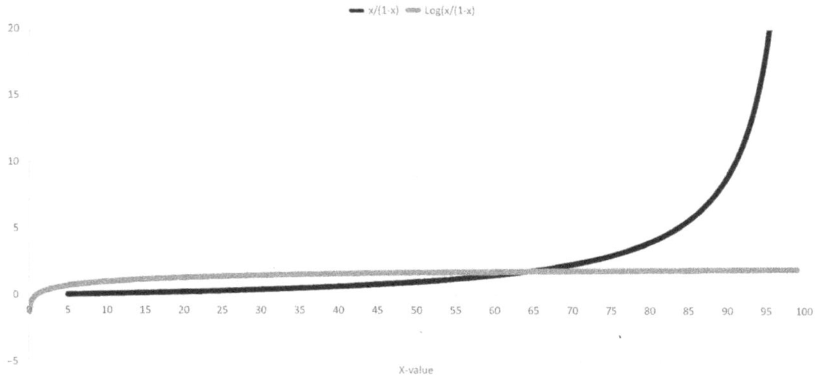

Figure 18.11 *Behavioural issues relating to the non linearity of the effector plot*

	5.0/16.6	15.0/17.2	20.0/20.1	40.0/28.6	20.0/17.4	
	Monetary	**Physical**	**Relational**	**Organisational**	**Human**	Row Sum
Monetary	1.5	1.1	0.9	1.3	0.2	**5.0**
Physical	4.7	2.3	3.7	3.5	0.7	**15.0**
Relational	2.0	1.5	5.2	6.0	5.3	**20.0**
Organisational	7.4	9.2	8.2	12.5	2.7	**40.0**
Human	1.0	3.1	2.1	5.3	8.5	**20.0**
Column Sum	**16.6**	**17.2**	**20.1**	**28.6**	**17.4**	**100.0**

Figure 18.12 *The principal calculation of effector ratios based on the resource transformation matrix in Figure 18.8*

	0.30	*0.87*	*0.99*	*1.40*	*1.15*	
	Monetary	**Physical**	**Relational**	**Organisational**	**Human**	Row Sum
Monetary	1.5	1.1	0.9	1.3	0.2	**5.0**
Physical	4.7	2.3	3.7	3.5	0.7	**15.0**
Relational	2.0	1.5	5.2	6.0	5.3	**20.0**
Organisational	7.4	9.2	8.2	12.5	2.7	**40.0**
Human	1.0	3.1	2.1	5.3	8.5	**20.0**
Column Sum	**16.6**	**17.2**	**20.1**	**28.6**	**17.4**	**100.0**

Figure 18.13 *The resulting effector ratios based on the resource transformation matrix in Figure 18.8 using the principal calculation outlined in Figure 18.12*

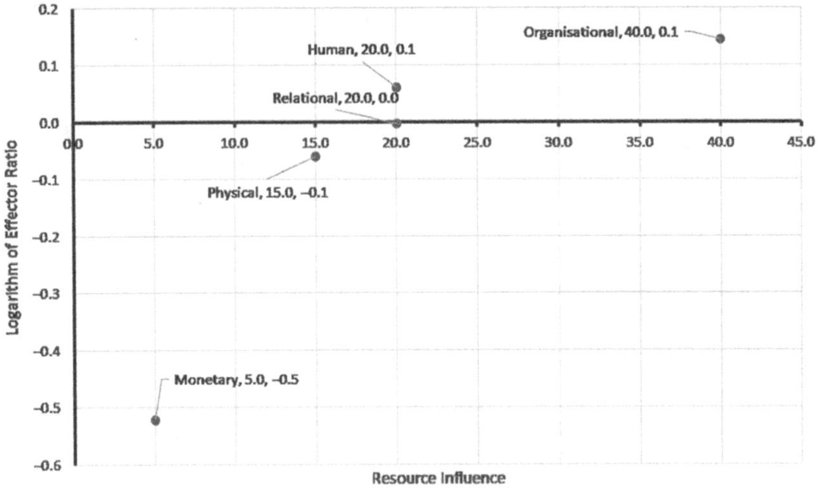

Figure 18.14 The resulting effector plot based on the resource category influence and effector ratios from the resource transformation matrix in Figure 18.13

it is desirable to accumulate a surplus monetary influence that can be used, for example, to influence shareholders through a dividend. Hence, monetary resources should always appear as a value sink in a for-profit organisation. Relational resources are neither a value sink nor a value source. Human and organisational resources appear as value sources, and physical resources appear as a value sink. It is normal for monetary resources to appear as a less influential value sink since monetary resources are an outcome in a for-profit organisation, whilst the other resource categories are the means through which this outcome is achieved. It is normal that the means are more important in generating the outcome than the resulting outcome is. The exception to this is in situations where the for-profit organisation is short on cash and facing an imminent crisis, when the perceived influence of monetary resources tends to increase dramatically.

To analyse the data provided by the effector plot, a least-square line fit is added to the effector plot in Figure 18.14, as shown in Figure 18.15.

Based on the discussion around the transformation matrix, the process by which the data is collected and generated, and the underpinning assumptions from the RBV and its associated theories of the firm including the intellectual capital view of the firm, it is possible to provide a framework for drawing conclusions from the visualisation in Figure 18.15:

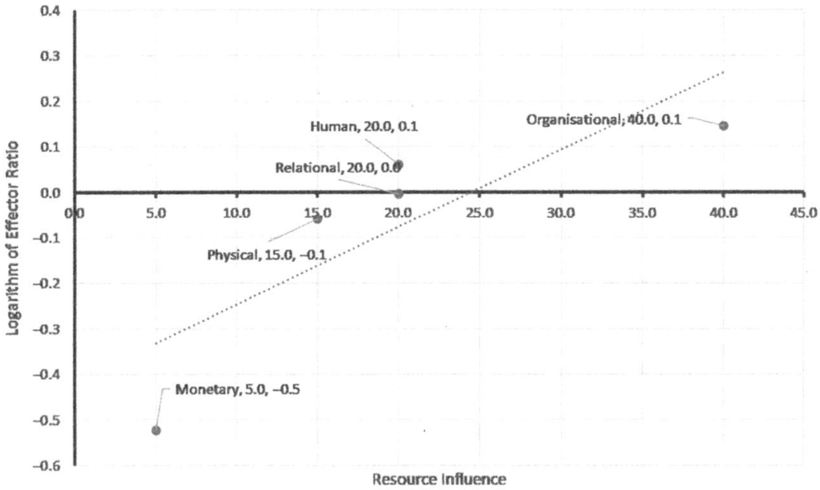

Figure 18.15 *The effector plot in Figure 18.14 with least-square line fit inserted*

- The more influential an intermediary resource is ('intermediary' meaning all resources except the output resource), the higher its effector ratio should be. This means that a curve or line fit should have a positive gradient (or first derivative). This in turn means that the resources that have the highest influence on value creation should be best leveraged (managed) and, as a consequence, appear as large value sources. This also means that the less influential an intermediary resource is (the further towards the left it appears in the effector plot), the less critical becomes its position on the y-axis in the effector plot. This means that the least-square line fit should be upward sloping (having a positive gradient or first derivative). As we can see in Figure 18.15, this is, to some extent, the case.
- The output resource – the resource form that embodies the value that the organisation is delivering – should be one of the left most resources, meaning one of the least influential. This is because greater or better output is achieved by focusing on the drivers of this output, not by focusing on the output itself, as highlighted in Figure 18.15.
- The output resource should also appear as a value sink, which means it should appear under the x-axis in the effector plot. This is because a sustainable resource transformation system needs to generate more effort into the output resource than it must draw from the output resource to keep the system working. If this is

the case, then there is an accumulation of effort in the output resource that can be used for other things; for example, influencing the shareholders by paying dividends. As can be seen in Figure 18.15, this is the case.

- The order in which the resources appear determines the value creating logic of the organisation. The most influential resource or resources should be the one(s) that form the basis for the organisation's competitive advantage:
  - In a value chain, the human resource cannot be the rightmost if the organisation is in the business of making money.
  - In a value shop, physical resources cannot be the rightmost if the organisation is in the business of making money.
  - In a value network, you would expect some combination of organisational and relational resources to appear as the rightmost if the organisation is in the business of making money.

Using the ternary plot approach, we can gain an understanding of the centre of gravity for the organisation captured in the effector plot illustrated in Figure 18.15 and the result shown in Figure 18.10. As can be seen from this figure, the organisation is predominantly a value network.

To further interpret the plots in Figure 18.15, an overlay provides further interpretation guidance. The first is a grid illustrated in Figure 18.16.

The purpose of the IC Navigator approach is to enable management to take actions that would improve the effectiveness of the firm's value creation. This will be exemplified by looking at the example used in Figure 18.8 and the assumption that management acts along the recommendations in the preceding two sections. This means that resources are redeployed to enhance the effectiveness of their use.

	Low Resource Influence	**High Resource Influence**
Value Source	**Problematic Stars** or **Irrelevant Value Generators** These resources are value sources but have low influence on the overall value generation of the organisation	**Expected Stars** These resources are value sources and have high influence on the overall value generation of the organisation
Insufficient Value Sources	**Necessary Resources, Loss Leader Resources,** or **Irrelevant Value Sinks** Excluding the monetary resource category that should sit in this grid cell these are value sinks with low influence on the overall value generation of the organisation	**The Dogs** These are value sinks or insufficient value sources with high influence on the overall value generation of the organisation

Figure 18.16 Analysis grid for the effector plot

The following values assume this has occurred, and illustrates one possible outcome after these redeployments have occurred (perhaps a year later). If these improvement potentials are acted upon, there would be a change in the numerical representation of the transformation matrix to something like what is shown in Figure 18.17.

The effector plots resulting from the transformation matrix in Figure 18.17 are shown in Figure 18.18.

	0.28	*1.00*	*1.16*	*1.32*	*1.05*	
	Monetary	**Physical**	**Relational**	**Organisational**	**Human**	Row Sum
Monetary	1.3	1.4	0.7	1.0	0.3	**4.6**
Physical	5.9	2.9	4.7	4.3	0.9	**18.6**
Relational	2.5	1.9	6.5	5.6	6.6	**23.1**
Organisational	5.6	8.6	6.2	9.4	2.3	**32.0**
Human	1.2	3.9	2.0	4.0	10.6	**21.7**
Column Sum	**16.5**	**18.6**	**20.0**	**24.2**	**20.6**	**100.0**

Figure 18.17 The numerical representation of the transformation matrix in Figure 18.13 after improving according to the identified improvement potentials using the logarithmic starting point

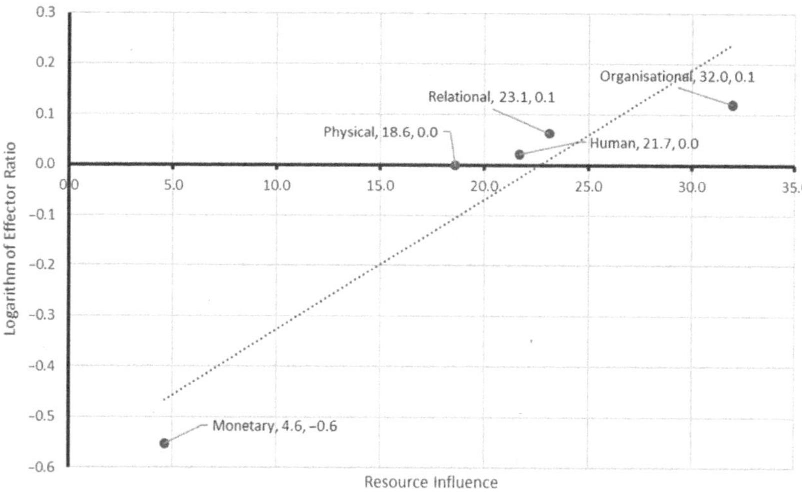

Figure 18.18 The effector plots of the transformation matrices shown in Figure 18.17

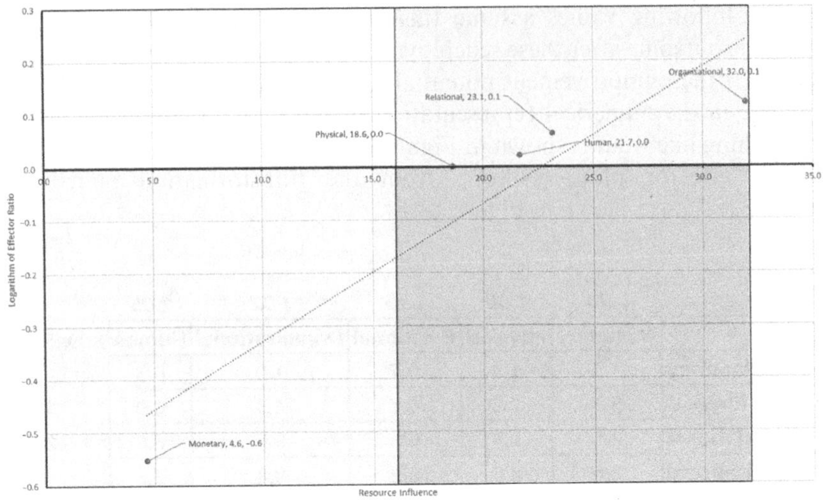

Figure 18.19 Figure 18.18 with evaluation framework overlaid

The overlay of the evaluation grid outlined in Figure 18.16 generates the result shown in Figure 18.19, which is a better situation than the original.

Using Figure 18.19 and the differences between the original transformation matrix, as shown in Figure 18.13, and the new proposed improved transformation matrix (calculated by subtracting the number in Figure 18.13 from the numbers in Figure 18.17, respectively), the proposed changes can be identified (Figure 18.20).

As can be seen in Figure 18.20, the changes are a decrease in the influence of the monetary and organisational resource categories and an increase in the influence of the physical, relational and human resource categories. This results in the change in centre of gravity in the strategic logic space, outlined in the ternary plot in Figure 18.21.

FUTURE RESEARCH DIRECTIONS

One potentially useful direction for further research is to extend the IC Navigator approach to cover networks of interacting organisations; for example, by creating and evaluating meta resource deployment systems, a form of network IC Navigator made up of IC Navigators for the network participants. This might provide answers to the question of how to

Difference between optimised and original	-0.02	0.13	0.16	-0.08	-0.10	
	Monetary	**Physical**	**Relational**	**Organisational**	**Human**	Row Sum
Monetary	-0.2	0.3	-0.2	-0.3	0.1	**-0.4**
Physical	1.2	0.6	0.9	0.8	0.2	**3.6**
Relational	0.5	0.4	1.3	-0.4	1.3	**3.1**
Organisational	-1.9	-0.6	-2.1	-3.1	-0.4	**-8.0**
Human	0.2	0.8	-0.1	-1.3	2.1	**1.7**
Column Sum	**-0.2**	**1.4**	**-0.1**	**-4.4**	**3.2**	**0.0**

Figure 18.20 Increases or decreases in resource influence, resource transformations and effector ratios in the improvements suggested

optimise network structures made up of simultaneously cooperating and competing organisations.

Another potentially useful direction for further research would be to look at the complexities of moving from managing resources within the traditional organisation to orchestrating resources that are partly inside and partly outside the organisational boundaries and thereby the organisation's control and influence. This is becoming more relevant as digital technologies allow traditional boundaries to dissolve between resources outside and resources inside the firm. Interesting discussions are already emerging in this arena, for example Sirmon et al. (2007), Helfat et al. (2009), Sirmon et al. (2011) and Roos (2017, 2018).

Longitudinal research around the changes suggested and implemented by the IC Navigator and the resulting changes in the performance of firms can form the basis for fruitful research around causality. This would require a large statistical sample but would be of great interest, especially around organisations changing their business model towards a more digital and/or lower resource footprint business model. This would further refine the RBV.

CONCLUSION

It is possible for an organisation to identify and evaluate the structure of its resource transformations by using the IC Navigator, which allows for the formulation of a set of hypotheses around the type of organisation and its value creating logics. This in turn allows for the identification of

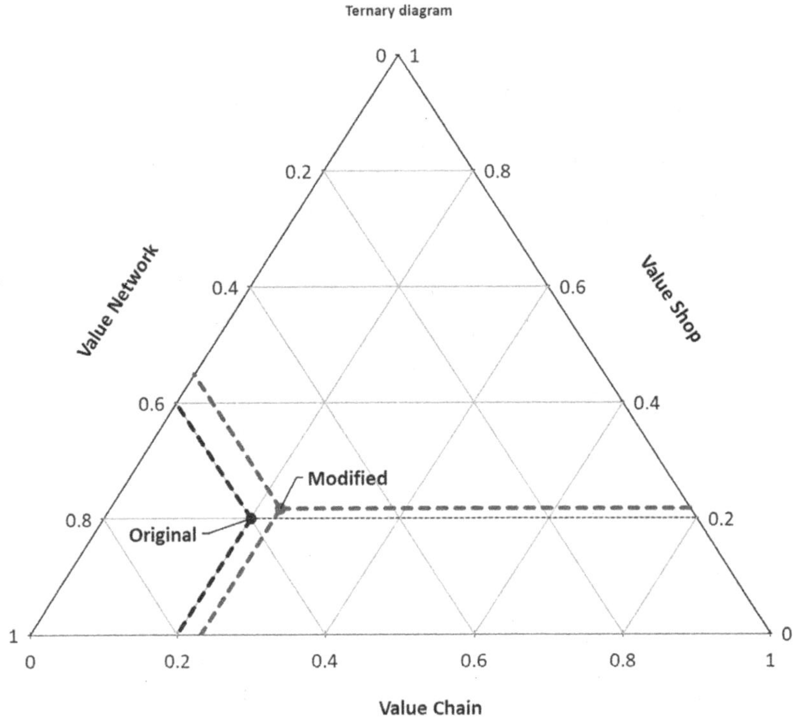

Figure 18.21 *Ternary plot outlining the changes in centre of gravity between the strategic logics following from the proposed changes in the resource transformation matrix outlined in Figures 18.14 to 18.20 (black and dotted is the situation before the change and grey and solid is the situation after the change)*

hypotheses around inconsistencies in the value creation structure and potential improvements in effectiveness in this value creating structure. The resulting effector plot forms the basis for evaluating hypotheses around future value creation strategies or business models.

This chapter introduces the IC Navigator as a tool that addresses key aspects of critiques made by Kraaijenbrink et al. (2010) (namely, points 6, 7 and 8) by:

- Identifying the value creation path and interactions between resources in resource deployment system; this addresses part of critique (6).

- Defining the concept of value and how it is embodied as a desired outcome of the operating resource deployment system; this addresses part of critique (7).
- Developing a behaviour-based characterisation system (or taxonomy) for resources in which any resource can fit; this addresses part of critique (8).
- Developing a tool that indicates actions that can be taken to increase the effectiveness of value creation using the bundle of resources available to the firm and, hence, ensure an effective resource deployment system; this may enable managers to strategise using the RBV framework.

Roos (2018) demonstrates how this tool may be applied within an RBV framework on the firm level, illustrating its usefulness in the migration to a digital value creating paradigm.

NOTES

1. The isolating mechanism that creates the *ex post* limits to competition is causal ambiguity limiting resource imitability (Ishikawa, 2006).
2. This system in practice can be the firm, its environment and the managerial decision-maker(s) (as the beholder(s) whose personal attributes and idiosyncrasies allow them to identify value creating opportunities that may not be obvious to other observers). The system could also, for example, be the system envisioned by an entrepreneur (as the beholder) given the value creating opportunities identified, given the resources available and the environment in which the venture is to operate.
3. All competitive advantages are by definition temporary.
4. This imposes no practical limitation since the solutions of (almost) any nonlinear system can be well-approximated by an equivalent linear system near its fixed points.
5. This statement is anchored in our understanding of sensemaking. Sensemaking is a continuous, retrospective, subtle, swift and social development of meaning that forms the basis for any action (Helms Mills, 2003; Weick et al., 2005). From a sensemaking perspective, a given reality is talked into existence within a given mediating social-psychological context (in the meaning of Blackler, 1993). This means that reality is also socially constructed within and about the firm (Taylor and Lerner, 1996). Sensemaking connects the abstract and impersonal with the concrete, idiosyncratic and personal (Paget, 2004); and sensemaking starts with immediate actions, local context and concrete cues (Weick et al., 2005). This means that sensemaking is less of a reflective process than might be assumed. 'Sensemaking is not about truth and getting it right. Instead, it is about continued redrafting of an emerging story so that it becomes more comprehensive, incorporates more of the observed data, and is more resilient in the face of criticism ... People may get better stories, but they will never get *the* story' (Weick et al., 2005, p. 415). Given that sensemaking is all-pervasive in organisations and among individuals in general, and given that it is action-oriented, people will act on 'the sense they have made of a reality' and not on whatever the underlying reality is in some true sense.
6. The alternative approaches are (Louviere, 1994): ranking alternatives in order of preference; series of paired comparisons; picking best and worst alternative; bundle selection

by choosing a given number of best alternatives; consider/not consider in making decision; and judgemental ratings.

7. A state variable is one of the set of variables that are used to describe the mathematical 'state' of a dynamic system. The state variables capture enough information about the system to determine the system's future behaviour in the absence of any external forces affecting the system. A state vector is a column vector having n rows (the resource column in the IC Navigator language) (Palm, 2005).
8. A system matrix is a square matrix having n rows and n columns (the transformation matrix in the IC Navigator language) (Palm, 2005).
9. The term 'effort' is introduced as a term encompassing all the different forms that influence can take.

REFERENCES

Bain, J.S. (1968), *Industrial organization*, New York: John Wiley.

Barney, J.B. (1986), 'Strategic factor markets: Expectations, luck, and business strategy', *Management Science*, 32 (10), 1231–1241.

Barney, J.B. (1991), 'Firm resources and sustained competitive advantage', *Journal of Management*, 17 (1), 99–120.

Barney, J.B. and R.W. Griffin (1992), *The management of organizations: Strategy, structure, behavior*, Boston, MA: Houghton Mifflin.

Blackler, F. (1993), 'Knowledge and the theory of organizations: Organizations as activity systems and the reframing of management', *Journal of Management Studies*, 30 (6), 863–884.

Bowman, C. and N. Collier (2006), 'A contingency approach to resource-creation processes', *International Journal of Management Reviews*, 8 (4), 191–211.

Carson, R.T., Louviere, J.J., Anderson, D.A., Arabie, P., Bunch, D.S., et al. (1994), 'Experimental analysis of choice', *Marketing Letters*, 5 (4), 351–367.

Collis, D.J. and C.A. Montgomery (1995), 'Competing on resources: Strategy in the 1990s', *Harvard Business Review*, 73 (4), 118–128.

Dagnino, G.B. (ed.) (2012), *Handbook of research on competitive strategy*, Cheltenham, UK and Northampton, MA, USA: Edward Elgar Publishing.

Davidsson, P., Steffens, P. and J. Fitzsimmons (2009), 'Growing profitable or growing from profits: Putting the horse in front of the cart?', *Journal of Business Venturing*, 24 (4), 388–406.

Dierickx, L. and K. Cool (1989), 'Asset stock accumulation and sustainability of competitive advantage', *Management Science*, 35 (12), 1504–1511.

Eisenhardt, K.M. and J.A. Martin (2000), 'Dynamic capabilities: What are they?', *Strategic Management Journal*, 21 (10–11), 1105–1121.

El Shafeey, T. and P. Trott (2014), 'Resource-based competition: Three schools of thought and thirteen criticisms', *European Business Review*, 26 (2), 122–148.

Foss, K., Foss, N.J., Klein, P.G. and S.K. Klein (2005), 'Austrian capital theory and the link between entrepreneurship and the theory of the firm', CKG Working Paper No. 5, Copenhagen: Center for Knowledge Governance, Department of Management, Politics and Philosophy, Copenhagen Business School.

Foss, N.J., Klein, P.G., Kor, Y.Y. and J.T. Mahoney (2008), 'Entrepreneurship, subjectivism, and the resource–based view: Toward a new synthesis', *Strategic Entrepreneurship Journal*, 2 (1), 73–94.

Foss, N.J. and T. Knudsen (2003), 'The resource-based tangle: Towards a sustainable explanation of competitive advantage', *Managerial and Decision Economics*, 24 (4), 291–307.

Grant, R.M. (2005), *Contemporary strategy analysis*, 5th edition, Hoboken, NJ: Blackwell Publishing.

Hamel, G. and A. Heene (eds) (1994), *Competence-based competition*, New York: Wiley.

Helfat, C.E., Finkelstein, S., Mitchell, W., Peteraf, M., Singh, H., et al. (2009), *Dynamic capabilities: Understanding strategic change in organizations*, Chichester: John Wiley & Sons.

Helfat, C.E. and M.A. Peteraf (2003), 'The dynamic resource-based view: Capability lifecycles', *Strategic Management Journal*, 24 (10), 997–1010.

Helms Mills, J. (2003), *Making sense of organizational change*, Abingdon: Routledge.

Ishikawa, I. (2006), 'The source of competitive advantage and entrepreneurial judgment in the RBV: Insights from the Austrian school perspective', SMG Working Paper No. 5/2006, Copenhagen: Center for Strategic Management and Globalization, Copenhagen Business School.

Kim, J. and J.T. Mahoney (2006), 'How property rights economics furthers the resource-based view: Resources, transaction costs and entrepreneurial discovery', *International Journal of Strategic Change Management*, 1 (1–2), 40–52.

Kor, Y.Y. (2003), 'Experience-based top management team competence and sustained growth', *Organization Science*, 14 (6), 707–719.

Kor, Y.Y., Mahoney, J.T. and S.C. Michael (2007), 'Resources, capabilities, and entrepreneurial perceptions', *Journal of Management Studies*, 44 (7), 1185–1210.

Kraaijenbrink, J., Spender, J.C. and A.J. Groen (2010), 'The resource-based view: A review and assessment of its critiques', *Journal of Management*, 36 (1), 349–372.

Lewin, P. and S.E. Phelan (2002), 'Rents and resources: A market process perspective', in J.N. Foss and G.P. Klein (eds), *Entrepreneurship and the firm: Austrian perspective on economic organization*, Cheltenham, UK and Northampton, MA, USA: Edward Elgar Publishing, pp. 221–247.

Lippman, S.A. and R.P. Rumelt (1982), 'Uncertain imitability: An analysis of interfirm differences in efficiency under competition', *Bell Journal of Economics*, 13 (2), 418–438.

Lockett, A., Thompson, S. and U. Morgenstern (2009), 'The development of the resource-based view of the firm: A critical appraisal', *International Journal of Management Reviews*, 11 (1), 9–28.

Louviere, J.L. (1994), 'Conjoint analysis', in R. Bagozzi (ed.), *Advanced methods of marketing research*, Cambridge, MA: Blackwell Business, pp. 223–259.

Mahoney, J.T. (1995), 'The management of resources and the resource of management', *Journal of Business Research*, 33 (2), 91–101.

Martín-de-Castro, G., Emilio Navas-López, J., López-Sáez, P. and E. Alama-Salazar (2006), 'Organizational capital as competitive advantage of the firm', *Journal of Intellectual Capital*, 7 (3), 324–337.

Mason, E.S. (1939), 'Price and production policies of large-scale enterprise', *American Economic Review*, 29 (1), 61–74.

Mathews, J.A. (2010), 'Lachmannian insights into strategic entrepreneurship: Resources, activities and routines in a disequilibrium world', *Organization Studies*, 31 (2), 219–244.

Nelson, R.R. (1991), 'Why do firms differ, and how does it matter?', *Strategic Management Journal*, 12 (S2), 61–74.

Nelson, R.R. and S.G. Winter (1982), *An evolutionary theory of economic change*, London: Belknap Press.

Newbert, S.L. (2007), 'Empirical research on the resource-based view of the firm: An assessment and suggestions for future research', *Strategic Management Journal*, 28 (2), 121–146.

Newbert, S.L. (2008), 'Value, rareness, competitive advantage, and performance: A conceptual-level empirical investigation of the resource-based view of the firm', *Strategic Management Journal*, 29 (7), 745–768.

Paget, M.A. (2004), *The unity of mistakes: A phenomenological interpretation of medical work*, Philadelphia, PA: Temple University Press.

Palm, W.J. (2005), *System dynamics*, Boston, MA: McGraw-Hill Higher Education.

Peppard, J. and A. Rylander (2001), 'Using an intellectual capital perspective to design and implement a growth strategy: The case of APiON', *European Management Journal*, 19 (5), 510–525.

Peteraf, M.A. (1993), 'The cornerstones of competitive advantage: A resource-based view', *Strategic Management Journal*, 14 (3), 179–191.
Peteraf, M.A. and J.B. Barney (2003), 'Unraveling the resource-based tangle', *Managerial and Decision Economics*, 24 (4), 309–323.
Porter, M.E. (1979), 'How competitive forces shape strategy', *Harvard Business Review*, 57 (2), 137–145.
Porter, M.E. (1980), *Competitive strategy: Techniques for analyzing industries and competitors*, New York: Free Press.
Porter, M.E. (1981), 'The contributions of industrial organization to strategic management', *Academy of Management Review*, 6 (4), 609–620.
Porter, M.E. (1985), *Competitive advantage*, New York: Free Press.
Porter, M.E. (1989), 'How competitive forces shape strategy', in D. Asch and C. Bowman (eds), *Readings in strategic management*, Basingstoke: Macmillan, pp. 133–143.
Porter, M.E. (1991), 'Towards a dynamic theory of strategy', *Strategic Management Journal*, 12 (S2), 95–117.
Porter, M.E. (1996), 'What is strategy', *Harvard Business Review*, 74 (6), 61–78.
Porter, M.E. (2008), 'The five competitive forces that shape strategy', *Harvard Business Review*, 86 (1), 79–93.
Roos, G. (2013), 'The role of intellectual capital in business model innovation: An empirical study', in P. Ordóñez de Pablos, R.D. Tennyson and J. Zhao (eds), *Intellectual capital strategy management for knowledge-based organizations*, Hershey, PA: IGI Global, pp. 76–121.
Roos, G. (2017), *Technology-driven productivity improvements and the future of work: Emerging research and opportunities*, Hershey, PA: IGI Global.
Roos, G. (2018), 'Resource deployment system implications of migrating the firm into a digital value creation paradigm', *Knowledge Management Research and Practice*, 16 (3), 281–291.
Roos, G. (2019), 'The IC Navigator as an answer to the critique directed at the resource based view of the firm framework', Unpublished dissertation, Adelaide: University of South Australia.
Roos, G. (2019), 'Optimising resource deployment within the firm: Overcoming theoretical problems with a practical application', Doctoral dissertation, Adelaide: University of South Australia.
Roos, G., Pike, S. and L. Fernström (2005), *Managing intellectual capital in practice*, Oxford: Butterworth-Heinemann.
Rumelt, R.P. (1984), 'Towards a strategic theory of the firm', in B. Lamb (ed.), *Competitive strategic management*, Englewood Cliffs, NJ: Prentice Hall, pp. 556–570.
Sanchez, R. (2008), 'A scientific critique of the resource-base view (RBV) in strategy theory, with competence-based remedies for the RBV's conceptual deficiencies and logic problems', in R. Sanchez (ed.), *Research in competence-based management, Vol. 4, A focused issue on fundamental issues in competence theory development*, Bingley, UK: Emerald Group, pp. 3–78.
Sanchez, R. and A. Heene (1997), 'Reinventing strategic management: New theory and practice for competence-based competition', *European Management Journal*, 15 (3), 303–317.
Seoudi, I. (2009), 'The resource–capability–competence perspective in strategic management: A reappraisal of the epistemological & theoretical foundations', PhD thesis, Cleveland, OH: Department of Economics, School of Graduate Studies, Case Western Reserve University.
Sirmon, D.G., Hitt, M.A. and R.D. Ireland (2007), 'Managing firm resources in dynamic environments to create value: Looking inside the black box', *Academy of Management Review*, 32 (1), 273–292.
Sirmon, D.G., Hitt, M.A., Ireland, R.D. and B.A. Gilbert (2011), 'Resource orchestration to create competitive advantage breadth, depth, and life cycle effects', *Journal of Management*, 37 (5), 1390–1412.

Taylor, J.R. and L. Lerner (1996), 'Making sense of sensemaking: How managers construct their organisation through their talk', *Studies in Cultures, Organizations and Societies*, 2 (2), 257–286.

Teece, D.J., Pisano, G. and A. Shuen (1997), 'Dynamic capabilities and strategic management', *Strategic Management Journal*, 18 (7), 509–533.

Tversky, B. (2014), 'Visualizing thought', in W. Huang (ed.), *Handbook of human centric visualization*, New York: Springer, pp. 3–40.

Warnier, V., Weppe, X. and X. Lecocq (2013), 'Extending resource-based theory: Considering strategic, ordinary and junk resources', *Management Decision*, 51 (7), 1359–1379.

Weick, K.E., Sutcliffe, K.M. and D. Obstfeld (2005), 'Organizing and the process of sensemaking', *Organization Science*, 16 (4), 409–421.

Index